ALLE · ZEIT · WACH · 1842

Alfred Schipke
Alan M. Taylor (Eds.)

The Economics of Transformation

Theory and Practice in the New Market Economies

With 13 Figures

Springer-Verlag
Berlin Heidelberg New York
London Paris Tokyo
Hong Kong Barcelona
Budapest

Alfred Schipke
Visiting Fellow
Department of Economics
Harvard University
Cambridge, Massachusetts 02138
United States

Correspondence address:
International Monetary Fund
Washington, D.C. 20431
United States

Alan M. Taylor
Academy Scholar
Harvard Academy for International and Area Studies
Harvard University
Cambridge, Massachusetts 02138
United States

Correspondence address:
Department of Economics
Northwestern University
Evanston, Illinois 60208-2600
United States

ISBN-13: 978-3-642-78617-4 e-ISBN-13: 978-3-642-78615-0
DOI: 10.1007/978-3-642-78615-0

Library of Congress Cataloging-in-Publication Data
The Economics of transformation : theory and practice in the new market economies / Alfred Schipke, Alan M. Taylor, eds. p. cm.
Includes bibliographical references and index. ISBN 3-540-57387-9 (Germany : alk. paper) : DM 148.00,- ISBN 0-387-57387-9 (U.S. : alk. paper)
1. Europe, Eastern--Economic policy--1989- 2. Former Soviet republics--Economic policy. 3. Capitalism--Europe, Eastern. 4. Capitalism--Former Soviet republics.
I. Schipke, Alfred, 1959- . II. Taylor, Alan M., 1964-
HC244.E2448 1994 338.947--dc20

Softcover reprint of the hardcover 1st edition 1994

2143/7130-5 4 3 2 1 0 - Printed on acid-free paper

Contents

Foreword

János Kornai

The collapse of the socialist system in eastern Europe and the Soviet Union is one of the major events of this century, perhaps the most important of all. The transformation now taking place is without any precedent in history.

The original development of capitalism was a process that lasted for centuries. The almost total liquidation of capitalism in the countries ruled by communist parties took place—in historical terms—in a very short period of time, but it was carried out by force and repressive methods. The transformation which has now begun is diverting these countries back onto the path of capitalist development and the hope is that the process will take place much faster than the original emergence of capitalism. And another hope can be expressed: that the governments of these countries will not resort during the process to the arsenal of political violence and repression in order to speed it up.

Although the post-socialist transformation is a historically *unique* phenomenon, some components and features of it show a similarity with other processes or events that took place under other circumstances. Other empires before the Soviet empire collapsed. The political structures of other countries took the path from dictatorship to democracy. Under other conditions, state assets have been privatized, inflation has been curbed, foreign capital has flowed in, new oligopolies have formed, and so on. The uniqueness lies in the new, specific configuration of these component processes and may other phenomena.

Under these circumstances, there are two mistakes that an active participant in the post-socialist transformation or a researcher analyzing it can commit. One is to discern the new, unique, unprecedented character of the process to the exclusion of everything else. Those who do this (and there are not a few of them, particularly among those who live where the process is occurring) are scorning the lessons to be learnt from history, other countries' experiences, or the theory of the capitalist market economy. The other mistake, the reverse of the first, is to assume that ready-made recipes can be found in the economic theory devised to explain the mature market economies or the historical experiences of other systems. The great virtue of this book is that it commits neither of these mistakes. The authors set an example of how to turn with sound intuition to analogous historical events (for instance the break-up of the Austro-Hungarian Monarchy, or the democratic transformations of Korea, Spain or Chile), or to certain chapters of economic theory (for instance the theory of general equilibrium, or the theories of integration or foreign direct investment). But they avoid drawing ill-considered or unqualified conclusions from them; their analysis is firmly embedded in the specific circumstances of the post-socialist transition. The eyes of the authors are open to the analogies, but they are aware of the unique, specific nature of this transition.

Another characteristic of these studies is their avoidance of the narrow-minded "technocratic" approach not infrequent in the economist's profession. Expressly in the foreground of several of the studies is an examination of the connection between politics and economics or a consideration of the sociological aspects of an economic process in the narrow sense. Although "economics" is the discipline named in the title of the book, I would have been inclined to describe it as dealing with the "political economy" of the post-socialist transition.

The post-socialist transition has its "prophets" who know beforehand just what to do. I think another virtue of this book is that it is free of such prophetic, messianic self-confidence. The attempt instead is to arrive at practical conclusions from a careful study of general theory and specific reality. Since it is not branded with the mark of a single theoretical school, the book displays an undoctrinaire pragmatism in the way in which it draws upon intellectual sources of various kinds.

The virtues are certainly explained by a number of factors, apart from the personal talent of the authors. Several of the contributors live in a country engaged in the process, or at least worked there for some time or belong to the staff of an institution dedicated to dealing with the post-socialist region. This ensures a rich background of experience. A high proportion of the authors are, for example, Germans witnessing and participating in the unique and vast effort being made to carry out the transformation of the former communist system within a reunited country consisting of capitalist and formerly socialist parts. Most of the authors of the book are young. Perhaps I, as a member of the older generation, may be allowed to say that their youth makes it easier for them to look on the emerging new world with fresh eyes.

I am sure that this volume will provide a great deal of useful knowledge to its readers and represents an intellectual stimulus and challenge to them.

Budapest and Cambridge, Massachusetts
June 1993

Editors' Introduction

Alfred Schipke and
Alan M. Taylor

The former socialist countries of eastern Europe are in the midst of transforming their political and economic systems. Since little is known about systemic transformation, both theoretically and empirically, policymakers in these countries have resorted to "trial and error" and measures that have allegedly been successful in market economies. The danger of such an approach is, of course, that erroneous and inconsistent policy measures could adversely affect the welfare of a large part of the population especially given the magnitude of the reforms in the New Market Economies.

This volume provides a systematic overview of standard areas of economic transformation such as price liberalization, privatization, and the reform of trade and financial markets. However, it also includes topics that have not received due attention thus far, yet are likely to be on the research agenda as the consequences of economic reform become more visible, namely the social implications and political dimensions of transformation. The book challenges widely-accepted conventional wisdom by presenting new empirical results.

The contributors to this volume have worked extensively on issues of economic transformation; most of them have experience in the field and worked either directly for east European governments or indirectly through international organizations such as the World Bank and the International Monetary Fund. The research backgrounds of the authors reflect a wide spectrum of issues in the field of economic transformation. The following part provides a brief outline of the main features of the book.

In Chapter 1 Holger Wolf focuses on aspects of institutional inertia in the former Soviet Union—a kind of "nostalgia trap" where short-term costs of adjustment create a hesitancy on the part of the authorities to fully implement and carry through reforms. Thus, the short-term costs may be prolonged and a vicious circle created where further delays jeopardize the entire transition process itself. Wolf draws parallels with the historical experience of Austria-Hungary and the collapse of its empire in the wake of World War One. Nascent self-interested nationalism almost thwarted the transition process, as the then-successor states (Austria, Hungary and Czechoslovakia) scrambled over the economic pie. As in the case of the FSU today, the protagonists resorted to beggar-thy-neighbor trade and monetary policies, and painted themselves into a corner with a sequence of retaliatory tariff increases. Wolf notes the key role played by the League of Nations in defusing this stand-off. Whilst the international community politely urged co-operation, it was the League's commissioners who strode into the midst of the conflict, and secured concessions through negotiation. Wolf outlines a possible course of treatment for the FSU's economic ills. Even so, he cautions that without co-ordination, such plans, predicated on inter-Republican co-operation, will reap little fruit. As in the case of Austria-Hungary, an external mechanism for policy co-ordination is needed to overcome the political tensions and the scope for free-riding. Given the success of the League in the 1920s, Wolf calls for an international body, most likely the IMF, to step in and enforce a mutually acceptable "code of conduct" governing inter-republican economic activity.

Joachim Ahrens takes a comparative, historical approach to understanding the transformation process in Chapter 2. He draws on late-twentieth century economic-reform experiences in a number of countries to illustrate the potential pitfalls for the countries of central and eastern Europe. Insights are drawn from Spain's reform after Franco and her integration into the European Community; from Germany's postwar experience with the unraveling of controls and the reconstruction of a market-type economy; from Korea's spectacular growth in the sixties and seventies predicated on a policy of "administrative guidance"; and from Latin America's numerous brushes with stabilization and reforms in the seventies and eighties, and the notable economic success case, Chile. Ahrens notes that the transferability of some of the components of these reforms to the present circumstances is problematic. Nonetheless, he identifies a number of key challenges that have been at the center of all economic reform packages, and which are likely prerequisites for success in central and eastern Europe today: political stability; social consensus; a commitment not to backslide; a popular acknowledgment of the hardships entailed; and reasonable expectations concerning future rewards.

In Chapter 3 Jonathan Morduch and Alan Taylor construct a general-equilibrium model of food markets in Russia prior to the economic reforms that began in 1992. The model is unusual in its explicit treatment of rationing, a pervasive feature of the Soviet system. Liberalization scenarios are simulated with often non-obvious results. For example, *ceteris paribus,* price liberalization should have entailed a general decline in free-market prices; this follows from the huge subsidy removal brought about by the end of rationing at fixed prices in large sections of the market. Pre-reform state prices offer no guide to the post-reform equilibrium price structure, particularly given the large income and substitution effects. The modelling is directed at distributional issues, it being known that the poorer groups in society depended relatively more on the former subsidized channels. Simulations indicate that flat income-compensation schemes would entail welfare losses for the poor, and gains for the richer groups, for just this reason. Only targeted schemes aimed at the poor could avoid this problem. However, narrow targeting is a strict condition, since any spillover into the large middle-class group rapidly erodes gains for the poorer minority. Most surprisingly, the subsidy system impaired equity both before and after reform. Prior to liberalization, richer groups were well-placed to gain access to subsidized channels; but, when removed, the subsidies, being a relatively small share of richer groups' total income, generated correspondingly small adverse income effects for said groups.

Bryan Roberts examines in Chapter 4 the initial welfare consequences of price liberalization in Poland, challenging the conventional wisdom that the immediate post-reform period was characterized by severe adverse welfare shocks relative to pre-reform conditions. Although such commonplace views may be questioned given the fragile empirical evidence, Roberts adopts a more formal approach in his critique, first developing a single-agent model of the pre-reform consumer sector which incorporates costs of queuing and procurement, each important elements of economic activity in state-market channels. He is then able to obtain an empirically useful formula for estimating such dead-weight losses, and, implicitly, the gains from liberalization arising from the elimination of inefficient allocation mechanisms. Roberts then explores Polish household budget data, and finds that these gains were potentially very large. Sensitivity analysis suggests that they were large enough to offset all but the most adverse estimates of the real income shock suffered in the first year of Poland's reform program. Although distributional issues are finessed, Roberts' careful and qualified analysis demonstrates that, contrary to the "short-term pain, long-term gain" view of reform, countries with costly and inefficient allocation mechanisms may even enjoy, in aggregate, immediate welfare gains from price liberalization.

In Chapter 5 Francesca Cornelli considers two central problems in the transition process: the privatization of existing firms and the need for large scale investments. Considered together, the two might yield a joint solution, since foreign capital will be needed to augment domestic savings, and foreign investors might acquire shares in the newly privatized firms. Cornelli presents a mechanism designed around these features. Governments ask foreign buyers to pay not in cash but directly with investments—which may be less costly for foreign companies given their technology and know-how. Also, the government does not commit beforehand to sell a given number of shares and only proceeds with the sale if it is deemed satisfactory. Given the political pressure not to undersell national assets to foreigners, such a strategy is credible. By pursuing such a strategy, the government realizes two advantages: it can threaten to renege the sale in order to obtain a higher payment and it can directly obtain infrastructural investments which are an optimal form of payment in terms of social welfare.

Paul Welfens analyzes in Chapter 6 the potential contribution of foreign investment and privatization in the former CMEA. He points out that newly industrializing countries with outward-oriented policies have benefitted especially from the presence of multinational companies, hence transforming former CMEA countries could benefit in similar ways. Welfens analyzes the economic and political role of FDI applying Dunning's FDI theory to eastern and central Europe. Introducing FDI in the traditional IS-LM macro model of the open economy suggests positive macroeconomic effects of foreign investors, but also points to specific risks associated with changing supply elasticities and links between FDI and exchange rate movement. Various theoretical aspects of FDI are considered and the role of emerging capital markets for a growth-oriented transformation are discussed. The interdependencies between FDI and privatization—both from above (privatizing state firms) and below (creating new firms)—are evaluated and specific problems of privatization analyzed.

In Chapter 7 Alfred Schipke points out that most of the research on privatization has focused on efficiency, that is, whether and under what circumstances private ownership is superior to its public counterpart and how companies are transferred to the private sector in the most efficient way. He argues, however, that privatization is first and foremost a political process. This is especially true in eastern Europe where privatization leads to a massive redistribution of wealth. In the search for an optimal privatization strategy, a number of eastern European countries have neglected to incorporate political constraints into their privatization rationale and are now struggling to secure the success not only of privatization, but the entire transformation of former socialist countries. Public choice arguments suggest that rapid privatization is necessary to take advantage of the institutional vacuum and the low degree of organized opposition to privatization at the beginning of the reform process. The more time elapses between the outset of the reform program and the beginning of large scale privatization, the more political opposition will mount. In any case, the government must be prepared to buy out vetoing interest groups to assure that privatization can take place at all. This is especially true if property rights are attenuated. Schipke uses two case studies to demonstrate the different approaches in dealing with the political constraints: Poland and Russia. In both cases he analyzes the different privatization approaches and whether they are apt in dealing with potential political opposition groups.

In Chapter 8 Oliver Fratzscher presents parallels between the southern and eastern European transformations in a horizontal perspective, focusing on macroeconomic effects and recent developments in trade and industry. His first objective is to draw some lessons as well as ideas and options for the eastern European transition. His second objective is to study the process of central and eastern European transformation within a larger perspective of European integration, by analyzing the evolving trade and industrial structures in the four central European countries. He shows that adequate comparison is hard to find, although, for example, the Spanish economy was about equal in size to the Polish economy in the 1960s, it has grown to about eight times that size today, and the Portuguese economy may be of more similar size. The Southern European transition has produced different results, more successful on the Iberian peninsula than in the case of Greece. Benefits from integration have materialized through reduced trade costs, increased competition, modernization of industry, factor mobility, and economies of scale, as well as through dynamic effects on economic growth through increased investment. Costs have been significant, but mostly transitional: high unemployment, high real interest rates, widening trade deficits, and increasing fiscal deficits. The distribution of benefits favored Southern European economies, and especially transport equipment sectors. Lessons for central Europe are complicated by political economy factors: past integration within the CMEA created political dependency, and future integration with the EC has to overcome protectionist barriers. Fratzscher argues that preparation for European integration should focus on stabilization (with the objective of meeting Maastricht criteria), reform fiscal and financial systems, and promote comprehensive structural reforms. A national social consensus may be the single most important factor for further progress, as was established by the Moncloa Pact in Spain in 1977. Prospects for membership in the EC involve political decisions in both West and East. For the EC, substantial financial costs and adjustments in sensitive sectors (especially agriculture) are involved. For central Europe, progress in restructuring, institutional reforms, and economic growth could facilitate integration. In the meantime, the Central European Free Trade Area (CEFTA) could become a catalyst for their integration into the EC, since it would expand intra-regional trade and promote the restructuring process.

Timothy Lane examines in Chapter 9 the objectives of and constraints on financial reform in the new market economies. He starts by identifying the unusual features arising from the neglect of the financial system under central planning: monobank structures, passive finance and extensive bad debt. Despite the burden of bad debt, Lane argues that debt overhang may play a helpful role during the transition, since it disciplines firm managers to make interest payments and, hence, act more in line with the objectives of firm owners. This forms an argument against complete debt cancellation, a "clean slate" approach advocated as a means to avoid costly bankruptcy procedures and allow potentially profitable enterprises to start over under a new price structure. Lane then draws out implications for the sequencing of reforms and the role of the banking system and non-bank finance. Portfolio reallocation, solvency, supervision and accounting reform all go hand-in-hand with a thorough shake out of the outdated monobank system and its ultimate privatization. Given the low liquidity levels in other financial sectors—for example, securities markets—bank finance is crucial to the structural adjustment process. However, reform will prove futile unless the bad debt problem is resolved: neither careful supervision nor enlightened regulation can keep a bank with negative capital from engaging in imprudent behavior.

In Chapter 10 Stephan Klasen addresses both short-term social issues relating to the current transformation process and the question of how the social fabric is affected by the reforms in the long run. The first section sets out a framework stressing the need to look beyond income growth to other important indicators of well-being such as adequate nutrition, good health, education, longevity—often referred to as *human development indicators*. Klasen uses case studies from developing countries and the experience of liberalization in China and shows that the introduction of a market economy, even if successful in terms of income growth, can lead to stagnating and worsening human development for a large part of the population. Eastern Europe and the CIS which, despite their poor overall economic performance, enjoyed impressive human development achievements (such as high levels of life expectancy and literacy) might now face a much more drastic reduction of human development unless measures are taken to protect these accomplishments. Since the former socialist countries displayed the highest labor participation rates for women in the world, women stand to lose the most from the establishment of new social and economic arrangements. In the current process of transformation, women are being pushed out of the labor force at much higher rates than men. Klasen argues that there is a close link between labor force participation of women and the share of resources they receive in the household. Hence, women might lose much of the economic and social independence they enjoyed before.

Sophia Eltrop examines in Chapter 11 the turmoil in the telecommunication industry in eastern Europe and the former Soviet Union, focusing on the role of foreign direct investment and the impediments to a competitive market outcome arising from a peculiar market structure. Eltrop notes that communication and information processing are key attributes of a well-functioning market economy. However, as an industry, telecommunication has very problematic attributes: large network externalities, natural monopoly properties and a mix of short- and long-term payoff investment opportunities. Eltrop argues that these features threaten to limit the scope of the market for telecommunication, an unfortunate outcome which is not easily avoided given the sometimes naive regulatory acts of governments. Oligopolistic behavior has been encouraged by the granting of multi-year licenses for operations that have already turned profits after only one or two years of investment. The cellular and fixed-wire telephone markets are segmented: foreign firms favor the fast profits to be made in the monopolistic cellular sector serving wealthy business clients, and the sector has expanded rapidly; by contrast, universal phone-service attracts relatively poor consumers and the improvement of the general-access fixed-wire networks is a tough challenge for credit-constrained governments. Yet if network externalities are large, the neglect of the fixed-wire service could be welfare damaging, and a case might be made for cross-subsidizing—either by taxing the highly-profitable foreign investment projects to sustain broad network expansion or by offering carrot-and-stick contracts at short-term license auctions to generate contributions for the state-run networks. Political uncertainty deters long-term commitment by private investors to a socially desirable fixed-wire network expansion: creative financing may be a way to surmount this major obstacle to network enhancement and wider competition.

In Chapter 12 Eugene Khartukov and Dimitry Surovtsev analyze one of the most important industries of the former Soviet Union: the oil industry. Since both the success of economic and ultimately political reform might depend on the future of the oil industry, at least in the oil-producing independent Republics, the question arises how the industry is affected by the current disintegration of the former Soviet Empire. The authors predict the effects of the disintegration on both the quantity and quality of FSU oil exports. By making different assumptions about the pace, speed, and depth of the market reforms Khartukov and Surovtsev project net oil exports from the FSU to be between 0.6 mmbd ("slow marketization" case) and almost 3.5 mmbd ("accelerated marketization" case). Based on these predictions, they argue that at the end of 1990s the estimated difference in the world oil price could amount to $8/b (in constant 1992 dollars).

Any publication is, naturally, the result not only of the efforts of the authors themselves but also of the inputs of numerous people that remain incognito. In this case, we depended particularly on assistance with our quantitative work since one of the major challenges to research on the New Market Economies is, of course, to obtain reliable qualitative and quantitative data. On behalf of all contributors, we would like to express gratitude to all those who, through their time and effort, made this task a little easier. In addition, we would like to thank our colleagues and friends, especially Bryan Roberts and Jonathan Morduch, for their advice and continued assistance. We must also thank Michael: certainly, this project would have been a different experience without his great sense of humor and infamous *Tasty* hot dogs at five o'clock in the morning.

Cambridge, Massachusetts
June 1993

List of Contributors

Joachim Ahrens	University of Göttingen
Francesca Cornelli	London School of Economics
Sophia Eltrop	Harvard University
Oliver Fratzscher	Harvard University
Eugene M. Khartukov	Moscow International Business School
Stephan Klasen	Harvard University
János Kornai	Harvard University and Collegium Budapest
Timothy D. Lane	International Monetary Fund
Jonathan J. Morduch	Harvard University
Bryan W. Roberts	Massachusetts Institute of Technology
Alfred Schipke	Harvard University
Dimitry A. Surovtsev	Moscow International Business School
Alan M. Taylor	Harvard University
Paul J. J. Welfens	University of Münster
Holger C. Wolf	New York University

1 The Economics of Disintegration in the Former Soviet Union

Holger C. Wolf

1.1 Introduction

The wave of political revolutions sweeping eastern Europe in 1989 wreaked havoc on the established economic arrangements for production and trade. Central planning, price controls and managed trade collapsed. Contrary to initial expectations, private initiative was often slow to fill the vacuum. The shift towards markets, in consequence, proved far more costly than initially expected: industrial production in the transition economies has fallen by 30%–40%. While a considerable fraction of the decline reflects the discontinued production of unwanted shoddy products, the shift to markets has undoubtedly lowered the living standards of sizeable social groups, in particular recipients of fixed incomes with limited outside employment opportunities.[1]

The Latin American experience over the last decade aptly demonstrates the political dangers inherent in falling living standards during economic reforms: looking back, the pre-reform situation gains appeal, providing a fertile ground for a populist backlash against the liberalization program. If strong enough, the *nostalgia trap* may lead to the abandonment of reforms. Latin America also provides hints on avoiding the trap: sustained liberalizations typically boast early signs of success safeguarding the political momentum—be they the availability of hitherto scarce goods (even at high prices), a wave of privatization giving individuals a stake in the continuation of reforms, or a rapid end to production

---

I thank John Flemming, Anne-Marie Gulde, Barbara Katz and Richard O'Brien for helpful comments. The chapter is an outgrowth of earlier work presented at the 1992 AMEX seminar in London.

[1] In Russia, the average pension of 4,275 rubles in January 1993 fell substantially short of the government estimate of the minimum subsistence level of 5,073 rubles, itself rather low at $8.87 per month.

declines followed by moderate growth.

Considered in this light, eastern Europe offers a mixed picture. While the central European economies—notably Poland, the Czech Republic and Hungary—have apparently passed the nadir without abandoning reform, the successor states of the Soviet Union suffer continuing output declines and appear by now to be caught in the nostalgia trap. Several republics have replaced reformist with conservative governments promising a "third way" towards markets and public support for continued reforms is at a low ebb.

The difference between central Europe and the successor states of the fragmented former Soviet Union (FSU) is striking. Why has the nostalgia trap proved so much more potent for the FSU? A large part of the answer can be found in the peculiar interconnection of politics and economics in disintegrating multi-nation empires. Whereas the central European transition economies focussed their energies on economic reconstruction, political emancipation in the former Soviet Union led to the reappearance of economic nationalism. The extreme interdependence between the republics translated such policies into large production and trade losses. Nor is the outlook particularly rosy: while production levels in the other post-socialist economies have stabilized at 20%–40% below the 1989 levels and are expected to grow in 1993, accelerating inflation and continued trade contraction threaten to further undermine production in the FSU (Tables 1.1 and 1.2).

The malaise reflects economic as well as political incentives. On the political side, nationalist themes have proved a lifesaver for endangered communist governments. On the economic side, free-rider incentives, uncertainty about the policies of other republics, and a desire to obtain bargaining chips for future negotiations all render expansionary monetary policy and restrictive trade practices attractive. Once in place these practices are hard to dislodge: while every republican government may support a joint move to free trade and sound money, no republic has an incentive to move first. The degree of mutual distrust between the republics makes a cooperative solution unlikely in the foreseeable future. Realistically, a cure for continued economic nationalism requires a coordination mechanism with credible sanctions.

Such a cure is urgently needed: a continued decline of production is likely to further strengthen the nostalgia effect, undermining the liberalization package. In this setting, the neoclassical paradigm—liberalize, decentralize, privatize—provides an attractive medium-term goal but offers little guidance in the short run.

Table 1.1
Output Losses Of Transition Economies

	1989	1990	1991	1992	1993	1989–93
Eastern Europe	−0.2	−7.1	−13.7	−9.7	2.4	−26.1
Former Soviet Union	2.5	−7.4	−9.0	−18.2	−6.5	−29.0

Source: IMF, *World Economic Survey* 2 (1992): 93.

Contrary to accepted wisdom, successful economic reform in the FSU may well require cautious macroeconomic *re*-centralization to ensure the success of microeconomic *de*-centralization.

I begin by looking back to 1918 and the dissolution of the multi-nation Austro-Hungarian empire, searching for insights into the dynamics of political and economic disintegration. I then turn to an assessment of the current situation in the FSU before considering institutional reforms capable of temporarily revitalizing trade and production and, thereby, of stabilizing the political support for a continuation of reforms.

1.2 The Past

History provides us with a case study of the disintegration of a multi-nation state. In 1918 the Austro-Hungarian dual monarchy dissolved into Austria, Czechoslovakia and Hungary as mutually hostile independence movements successfully exploited the collapse of central authority. The disintegration of the Habsburg empire exhibits striking parallels to today's events in the FSU:

> Coming into existence as a result of the violent disruption of old relationships, in a strained atmosphere of war and revolution, the new...countries could not escape extreme manifestations of political nationalism, which was intensified by the fact that large numbers...found themselves...in the condition of minorities in the newly created states. And side by side with this aspect of their new nationhood these countries were confronted with economic problems of great magnitude and complexity. (Pasvolsky 1928, 24)

The emergent political nationalism soon spilt over into the economic sphere. Prior to the split-up, the dual monarchy enjoyed near self-sufficiency, with Hungary specializing in agriculture and Austria producing industrial goods: more than 70 percent of Hungary's exports were destined for Austria and vice versa. In principle,

Table 1.2
Output and Inflation in the Former Soviet Union

	Output				
	1990	1991	1992	1990–92	Inflation
Belarus	−3.0	−3.0	−15.0	−20.1	606
Russia	1.2	−9.0	−20.0	−26.3	651
Ukraine	−3.4	−11.2	−12.0	−24.5	530
Armenia	−8.5	−11.8	−44.7	−55.3	193
Moldova	−1.5	−11.9	−22.5	−32.7	403
Kazakhstan	−1.5	−10.0	−20.3	−29.3	512
Azerbaijan	−11.7	−0.7	−21.8	−31.4	326
Kirgizia	4.0	−2.0	−25.2	−23.7	333
Turkmenistan	1.5	−5.9	−10.5	−14.5	460
Uzbekistan	4.3	−0.5	−20.5	−17.4	339
Tajikistan	−0.6	−8.7	−17.1	−24.7	266

Notes: Tajikistan figures for 1992 are industrial production. The 1992 data are for the January–August period.
Sources: IMF, *World Economic Outlook* 2 (1992): 46; *Financial Times,* 20 January 1993, 2.

political separation need have had little impact on economic interaction between the successor states since the efficient trade pattern was unchanged by the creation of new political boundaries. Yet economic reasoning proved secondary to political priorities as new-found sovereignty was held to require economic autonomy: "Political independence appeared most precarious without economic independence ....Political subjection had too long been identified in their minds with economic domination, and political nationalism found an equally distinct counterpart in economic nationalism" (Pasvolsky 1928, 24).

Economic nationalism found its expression principally in two areas, money and trade. On the trade side, several rounds of retaliatory tariff increases translated minor impediments into prohibitive barriers, promoting government barter at the expense of sharply curtailed private trade. While the tariff rates were raised at least partly to obtain bargaining chips for future negotiations, later attempts to achieve a coordinated reduction in barriers proved futile. The resistance of trade barriers to reform reflected the lack of a credible coordination device: although the successor governments concurred in lamenting the effects of high tariff walls and agreed that, in principle, a liberalization would be mutually advantageous, no individual government was willing to take the initiative in dismantling barriers (Berger 1982).

Monetary instability worsened the contraction (Dornbusch 1992; Flood, Garber, and Spence 1992). The successor states initially adopted the institutional remnants of the Austro-Hungarian system, including the crown as legal tender. However, the fragile union did not last long as the sound-money objectives espoused by Czechoslovakia clashed with the deficit-monetization strategies pursued in Austria and Hungary. In 1919 Czechoslovakia seceded from the crown zone by stamping the notes on her own territory, triggering monetary reforms by the other successor states. The resulting profusion of internationally unrecognized new currencies created further havoc in internal and external trade relations. Continued deficit monetization over the next years drove both Austria and Hungary into hyperinflation, causing further economic contraction and political polarization. Czechoslovakia avoided such extreme monetary instability by dint of her fiscal and monetary conservatism; nevertheless she suffered from the monetary disintegration as the Czechoslovakian crown was first driven down by a contagion effect in unison with the mark and Austrian crown only to later suffer a substantial *overvaluation* as it became the "dollar of central Europe."

The decision to subjugate economic policy to the dictates of political expediency, particularly the pursuit of independence, thus came at a very substantial economic and—via the impoverishment of a large part of the Austrian and Hungarian middle class—political cost. The international community recognized the consequences of economic nationalism, yet its advice remained apolitical, recommending the return to free trade without addressing the political dynamics. The exhortations went unheeded as ethnic conflicts spilt over into the economic sphere.[2]

The experience of Austria-Hungary suggests that although—in principle—economic cooperation need not suffer from changes in political frontiers, the spillover of political nationalism into the economic sphere can easily lead to a negative-sum game with escalating trade conflicts and beggar-thy-neighbor monetary policies. Well-meaning exhortations from abroad—unless followed up by deeds—may have little impact on the political dynamics as long-suppressed opposition and conflict become dominant factors.

1.3 The Present

The dissolution of the Soviet Union resembles in many respects the interwar experience of the dual monarchy. Long suppressed ethnic conflicts are again flaring

[2] "The states which have been created .. should at once re-establish full and friendly cooperation .. in order that the essential unity of European economic life may not be impaired by the erection of artificial economic barriers" (Allied Supreme Council Declaration, 8 March 1920).

up, relentless pursuit of independence has been the key to election success, and political nationalism plays a prominent role in economic policy decisions.

In the aftermath of the collapse of central authority, republican governments have introduced export prohibitions in an attempt to conserve raw materials and establish de facto claims to the resources of the FSU. The attempt proved costly as the extreme degree of economic interdependence of the republics, a legacy of the period of central planning, made the economies of the successor republics extraordinarily sensitive to the severance of established supply links (Table 1.3). In response to shortages, republican governments have resorted to inter-governmental barter deals with bilateral trade-balancing. Trade restrictions are particularly severe for the most heavily subsidized sectors—energy and agriculture—where concessions on the speed of convergence to world prices have been offset by de facto export quotas.

The trade collapse is worsened by monetary disintegration. On the cash side, Russia's unilateral decision to (re)nationalize the ruble has deprived the other republics of seignorage, monetary control and, not least, cash—prompting both the issue of temporary coupons as complementary monies and outright secessions from the ruble zone. Most of the new monies enjoy at best limited local acceptance; few serve as acceptable means of payments in inter-republican trade. The credit side presents an equally bleak picture. The initial institutional set-up actively encouraged a fiscal deficit-race since the inflation tax could be partly shifted to the other republics. While Russia has maintained the monopoly on printing ruble notes, republican central banks were able to create ruble credit to settle inter-republican import bills. The structure of intra-FSU trade rendered the net exporters of energy—Russia and Kazakhstan—net losers in this game: in the first six months of 1992 alone, Russia accumulated a surplus of 320 billion rubles against the other republics, settled in (de facto) increasingly worthless bank deposits.

The trade-induced credit explosion further fueled the rapid growth of the Russian money-supply and accelerated inflation. In response, credit extension by the Russian central bank to the republican central banks was curtailed in the summer of 1992 and the clearing process was transferred to commercial banks with "republican rubles" trading on the open market at discounts reflecting their trade position (Table 1.4). In combination, the two measures have effectively rung the death knells of the ruble clearing system.

The successor monies, hobbled by economic and political uncertainty, have so far failed to fill the gap left by the collapse of ruble clearing. The

Table 1.3
Regional Dependence in the Former Soviet Union

	Gross State Product per capita (relative)	Total trade (% of Gross State Product)	FSU trade (% of total trade)
Latvia	130	54.1	86.7
Estonia	120	58.9	85.1
Belarus	115	52.0	85.8
Russia	115	22.3	57.8
Lithuania	115	54.5	86.8
Georgia	95	43.8	86.5
Ukraine	90	34.0	79.1
Armenia	90	53.7	89.2
Moldova	80	52.2	87.9
Azerbaijan	80	41.3	85.7
Kazakhstan	75	34.2	86.3
Turkmenia	70	42.2	89.1
Kirgyzystan	60	45.6	87.1
Uzbekistan	55	39.7	85.9
Tadjikistan	50	43.7	86.3

Sources: Pisani-Ferry and Sapir 1992, 15; IMF; Deutsche Bank 1991, 45.

alternative—settlement of bilateral balances in hard cash—remains unattractive as scarce dollar holdings are largely spent on imports from the West. The end result is an increasing reliance on economically inefficient bilaterally-balanced trade which, given the extreme degree of inter-republican dependence and the structural surpluses of Russia and Kazakhstan, can only be found at a low fraction of previous trade levels.[3]

1.4 A Reform Package

Trade and production have collapsed in the former Soviet Union. Part of the decline reflects the unavoidable costs of transition, yet a significant fraction must be attributed to the avoidable resurgence of economic nationalism. As in the 1920s, the successor states agree—in principle—that a reduction in trade barriers and monetary hardening would be desirable. Indeed, the communiqués of the Brussels conferences are strikingly reminiscent of their antecedents in the Portrose conference of 1922. Yet now, as then, progress towards implementation proceeds at a snail's pace, raising the specter of a repeat appearance of the interwar dilemma: agreement in

[3] Fischer (1992) estimates a 44% first round decline in trade from moving to bilateral balance.

Table 1.4
Republican Exchange Rates, September 1992

Republic	Exchange rate vis-a-vis Russia	Trade deficit with Russia
Kazakhstan	0.32	46.7
Ukraine	0.32–0.42	159.3
Belarus	0.74–1.05	22.0
Moldova	0.73–0.84	12.5
Tajikistan	0.84–1.05	3.7

Source: *Economist,* 19 September 1992, 96.

principle and inaction in the particulars.

The behavior of republican governments is rational at the individual level, although it becomes increasingly detrimental at the systemic level. Uncertainty about the policies of other republics, coupled with a desire to obtain bargaining chips for future negotiations, renders the hoarding of scarce goods within a republic's boundary an attractive choice. Export controls are made even more attractive by inflation variability across republics. Within the common currency area which existed until last summer, achieving inflation rates below the average implied arbitrage inflows of money from other republics and, hence, outflows of goods—a trend countered by additional restrictions including export limitations and residency requirements for buyers.

In contrast to free trade, the resulting protectionism is self-sustaining. Even though all republics may (indeed, do) agree that a joint move to freer trade would be mutually beneficial, the first republic to liberalize may find itself denuded of her hoards without much compensation if the other republics choose not to follow suit. The stability of the protectionist equilibrium reflects the principle of second best: starting from a situation of general excess demand, removing the barriers in one region only leads to a manifestation of the entire excess demand in that region. The lesson was learned the hard way by postwar Great Britain upon the unilateral introduction of Sterling convertibility. It applies with equal force today to the republics of the former Soviet Union. In like vein, monetary beggar-thy-neighbor policies remained individually attractive as long as Russia accepted credit created by republican central banks as payments for republican imports, even though a joint return to sound money might have been globally more beneficial.

Once reached, the protectionist outcome thus becomes hard to dislodge without a formal coordination and enforcement mechanism, a stick to complement the carrot of greater access to export markets and monetary stability. Two candidates for the role of central coordinator come to mind, one internal and one external. Internally, Russia, given her dominant role in the FSU, may wield sufficient power to successfully lead a drive towards lower trade barriers. Externally, the International Monetary Fund (IMF), through its influence on the availability of external credit, may achieve the same goal.

The Russian leadership approach relies on exploiting the asymmetry of bargaining power within the FSU: Russia suffers relatively little from any unilateral trade conflict and thus may be able to credibly threaten retaliation against non-conforming republics. Table 1.5 provides a rough and ready measure of bargaining power by calculating the effects on production of curtailing trade between the republics. The first column reports the loss (as a fraction of total output) a republic would incur if trade in "soft" goods were to stop (without alternative markets outside the FSU). With the exception of Russia and Kazakhstan, republics stand to lose between a quarter and half of their production, underlining the prime importance of intra-republican trade. Column two reports the loss to Russia (as a fraction of total output) if trade with the particular republic were to stop, and column three reports the ratio of absolute losses to the republic and to Russia. While the precise numbers are clearly subject to substantial measurement error, the qualitative result is likely to be sturdy: with the exception of Ukraine, losses to Russia from particular bilateral trade disturbances are fairly minor; with the exception of Kazakhstan, the loss to the republic exceeds the loss to Russia itself.

Reliance on Russia as a means to achieve internal coordination, however, appears increasingly risky. First, the Russia option assumes continued progress towards marketization in Russia itself. The reintroduction of price controls, sluggish privatization and an unwillingness to enforce hard budget-controls cast doubt on the political support for free markets at present. Second, the internal approach assumes that Russia is willing not to exploit her relative power to achieve gains at the cost of the FSU as a whole. The very fact of Russia's dominant position however will render individual welfare maximization a tempting option for any Russian government. Thirdly, the very existence of a consistent Russian policy is increasingly questionable as independence movements in the regions, encouraged by attempts of the feuding central government and parliament to garner support by promising more regional independence, threaten a disintegration of the Russian

Table 1.5
Relative Bargaining Power of the Republics

	Loss from disruption of trade (% of Net Material Product)			Index of bargaining power (Asilis & Brown)
	Republic	Russia	Ratio	
Russia	11.5	—	—	8.0
Kazakhstan	12.5	1.3	0.7	5.0
Ukraine	24.2	4.8	1.3	7.3
Uzbekistan	26.6	1.0	1.5	4.1
Turkmenistan	28.2	0.2	1.6	3.9
Tajikistan	31.7	0.2	1.8	2.4
Georgia	35.9	0.5	2.0	4.9
Azerbaijan	36.4	0.5	2.0	5.1
Kirgizia	38.3	0.2	2.1	2.8
Moldova	45.0	0.4	2.5	3.5
Lithuania	46.2	0.4	2.6	4.4
Armenia	50.3	0.3	2.8	4.0
Estonia	51.1	0.2	2.8	4.6
Latvia	52.1	0.3	2.9	5.0
Belarus	52.9	1.2	2.9	4.4

Source: Nuti and Pisani-Ferry 1992, 25; Asilis and Brown 1991, 19.

federation.[4] Lastly, a Russia- (Moscow-) led reform will, rationally or not, encounter substantial political resistance from republican governments deriving a large part of their legitimization from opposition to the pervasive influence of Moscow.[5] Internal coordination failed in Austria-Hungary in the 1920s. As of today, there is little reason to expect a better fate in the 1990s.

Can external coordination work? In the 1920s, following severe economic disruptions, the successor states accepted the appointment of League of Nations commissioners with effective veto-power over fiscal and monetary decisions as a precondition for foreign loans. The commissioners proved instrumental in returning Austria and Hungary to sound policies (Dornbusch 1992; Flood, Garber and Spence 1992). Today, foreign economic dictators—of the benevolent kind—are not (yet?) in the political picture. External credits are granted without much regard to inter-republican conduct in trade and monetary matters. Not surprisingly, external

[4] Paul Goble of the Carnegie Endowment for Peace estimates that *oblasts* to date have issued some 14,000 regulations which directly contradict central law, casting increasing doubt on the ability of the central Russian government or of Parliament to implement policy.
[5] Ukraine's Leonid Kravchuk exemplifies the caution vis-a-vis Russia: "We are sharing a bed with an elephant: if it rolls over it can smother us" (*Financial Times,* 20 January 1993).

exhortations go largely unheeded.

The lessons of the past encourage a more forceful approach to trade and monetary reform. The IMF, combining a pool of technical knowledge with neutrality regarding inter-republican conflicts and a strong bargaining chip in its ability to affect access to international capital markets, provides a natural candidate for external coordinator. An extension of IMF conditionality to include inter-republican relations offers a promising mechanism. Undoubtedly, a significant role for the IMF in the external relations of the newly independent republics will meet with substantial political opposition. Yet, if history provides a lesson, in the end the cost of inaction will outweigh political reservations; furthermore, the IMF provides a politically convenient scapegoat on which to blame politically unpopular but necessary actions.

The policy challenge is twofold. A continuation of the present trade and production collapse for another year or two risks undermining the already fragile political support for ongoing liberalization. A resuscitation of trade in the short term (even in the absence of a healthy monetary system) may prove crucial in ensuring the survival of reforms. However, long-term success of the reforms requires wrenching changes in trade patterns as enterprises adjust to a new environment with radically different relative prices, higher transportation and energy costs, and increased access to other trading partners. Economic policy advice must thus aim to devise structures bounding the short-term contraction while not impeding long-term adjustment. Contrary to accepted wisdom, successful economic reform in the FSU may well require cautious macroeconomic re-centralization along the lines described below to ensure the success of microeconomic de-centralization. The rapid introduction of a payments union between the republics serves to achieve this objective. However, the union will provide at best a short-run solution. In the medium run, a return to sound money and a substantial softening of trade barriers are prerequisites for a successful transition to markets. To a degree, the very introduction of a payment union serves to facilitate the transition by providing a natural coordinating institution. The adoption of a minimal code of conduct regarding trade among the successor republics completes the reform package by determining the dynamics of trade policy after the payments union is established.

The Payments Union

The trade situation in the FSU is rapidly deteriorating. Ruble-based trade has shrunk dramatically as secessions and competitive money-issues have eroded the ruble zone. Settlement in hard currencies provides no alternative as republics attempt to preserve scarce reserves for purchases of hard goods. The result is a regression to bilaterally-balanced barter and, consequently, severe trade contraction. In the medium run, stabilization will do much to revive monetary trade. However, a return to monetary stability cannot be expected for some time. A continued trade and production collapse imposes severe political costs, motivating the search for a temporary arrangement enabling a limited revival of multilateral trade even in the absence of a sound monetary system. The proposal for a payments union aims to fill that role.

A payments union along the lines advocated in the by-now sizeable literature enables a return to multilateralism. At the end of each month, surpluses and deficits within the union are offset; temporary imbalances are financed by prespecified credit quotas; fundamental disequilibria can be addressed by additional conditional loans. In addition, a payments union provides a natural coordination mechanism for reducing trade barriers: a gradual reduction of the credit quotas beyond which settlement in hard currency is required allows a smooth convergence towards full convertibility. The European Payments Union of postwar western Europe provides a useful model for such a flexible approach towards gradual, coordinated trade reform.

A Code of Conduct

The payments union, by allowing a return to multilateralism despite monetary instability acts as a short-run tranquilizer. It does not, however, address the underlying causes of trade imbalances. Trade liberalization must urgently follow if the transition to markets is to succeed. The dissimilarity between the republics in combination with nationalist politics suggests that highly-integrated trade reforms are unlikely. In the medium run, substantial variability in trade regimes and the soundness of republican monies must be expected. The adoption of a code of conduct aims to eliminate the most harmful variants of trade policies while creating a policy structure which permits a gradual convergence towards lower trade barriers and sound money.

The proposed code of conduct for trade policy is based on two core principles: a default of non-intervention and non-discrimination. Based on these principles, the code specifies the conditions under which restrictions can be introduced, the instruments that can be used, the manner in which they can be used and, finally, the procedure in case of disputes. Table 1.6 presents an outline of such

Table 1.6
A Code of Conduct

Non-intervention default	Individuals and enterprises are allowed to freely trade in goods and services unless specifically prohibited from doing so.
Symmetry	Trade regulations apply equally to all republics.
Unrestricted passage	Goods in transit are not subjected to unwarranted delay. Transport fees do not exceed reasonable costs.
Imports restrictions	Tariffs take preference over quotas. If imposed, quota allocations are sold by unrestricted auction.
Export restrictions	Export restrictions may only be imposed on products with regulated prices. Price reform is to be urgently implemented.
Uniformity	Goods are grouped into three groups for tariff purposes.
Disputes	Disputes will be decided by an arbitration council. The decision is binding.

a code.[6] The effectiveness of the code will be determined by the power of the arbitration council, a body to be staffed by independent experts with representation (but no voting rights) for the republics. Institutionally, the GATT would provide an obvious choice for locating the council. A temporary halt to international financial assistance for republics ruled to be in violation of the code would provide the necessary bite.

1.5 Conclusion

Economic reform of the type witnessed in the formerly-planned economies invariably entails sizeable initial welfare-losses for at least part of the population. Declining standards of living render the previous (dismal but stable) system more attractive in retrospect, creating political resistance to the continuation of pro-market reforms. If sufficiently strong, the nostalgia trap may even topple the reform process. In sharp contrast to the experiences of the transition economies of central Europe, notably Poland and the Czech Republic, the recent resurgence of conservative leaders in Russia and Ukraine suggests that the nostalgia trap may have snapped shut on many of the former Soviet Republics.

[6] See Gross, Pisani-Ferry, and Sapir 1992 for a very similar proposal made for the Brussels Conference.

In this essay, I argued that an explosive mixture of political and economic nationalism has played a major role in depressing production and trade in the FSU further than in the other transition economies, thus promoting the nostalgia effect. The politics of disintegration made the achievement of "independence" paramount for republican governments keen on survival. Political independence, now as in the 1920s, could not be envisaged without a drastic reduction in economic interdependence, resulting in increasing trade barriers reinforced by monetary instability.

Economic recovery in the FSU ultimately depends on individuals grasping the opportunities offered by the market environment. Their ability to assume the initiative depends on a return to sound monetary policies and a reduction of the protectionist mood. It is here that the West, seeking to safeguard the transition to democratic market economies, has a crucial role to play in prodding the republics into action. Rendering continued financial assistance conditional on the adoption of a minimal code of conduct for inter-republican trade relations can provide the necessary impulse. The conditionality needs to be strictly applied: the close linkages between the republics implies that failure in one republic could reduce the recovery potential of all the other republics. To stabilize trade in the short run, the code of conduct should be augmented by a self-liquidating payments union. While my arguments addressed the issue of inter-republican trade, they directly extend to intra-republican trade conflicts that may assume increasing importance, particularly in Russia.

References

Asilis, C., and S. Brown. 1991. Western Aid and Soviet Reform: The Role of Coordination. Department of Economics, Georgetown University. Working Paper.

Berger, P.-R. 1982. *Der Donauraum im Wirtschaftlichen Umbruch nach dem Ersten Weltkrieg*. Vienna: VWGO.

Deutsche Bank. 1991. *Die Sovietunion im Umbruch*. Frankfurt: Deutsche Bank.

Dornbusch, R. 1992. Monetary Problems of Post-Communism: Lessons from the End of the Austro-Hungarian Empire. MIT. Photocopy.

Fischer, S. 1992. Russia and the Soviet Union Then and Now. NBER Conference paper. Forthcoming.

Flood, R. P. , P. M. Garber, and A. M. Spence. 1992. The Dissolution of the Austrian

Hungarian Empire: Lessons for Currency Reform. IMF. Photocopy.

Gros, D., J. Pisani-Ferry, and A. Sapir. 1992, eds. Inter-State Economic Relations in the Former Soviet Union. Brussels: CEPS Working Document, no. 63.

Nuti, M., and J. Pisani-Ferry. 1992. Post-Soviet Issues: Stabilization, Trade and Money. In CEPR. *The Economics Consequences of the East.* London: CEPR.

Pasvolsky, L. 1928. *Economic Nationalism Of The Danubian States.* New York: Macmillan.

Pisani-Ferry, J., and A. Sapir. 1992. Trade and Transition to the Market: A Survey of the Key Issues. In Gros, Pisani-Ferry and Sapir 1992.

2 The Transition to a Market Economy: Are there Useful Lessons from History?

Joachim Ahrens

2.1 Introduction

The mostly peaceful revolutions in central and eastern Europe at the end of the 1980s marked the ultimate breakdown of the traditional socialist systems in the region. Following many years of half-hearted and inconsistent reforms and growing popular pressure for more political freedom, the transformation of the entire social system came to be seen as the only way of overcoming the prevailing political and economic problems. The former European members of the Council for Mutual Economic Assistance (CMEA)[1] decided to transform both their centrally-planned economies and their socialist political systems. The transition towards a democratic constitutional state, a market-type economy and social pluralism reflects the growing desire for a liberal way of life in eastern Europe.

In such transformation processes a highly sensitive interaction emerges between the political, economic and cultural subsystems. Within a short time-period this interaction challenges the entire organizational framework of society. The systemic change represents a unique historical challenge, although possible models of orientation and patterns of explanation appropriate for the Newly Liberalizing Countries (NLCs) in central and eastern Europe are not entirely based on new utopian visions of the future, but, to some extent, on lessons from the past.[2]

I am grateful to Karl-Heinz Ahrens and Christina Daseking for critical comments and helpful suggestions.

[1] In Europe, there were seven full and active members of the CMEA: Bulgaria, former Czechoslovakia, the former German Democratic Republic, Hungary, Poland, Romania and the former Soviet Union (van Brabant 1990).

[2] In this study the terms "Newly Liberalizing Countries" and "central and eastern European countries" refer to former Czechoslovakia, Poland, Hungary, Bulgaria, Romania and the successor states of the former Soviet Union.

Since a general theory of the transformation of centrally-planned economies into market-type economies has not yet been developed, policy makers in central and eastern Europe and their Western consultants still seek appropriate strategies. A number of Western economists suggest that the development patterns of some economies in Latin America or Asia might serve as models for the restructuring in central and eastern Europe. Others believe that there are useful lessons to be drawn from postwar-Germany's economic miracle or from Spain's political and economic transition during the last thirty years.

The key question addressed in this paper is to what extent there are useful lessons from history for the east European transformation processes. If suitable lessons can be drawn, the NLCs could reduce the adjustment costs of their own transitions. In order to evaluate the usefulness of historical comparisons, the initial conditions for the transformation in central and eastern Europe have to be taken into account first, as well as the requirements for a *systemic* transformation. Subsequently, I will discuss to what extent it is possible to learn from the economic successes and failures of Spain, Germany, the Newly Industrialized Countries, and Latin America—countries which at times carried out similar broad economic reforms or transformations.[3, 4]

2.2 Initial Conditions

Although the initial conditions have not been the same throughout central and eastern Europe, the basic structures and the fundamental economic and political problems show great similarities. In all NLCs the fundamental economic and political problems at the beginning of the transformation process largely reflect systemic, functional failures of a soviet-type economy, insufficient and inconsistent reforms during the 1980s, as well as the vacuum of order—a half-way-house somewhere between plan and market—which evolved in the course of the breakdown of the socialist systems.[5]

The Economic Situation on the Eve of Transformation

The actual economic situation in central and eastern Europe at the beginning of the

---

[3] The group of Newly Industrialized Countries includes South Korea, Taiwan, Hong Kong and Singapore, of which only South Korea has been explicitly considered in this study.

[4] The German unification of 1990 and the transformation of the former-GDR economic system have not been taken into account in this analysis. Possible lessons of German unification for central and eastern Europe have been discussed by Siebert, Schmieding, and Nunnenkamp 1992.

[5] For detailed information on the nature of the socialist systems see Ericson 1991 and Wolf 1991.

1990s is characterized by an accelerating decline in output (except in Poland) in 1991, a decline which had already started in 1989 (Table 2.1).[6, 7] Estimates for 1992 predict continuing negative growth rates of GDP throughout the region, albeit not as large.[8] Contraction has reflected the breakdown of the old command system, the lack of functioning market mechanisms, political instability, and the tight financial policies in the first stabilization efforts. As a result of continued labor hoarding, limited success in the privatization and commercialization of production, and a significant fall in real wages, unemployment is still relatively low (IMF 1992a).

However, the fall in output has not only been the result of domestic problems and policies, but also of international developments. The breakdown of the traditional trading arrangements of the CMEA and a substantial deterioration in most countries' terms of trade (a consequence of settling former CMEA trade on a hard-currency basis and at world market prices) seriously affected the economies' import capacities, domestic production, and export opportunities, since—as a result of the socialist division of labor—a strong economic interdependence had evolved among the central and eastern European states (IMF 1992a). In 1988, the share of CMEA trade in total trade ranged between 41% for Poland and 81% for Bulgarian exports (Collins and Rodrik 1991).[9] Besides the terms-of-trade effect, the payments difficulties of the Soviet Union were a principal source of the growing current-account deficits of the central and eastern European countries.

Except for Romania and former Czechoslovakia, the scale of foreign debt has reached an alarming level (Table 2.2). The ratio of net debt to hard-currency exports (generally accepted as an appropriate indicator for evaluating a country's position as international debtor) has significantly deteriorated for all countries but Poland. In 1991, only Hungary and Czechoslovakia were able to borrow in international capital markets (IMF 1992a). Coupled with insufficient or delayed economic reforms, the debt boom will further impair the region's creditworthiness and, thereby, threaten to retard the transformation process. Only the better

---

[6] A comprehensive analysis of the economic situation in central and eastern Europe in early 1992 has been provided by Gabrisch et al. 1992.

[7] Welfare losses implied by the decline in output may be overestimated because output losses also reflect cutbacks for unwanted production.

[8] However, the successor states of the Soviet Union are supposed to perform even worse than in 1991 due to the great extent of political instability, the relatively late starting point of transformation policies, and inconsistent economic reforms in 1992 (Gabrisch et al. 1992).

[9] In the meantime, only Czechoslovakia, Hungary, and Poland were able to expand exports to OECD countries, especially to western Europe.

Table 2.1
Central and Eastern Europe: Macroeconomic Indicators

	Real GDP		Consumer Prices		Employment		Current Acount[a]	
	1990	1991	1990	1991	1990	1991	1990	1991
Central and Eastern Europe (5)[b]	−2.9	−16.9	22.0	92.8	−0.8	−2.6	−1.1	−0.7
Central and Eastern Europe[b]	−7.1	−16.6	149.1	134.7	−1.6	−5.8	−0.5	−2.2
Bulgaria	−10.6	−25.0	26.3	460.4	−6.5	−13.9	−5.3	−12.1
Czechoslovakia	−0.4	−16.4	10.8	58.7	−0.1	−6.6	−2.9	2.1
Hungary	−4.0	−7.5	33.4	33.0	−0.7	−1.1	1.2	1.4
Poland	−11.6	−8.0	585.8	70.3	−1.6	−2.4	4.0	−2.1
Romania	−7.4	−12.0	4.7	164.3	−1.0	−2.5	−8.7	−7.7
Former Soviet Union[c]	−2.0	−17.0	5.6	86.0	−0.6	−2.0	−1.2	−0.2
Russia	0.4	−9.0	5.0	90.4	−1.1	−1.1	−0.8	0.7
Belarus	−3.0	−3.1[d]	4.5	80.0	−0.9	−2.0	−2.0	3.4
Ukraine	−3.4	−9.6[d]	4.2	84.2	−3.0	−0.4	−4.9[e]	−6.4[f]

Changes in percent, unless otherwise noted.
[a] Current account in convertible and nonconvertible currencies. The aggregates have been calculated as combined current account in percent of aggregate GDP or NMP.
[b] Including Yugoslavia as it existed in 1990. (5) refers to the central and eastern European economies excluding the former Soviet Union.
[c] Reliable, comparable data for the republics of the former Soviet Union are not generally available; the estimates presented above should be interpreted as indicative of broad orders of magnitude.
[d] Net material product.
[e] State sector.
[f] Trade balance as a percent of NMP or GDP. For Ukraine, balance of foreign and inter-republic trade.
Source: IMF 1992a, 31.

reformers, which might be capable of improving their future ability to service debt, can be expected to increase their creditworthiness.

Given such tremendous macroeconomic difficulties, underlying microeconomic problems with respect to the still-distorted price structure, insufficient reforms of property rights and a lack of financial discipline, the enormous requirements for systemic change cannot be met overnight. Assuming average growth of per-capita income in the OECD economies amounts to 2.5% per annum, the central and eastern European countries have to attain growth rates of

Table 2.2
Indicators of Foreign Debt in Convertible Currency, 1990

	Net debt (million US $)	Net debt per capita (US $)	ND/X[a] (%)
Czechoslovakia	6,300	403.8	111
Hungary	20,300	1,915.1	343
Poland	41,800	1,102.9	418
Bulgaria	9,800	1,088.9	468
Romania	1,300	56.0	38
Former Soviet Union	43,400	151.4	139

All data are preliminary at the time of writing.
[a] (Net debt − reserves)/hard-currency goods exports
Source: OECD 1991, 20, 24; World Bank 1991,205.

7.5% (15.6%), in order to catch up within fifty (twenty) years.[10] This might be interpreted as a rough estimate of the time necessary to transform the economies in central and eastern Europe successfully. However, a growth rate of 7.5% over fifty years is historically unprecedented, suggesting an even longer convergence period.

Political Starting Conditions and Sociopolitical Aspects

The political landscape before and during the transitional process plays an important, maybe crucial, role in the success or failure of the systemic change. In almost all central and eastern European countries forces have come into power whose objectives include abolishing the socialist economic system and creating a market economy. The majority of the NLCs sought to create a democratic political system, following the Western model, and many have already conducted free and general elections.[11] However, a working democracy is not only based on democratic institutions such as a parliament and free elections, but, even more important, on a certain system of social values, on specific attitudes and convictions shared by all citizens. Such preconditions have not fully evolved as yet.

The lack of rational collective decisions endangers political stability and the

[10] This calculation has been based on per-capita income data reported by the World Bank 1992. Per-capita income of the former USSR in 1990 has been estimated as $1,780 (IMF et al. 1990).

[11] In this context, the majority of the successor states of the Soviet Union represents a notable exception. Whereas former republics such as Russia and Ukraine are still struggling to establish sustainable democratic structures, other republics are not yet on their way to democracy. Either they are still ruled by old communists or by new nationalists, or they are plagued by civil war.

elaboration of a transformation strategy, which is based on a broad social consensus. A great variety of political and social groups and parties generally emerge in systems which are at the very beginning of their democratization process. For example after Polish elections in 1991, 29 political parties were represented in the *Sejm* in Warsaw. Such a development adversely affects the prospects for social and political consensus, placing at risk the development and realization of comprehensive and rational economic transformation programs. Inconsistent populist compromises may then dominate and important steps of the transformation may be delayed again and again.

Moreover, the systemic change in central and eastern Europe is confronted with numerous forces of resistance coming from different social groups. Orthodox communists wielding considerable political power in some countries try to parályze the transformation process. The same is true for large segments of the wide-spread bureaucracy, fearing the loss of influence, power, and (not least) their jobs in the course of transformation. Large parts of the so-called *nomenklatura* still exist and seek to counteract the realization of political reform measures especially on the microeconomic level (Csaba 1991).

In some countries, the transition to a market economy is further delayed and hampered by geopolitical problems and domestic disintegration. Inter-republic trade almost totally broke down due to a lack of economic coordination between the members of the Commonwealth of Independent States (IMF 1992b). Russia is subject to various kinds of separation movements. Czechoslovakia was separated into two countries in January 1993. Former Yugoslavia and some former republics of the Soviet Union suffer from civil war. These concerns direct attention to (geo)political, rather than economic, objectives.

Finally, the population has to play a key role during the transition. A broad acceptance of the necessity to transform the whole system is as important as appropriate ways of thinking and acting to meet the requirements of the transformation. Such consensus is quite fragile and problematic in central and eastern Europe, essentially for two reasons: first, the willingness to bear poverty and social uncertainty is limited; second, transition to a market economy requires the development of a market-oriented pattern of individual behavior. In this respect, one still observes fundamental deficits in central and eastern Europe—more so in eastern Europe and Eurasia than in central Europe, the latter indoctrinated by the socialist dogma for *only* forty years or so. In general, peoples' thinking is still dominated by the goal of (socialist) equality instead of individual freedom. The consequences of socialist education consist of a lack of self-responsibility and an unwillingness and incapability to take individual risks. However, these are essential characteristics for a working market economy. At present, helplessness and myopia dominate wide ranges of individual activities. Political leaders have to take these facts into consideration when they design a transformation strategy.

2.3 Economic Requirements of a Systemic Transformation

The economic objective of the systemic change in central and eastern Europe clearly consists of creating a market economy. In the Western world, three basic prototypes of successful market economies can be identified, exemplifying the possibility of building a market economy in different historical, political, economic, and socio-cultural environments. According to Paul Marer (1991), these prototypes include: the social market economies in western Europe; the consumer-directed market economies, of which the most important example is the United States; and the market economies of the Far East, which are dominated by the philosophy of administrative guidance.

Despite substantial differences among the various types, there are some common features of the different systems which are unalterable prerequisites for a well-functioning market economy. Irrespective of their setting, these systemic features and the underlying policies have to be duplicated by the central and eastern European countries, if they want to improve their economic performance and successfully transform into market economies. Marer identified the following fundamental features of a market economy:

- Basic constitutional rights and a market-oriented institutional setting: Besides basic political rights combined with economic freedom, these include the guarantee of private-property rights, appropriate business laws, and the like.
- Private-property rights: Serve as a basis of a market-oriented incentive structure, an efficient production of goods and allocation of factors of production.
- Competition: The key characteristic of a working market economy. It requires a comprehensive and stable framework of regulations and rules in all fields of economic activity. In this context, relatively small countries have to open their economies to the world market, whereas big economies with large domestic markets may be able to afford protectionist policies.
- A sound currency: The most important precondition for competition. A structure of relative prices reflecting relative scarcities and tastes, a low rate of inflation and convertibility are elementary for avoiding microeconomic distortions, for an

efficient allocation of goods, services, and factors of production, and for providing appropriate incentives to economic agents.

- An adequate-to-high level of savings, an appropriate tax system which does not destroy private incentives, and efficient financial intermediation: Essential features for sustained economic performance and growth.
- A well-functioning infrastructure: Necessary for efficient economic activities. It serves (like the protection of the environment) as a basis of economic growth, and raises the standard of living.
- A stable political system based on pluralism and individual freedom: Necessary in order to provide comprehensive opportunities for the individual activities and personal fulfillment of producers, consumers, investors, and employees. Additionally, the state has to guarantee a certain minimum of social security, and a fair (not equal) distribution of income.

Any economic transformation process in central and eastern Europe has to take into account such basic features of a market economy. The key issues that have to be addressed in the transition process can be divided into four broad categories (Table 2.3): macroeconomic stabilization; microeconomic liberalization; restructuring and privatization; and the role of the state in economic affairs.[12]

It is widely agreed that macroeconomic stability is a precondition for most stages of economic transformation. Stabilization here means eliminating large disequilibria and balancing total domestic demand with domestic production. Price stability can then be realized with no need for the economy to borrow from abroad beyond its medium-run capacity to service debt. Without macroeconomic stability, it is extremely difficult for prices to reflect relative scarcities and tastes—a central aspect of a working market economy (Collins and Rodrik 1991).

Internal liberalization means free domestic prices as well as open domestic markets for residents and foreigners, that is, the guarantee of free entry and exit in all kinds of markets. External liberalization includes decentralizing foreign trade, reducing trade protection, and establishing currency convertibility. Restructuring and privatization are further crucial steps toward a market economy. The central and eastern European economies still show a very high degree of monopolization and a strong bias toward heavy industry. Restructuring is necessary to avoid continued rent-seeking and to build up new industrial structures based on light

[12] For a more complete analysis of the major economic steps that must be undertaken during the transition to a market economy see Blanchard et al. 1991.

Table 2.3
Economic Elements of Systemic Transformation

Macroeconomic stabilization	Reduction of macroeconomic imbalances; hardening budget constraints; tight monetary and fiscal policies; emergency safety net.
Microeconomic liberalization	Price reform (including wages and interest rates); deregulation of goods and factor markets; international trade liberalization; currency convertibility; reform of the distribution system.
Restructuring and privatization	Small- and large-scale privatization; building up new private enterprises; privatization of land and housing; commercialization of still-existing state enterprises; industrial policy to build up non-heavy industries (including services).
The role of the state in economic affairs	Market-oriented legal system (including property rights protection); providing market-oriented institutions (independent central bank, two-tier banking system, anti-monopoly authorities, etc.); reforms of the administration, establishing a comprehensive social-security system; creation of tools for indirect macroeconomic policy making.

industry and the service sector. Furthermore, private property creates incentives for the individual to work harder, increases efficiency, and represents a precondition for foreign direct investment as well as for eliminating the monopolistic structure of the economies. The government has to take care that small- and large-scale privatization is put into motion as soon as possible. Additionally, it should promote the foundation of new private enterprises.

Last but not least, the economic role of the state has to be newly defined. The state has to concentrate on institutional reforms, on establishing information systems, and on creating tools and institutions for *indirect* economic management, such as a simple, but effective, tax system, budgeting control, and sensible monetary and fiscal policies. The authorities have to stop subsidizing enterprises and establish hard budget-constraints for all economic units. A decisive factor is the creation of a social safety net to soften the adjustment process; therefore, incomes policy will play a major role in the transformation process.

Despite the broad consensus among western and eastern economists and most reform-minded politicians with respect to the key economic elements that have to be addressed in the transition period, there is no similarly broad agreement on the timing and sequencing of the transformation process. The pace of the transformation strategy, however, determines the consistency and credibility of the policies of systemic change and, finally, the success of the entire transformation process itself.

Moreover, evidence from history suggests that a set of issues exists which are crucial for the elaboration of a successful transformation strategy. These include non-economic factors of strategic relevance for the systemic change and aspects concerning the elements and conceptual underpinnings of economic reforms. The former imply questions regarding the design of the political system, the vision of policy making, and the reputation and authority of government (Ritter 1991). The latter encompass the design of economic reforms, the institutional setting, the role of expectations and wage policy, the determinants of economic growth, as well as the question of external liberalization (Giersch 1991a; Nunnenkamp 1992).

The following case studies are examined in the light of these issues. Corresponding findings will be summarized in the last section by identifying possible implications for central and eastern Europe.

2.4 Lessons from History

Uncertainties among economic agents and politicians might be reduced, future adjustment costs cut down and benefits increased by drawing lessons from countries which have undergone similarly comprehensive reforms. In this respect, Spain, postwar Germany, the Newly Industrialized Countries, and some Latin American countries are often referred to as suitable models for central and eastern Europe. The question arises to what extent the experiences of these economies are relevant for the systemic change in central and eastern Europe.

Experiences of Non-CMEA Countries

To begin with, the economic conditions prior to reform and the subsequent development patterns of these "reference" countries are briefly outlined. However, only those aspects of economic development are taken into consideration which promise to offer a relevant lesson for central and eastern Europe. Subsequently, possible implications for the transformation process of the NLCs are discussed.

SPAIN

Since Franco's death, in November 1975, Spain has undergone a radical and successful economic and political transformation. Despite partial reforms since the 1950s, Spain still was an authoritarian and bureaucratic state in the mid-70s. Absent the characteristics of a civil society, absolutist, traditionalist, and authoritarian values—coupled with anticapitalist sentiments—determined social life. At that time Spain had a relatively-closed, mixed economy with substantial macroeconomic imbalances and microeconomic distortions. The administered part of the economy was of much greater importance than the area based on market forces. It was basically a rural economy, and the underdeveloped production structure was largely obsolete and highly protected. Factor markets, especially the labor market, showed considerable rigidities (de la Dehesa 1991).

Sustainable reforms started only in 1975. They were broadly based on the solidarity of the major social groups, namely political parties, trade unions, and employers. Keeping the disaster of the 1930s' civil war in mind, there was, from the very beginning, a consensus of all social and political forces on the model the country should emulate. Building up both a Western style democracy and a market economy became the primary political goal. Economically, as well as politically, the vision of the Spanish people was the country's integration into the European Community (EC).

Although the new political leadership showed considerable lack of experience in government and responsible opposition, the authorities attained their objectives within a fairly short time-period. The rational and coherent political agenda, which was realized by the rigorous measures of the leadership, increased the authorities' credibility and supported the development of social containment (an appropriate social framework reducing uncertainties and social conflicts). In this context, the democratic legitimization of the government and other elected representatives in different organizations proved to be of major importance (Ritter 1991). The main reasons for Spain's economic success consisted of the strong will to join the EC, the explicit readiness of the EC to integrate Spain into the community, the quick external opening, and radical and consistent economic reforms.[13] The latter included tight monetary and fiscal policies oriented to the balance of payments, followed by the comprehensive liberalization of markets, and the adoption of obligations imposed by international organizations. Finally, politicians placed special emphasis on building up a competitive economic environment, modernizing infrastructure, and improving general education and management skills (de la Dehesa 1991).

---

[13] Due to Spain's political history, the EC members showed great political interest in integrating Spain into the community. Hence, various political parties of western Europe massively supported Spain's political reorientation.

POSTWAR GERMANY

After World War Two, Germany resembled a classical Soviet-type economy in numerous respects. The economy was characterized by a distorted production structure, price controls, large macroeconomic disequilibria and latent mass unemployment. Between 1945 and 1948, a mixture of allocation systems existed which was, however, dominated by elements of central planning. This induced an extremely inefficient allocation of resources (especially of the labor force) and a considerable repudiation of the legal tender. As a result of the war, the material and financial infrastructures were destroyed. Moreover, the German economy was relatively closed. The currency was non-convertible and foreign trade was a government monopoly. Deficits in the trade account evolved (Wolf 1992; Schmieding 1991).

On the other hand, industrial capacities had been hardly damaged, so that the capital stock showed almost up-to-date technology in 1948. The old, market-oriented institutional infrastructure (banking system, commercial laws, private property rights, and such) was still in place, and public administration worked properly after a relatively short period of adjustment. Further factors positively affecting economic development consisted of the relatively low degree of monopolization, a strong medium-sized industry, and skilled managers and entrepreneurs. Besides general education and skills, the experience and motivation of the German people became decisive factors in generating sustained economic growth (Giersch, Paqué, and Schmieding 1992; Schmieding 1991).

Under the auspices of the allies, especially the United States, political stability was quickly achieved, and a broad social and political consensus evolved for establishing a market economy based on a democratic political system (Watrin 1990). As of June 1948, authorities conducted a radical reform of the economic constitution. In this context, the absent need of privatizing the means of production certainly facilitated the transformation. The reform package included, above all, a currency reform, the restructuring of the financial system, tax releases, price liberalization, and comprehensive deregulation of markets (Wolf 1992; Schmieding, 1991).[14] These measures caused a sudden and drastic regime switch, which initiated a sustained process of economic growth. Monetary policy was strictly aimed at price stability, thereby reducing expectations of inflation. Another

[14] For social reasons several industries were not liberalized during the reconstruction phase (agriculture, mining, housing). It is argued that this caused substantial economic and political problems in the further economic development of Germany (Schmieding 1991).

precondition for the fast long-term growth process was the German populations' high propensity to save. Additionally, authorities gave high priority to measures which encouraged private savings and investments, cognizant of the high social-productivity of capital during the transformation. Steps towards currency convertibility as well as trade liberalization were only gradually taken. Germany could afford to separate internal and external liberalization, because foreign economic relations were of minor importance at the beginning of the transformation (Schmieding 1991; Helliwell 1991).

A crucial factor for the extraordinarily good performance of the German economy between 1948 and the late fifties was the role of expectations. Since these had been more modest than actual economic performance, a *circulus virtuosus* evolved. In particular, the results at the wage-bargaining table were of major importance. As both trade unions and employers had systematically underestimated future productivity gains, real wages increased less than productivity. This development not only maintained social peace and political stability by avoiding distributional conflicts (among residents and between residents and immigrants), but, even more important, induced relatively high profits and comprehensive private investment. Thus, capital-shortage unemployment was reduced and the basis for an economic upswing strengthened (Giersch 1991a).

Another important aspect supporting the economic upswing consisted of two exogenous factors.[15] First of all, the production and export structure exactly met the requirements of international demand in the 1950s, because Germany traditionally had a comparative advantage in the production of investment goods. Favorable international conditions and improvements of the terms of trade additionally supported domestic growth (Giersch, Paqué, and Schmieding 1992). Secondly, the significant number of highly-motivated and well-qualified immigrants (mainly refugees and expellees) improved the stock of human capital inducing further productivity gains. Finally, immigration led to excess supply on the labor market, which implied a greater flexibility in production without jeopardizing price stability (Wolf 1992).

Finally, returning to a market economy was facilitated by the still-existing familiarity of most economic agents with the elements of a market economy and the principles of market-oriented thinking and acting. Since the phase of central planning had been limited to twelve years, hysteresis in individual behavior

---

[15] For more detailed information see Wolf 1992.

positively affected the systemic change, because the transition to a competitive economy could be undertaken with economic agents who had the appropriate knowledge and experience (Wagener 1992). Hence, the traditional work ethic in terms of individual initiatives and readiness to work, as well as the capitalist spirit, which soon re-emerged, became crucial factors for sustainable economic development.

Newly Industrialized Countries: The Case of South Korea

The development of South Korea during the last thirty years has to be regarded as one of the most successful cases of industrialization and economic growth. After the Korean war, South Korea was one of the world's poorest countries. Driving forces for sustained and self-reliant economic development did not exist (Serfas 1987). The economy was highly protected, with considerable supply bottlenecks, relatively low investment, a repressive financial system, a distorted price structure, and an underdeveloped infrastructure and industrial base. Moreover, large budget deficits, a lax monetary policy, and an overvalued currency imposed a serious burden on the economy. The government's inward-oriented policies entailed a highly restrictive trade regime with numerous quantitative import restrictions, high tariffs, and multiple exchange rates (Serfas 1987; Park 1991).

Following the *coup d'état* in May 1961, military forces came to power, built up an authoritarian regime, established political stability and started economic reforms. The first five-year economic development plan (1962) introduced a new orientation in Korean economic policy-making and marked the starting point of sustained economic reforms. The government's policy transcended political ideology and concentrated on economic modernization and growth. Most notably, administrative guidance thereafter became the underlying philosophy of economic policy in South Korea (Serfas 1987).

Although political leaders basically accepted the advantages of a market economy, state interventions—in terms of obligatory planning targets, state orders, and direct incentives—have been regarded as suitable, temporary elements of an economic development strategy. However, the private sector has been intensely involved in the economic decision-making process, taking advantage of the widespread network in the political and economic spheres. Economic policy-making has distinguished itself by single-mindedness, clear policy objectives, and by creating an incentive system which has encouraged entrepreneurship and efficiency.

With respect to internal reforms, the government took a substantial part in providing guidance for key industries, especially for those which were necessary for the development of self-supporting industry. In addition, high priority has been given to monetary stability and decentralization. Economic liberalization was undertaken only gradually. In particular, strict and pervasive controls have been maintained in the financial sector for a long time (Serfas 1987).

The government placed heavy emphasis on reforms of the trade sector from the very beginning. The authorities initiated a successful opening strategy that consisted of a mixture of broad export-promotion and selective import-substitution policies. Subsidies and tax releases for import-substitution industries were temporarily granted with regard to future export potential. They were rapidly removed in cases where the industry could not compete successfully in the world market (Helliwell 1991; Park 1991).

The most important forces in the sustained economic upswing consisted of the economy's rapid participation in the international division of labor, the mobilization of domestic (public and private) savings, and, finally, certain non-economic factors. The early endeavor to integrate South Korea into the world economy substantially eased the country's employment problems. Moreover, the greater openness increased domestic efficiency and growth by encouraging competition. The sustained increase in exports made the import of both investment goods and foreign technology possible, and facilitated South Korea's access to the international capital market. Public and private savings were mobilized by tight fiscal and monetary policies, inducing positive real interest rates, and by the improvement of the banking system. Thus, domestic investment could be increased significantly (Serfas 1987).

Finally, non-economic factors played a major role in the country's economic development. Stimulating impulses for the economic upswing came from the time when Japan was a colonial power in Korea. The Japanese contributed to the economy's modernization: they introduced an efficient education system and familiarized the Korean population with modern methods of production, organization, and administration (Serfas 1987). In addition, a stable political environment and social factors such as ethnic homogeneity, social mobility, a powerful work ethos, and a broad pursuit of better education facilitated the adoption of foreign technology and supported the successful development pattern.

Latin America: The Case of Chile

For several reasons Chile has been regarded as a suitable Latin American model for central and eastern Europe. In 1973, Chilean economic conditions showed great similarities to those in central and eastern Europe today. Unlike other Latin American countries, Chile carried out comprehensive economic reforms in the 1970s and 1980s, including stabilization, liberalization and privatization. Finally, the country's transition from a tightly-controlled and highly-inflationary economy into a stable market economy was successful in contrast to the reforms in, say, Brazil or Argentina.

Initial conditions were characterized by substantial fiscal deficits financed by money creation. In 1973, the budget deficit amounted to 26% of GDP. At the end of the Allende era the economy faced a large monetary overhang and general scarcities. The system of relative prices showed considerable distortions, and, despite price controls, severe inflation emerged inducing negative real interest rates. The financial sector was tightly controlled. Numerous banks and enterprises had been nationalized under Allende. Unemployment was virtually non-existent, and labor productivity declined rapidly. There was no hard budget-constraint, neither for enterprises nor for the state budget. In addition, the external sector was strongly regulated by differentiated tariffs, multiple exchange rates and extensive quantitative restrictions. A large current-account deficit emerged reflecting the severe balance-of-payments crisis (Corbo 1992; Edwards 1991).

In 1973 Pinochet assumed power in a long-lived dictatorship, which, especially at its beginning, made use of brutal repression. Economically, the leadership distinguished itself as an outrider of neo-liberal policy making in Latin America. Chilean authorities undertook a successful strategy of economic reform encompassing stabilization, liberalization and structural adjustment. Stabilization was primarily aimed at the reduction of the budget deficit and a real devaluation in order to restore internal and external balance. A comprehensive price-reform supported the stabilization program by reducing subsidies and creating a price structure that reflected opportunity costs. Economic efficiency increased significantly. Structural elements of the reform tackled the fundamental causes of Chile's crisis, established hard budget constraints and a market-oriented incentive structure (Corbo 1992). Tight fiscal and monetary policies in connection with substantial trade liberalization (including partial convertibility for commercial transactions), a major privatization program and a reform of the tax system stimulated private investment and improved the economy's export performance (Nunnenkamp 1992; Edwards 1991).

The exchange-rate stabilization measures, which were undertaken by pegging the peso to the US dollar in June 1979 aimed to stop inflation. However, although the fiscal deficit had been substantially reduced, this policy led to a significant real overvaluation of the domestic currency in Chile, thereby jeopardizing the country's international competitiveness. The primary objective of greater price stability could be attained only in the long run (Edwards 1991). There is broad agreement that the persistent inflationary pressures and the economic crisis at the beginning of the 1980s were not a failure of the conceptual underpinnings of the reform but, rather, caused by persistent inconsistencies and mistakes in economic policy making. In particular, stubborn inflationary expectations and backward wage indexation, combined with a fixed exchange rate, were responsible for substantial inertia in the Chilean economy (Nunnenkamp 1992).

Implications for Central and Eastern Europe

The timing and sequencing of the transition toward a market economy represent the most urgent problems of policy making in central and eastern Europe. By drawing suitable lessons from the historical experiences of countries which have faced similarly comprehensive policy challenges, it might be possible to reduce future adjustment costs. However, if one tries to identify appropriate implications for the pace of transformation in central and eastern Europe, one has to take certain facts into consideration which *a priori* limit the outcome of the endeavor. First of all, there are no sound theoretical underpinnings concerning optimal timing and sequencing. Secondly, also empirically, it is hardly possible to elaborate well-grounded maxims for policy making as the transformation process started only two or three years ago. Thirdly, the economic reforms of countries in western Europe, Southeast Asia or Latin America can basically serve as a reference point; however, in transferring experiences one has to take several fundamental differences between these states and the NLCs into consideration, including socio-cultural, economic, geopolitical and ethnic aspects.

Socio-cultural differences exist with respect to individual attitudes, thinking and acting. In central and eastern Europe there was no need for the individual to take initiatives, as the state took care of the people. Hence, a situation of "learned helplessness" (Zon 1992, 474) evolved. Additionally, economic actors in the NLCs lack entrepreneurial spirit and knowledge concerning the functioning mechanisms of a market economy. Next, a tradition of lawlessness and corruption evolved hampering the acceptance of new institutional regulations. Finally, the organizational structure of the entire social system has to be changed, so that the problem of the diffusion of a new organizational paradigm evolves.

In economic respects, differences in starting conditions between the central and eastern European countries and the reference economies have to be taken into account. Above all, market-oriented institutions (such as private-property rights, a two-tier banking system, a capital market) existed in the reference countries, whereas they are unknown, or significantly underdeveloped, in central and eastern Europe. Another important aspect is that substantial differences exist even among the NLCs; namely with respect to their history, culture, present policy objectives, and economic conditions prior to transformation.

Finally, in contrast to our historical models, several NLCs are confronted with ethnic and national tensions and geopolitcal problems jeopardizing territorial integrity. Therefore, the potential for massive migration, minority conflicts, and secessionist movements endangers political stability and economic transformation.

Again, these considerations reveal that the transformation in central and eastern Europe has no precedent in history, as the entire social system has to be reformed, including a change of social orientations and of the underlying values of the societies. Thus, a detailed and country-specific formulation of a transformation strategy based on historical lessons from other countries is not feasible. The implications for a transformation strategy have to be restricted to an outline of a more general pattern of systemic change, addressing only those key aspects which are transferable from our reference countries to central and eastern Europe.

Experiences in reference countries clearly reveal that political stability is an unalterable prerequisite for comprehensive reforms. Therefore, in all NLCs, a strong government (that is, one which is not subject to political or social pressure groups) is urgently needed. According to historical evidence, the establishment of a Western-style democracy does not seem to be a necessary precondition for a systemic change. Successful economic transformations in Chile, South Korea and (to some extent) even in postwar Germany and Spain took place under fairly authoritarian regimes. Assuming gains in political freedom to carry economic costs, an authoritarian government as an intermediate step on the road to democracy might have comparative advantages in overcoming economic problems of the transformation (Schwarz 1992). Authoritarian regimes without ideological claims or limited democracies based on substantial presidential powers might be more appropriate the less people are capable of taking advantage of their new individual freedom, and the more active the resistance of pressure groups and old communists to the systemic change.

Governmental power does not only depend on the form of government but also on the relationship between the state authorities and the various social groups. Therefore, the shielding of policy making from the specific claims of social groups which are badly affected by the transformation and the dissolution of reactive pressure groups represent necessary prerequisites for the pursuit of long-term objectives. In this context, it becomes particularly important to identify and organize potential beneficiaries of the transformation. Furthermore, short-term adjustment costs of potential losers have to be rapidly reduced by implementing a social safety net (Nunnenkamp and Funke 1991).

Sustainable, successful transformation policies require a high degree of credibility, consistency and continuity in policy making. The experiences of the reference countries reveal four aspects of political strategy, which play a crucial role: the political and economic vision of the systemic change, as well as the concrete definition of the reforms' objectives; the authority and leadership of the government; the containment of the transformation in terms of an appropriate social framework reducing uncertainties and social conflicts and thereby flanking the adjustment process; and the conceptual approach of the economic reform package.

In Argentina, Menem's vision of the *Revolución Productiva* turned out to be an empty formula, and in Brazil de Mello's plan *Novo Brazil* proved to be unsustainable. On the contrary, Spain's idea of integrating the country into the EC became the leading and broadly accepted vision of the Spanish people and supported the reform process emphatically (Ritter 1991). The creation of a vision of the systemic change in central and eastern Europe will be of crucial importance. In this respect, the proposed EC-integration of Hungary, Poland, the Czech Republic, and (to a limited extent) Slovakia might lead to positive effects, as in the Spanish case. However, the realization of this vision strongly depends on the willingness of the EC to integrate these countries. In this respect, the association agreements of 1991 between the EC and the central European states represent steps in the right direction. On the other hand, due to their own economic interests, one can hardly expect the EC to promote these countries' integration as rapidly and energetically as in the Spanish case. Concerning Romania, Bulgaria and the successor states of the Soviet Union, the likelihood of close international cooperation is even less evident. In particular, the West's interest in the economic and political development of the FSU has been decreasing since late 1992. A return to Europe does not seem to be a realistic opportunity for such countries in the near future.

At present, after the break with communist ideology, governments in central and eastern Europe, except in the FSU, have a relatively good reputation. However, Third World experience illustrates that government reputation can be easily destroyed, but that its restoration is time-consuming and difficult. The history of economic reforms especially in Brazil and Argentina reveals that private economic agents will not believe in announced reforms when previous reform efforts have often been revised. Entrepreneurs, investors, and other economic agents will not be willing to bear short-term adjustment costs if they expect a revision of announced policies. As a consequence, the danger of half-hearted and only-partial reforms is increasing and the authorities' reputation is decreasing (Nunnenkamp and Funke 1991).

In order to attain and maintain its authority, the government has to restructure the public administration as an efficient instrument of policy making as soon as possible. The governmental bodies have to be headed by competent experts, who are able and willing to accept responsibilities. All activities, measures, and operations of political leaders and experts are to be clearly oriented—without any compromises—toward the ultimate goals of the transformation process, thereby making the people aware of the necessity of radical reforms. Furthermore, leadership also implies delegating suitable tasks and duties to subordinated levels of the decision-making process, including the operational units at the microeconomic level. By this way, the efficiency of transformation policies can be enhanced and possible resistance to the systemic change can be headed off.

Moreover, establishing political stability and efficient mechanisms of policy making in central and eastern Europe requires a completely new institutional setting, including norms, rights and sanctions. The rules of the game have to be implemented at the very beginning of the transformation process. They represent the obligatory framework of political, economic and social life, imply a new incentive structure, and establish social containment, which guarantees security and backing for individual activities. Implementing a clear and consistent, formal and informal regulatory framework—and avoiding unexpected changes in political orientations—increase the people's confidence in the continuity and sustainability of political decision-making.

With respect to the success or failure of the economic transformation, expectations play a decisive role. In particular, the experience of postwar Germany underlines this hypothesis, as modest expectations of the people concerning future economic development initiated an economic *circulus virtuosus*. However, due to deficient information about the characteristics of a market economy, unrealistic perceptions of the people and exaggerated promises of political leaders and their (foreign) advisors, expectations are relatively high in the NLCs today. In order to hold expectations in check, politicians must not make unrealistic economic promises, as they did, for example, in Russia in 1992.

The standard of living was very low in Europe after World War Two and in many developing countries at the beginning of their reforms. Hence, the population could only gain by economic reforms. With respect to central and eastern Europe, this assumption does not hold. In the first instance, transformation implies a serious deterioration of welfare—in this regard, it makes no difference whether the political leaders carry out shock therapy or a piecemeal approach. Therefore, state authorities should clearly articulate that personal hardship and considerable individual effort are necessary adjuncts to the reform process. In order to strengthen the people's confidence in an economic recovery, political leaders and economists have to explain the functioning mechanisms of a market economy as well as the role of the individual within the new system. The short- and long-term reform objectives need to be clearly defined and single-mindedly pursued. In addition, an outline and public preannouncement of the conceptual underpinnings and different phases of the economic reform will increase the transparency of policy making and thereby encourage its public acceptance.

Albeit there was broad agreement with respect to a growth-oriented package of economic reforms, numerous attempts to overcome stabilization and structural problems often failed in Latin America. This was mainly the result of inconsistencies in economic reforms and a lack of credibility (Nunnenkamp and Funke 1991). A similar lesson can be drawn from the Soviet experiences in the *perestroika* era, when partial reforms and numerous policy changes proved to be unsustainable. According to empirical evidence, these inconsistencies can be reduced and credibility can be enhanced, if *persistent* and *comprehensive* reform measures are implemented. The Chilean example reveals that a *stabilization-cum-adjustment* approach is more credible and sustainable than one of partial reforms (Nunnenkamp 1992), the more so as a broadly-formulated reform program takes the interdependencies of the various reform steps into account. Stabilization policies, which are not accompanied by microeconomic liberalization and structural reforms, are doomed to fail, because microeconomic distortions—in terms of soft budget-constraints, controlled prices and the like—are often the essential causes of macroeconomic imbalances. Finally, in the case of the NLCs—and especially the FSU—a radical and comprehensive transformation seems to be necessary in order to weaken the influence of pressure groups, thereby reducing the latent danger of a policy reversal and a return to old paradigms.

Imposing hard budget-constraints on enterprises, banks and the public sector, as well as controlling inflation and creating competitive market structures require—first of all—a tight monetary policy carried out by an independent central bank. Furthermore, massive import protection and preferential access to credits have to come to an end. Budget deficits need to be rigorously reduced, and an efficient tax system, which improves tax enforcement and is not vulnerable to inflation, must be built up. In the case that political leaders decide (as they did in South Korea) to maintain selected subsidies to support single branches of industry which promise to perform well in the world market after restructuring, the incentives have to be credible, sufficiently sustained, yet temporarily limited (Helliwell 1991). Finally, privatization and deregulation are of particular importance. Privatizing state-owned enterprises is not only essential for increasing efficiency and competition, but also for avoiding negative effects on the capital stock and the long-term viability of firms. As long as the question of ownership is not clearly settled, the imposition of hard budget constraints may increase the probability of enterprise closing and, thereby, jeopardizing employees' jobs. This danger would impel managers and workers to maximize short-term revenues at the cost of depleting the firms' capital stock (Kiguel and Liviatan 1991).

Due to the former interventionist policy-regime in central and eastern Europe and the extremely high degree of monopolization, deregulation and demonopolization represent further urgent policy needs. With respect to the deregulation of goods and factor markets, the NLCs should not simply copy the piecemeal approach of Western countries, but, rather, decontrol markets quickly and comprehensively, the more so as the fear of low supply elasticities is warranted in the short run only. In this way, they might avoid "government-induced sclerosis" (Giersch 1991a, 18), such as hampered economic development in Germany, where sectors such as mining, transport and agriculture have not been liberalized.[16]

Important lessons concerning wage policies can be drawn from experiences in Latin America and postwar Germany. Stabilization efforts will be endangered, if wages are linked to (past) inflation. In Chile backward indexation in 1976 led to substantial inertia, which accelerated inflation. Hence, successful stabilization

---

[16] However, for social reasons it might be inevitable to maintain certain regulations with respect to basic goods (for example, foods and drugs) in central and eastern Europe.

programs must maintain the deindexation of the labor market throughout the program (Edwards 1991). In postwar Germany, rapid productivity gains were not anticipated by trade unions and employers, so that positive surprises evolved. Wage moderation became one of the key elements for fast growth, because increasing profits and profit expectations stimulated private investment. Additionally, low unit-labor costs are preconditions to attract foreign direct-investment and to improve export performance.

Rapid growth is to be regarded as an unalterable prerequisite for maintaining economic and political stability in central and eastern Europe. Besides wage moderation and investment, private and public savings, functioning capital markets as well as human capital determine the growth potential of the NLCs. A high propensity to save is to be considered almost as a guarantee of sustainable long-term growth (Giersch 1991a). Due to the high social productivity of capital during the transitional period, reform policies should encourage both private and public savings, as they did in Germany and the Newly Industrialized Countries. Moreover, the central and eastern European countries cannot afford to follow Germany's policy of maintaining financial regulation. As major parts of the capital stock are to be rebuilt, the creation of capital markets is of paramount importance. Due to the massive structural change, the NLCs cannot rely on the self-financing of existing enterprises as did Germany where most investment was financed via retained earnings (Schmieding 1991).

With respect to human capital, alarming developments might occur in central and eastern Europe. Whereas in Germany numerous immigrants with considerable human capital and valuable skills increased the growth potential, professional and skilled workers in the NLCs, who are mobile across borders, are expected to emigrate. Therefore, these workers must be offered a relatively high return on their human capital in terms of high wages and earning prospects. Hence, the wage structure has to be considerably differentiated, causing the income distribution to be relatively unequal during the period of economic reconstruction (Giersch 1991b). In this context, a special problem occurs. Due to socialist education during the past 40 to 70 years, equality still is a dominating value among economic agents in central and eastern Europe. Therefore, it will require substantial efforts to have the people accept an unequal distribution of income, which is typical for market economies and unalterable in the process of catching up. The acceptance of inequality is based on three pillars in market economies, namely the capitalist spirit, sustained economic growth, and the emergence and maintenance of business ethics.

Economic growth will not only compensate possible losers of the transformation, but it gives hope to everybody to catch up to other economic agents, who are better-off in terms of individual welfare. Market-oriented business ethics correspond to equality of opportunity. This includes fair contracts, private-property rights, and prudent regulations, as well as the absence of rent-seeking and monopolistic exploitation (Marer and Zecchini 1991). Rebuilding of these pillars will take a long time in the NLCs, but this process might be accelerated by opening the economy to the world market and by support from abroad.

Last but not least, a valuable lesson can be drawn from all reference countries with respect to external liberalization. The central and eastern European countries cannot afford—as postwar Germany did—to separate domestic reforms from external liberalization without affecting their growth prospects negatively. Unlike postwar Germany, all NLCs have been strongly involved in the international (socialist) division of labor. Given the strong dependence of all former-CMEA members on external economic relations and the need to reduce the power of domestic monopolies by exposing them to the competition in the world market, opening up has to be a major part of the transformation (Schmieding 1991).

The integration of central and eastern Europe into the international division of labor requires the decentralization of foreign trade, the cut of import barriers (especially of quantitative restrictions), a convertible currency, and a competitive exchange rate. As in Mexico in 1988 and Poland in 1990, trade liberalization may emphatically support stabilization efforts and the creation of competitive domestic markets (Corbo 1992). However, experiences of developing countries clearly reveal that the external liberalization is doomed to fail, if it is not accompanied by suitable domestic reforms. Above all, a competitive domestic price-structure, non-inflationary macroeconomic policies, private-property rights and a functioning capital market are unalterable prerequisites for a successful external liberalization (Nunnenkamp 1992).

According to the experience of developing countries, the program of external liberalization should be bold, especially in central and eastern Europe, in order to signal the ultimate break with the socialist regime (Nunnenkamp and Funke 1991). If possible, politicians should start the liberalization with a bang and a significant real depreciation of the domestic currency. Quantitative restrictions have to be basically abandoned and partly substituted by tariffs, the more so as additional tariffs will increase fiscal revenues; the reduction of quantitative restrictions will promote exports by increasing imports of inputs (Papageorgiou, Choksi, and

Michaely 1990). Furthermore, liberalization of imports is expected to increase competition, thereby reducing costs of production in the import-substitution sector, and to induce a shift of resources to export industries (Giersch 1991a).

The change from import-substitution to export-led growth policies is to be carried out as soon as possible. However, in central and eastern Europe it might be reasonable to follow the model of the Newly Industrialized Countries with respect to a prolonged protection of certain industries which promise to perform well in the world market after their reconstruction. In addition, as exports respond to incentives, the government should show a sustainable commitment to an outward-oriented strategy in order to convince future exporters of the long-term continuation of this policy (Park 1991).

With regard to the liberalization of international capital flows, considerable disagreement exists among economists. Whereas some experts point out that convertibility for capital account transactions is to be postponed *inter alia* due to the danger of a real appreciation, which reduces the country's international competitiveness, others call for rapid liberalization. However, real appreciations, which have been often observed in Latin America, have not been the result of an early liberalization of international capital flows but rather the consequence of deficient domestic policies. First of all, appreciation effects caused by capital imports are reduced if these are used for investments, thereby inducing an increase in imports. Secondly, the exchange-rate regime is of major importance. Several Latin American economies fixed the nominal exchange rate to other important currencies as part of their stabilization programs. The main objective was to control inflation by reducing the degree of inertia in the economy. In this context, the real appreciation of the currency could be explained by persistent distortions in goods and factor markets as well as by lax monetary policies. Mexico, however, carried out a rather successful exchange-rate based stabilization program by avoiding these mistakes, supplementing this strategy with incomes policies and starting the stabilization program at a point of undervaluation of its currency in 1988 (Edwards 1991; Nunnenkamp and Schmieding 1991).

Furthermore, due to substantial political and economic instabilities, one can hardly expect massive capital imports in the NLCs in the near future (Nunnenkamp and Schmieding 1991). Therefore, international capital flows should be liberalized in an early phase of the transformation process, the more so as economic agents would be capable of circumventing possible regulations anyway due to the high degree of corruption in many NLCs.

2.5 Conclusion

The social revolutions in central and eastern Europe at the end of the 1980s have initiated a political, economic, and cultural process of restructuring which is without precedent in history. The comparison to historical experiences of countries which have undertaken similarly comprehensive reforms is expected to provide ways softening the painful adjustment process.

However, no single country is suited as a development model for the complex changes of the former socialist societies. Single experiences have been determined by country-specific characteristics, so they cannot be generalized. Therefore, we needed to identify possible implications and lessons from different theoretical fragments and historical experiences and, thereby, separate peculiarities from transferable developments. Moreover, it has to be taken into consideration that central and eastern Europe has a different tradition, culture, and (political) history.[17] In addition, the transformation of the former centrally-planned economies requires a restructuring of the entire social system, unlike reforms in western Europe or the developing countries which did not affect the social system *per se*. Finally, the well-known radical economic reforms in Latin America, Germany, and elsewhere were undertaken in an economic and political environment where economic actors were much more familiar with the characteristics of a market economy than the populations in eastern Europe today. These considerations reveal the difficulties of transferring any Western experiences, even if they are regarded as useful from an economic point of view.

Of course, this study did not attempt and could not hope to elaborate a blueprint for the systemic transformation in central and eastern Europe. However, despite the considerable differences between the NLCs and the reference countries, some broad guidelines for the transformation could be identified by drawing suitable lessons from history. All country-specific experiences place great emphasis on the necessity of political stability as an unalterable prerequisite for successful systemic change, regardless of the concrete form of government. Furthermore, the experiences of the reference countries clearly reveal that the success of the transformation strongly depends on the conceptual underpinnings of the reforms. In particular, the sustainability of the transformation policies requires a transparent

[17] Furthermore, it has to be taken into account that there are also substantial historical, political and social differences between the central and eastern European countries, especially if one compares the central European countries with the Slavic states and even more in case of the Central Asian republics of the former Soviet Union.

and credible strategy, which avoids inconsistencies by an appropriate timing and sequencing. Economic transformation should be based on a bold and radical program. Piecemeal social engineering has to be regarded as an unsustainable strategy. At least the most important elements of macroeconomic stabilization, microeconomic liberalization, competition-increasing structural reforms—including privatization and the imposition of hard budget-constraints—and social containment have to be introduced simultaneously, as the effectiveness of each depends on the existence of the others.

Finally, the systemic change has to change the mentality and the work ethic of the individuals. Due to the lack of capitalist tradition, it might take a generation or more to create functioning markets based on dynamic competition. Trade liberalization and foreign direct investment are supposed to support this process in the medium run. In order to attain significant progress rapidly, the adoption of obligations by the government vis-à-vis international organizations and the support of the industrialized countries are to be regarded as unalterable prerequisites. International obligations will impose, reinforce and maintain the transformation policies carried out by central and eastern European governments, thereby enhancing their credibility. Financial and technical assistance from abroad might help to rebuild the capital stock and accelerate the development of market-oriented thinking and acting. In this respect, teaching of business administration and economics, hiring temporarily foreign managers and experts, having people of central and eastern Europe go abroad, and admitting the NLCs to western markets are of major importance.

References

Blanchard, O. J., et al. 1991. *Reform in Eastern Europe.* Cambridge: MIT Press.

Brabant, J. M. van. 1990. *Remaking Eastern Europe—On the Political Economy of Transition.* Dordrecht: Kluwer Academic Publishers.

Collins, S. M. and D. Rodrik. 1991. *Eastern Europe and the Soviet Union in the World Economy.* Policy Analyses in International Economics no. 32. Washington, D.C.: Institute for International Economics.

Corbo, V. 1992. Economic Transformation in Latin America: Lessons for Eastern Europe. *European Economic Review* 36: 407–16.

Csaba, L. 1991. Systemic Change: Constraints and Driving Forces. In A. Köves and P. Marer, eds. *Foreign Economic Liberalization. Transformations in Socialist and Market*

Economies. Boulder, Colo.: Westview Press.

de la Dehesa, G. 1991. Excerpts from Selected Country Studies: Spain. In P. Marer and S. Zecchini, eds. *The Transition to a Market Economy*. Vol. 1, *The Broad Issues*. Paris: OECD.

Edwards, S. 1991. *Stabilization and Liberalization Policies in Central and Eastern Europe: Lessons from Latin America*. NBER Working Paper no. 3816. Cambridge, Mass.

Ericson, R. E. 1991. The Classical Soviet-Type Economy: Nature of the System and Implications for Reform. *Journal of Economic Perspectives* 5: 11–27.

Gabrisch, H., et al. 1992. *Advanced Reforming Countries Might Reach End of Recession: The Economic Situation in Central-East European Countries, ex-USSR and ex-Yugoslavia in Early 1992*. Vienna: WIIW Forschungsberichte.

Giersch, H. 1991a. Some General Lessons from West Germany's Postwar Experiences. In H. Giersch, ed. *Towards a Market Economy in Central and Eastern Europe*. Berlin: Springer-Verlag.

Giersch, H. 1991b. Selected Country Studies: Germany. In P. Marer and S. Zecchini, eds. *The Transition to a Market Economy*. Vol. 1, *The Broad Issues*. Paris: OECD.

Giersch, H., K.-H. Paqué, and H. Schmieding. 1992. Der wirtschaftliche Wiederaufbau Westdeutschlands nach dem Zweiten Weltkrieg: Eine Übersicht. In R. Dornbusch, W. Nölling and R. Layard, eds. *Der Wiederaufbau Deutschlands nach dem Zweiten Weltkrieg—Lehren für Osteuropa*. Hamburger Beiträge zur Wirtschafts- und Währungspolitik in Europa no. 10. Hamburg.

Helliwell, J. 1991. Lessons from the West. In P. Marer and S. Zecchini, eds. *The Transition to a Market Economy*. Vol. 1, *The Broad Issues*. Paris: OECD.

IMF (International Monetary Fund). 1992a. *World Economic Outlook* (May). Washington, D.C.: IMF.

IMF. 1992b. *Economic Review: Common Issues and Interrepublic Relations in the Former U.S.S.R.* Washington, D.C.: IMF.

IMF et al. 1990. *The Economy of the USSR: Summary and Recommendations*. Washington, D.C: IMF.

Kiguel, M. A., and N. Liviatan. 1991. Stopping Inflation: The Experience of Latin America and Israel and the Implications for Central and Eastern Europe. In V. Corbo, F. Coricelli, and J. Bossak, eds. *Reforming Central and Eastern European Economies: Initial Results and Challenges*. Washington, D.C.: World Bank.

Marer, P. 1991. Models of Successful Market Economies. In P. Marer and S. Zecchini, eds. *The Transition to a Market Economy*. Vol. 1, *The Broad Issues*. Paris: OECD.

Marer, P., and S. Zecchini. 1991. Summary of the Discussion. In P. Marer and S. Zecchini, eds. *The Transition to a Market Economy*. Vol. 1, *The Broad Issues*. Paris: OECD.

Nunnenkamp, P. 1992. Critical Issues of Macroeconomic Stabilization in Post-Socialist Countries—What Can We Learn from Past Failures? Paper presented at conference, Reintegration of Poland into the West European Economy by External and Internal Liberalization, Warsaw, 26–27 March.

Nunnenkamp, P., and H. Schmieding. 1991. *Zur Konsistenz und Glaubwürdigkeit von Wirtschaftsreformen. Einige Erfahrungen und Lehren für die Systemtransformation in Mittel- und Osteuropa*. Kiel Discussion Papers no. 166. Kiel: Institut für Weltwirtschaft.

Nunnenkamp, P., and N. Funke. 1991. Woran scheitern Stabilisierungs- und Liberalisierungsprogramme? Lehren aus Entwicklungsländern für den Transformationsprozeß in Osteuropa. In R. Herrmann and F. R. Sell, eds. *Wirtschaftliche Liberalisierung in Industrie- und Entwicklungsländern*. Hamburg: Verlag Weltarchiv.

OECD (Organization for Economic Cooperation and Development). 1991. *Financial Market Trends* 48. Special Feature: The International Financial Situation of the Central and Eastern European Countries. Paris: OECD.

Papageorgiou, D., A. M. Choksi, and M. Michaely. 1990. *Liberalizing Foreign Trade in Developing Countries: The Lessons of Experience*. Washington, D.C: World Bank.

Park, Y. C. 1991. Liberalization in Korea and Taiwan. In A. Köves and P. Marer, eds. *Foreign Economic Liberalization: Transformations in Socialist and Market Economies*. Boulder, Colo.: Westview Press.

Ritter, U. P. 1991. Überlegungen zu einer Theorie wirtschaftspolitischer Reformen anhand ausgewählter Beispiele. In H. Sautter, ed. *Wirtschaftspolitische Reformen in Entwicklungsländern*. Schriften des Vereins für Socialpolitik Neue Folge no. 209. Berlin: Duncker & Humblot.

Schmieding, H. 1991. West Germany's Economic Reforms of 1948: The Lessons for Central and Eastern Europe Today. In H. Giersch, ed. *Towards a Market Economy in Central and Eastern Europe*. Berlin: Springer-Verlag.

Schwarz, G. 1992. Marktwirtschaftliche Reform und Demokratie—Eine Haßliebe? Überlegungen zur Interdependenz der Ordnungen beim Übergang von der Kommando- zur Wettbewerbswirtschaft. *Ordo. Jahrbuch für die Ordnung von Wirtschaft und Gesellschaft* 43: 65–90.

Serfas, A. 1987. *An der Schwelle zum Industrieland: Die wirtschaftliche Entwicklung Südkoreas 1963–1983*. Frankfurt am Main: Verlag Peter Lang.

Siebert, H., H. Schmieding, and P. Nunnenkamp. 1992. The Transformation of a Socialist Economy: Lessons of German Unification. In G. Winckler, ed. *Central and Eastern*

Europe: Roads to Growth. Washington, D.C.: International Monetary Fund and Austrian National Bank.

Wagener, H.-J. 1992. Wieweit ist Systemtransformation plaubar? In H. Albeck, ed. *Wirtschaftsordnung und Geldverfassung: Symposion zum 65. Geburtstag für Norbert Kloten*. Göttingen: Vandenhoeck and Ruprecht.

Watrin, C. 1990. Der schwierige Weg von der sozialistischen Planwirtschaft zur marktwirtschaftlichen Ordnung. In J.M. Graf von der Schulenburg, H.-W. Sinn, eds. *Theorie der Wirtschaftspolitik: Festschrift zum 75, Geburtstag von Hans Möller*. Tübingen: Mohr.

Wolf, H. C. 1992. Ordoliberalismus: Ein Rezept für die neunziger Jahre? In R. Dornbusch, W. Nölling and R. Layard, eds. *Der Wiederaufbau Deutschlands nach dem Zweiten Weltkrieg—Lehren für Osteuropa*. Hamburger Beiträge zur Wirtschafts- und Währungspolitik in Europa no. 10. Hamburg.

Wolf, T. A. 1991. The Lessons of Limited Market-Oriented Reform. *Journal of Economic Perspectives* 5: 45–58.

World Bank. 1991. *World Development Report 1991*. Washington, D.C.: World Bank.

Zon, H. van. 1992. Alternative Scenarios for Central Europe. *Futures* (June): 471–82.

3 A Model of Price Liberalization in Russia

Jonathan J. Morduch and
Alan M. Taylor

3.1 Introduction

While the world focused on the hasty disassembly of the Soviet Union, the people of the Russian Republic focused on the next revolutionary transformation: the radical reform of their economic system. On 2 January 1992 the government eliminated most price subsidies, allowing prices to be determined by market forces. As a result, most prices paid by consumers rose dramatically. While the price increases were politically unpopular, elimination of subsidies was necessary to avoid the collapse of the food sector.[1] While such a collapse was averted, the liberalization still ignited impassioned debates in the Kremlin and in households and firms throughout the republic. The debates have had special charge since, in the short run, many have faced hardships as a result of the liberalization, while, over the longer run, the ability to sustain better living conditions hinges on the establishment of a price structure which rapidly conveys accurate information about the changing economy.

Despite these concerns, there has been little concrete analysis of even the most basic elements of the liberalization: how relative prices change and how these changes affect the purchasing power of different segments of the population. This work presents analysis designed to help address these issues, with particular focus

---

This work was started during a World Bank mission to Moscow in December 1991 under the direction of Karen Brooks, in consultation with Jakov Urinson, Alexei Gendarov, and Alla Moshkina of the Center of Economic Analysis and Forecasting at the Ministry of Economics. We are also grateful to Igor Dimitrichev of the Department of Social Statistics (*Goskomstat*) for making household budget data available to us. In addition, we have benefitted from discussions with Harold Alderman, Jeffrey Hammer and Jeffrey Williamson. The views expressed here are those of the authors only.

[1] Other elements of the stabilization program included privatization of land and enterprises, imposition of a value-added tax, convertibility of the ruble, and monetary and fiscal discipline.

on the food sector. Our aim is: (i) to aid in the understanding of relative price movements in the first few months following the liberalization; (ii) to show the (often non-obvious) consequences of policy alternatives; and (iii) to demonstrate a modelling strategy which can be used in considering price liberalizations in other contexts. The model identifies changes in prices, real income, and consumption between approximately June 1991 and March 1992, but the mechanisms described have continued to play a role in the "middle" stage of reform in Russia and in other formerly socialist economies.

The modelling exercise begins by recognizing of the magnitude and complexity of the proposed policy changes and their relation to the economy. With a reform so fundamental, success and failure have many dimensions, and policies have multiple direct and indirect effects, attenuating and intensifying tendencies through their interaction. For example, although two commodities might not be substitutes for each other in demand, removal of the price subsidy for one will affect the price of the other through a change in the household's full income (cash income plus the sum of subsidies). While considering each effect is quite straightforward on its own, consideration of all the pieces simultaneously is not feasible without a computer. To this end, we have designed a computable mathematical model which allows interactions between up to twelve main markets for consumer commodities and allows simulation of both full and partial price liberalization, exogenous supply shocks, and government income transfer programs. We consider the effects on three separate income groups within the population.

In large part, the liberalization served to collapse the many channels through which consumers made purchases into one "free" market. Prior to liberalization, most consumers bought a fraction of purchases at subsidized prices from state stores, another fraction at subsidized prices at cooperative stores, and another fraction on "free," unsubsidized markets.[2] Thus *average prices* paid for a given good were always less than the "free" *market prices*, but, after the elimination of subsidies, the two concepts of price came into line. This distinction, while elemental, has often been blurred, and our analysis shows that tracking changes of average and market prices provides a simple way to characterize the distributional impacts of the liberalization.

At the same time that we have incorporated these degrees of complexity, we have kept the model as simple as possible without too greatly compromising its

[2] Below we discuss other important channels which operated before the liberalization.

usefulness. We view the model as a tool, not a replacement, for the policymaker, and an important aim of the exercise is to help policymakers build intuition about the workings of the economy.[3] One source of the relative simplicity is our exclusive focus on short-term demand movements. Supply is assumed to be fixed at current levels or changed exogenously, and returns to factors are also constant (although wages can be changed exogenously as well). These limitations arose in response to the needs of policymakers who were concerned primarily with how well the country would survive the early phase of the reforms. At the same time, by carefully setting out the pieces of the present model, we have anticipated issues which have arisen in consideration of longer term changes.

Several non-obvious conclusions emerge from this exercise. Notably, the impact of the price liberalization on different segments of the population depends critically on the distribution of transfers which accompany the liberalization. First, while the removal of subsidies meant increased *average prices* paid by consumers, *market prices* actually fell immediately after the liberalization. The decline in market prices stemmed from demand contractions in the wake of declining effective purchasing power caused by the elimination of subsidies. Second, due to subsequent price effects, the poor and other vulnerable groups would have been hurt by biasing relative compensation toward wealthier groups, even if absolute transfers to the poor had been held constant; we show that, in general, only a targeted scheme biased toward the poor can adequately protect low-income groups from the adverse effect of liberalization on their welfare.[4]

Third, the richer groups fared relatively well after liberalization, and, in this way, the liberalization intensified inequality. Before the reform, richer groups made relatively more of their purchases at market prices, even though they generally had ample access to goods at subsidized prices as well. On the other end of the spectrum, poorer groups, which had relied heavily on price subsidies, were hit hard by the liberalization and gained little from declining market prices. Since most market prices fell with liberalization, the rich saw an increase in their relative

---

[3] Thus we have made all the assumptions as clear as possible, and we have written a relatively user-friendly version of the model for use on a personal computer. In the resulting model it is easy for users to change any or all parameters in order to simulate different economic environments and to conduct sensitivity analyses. Once parameters and policy changes have been selected, the system can be solved in less than a minute.

[4] On the other hand, it may be argued that since many of the poorer groups had ample diets before liberalization, a decline in their consumption levels may be tolerable from a policy perspective.

purchasing power.[5]

The paper is organized in five sections. The next section describes the key elements of the model, detailing the impact of price reform on a single market with a single, representative consumer. Here, we pay particular attention: to (a) the role of rationing; (b) the role of partial and full liberalization; and (c) ways to consider the non-linear effects of large changes in incomes and prices. In Section 3.3 we consider price reform when there are many markets and many consumers. In Section 3.4 we present simulations based on data suggestive of Russia in 1991 and the proposed policy changes. Concluding comments and extensions are discussed in Section 3.5.

3.2 Price Liberalization in a Single Market with a Representative Consumer

While the motivation for constructing a model is that interactions between markets are important, much intuition can be gained by first examining price liberalization in a single market with a homogeneous population (or, equivalently, with a single, representative consumer). Both of these assumptions are relaxed in Section 3.3.

In the next section we consider a typical market before the liberalization. Here, we focus on characterizing the effects of rationing on consumer demand. We then consider a typical market after the liberalization, focusing on the effects of full and partial liberalization. Next we discuss strategies to address large policy changes; the boldness of the liberalization raises the possibility of highly non-linear responses to changes in prices and quantities, and these non-linearities must be either incorporated in the choice of parameters or embedded in the structure of the model. Finally, we outline several caveats to be borne in mind before moving on to consider the more general model of Section 3.3.

Characterizing Rationing

Obtaining food and other basic commodities had involved a complicated process in Russia. Under the former regime, the total consumption of a typical good was the sum of quantities obtained through a variety of channels at a variety of prices (or shadow prices). Some was bought at state stores at subsidized prices. Some was obtained through the workplace. Some may have been purchased through cooperatives. Some was produced on private plots. Another part might have been

[5] These effects partially offset the tax burdens which have fallen particularly heavily on the richer groups, and the conclusions should be considered in the context of the net changes in cash income which emerge from all the tax and transfer policies implemented alongside price liberalization.

obtained through barter. And still more was purchased at "free market" prices through the *kolkhoz* (collective) market. In 1988, state markets accounted for 71% of total retail sales, cooperative markets accounted for 26% and *kolkhoz* markets accounted for less than 3%.[6]

The multiplicity of channels stems from the fact that households faced restrictions on the quantities which they could purchase from any particular source. But because many channels existed, households were often able to satisfy total demands. As a result, despite the presence of rationing in some markets, *marginal* purchases were often made without restrictions; that is, there was no excess demand at prices on the marginal market. Most often the marginal market was the *kolkhoz* (collective) market, in which prices were determined by market forces—and we have built the model around this assumption.[7] In considering the channels, for now we will concentrate on the state and *kolkhoz* markets only, although in the actual model we allow a third channel (purchases from cooperatives). Households will be in one of two situations: either they face rationing on the margin (they have no access to the *kolkhoz* market) or rationing is infra-marginal (marginal purchases are made from the *kolkhoz*). We take these situations in turn.

Rationing on the Margin

When households face rationing on the margin, they would like to purchase more goods than permitted at the going prices. Thus, up to a point, prices can rise or fall without affecting the quantities demanded. Unlike the situation with infra-marginal rationing, markets do not clear here and a modelling strategy based on market-clearing equations might appear inappropriate.

However, this need not be. Following Rothbarth's discussion of the uses of virtual prices, Neary and Roberts (1980) showed that the demand problem under rationing can be recast and placed within a market-clearing framework. Neary and Roberts show that the basic tools of demand analysis can be used without modification if instead of working with observed prices we work with *virtual prices* and *virtual income* (defined as prices and income which would have to prevail without rationing in order to induce households to purchase the same quantities as

---

[6] It is likely, however, that the size of *kolkhoz* markets has been underestimated in the official data; see Morduch, Brooks, and Urinson 1993.

[7] Although *kolkhoz* markets reflect monopoly power on the part of sellers, prices are still determined by market forces and prices still reflect the opportunity cost of purchases on subsidized markets. Thus these prices are the appropriate ones to use in the analysis, as described below.

they do under rationing). This allows the use of equations in which markets "clear" at virtual prices.

A difficulty with this approach is that since virtual prices are not observed, they must be estimated. This is a modelling exercise in itself, requiring specific assumptions about the functional form and parameters of the demand system. While such an exercise may be necessary in investigating price liberalizations elsewhere, it was not deemed to be critical in analyzing demand for most goods in Russia. Aggregating across the Russian Republic, all groups make at least some purchases of most goods on the *kolkhoz* markets so that the assumption of infra-marginal rationing provides a reasonable starting point for the present analysis. However, where goods are generally not available through *kolkhoz* markets (for example, fish, sugar, and oil), we have estimated virtual prices.

For simplicity of exposition, then, we assume below that all rationing is infra-marginal—but the equations hold when marginal purchases are rationed instead. In that case one can just substitute virtual prices for *kolkhoz* prices (p^k) in all equations and proceed without further modification.

Infra-Marginal Rationing

As discussed above, while households purchase goods through a variety of channels at a variety of prices, it is the price of their marginal purchases which is critical for the present purpose. While households may face constraints in the amount of goods which they can purchase through official channels at subsidized prices, if they do not face constraints in the total amount of purchases which can be made, they are infra-marginally rationed. Here we give careful consideration to the income transfer implicit in the price subsidy, but beyond this accounting, the fact of rationing does not enter the basic analysis.

Essentially, although households face a complicated pattern of non-linear prices, we can treat prices as if they were linear (at p^k) by appropriately augmenting income to account for the implicit subsidy.[8] The problem to be solved by the model is then just how to determine the new set of prices which will occur for marginal purchases. Together with changes in full income (defined below), these prices are all that is necessary to determine changes in quantities demanded.

The calculation of full income is thus critical. We define "full" (or virtual)

---

[8] See Hausman 1985 for discussion of a similar procedure used in analyzing the effect of taxes on labor supply.

income (Y^f) as cash income (Y) plus the income transfer implicit in the subsidy.[9] This implicit transfer equals the difference between the subsidized purchase price of rationed goods (p^s) and the opportunity cost, the *kolkhoz* price (p^k), multiplied by the quantity purchased at the subsidized price (D^s):

$$Y^f = Y + (p^k - p^s)D^s. \tag{1}$$

This implicit transfer corresponds to the shaded rectangle in Figure 3.1. We turn now to how full income changes under price liberalization.

Full and Partial Price Liberalization

Whether or not rationing is infra-marginal, following the discussion above, we begin by assuming that markets clear (at p^k with full income Y^f). Thus, supply is equal to demand for the given good:

$$D(p^k, Y^f) = Q. \tag{2}$$

As discussed above, quantities demanded are solely a function of *kolkhoz* prices and full income. Taking the logarithm and then differentiating equation (2) yields:

$$\hat{D} = \epsilon^P \hat{p}^k + \epsilon^Y \hat{Y}^f = \hat{Q}. \tag{3}$$

where ϵ^P is the (uncompensated) price elasticity and ϵ^Y is the income elasticity. A hat above a variable denotes percentage changes (dX/X).[10]

If we consider the short run, so that there are no changes in supply, then

$$\hat{Q} = 0 \Rightarrow \hat{p}^k = -\frac{\epsilon^Y}{\epsilon^P} \hat{Y}^f. \tag{4}$$

Equation (4) captures the essence of many results in the model. Most significantly, we see how the percentage change in the price is related to the percentage change in full income. Since $\epsilon^P \leq 0$ and $\epsilon^Y \geq 0$ (assuming that the good is not inferior), the relationship is positive: when full income falls, so does the price. Given the elasticities, the determination of price movements is just a matter of determining full income movements. For example, if $\epsilon^Y = 0.3$ and $\epsilon^P = -0.2$, a 10% decline in full income leads to a 15% drop in the *kolkhoz* price. If instead the income

---

[9] Cash income includes wages, salaries, gifts, and pensions plus (explicit) transfers received directly from the government. All prices and income in the model are net of taxes.

[10] Strictly, the analysis which follows is only appropriate for investigating very small, or local changes. This issue, and strategies to address it, are discussed below.

Figure 3.1
Full Liberalization, Complete Elimination of Subsidy

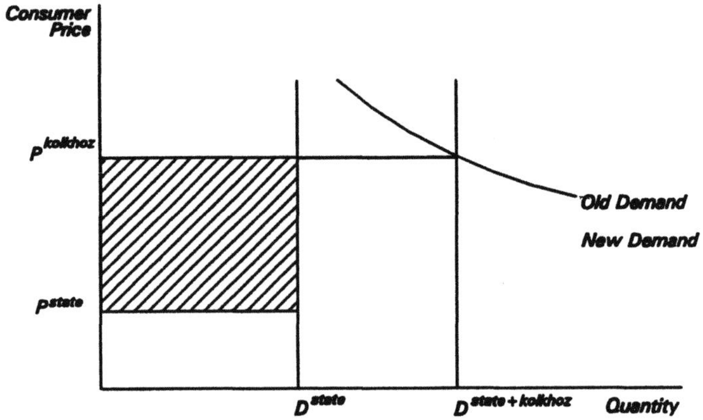

Figure 3.2
Partial Liberalization, Reduction of Subsidy

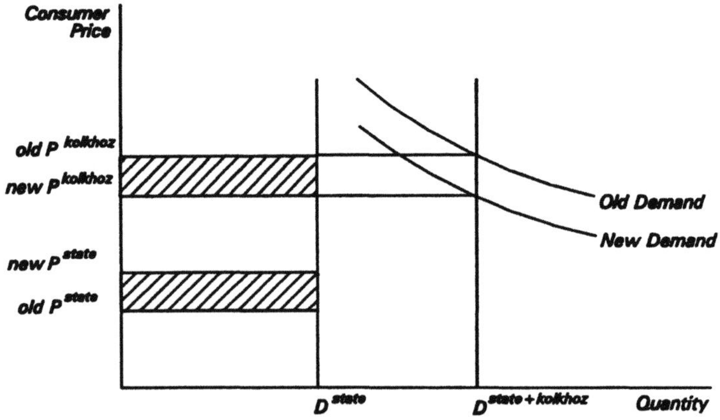

elasticity is 0.4, the 10% decline in full income results in a 20% price drop. This simple example shows the importance of choosing reasonable elasticities; when elasticities are not known with much confidence, it will be important to conduct sensitivity analyses to ascertain how price changes vary over a range of parameter choices. While elasticities are inputs to the model, any change in full income is calculated within the model. We turn to that now.

FULL LIBERALIZATION

Full liberalization entails completely eliminating subsidies, taking away from households the implicit income transfer. Thus, full income falls by the full amount of the subsidy:

$$\hat{Y}^f = dY^f/Y^f = [dY-(p^k-p^s)D^s]/Y^f. \tag{5}$$

Here, dY reflects exogenous changes in cash income, such as wage supplements made by the government to offset some of the effects of the price reform. Note that in Russia cash income will be affected both positively by transfers and negatively by taxation. Thus dY reflects *net* income augmentation.

PARTIAL LIBERALIZATION

When liberalization is partial, part of the subsidy is retained, so full income falls less far than under full liberalization. Assuming that the household purchases the same quantity of the commodity on the subsidized market, the implicit income transfer is changed to the extent that subsidized prices and *kolkhoz* prices move:

$$\hat{Y}^f = [dY + (dp^k-dp^s)D^s]/Y^f. \tag{6}$$

These changes reflect the upper and lower shaded rectangles in Figure 3.2. While dY and dp^s are exogenous, dp^k is endogenous, so part of the change in full income is endogenous when liberalization is partial. This contrasts with the case of full liberalization above, where the change in full income is entirely exogenous.[11]

[11] Note that we assume that, under partial liberalization, households remain constrained at the former quantity restriction, D^s.

Large Policy Changes

The approach that we have outlined is quite general in that we do not require assumptions about the functional form of the utility function. The data requirements are also relatively parsimonious; the minimum data required is knowledge of current prices and quantities consumed and estimates of price and income elasticities. Since we begin by only assuming that markets clear (at *kolkhoz* or virtual prices), the model does not have to be calibrated to match theoretical constraints and weights used in optimization routines. The fact that the model does not need to be recalibrated for each new set of base date makes repeated experimentation with different parameters both simple and quick.[12]

However, these attributes are counterbalanced by the restriction that the analysis above is only truly appropriate for very small (indeed, infinitesimal) changes. This poses a large problem in considering the Russian price liberalization, possibly the most radical change in pricing policy attempted in world history. Below we discuss three ways to address issues bound up with large changes, and we ultimately argue for solving the model iteratively in many small steps. We leave consideration of other approaches to future work.

ARC ELASTICITIES VERSUS POINT ELASTICITIES

Since the point elasticities used above are based on derivatives, they are only appropriate for analyzing local changes. When analyzing larger changes, predictive performance can be improved by using arc elasticities, reflecting changes between fairly distant points on the demand curve. A problem is that choice of the appropriate distance requires an assumption about the extent of the price change—but this is what we are trying to estimate in the first place. Moreover, careful choice of arc elasticities requires an assumption about the specific functional form of the utility function which gives rise to the demand curve. Still, use of arc elasticities may yield reasonable approximations when analyzing large changes—without requiring modification of model structure. The apparent advantages of this approach are the maintenance of simplicity and transparency, but these benefits are obtained by making hidden (extra-model) assumptions. Perhaps more problematic, new arc elasticities must be calculated each time substantially different policies are simulated.

[12] See Ahmad and Stern 1991 for an application of local analyses to tax reform and Braverman, Hammer and Gron 1987 and Braverman, Hammer, and Morduch 1987 for applications to pricing policy in Brazil and Hungary, respectively. See Deaton 1984 for a general theoretical argument.

EMBEDDED NON-LINEARITIES

The need for recalculating elasticities is avoided by a second approach. Here we could take the other tack, embedding non-linear responses to price and income changes within the model structure. However, this requires specific assumptions about functional form, and it risks moving the model closer toward being a "black box" in which it is difficult to relate inputs to results. In addition, computable general equilibrium models equipped to address large changes often require calibration of the data and model parameters with each change in base levels. This makes it more difficult to complete sensitivity analyses and comparisons of alternative scenarios. More important from a policy perspective, the greater complexity required by this approach means that the model builder is generally the only user of the model, and it is difficult to construct such models in the limited time horizon allowed for operational work.

ITERATIONS ON LOCAL CHANGES

Having weighed the concerns above, our compromise approach is to retain the linear structure of the basic model but to analyze a series of small changes, updating prices, incomes, and quantities at each iteration (specifics are described in Section 3.3). In this way we maintain the flexibility of the linear model while accommodating substantial shifting of budgets which leads to non-linearities. The usefulness of the results will depend on how good an approximation the iterative approach is to the actual process of making decisions, and sensitivity analysis of changes in the number of iterations should be done. It would be worthwhile to compare results based on the three approaches in future research.

Other Considerations

While we have accommodated considerable complexity, there is much from which we have abstracted. In this section we briefly describe the implications of considering only a subset of household consumption items, the effects of hoarding and speculative behavior, and supply and factor market effects.

Since we are focusing on small changes from given base levels, we have not had to specify adding-up constraints. This means that we can obtain sensible results without considering all commodities unrelated in demand. However, because interdependence is driven by both price and income effects, the results will be biased if we do not consider carefully *all* changes in implicit income transfers. To minimize this problem, the set of goods included in the demand system was chosen partly to account for important budget items which receive large subsidies. But due to computational constraints, we have left out some important subsidized items, for example, clothing. However, we suspect that the resulting biases will not be large. This is because the removal of subsidies on clothing (which decreased full income) was counterbalanced by short-term shifts out of clothing in the budget (increasing the amount of full income available for purchasing the included items). The two effects roughly wash each other out, and this would have been exactly so if the previous expenditure on clothing (at low, subsidized prices) equaled the new expenditure (at higher, market prices).

Along the same lines, we do not treat the consumption-saving decision explicitly. Rather, savings are determined residually: households first choose new consumption levels, and the difference between income and expenditures is saved (or borrowed). This is a reasonable approximation of behavior during this period of relative hardship in Russia, where maintenance of current consumption levels has been of prime importance for most people.

We also abstract from some forces which matter in the very short run—notably the speculation and hoarding which marked the weeks immediately preceding and following the liberalization. These forces fueled demand and drove up prices. However, as consumers better gauged the expected new price structure and started to draw down their caches, rather than build them up, prices began to fall, *ceteris paribus*, offsetting the initial price rises fueled by speculation. This is one reason we stress that our results should be viewed as being most appropriate to changes occurring in the "medium short run," approximately two to three months after the liberalization was enacted.

By taking the current level of supply as fixed (or changeable exogenously), we have abstracted from how changes in prices and incomes affect factor markets and, through them, production. After the liberalization, wages were bid up in response to the price rises, and while we can capture this by exogenously increasing cash income, we do not explicitly model the effect of wage increases on production costs and thus on prices. Nor do we capture the effect of price movements for goods which are inputs into the final production of other goods. However, neither of these concerns should be critical in the limited time horizon that we are analyzing—although they will matter significantly beyond the short run.

3.3 Price Liberalization in Many Markets with Many Consumers

In this section we generalize the analysis of Section 3.2 to consider price liberalization when there are H consumers, $h = 1,\ldots, H$, purchasing J commodities through $S+1$ possible channels. We assume that the $S+1$st channel is the *kolkhoz* market and that purchases on the other S channels are made at subsidized prices. As before, total supply of each good (Q_i) equals total demand at *kolkhoz*/virtual prices (p_j^k)and full income (Y_h^f):

$$D_i = \sum_{h=1}^{H} D_{ih}(p_1^k, p_2^k, \ldots, p_J^k, Y_h^f) = Q_i \quad \text{for } i = 1, 2, \ldots, J, \tag{7}$$

where the total demand for a given household (D_{ih}) equals the sum of infra-marginal purchases at subsidized prices (D_{ih}^s) plus purchases on the marginal market (D_{ih}^k):

$$D_{ih} = \sum_{s=1}^{S} D_{ih}^s + D_{ih}^k. \tag{8}$$

and full income equals cash income (Y_h) plus the sum of implicit subsidies across commodities and channels:

$$Y_h^f = Y_h + \sum_{j=1}^{J} \sum_{s=1}^{S} (p_j^k - p_j^s) D_{jh}^s. \tag{9}$$

Log differentiation yields equations for percentage changes in demand:[13]

$$\hat{D}_i = \sum_{h=1}^{H} \omega_{ih} \hat{D}_{ih} = \sum_{h=1}^{H} \omega_{ih} [\sum_{j=1}^{J} \epsilon_{ij}^P \hat{p}_j^k + \epsilon_i^Y \hat{Y}_h^f] = \hat{Q}_i \quad \text{for } i = 1, 2, \ldots, J, \tag{10}$$

where the fraction of total demand of a good purchased by a household is

$$\omega_{ih} = D_{ih} / \sum_{h=1}^{H} D_{ih}, \text{ where } \sum_{h=1}^{H} \omega_{ih} = 1, \tag{11}$$

and the percentage change in income is given by

---

[13] While we have tried to keep theoretical restrictions to a minimum, we impose symmetry of the Slutsky matrix on the demand system. That is,

$$s_{ij} = \epsilon_{ij}^P + \alpha_j \epsilon_i^Y = \epsilon_{ji} + \alpha_i \epsilon_j^Y = s_{ji}$$

where s_{ij} is the compensated elasticity of demand for good i with respect to the price of good j and α_i gives the population weighted average budget share of good i. Accordingly, half of the cross-price elasticities are calculated so that:

$$\epsilon_{ij}^P = \epsilon_{ji} + \alpha_i \epsilon_j^Y - \alpha_j \epsilon_i^Y.$$

$$\hat{Y}_h^f = \{dY_h - \sum_{j=1}^{J}\sum_{s=1}^{S}[L_j^s(p_j^k - p_j^s)D_{jh}^s - (1-L_j^s)(dp_j^k - dP_j^s)D_{jh}^s]\}/Y_h^f. \tag{12}$$

The degree of liberalization is captured by L_j^s, a dummy variable which equals one if the market for good j through channel s is completely liberalized. When L_j^s equals zero, there is partial liberalization (and if $dp_j^s = 0$ for all s while $L_j^s = 0$, there is no change in market j at all). Substituting equation (12) into equation (10) and taking endogenous terms to the left hand side and exogenous terms to the right hand side yields:[14]

$$\sum_{j=1}^{J}\hat{p}_j^k\{\epsilon_{ij}^P + \sum_{h=1}^{H}\sum_{s=1}^{S}\omega_{ih}\epsilon_i^Y p_j^k(1-L_j^s)D_{jh}^s/Y_h^f\} = \hat{Q}_i - \sum_{h=1}^{H}\omega_{ih}\epsilon_i^Y\hat{Y}_h^{fx}, \quad \text{for } i = 1, 2,\ldots, J, \tag{13}$$

where we have simplified by denoting the percentage change in full income due to exogenous factors as:

$$\hat{Y}_h^{fx} = \{dY_h - \sum_{j=1}^{J}\sum_{s=1}^{S}[L_j^s(p_j^k - p_j^s)D_{jh}^s + (1-L_j^s)\,dP_j^s D_{jh}^s]\}/Y_h^f. \tag{14}$$

Putting equation (13) into matrix format yields a system of J equations which can now be solved via matrix inversion:

$$\begin{bmatrix} \epsilon_{11}^P + \sum_{h=1}^{H}\sum_{s=1}^{S}\omega_{1h}\epsilon_1^Y p_1^k(1-L_1^s)D_{1h}^s/Y_h^f & \cdots & \cdots \\ \cdots & \cdots & \cdots \\ \cdots & \cdots & \epsilon_{JJ}^P + \sum_{h=1}^{H}\sum_{s=1}^{S}\omega_{Jh}\epsilon_J^Y p_J^k(1-L_1^s)D_{Jh}^s/Y_h^j \end{bmatrix} \begin{bmatrix} \hat{p}_1^k \\ \cdots \\ \hat{p}_J^k \end{bmatrix} = \begin{bmatrix} \hat{Q}_1 - \sum_{h=1}^{H}\omega_{1h}\epsilon_1^Y\hat{Y}_h^{fx} \\ \cdots \\ \hat{Q}_J - \sum_{h=1}^{H}\omega_{Jh}\epsilon_J^Y\hat{Y}_h^{fx} \end{bmatrix}. \tag{15}$$

After solving for the endogenous changes in *kolkhoz*/virtual prices, changes in demands and full income for each household can be derived from equation (10).

---

[14] Note that we have gained considerable simplification by assuming that price elasticities are equal for all households. Generalizing this assumption is straightforward but tedious.

When the model is solved iteratively, the absolute changes in the policy variables (exogenous changes in supply, cash income, and full income) are first divided by the chosen number of iterations. In the first step, the percentage changes in the policy variables are calculated using the original base levels, but subsequent percentage changes are calculated using the new levels computed after each step.

3.4 Base Data and Simulation Exercises

We now describe how the multi-market model of the Russian food sector is implemented and present some illustrative simulation exercises.

Base Data

Table 3.1 displays the base data for the simulations. The base data were chosen in consultation with experts at *Gosplan*.[15] First we consider base consumption levels by channel for ten goods and three income groups. The three channels are the state market, the cooperative market, and the *kolkhoz*/free market. The ten goods are the following products and aggregates (in the given units), with abbreviations as indicated:

Meat:	meat and meat products (kilograms);
Milk:	milk and milk products (milk equivalent liters);
Eggs:	eggs (number of eggs);
Fish:	fish and fish products (kilograms);
Sugar:	sugar (kilograms);
Oils:	vegetable oils (kilograms);
Pota:	potatoes (kilograms);
Vegs:	vegetables (kilograms);
Fruit:	fruit (kilograms);
Bread:	bread (kilograms).

While we do not consider them explicitly here, an important extension would be to consider alcohol purchases and an "other goods" residual category. The three income groups are "low," "middle" and "high." In places where an "average" is indicated across income groups this denotes a population-weighted arithmetical average.

We next consider base income and price data. The state buying price ("State buy") is not used in this model, but could be used in a simple extension of the

[15] *Gosplan* refers to the former planning ministry of the Soviet Union.

Table 3.1
Base Data

		Meat (kg)	Milk (l)	Eggs (#)	Fish (kg)	Sugar (kg)	Oils (kg)	Pota (kg)	Vegs (kg)	Fruit (kg)	Bread (kg)
Consumption per person annual: state market											
low		30.7	226.0	129.0	6.2	18.0	5.3	60.7	44.5	14.6	90.5
middle		47.2	253.0	151.0	12.0	27.0	6.0	61.4	58.0	25.7	87.0
high		57.0	253.0	154.0	20.0	23.0	8.0	37.4	42.8	21.6	95.0
average		46.7	249.0	149.0	12.6	25.1	6.2	57.2	53.7	23.5	89.4
Consumption per person annual: cooperative market											
low		0.0	0.0	0.0	0.0	0.0	0.0	0.0	0.0	0.0	0.0
middle		7.9	42.1	25.3	1.7	0.0	0.0	10.2	9.7	4.3	0.0
high		0.0	0.0	0.0	0.0	0.0	0.0	0.0	0.0	0.0	0.0
average		5.5	29.5	17.7	1.2	0.0	0.0	7.2	6.8	3.0	0.0
Consumption per person annual: kolkhoz/free market											
low		3.4	25.2	14.4	0.0	0.0	0.0	6.8	5.0	1.6	0.0
middle		7.9	42.1	25.3	0.0	0.0	0.0	10.2	9.7	4.3	0.0
high		37.0	169.0	103.0	0.0	0.0	0.0	56.1	64.2	32.4	0.0
average		12.2	61.5	37.1	0.0	0.0	0.0	17.5	18.3	8.7	0.0
Prices (rubles)											
State buy		0.0	0.0	0.0	0.0	0.0	0.0	0.0	0.0	0.0	0.0
State sell		7.0	0.7	0.3	1.5	2.4	3.0	1.0	1.0	3.0	1.2
Coop		14.0	0.7	0.3	1.5	3.5	6.0	1.5	4.0	6.0	1.2
Free/virtual		25.0	2.0	0.7	1.7	5.0	12.0	1.5	5.0	12.0	1.2
Base demand elasticities											
	Meat	−0.50	0.02	0.06	0.02	0.00	0.01	0.00	0.00	0.00	0.00
	Milk	0.00	−0.20	0.04	0.00	0.00	0.00	0.00	0.00	−0.02	0.00
	Eggs	0.05	0.05	−0.20	0.01	0.00	0.00	0.00	0.00	−0.01	0.00
	Fish	0.00	0.01	0.01	−0.30	0.00	0.00	0.00	0.00	−0.02	0.00
	Sugar	0.00	0.00	0.00	0.00	−0.40	0.00	0.00	0.00	0.05	0.00
with	Oils	0.00	0.01	0.00	0.00	0.00	−0.20	0.00	0.00	0.01	0.00
respect	Pota	0.00	0.01	0.00	0.00	0.00	0.01	−0.10	0.00	0.01	0.00
to	Vegs	0.00	0.00	0.00	0.00	0.00	0.00	0.00	−0.70	0.12	0.00
price	Fruit	0.00	0.00	0.00	0.00	0.05	0.00	0.00	0.10	−0.80	0.00
of:	Bread	0.00	0.00	0.00	0.00	0.00	0.00	0.00	0.00	0.00	−0.10
with respect to income:		0.50	0.20	0.20	0.30	0.20	0.20	0.02	0.30	0.50	0.10

Income levels

	Total earnings per capita (rubles)	Population share
low	1,200	0.13
middle	2,700	0.70
high	6,000	0.17
average	3,066	

model to calculate the impact of changes in subsidies on the fiscal balance of the state. The state selling price ("State sell") is the purchase price for consumers in state markets. The cooperative price ("Coop") is the consumer price in cooperative markets. The "Free/virtual" price represents either the *kolkhoz*/free market price or the estimated virtual price, as appropriate (see Section 3.3).[16]

We consider the distributional consequences for three groups within society: a small poor population (13% of the total), a large middle group (70%) and a high-income group (17%).[17] Before the liberalization, their total annual nominal income per capita was assumed to be 1,200, 2,700, and 6,000 rubles, respectively, not inclusive of the value of food or other subsidies. Table 3.2 shows that once food subsidies are considered, full income increases by 52%, 43%, and 24% for each group. The proportionate importance of food subsidies is thus greatest for the poor, even though the rich receive a greater absolute amount of subsidy.

Table 3.2 also shows that when cash income is increased by 50% at the same time that subsidies are eliminated, the poor group's full income (not deflated by the price increase) falls by 29%, and when cash income is doubled, their full income falls by just 5%. However, increases in cash income, as for example in wage and pension escalators, help the richer groups more, since relatively more of their full income comes from wages and pensions. Thus, subsidy elimination coupled with a doubling of wages and pensions *increases* the full income of the richer groups by half, while the poorest group suffers a slight income loss under the same policy. The implications of these price and income changes are the subject of the simulations discussed below.

Next we consider all the information on demand elasticities necessary to solve the model. Price and income elasticities are exogenous to the model and are estimated independently. The task is made somewhat simpler by invoking Slutsky symmetry to derive the upper-diagonal terms of the price-elasticity matrix, as explained above (Section 3.4). Lacking appropriate raw data, the elasticity estimates for the simulations were again chosen in consultation with economists at *Gosplan*.[18]

---

[16] The prices are not necessarily those in Moscow or St. Petersburg; for example, the *kolkhoz* prices are based on November 1991 mid-point prices in 70 cities in Russia.

[17] This paragraph and the next draw heavily on Morduch, Brooks, and Urinson 1993.

[18] The model also derives summary statistics to provide statistical checks to verify the base data. The derived figures include implied budget shares for each income group by good; implied shares of purchases by channel; implied average consumer prices for each income group (weighted by the quantity consumed from each channel); and implied subsidy levels as a share of expenditure.

Table 3.2
Benchmark Data: Income and Subsidies

Income group	Cash income (rubles)	Value of subsidies (rubles)	Full income (rubles)	Percentage change in full income after removal of subsidies and money income increase by:		
				0%	50%	100%
low	1,200	1,337	2,537	−53	−29	−5
middle	2,700	2,049	4,749	−43	−14	+14
high	6,000	1,938	7,938	−24	+13	+51

Simulation Exercises: Policy Options

With the base data presented in Table 3.1, we move on to Table 3.3 to view the model in action (a wider set of policy simulations is considered in Morduch and Taylor 1992). Prices for each good may be set free (full liberalization) or set at some new fixed level (partial liberalization). Supplies may be augmented by the release of stocks or by imports. Income transfers may be set for each of the three income groups to provide a compensation scheme. These transfers may arise from augmented wages in enterprises, increased state pensions or direct payments, but are thought of as a simple "helicopter-drop" of money.

Lastly, the model may be solved in arbitrarily many iterations. In almost all examples, ten iterations are used. The qualitative results are robust to increasing the number of iterations, but coarse, even nonsensical, results may result from insufficient iteration.

Complete Elimination of Subsidies without Compensation

The policy simulations which we consider here center on the role of increasing transfers which accompanied the price reform. First we consider the results in Table 3.3, in which all subsidies have been eliminated and no compensation has been made. Under this scheme, the removal of all subsidies from food constitutes a large negative income effect on all consumers. Consequently, *ceteris paribus*, we expect market prices for most goods to fall, which is indeed the case. We find price declines for all goods between 24% and 70%. In some cases, these declines even bring the new free market price below the level of the base state prices: this is the case for milk, eggs, fish and bread. These price changes are summarized in the Laspeyres price indices shown below (base index level is 1.0); the market price

Table 3.3
All Prices Free; No Compensation

Price changes

		Old price (rbls.)			New market price (rbls.)	Percent change from old market price	Percent change from old state price
		State	Coop	Market			
Meat	(kg)	7.00	14.00	25.00	9.60	−62	37
Milk	(l)	0.65	0.65	2.00	0.60	−70	−10
Eggs	(#)	0.26	0.27	0.70	0.20	−66	−11
Fish	(kg)	1.50	1.50	1.70	1.00	−38	−30
Sugar	(kg)	2.40	3.50	4.00	3.70	−26	55
Oils	(kg)	3.00	6.00	12.00	7.00	−42	133
Pota	(kg)	1.00	1.50	1.50	1.10	−30	6
Vegs	(kg)	1.00	4.00	5.00	3.80	−24	278
Fruit	(kg)	3.00	6.00	12.00	8.40	−30	179
Bread	(kg)	1.19	1.19	1.19	0.70	−42	−42

	Meat (kg)	Milk (l)	Eggs (#)	Fish (kg)	Sugar (kg)	Oils (kg)	Pota (kg)	Vegs (kg)	Fruit (kg)	Bread (kg)
New consumption per person annual: all sources										
low	30.4	241.0	137.0	5.8	17.2	5.1	67.2	46.2	14.4	93.1
middle	61.1	334.0	200.0	13.4	26.8	5.9	81.8	76.2	33.1	96.7
high	104.0	441.0	268.0	21.3	24.1	8.4	94.0	114.0	59.9	97.3
average	64.5	340.0	204.0	13.7	25.1	6.2	82.0	78.8	35.2	89.4
Percent change in consumption										
low	−10	−4	−4	−7	−4	−4	0	−6	−11	−2
middle	−3	−1	−1	−2	−1	−1	0	−2	−3	0
high	11	5	5	7	5	5	0	7	11	2
average	0	0	0	0	0	0	0	0	0	0

Income and welfare

Cash income

	Nominal			Real: avg. price deflator		
	Base	New	Percent change	Base	New	Percent change
low	1,200	1,200	0	1,200	1,107	−8
middle	2,700	2,700	0	2,700	1,800	−33
high	6,000	6,000	0	6,000	7,131	19
average	3,066	3,066	0	3,066	2,407	−21

Laspeyres indices

Market price	Avg. price	Qty.
0.48	1.08	0.927
0.48	1.08	0.980
0.48	0.84	1.086

Full income (cash and subsidies)

	Nominal			Real: avg. price deflator		
	Base	New	Percent change	Base	New	Percent change
low	2,538	1,200	−53	2,538	2,510	−1
middle	4,749	2,700	−43	4,749	5,648	19
high	7,938	6,000	−24	7,938	12,542	58
average	5,004	3,066	−39	5,004	6,414	28

index falls to 0.48, and new average price indices are (1.08, 1.08, 0.84) by income group.

We also can see detailed consumption data on the impact of the change which suggests that low income consumers lose most (up to 11.2%), middle income consumers lose a little (up to 3.2%) and high income consumers gain (up to 11.1%). These welfare changes are verified in the summary Laspeyres quantity indices (base 1.0) calculated for each group: (0.927, 0.980, 1.086).

That the low income group loses and the high group gains follows from the fact that supplies are fixed (so some consumers can only gain at the expense of others) and the tendency of lower income groups to purchase more through state channels. When state subsidies are removed, the negative income effect is much greater for the groups most reliant on the subsidized channels.

COMPLETE ELIMINATION OF SUBSIDIES WITH COMPENSATION BIASED TOWARD THE POOR

Since poorer groups are adversely affected by a full liberalization without a compensation scheme, we now explore the implications of a set of income augmenting transfers biased toward the poor. As argued above, a proposal to raise all income across the board would be futile: since supplies are fixed, a general increase in the price level will result, and, as in the above no-compensation scheme, the poorer groups most reliant on subsidized channels will lose out. Thus, we first experiment with a policy where poor incomes are doubled (a 100% income gain in the low income group) and other incomes are raised by half (a 50% gain in middle and high income groups). This is, of course, a narrowly targeted relief scheme: recall that the low income group is only 13% of the population.

With nominal income transfers in place, we expect a much higher price level to result. This is indeed the case: Table 3.4 shows that now market prices fall between 4% and 20%, and, except for bread, the new market price is above the former state price, by up to 378% in the case of vegetables. This poor-biased policy is effective in protecting the welfare of the low income group: their consumption levels do not decline. In this case only the middle group loses, and, once again, the high income group enjoys large gains. The summary Laspeyres indices indicate a new market price index of 0.87 and average price indices of (2.15, 1.95, 1.54) by income group. Quantity indices are (1.008, 0.972, 1.082) by income group which confirm the gain of low and high groups at the expense of the middle group.

Table 3.4
All Prices Free; Compensation 100%-50%-50%

Price changes

		Old price (rbls.) State	Old price (rbls.) Coop	Old price (rbls.) Market	New market price (rbls.)	Percent change from old market price	Percent change from old state price
Meat	(kg)	7.00	14.00	25.00	21.20	−15	203
Milk	(l)	0.65	0.65	2.00	1.60	−20	141
Eggs	(#)	0.26	0.27	0.70	0.60	−17	114
Fish	(kg)	1.50	1.50	1.70	1.60	−8	5
Sugar	(kg)	2.40	3.50	4.00	4.70	−6	97
Oils	(kg)	3.00	6.00	12.00	11.00	−9	266
Pota	(kg)	1.00	1.50	1.50	1.40	−6	41
Vegs	(kg)	1.00	4.00	5.00	4.80	−4	378
Fruit	(kg)	3.00	6.00	12.00	11.40	−5	278
Bread	(kg)	1.19	1.19	1.19	1.10	−9	−9

	Meat (kg)	Milk (l)	Eggs (#)	Fish (kg)	Sugar (kg)	Oils (kg)	Pota (kg)	Vegs (kg)	Fruit (kg)	Bread (kg)
New consumption per person annual: all sources										
low	34.5	253.0	144.0	6.2	18.1	5.3	67.5	49.8	16.4	35.3
middle	60.4	332.0	199.0	13.3	26.7	5.9	81.7	75.6	32.8	86.4
high	104.0	440.0	268.0	21.2	24.0	8.3	94.0	113.0	59.7	97.0
average	64.5	340.0	204.0	13.7	25.1	6.2	82.0	78.8	35.2	89.4
Percent change in consumption										
low	1	1	6	1	1	1	0	1	1	0
middle	−4	0	−1	−2	−1	−1	0	−2	−4	−1
high	11	4	4	6	5	4	0	6	10	2
average	0	0	0	0	0	0	0	0	0	0

Income and welfare

Cash income

	Nominal Base	Nominal New	Nominal Percent change	Real: avg. price deflator Base	Real: avg. price deflator New	Real: avg. price deflator Percent change
low	1,200	2,400	100	1,200	1,117	−7
middle	2,700	4,050	50	2,700	2,578	−5
high	6,000	9,000	50	6,000	5,859	−2
average	3,066	4,677	53	3,066	2,922	−5

Full income (cash and subsidies)

	Nominal Base	Nominal New	Nominal Percent change	Real: avg. price deflator Base	Real: avg. price deflator New	Real: avg. price deflator Percent change
low	2,538	2,400	−5	2,538	2,751	8
middle	4,749	4,050	−15	4,749	4,642	−2
high	7,938	9,000	13	7,938	10,319	30
average	5,004	4,677	−7	5,004	5,361	7

Laspeyres indices

Market price	Avg. price	Qty.
0.87	2.15	1.008
0.87	1.95	0.972
0.87	1.54	1.087

COMPLETE ELIMINATION OF SUBSIDIES WITH COMPENSATION BIASED TOWARD THE POOR AND MIDDLE INCOME GROUPS

It will be remembered that the middle group is a large share of the population, at 70%, and since they lose in the above scenarios, it is interesting to ask what might happen when a 100% income gain is extended to this group, as well as to the poor. We would expect transfers to this large group in the population to have profound effects on the structure of prices and welfare outcomes, and this is certainly confirmed by this policy exercise.

In this case, shown in Table 3.5, with yet more cash income in circulation, a still more inflationary outcome results. We find all market prices rising, between 6% and 36%, and all new market prices above the former state levels, by between 11% and 432%. The summary price indices are 1.22 for market prices, and (2.83, 2.83, 2.00) for average prices by income group.

Since the poor and rich have received no extra compensation whilst the middle have gained, relative to the previous example, we expect these two groups to lose as the middle group gains. Consumption patterns confirm that overall the low group loses now, although the high group, less adversely affected by subsidy removal, still gains a little. Significantly, the middle groups manages a slight gain too. The summary quantity indices are (0.944, 1.005, 1.004), and these illustrate that the large middle group can only make even modest gains at a relatively large cost to smaller groups: in this case, the poor.

SUPPLY SHOCKS

A second set of policy exercises explores the impact of adverse supply shocks in the three compensation scenarios. A set of plausible supply shocks is shown in Table 3.6, ranging from a 20% decline in oil supply to a 1% decline in bread supply. These figures represent diminished production, impaired distribution of goods and wastage. In all cases we examine the impact of these new scarcities on a fully liberalized price structure.

Under a scheme without compensation, shown in Table 3.7, added scarcities serve to raise the general price level and raise individual prices in line with the scarcity of the given good relative to the previous case where no supply shocks apply. The new market price level index is 0.95 and average price indices are (1.93, 1.84, 1.41) by group. Quantity indices suggest that adverse supply shocks without compensation will still harm the low income group most, and the high income group least, and the actual indices are (0.801, 0.839, 0.926). The general

Table 3.5
All Prices Free; Compensation 100%-100%-50%

Price changes

		Old price (rbls.)			New market price (rbls.)	Percent change from old market price	Percent change from old state price
		State	Coop	Market			
Meat	(kg)	7.00	14.00	25.00	31.80	27	355
Milk	(l)	0.65	0.65	2.00	2.70	36	309
Eggs	(#)	0.26	0.27	0.70	0.90	29	233
Fish	(kg)	1.50	1.50	1.70	1.90	13	28
Sugar	(kg)	2.40	3.50	4.00	5.30	7	122
Oils	(kg)	3.00	6.00	12.00	13.50	12	350
Pota	(kg)	1.00	1.50	1.50	1.60	8	63
Vegs	(kg)	1.00	4.00	5.00	5.30	6	432
Fruit	(kg)	3.00	6.00	12.00	13.10	9	335
Bread	(kg)	1.19	1.19	1.19	1.30	11	11

	Meat (kg)	Milk (l)	Eggs (#)	Fish (kg)	Sugar (kg)	Oils (kg)	Pota (kg)	Vegs (kg)	Fruit (kg)	Bread (kg)
New consumption per person annual: all sources										
low	31.3	243.0	139.0	5.9	17.4	5.1	67.2	47.0	14.8	93.5
middle	63.4	338.0	203.0	13.7	27.0	6.0	81.9	77.7	34.4	87.2
high	94.4	423.0	257.0	20.0	23.0	8.0	93.6	107.0	54.2	95.2
average	64.5	340.0	204.0	13.7	25.1	6.2	82.0	78.8	35.2	89.4
Percent change in consumption										
low	−8	−3	−3	−5	−3	−3	0	−5	−8	−2
middle	1	0	0	0	0	0	0	0	1	0
high	1	0	0	0	0	0	0	0	0	0
average	0	0	0	0	0	0	0	0	0	0

Income and welfare

Cash income

	Nominal			Real: avg. price deflator		
	Base	New	Percent change	Base	New	Percent change
low	1,200	2,400	100	1,200	849	−29
middle	2,700	5,400	100	2,700	3,104	15
high	6,000	9,000	50	6,000	4,495	−25
average	3,066	5,622	83	3,066	2,969	−3

Laspeyres indices

	Market price	Avg. price	Qty.
low	1.22	2.83	0.944
middle	1.22	2.83	1.005
high	1.22	2.00	1.004

Full income (cash and subsidies)

	Nominal			Real: avg. price deflator		
	Base	New	Percent change	Base	New	Percent change
low	2,538	2,400	−5	2,538	1,960	−23
middle	4,749	5,400	14	4,749	4,410	−7
high	7,938	9,000	13	7,938	7,349	−7
average	5,004	5,622	12	5,004	4,591	−8

Table 3.6
Supply Shocks, Percent of Base Supply

Meat	Milk	Eggs	Fish	Sugar	Oils	Pota	Vegs	Fruit	Bread
−15	−10	−5	−10	−15	−20	−10	−15	−25	−1

pattern of consumption shows that the low income group experiences the most severe cutbacks in all goods.

Table 3.8 illustrates that even a poor-biased compensation scheme leaves the high income group least harmed by the adverse supply shocks, as in Table 3.4 when these shocks were absent. The bias to the poor comes now at the expense of the middle group, which experiences the biggest decline in consumption levels. Quantity indices are now (0.872, 0.832, 0.923) and the outcome is seen to be more inflationary than the previous example, as expected. The market price index rises to 2.19 and average price indices to (4.95, 4.27, 3.22) by group.

Finally, Table 3.9 illustrates that, as in Table 3.5, compensation of the middle group comes at the expense of both low and high groups. The 100%-100%-50% scheme is more inflationary, but, with their incomes better protected, the large middle group has a large impact on the price level, depressing the welfare of the other groups. Quantity indices are now (0.817, 0.861, 0.856) and the new market price index jumps to 3.80. By group, average price indices rise to (8.91, 7.78, 5.15).

3.5 Conclusions

It should be reiterated that these results pertain only to changes in the relatively short term. This has enabled us to abstract from otherwise important interactions between demand, supply and factor markets. Moreover, the model has been designed to facilitate understanding of the key market forces, and we have not modelled important short-term phenomena like hoarding and speculation. We also abstract from monetary expansion as a source of inflation and changes in the general price level. Furthermore, the analysis pertains to a region typical of the Russian Republic and masks important regional differences within Russia. These simplifications have allowed us to focus on several important mechanisms which characterize price liberalizations. In particular, we have shown that, while not obvious at first glance, the distributional impact of price liberalization hinges on policies regarding compensation and interactions between key markets. These

Table 3.7
All Prices Free; Adverse Supply Shock; No Compensation

Price changes

		Old price (rbls.)			New market price (rbls.)	Percent change from old market price	Percent change from old state price
		State	Coop	Market			
Meat	(kg)	7.00	14.00	25.00	19.50	−22	179
Milk	(l)	0.65	0.65	2.00	1.80	−6	182
Eggs	(#)	0.26	0.27	0.70	0.50	−33	73
Fish	(kg)	1.50	1.50	1.70	1.40	−20	−9
Sugar	(kg)	2.40	3.50	4.00	5.70	14	137
Oils	(kg)	3.00	6.00	12.00	21.40	78	613
Pota	(kg)	1.00	1.50	1.50	3.90	158	287
Vegs	(kg)	1.00	4.00	5.00	5.10	3	414
Fruit	(kg)	3.00	6.00	12.00	12.80	7	327
Bread	(kg)	1.19	1.19	1.19	0.80	−35	−35

	Meat (kg)	Milk (l)	Eggs (#)	Fish (kg)	Sugar (kg)	Oils (kg)	Pota (kg)	Vegs (kg)	Fruit (kg)	Bread (kg)
New consumption per person annual: all sources										
low	25.8	217.0	130.0	5.2	14.6	4.1	60.4	39.2	10.7	92.2
middle	51.9	301.0	190.0	12.0	22.8	4.8	73.6	64.7	24.8	85.9
high	88.9	397.0	255.0	19.1	20.5	6.7	84.6	97.3	45.0	96.3
average	54.8	306.0	193.0	12.4	21.3	5.0	73.8	66.9	26.4	88.5
Percent change in consumption										
low	−24	−13	−9	−16	−18	−23	−10	−20	−34	−3
middle	−17	−10	−6	−11	−15	−20	−10	−16	−27	−1
high	−5	−6	−1	−4	−10	−16	−10	−9	−17	1
average	−15	−10	−5	−10	−15	−20	−10	−15	−25	−1

Income and welfare

Cash income

	Nominal			Real: avg. price deflator			Laspeyres indices		
	Base	New	Percent change	Base	New	Percent change	Market price	Avg. price	Qty.
low	1,200	1,200	0	1,200	623	−48	0.95	1.93	0.801
middle	2,700	2,700	0	2,700	2,088	−23	0.95	1.84	0.839
high	6,000	6,000	0	6,000	4,265	−29	0.95	1.41	0.926
average	3,066	3,066	0	3,066	2,237	−27			

Full income (cash and subsidies)

	Nominal			Real: avg. price deflator		
	Base	New	Percent change	Base	New	Percent change
low	2,538	1,200	−53	2,538	1,259	−50
middle	4,749	2,700	−43	4,749	2,833	−40
high	7,938	6,000	−24	7,938	6,295	−21
average	5,004	3,066	−39	5,004	3,217	−36

Table 3.8
All Prices Free; Adverse Supply Shock; Compensation 100%-100%-50%

Price changes

		Old price (rbls.)			New market price (rbls.)	Percent change from old market price	Percent change from old state price
		State	Coop	Market			
Meat	(kg)	7.00	14.00	25.00	44.70	79	538
Milk	(l)	0.65	0.65	2.00	8.30	324	1,172
Eggs	(#)	0.26	0.27	0.70	1.30	93	396
Fish	(kg)	1.50	1.50	1.70	2.00	20	37
Sugar	(kg)	2.40	3.50	4.00	7.10	42	196
Oils	(kg)	3.00	6.00	12.00	33.30	178	1,011
Pota	(kg)	1.00	1.50	1.50	5.60	275	462
Vegs	(kg)	1.00	4.00	5.00	6.40	29	544
Fruit	(kg)	3.00	6.00	12.00	17.10	43	471
Bread	(kg)	1.19	1.19	1.19	1.20	1	1

	Meat (kg)	Milk (l)	Eggs (#)	Fish (kg)	Sugar (kg)	Oils (kg)	Pota (kg)	Vegs (kg)	Fruit (kg)	Bread (kg)
New consumption per person annual: all sources										
low	29.3	228.0	137.0	5.6	15.4	4.3	60.7	42.4	12.3	94.3
middle	51.3	299.0	189.0	12.0	22.6	4.7	73.6	64.2	24.6	85.5
high	88.5	396.0	254.0	19.1	20.4	6.7	84.6	96.9	44.9	96.1
average	54.8	306.0	193.0	12.4	21.3	5.0	73.8	66.9	26.4	88.5
Percent change in consumption										
low	−14	−9	−4	−9	−14	−19	−10	−14	−24	−1
middle	−18	−11	−6	−12	−15	−21	−10	−16	−28	−2
high	−6	−6	−1	−4	−10	−16	−10	−9	−17	1
average	−15	−10	−5	−10	−15	−20	−10	−15	−25	−1

Income and welfare

Cash income

	Nominal			Real: avg. price deflator		
	Base	New	Percent change	Base	New	Percent change
low	1,200	2,400	100	1,200	485	−60
middle	2,700	4,050	50	2,700	3,340	24
high	6,000	9,000	50	6,000	2,792	−53
average	3,066	4,677	53	3,066	2,255	−26

Laspeyres indices

	Market price	Avg. price	Qty.
low	2.19	4.95	0.872
middle	2.19	4.27	0.832
high	2.19	3.22	0.923

Full income (cash and subsidies)

	Nominal			Real: avg. price deflator		
	Base	New	Percent change	Base	New	Percent change
low	2,538	2,400	−5	2,538	1,097	−57
middle	4,749	4,050	−15	4,749	1,852	−61
high	7,938	9,000	13	7,938	4,115	−48
average	5,004	4,677	−7	5,004	2,138	−57

Table 3.9
All Prices Free; Adverse Supply Shock; Compensation 100%-100%-50%

Price changes

		Old price (rbls.)			New market price	Percent change from old market price	Percent change from old state price
		State	Coop	Market	(rbls.)		
Meat	(kg)	7.00	14.00	25.00	36.90	48	427
Milk	(l)	0.65	0.65	2.00	25.60	1,212	3,835
Eggs	(#)	0.26	0.27	0.70	2.20	227	743
Fish	(kg)	1.50	1.50	1.70	2.50	49	69
Sugar	(kg)	2.40	3.50	4.00	7.90	59	231
Oils	(kg)	3.00	6.00	12.00	41.90	249	1,296
Pota	(kg)	1.00	1.50	1.50	7.00	370	605
Vegs	(kg)	1.00	4.00	5.00	7.10	43	614
Fruit	(kg)	3.00	6.00	12.00	19.60	63	553
Bread	(kg)	1.19	1.19	1.19	1.50	22	22

	Meat (kg)	Milk (l)	Eggs (#)	Fish (kg)	Sugar (kg)	Oils (kg)	Pota (kg)	Vegs (kg)	Fruit (kg)	Bread (kg)
New consumption per person annual: all sources										
low	22.6	219	132.0	5.3	14.7	4.1	60.5	39.9	11.1	92.5
middle	53.9	304	193.0	12.3	23.0	4.8	73.7	66.0	25.8	86.3
high	80.3	380	244.0	18.0	19.6	6.4	84.2	91.3	40.7	94.2
average	54.8	306	193.0	12.4	21.3	5.0	73.8	66.9	26.4	88.5
Percent change in consumption										
low	−22	−12	−8	−14	−17	−22	−10	−19	−31	−3
middle	−14	−10	−5	−10	−14	−19	−10	−14	−25	−1
high	−14	−10	−5	−10	−14	−19	−10	−14	−25	−1
average	−15	−10	−5	−10	−15	−20	−10	−15	−25	−1

Income and welfare

Cash income

	Nominal			Real: avg. price deflator		
	Base	New	Percent change	Base	New	Percent change
low	1,200	2,400	100	1,200	269	−78
middle	2,700	5,400	100	2,700	3,732	38
high	6,000	9,000	50	6,000	1,749	−71
average	3,066	5,622	83	3,066	1,829	−40

Laspeyres indices

Market price	Avg. price	Qty.
3.80	8.91	0.817
3.80	7.78	0.861
3.80	5.15	0.856

Full income (cash and subsidies)

	Nominal			Real: avg. price deflator		
	Base	New	Percent change	Base	New	Percent change
low	2,538	2,400	−5	2,538	632	−75
middle	4,749	5,400	14	4,749	1,421	−70
high	7,938	9,000	13	7,938	2,369	−70
average	5,004	5,622	12	5,004	1,480	−70

results yield several broad conclusions concerning the implications of full and partial liberalization, and various compensation schemes, as well as the consequences of adverse supply shocks.

First, since subsidy removal involves a negative income impact on all groups, liberalization, *ceteris paribus,* will entail a general decline in the market price level. Thus, pre-reform market prices in no way give an accurate prediction of the stable post-reform price structure. Indeed, unless inflationary monetary policy or some other forces, such as hoarding or speculation, serve to drive up prices in the interim, an uncompensated full price liberalization should entail a post-reform price level well below the pre-reform free-market price level. In this regard, our model is obviously to be viewed as an analysis of the stable post-reform price structure since it does not account for temporary destabilization due to hoarding and speculative transactions. The time-horizon is therefore best envisaged as around two or three months, looking forward to a time when the considerable stocks hoarded have been run down, and when speculative activity has ceased: at such a time prices should begin to fall from their currently inflated level during the immediate post-reform confusion.

Second, our policy analysis suggests that only a targeted compensation scheme, biased to the poor, can adequately protect low income groups from the adverse effects of liberalization on their welfare. Expressed as a proportion of their pre-reform full income, the subsidies to the poor were considerably larger than in any other group; consequently, subsidy removal is most acutely felt by this group as a negative income effect, and, in a zero-sum game where supplies are fixed, the low income group will necessarily suffer more whilst the rich gain. Indeed, the middle group loses in some small measure when not compensated too, reflecting their relatively heavy reliance on subsidies. Obviously, a flat compensation scheme (say, doubling all incomes) is futile in such a zero-sum scenario: raising the general price level and not redistributing income still leaves the low group much worse off, and consumption outcomes little changed.

Third, the consumption outcomes are very sensitive to the amount of compensation granted the middle group. Since the group is relatively numerous (a 70% share of population) changes in their demands have large impacts on the price level. Thus, extending a biased compensation scheme to this group effectively undoes the compensation of the poor, as well as harming the high income group. This suggests that widespread compensation schemes which include the middle classes must be carefully designed to take this sensitivity into account.

Finally, and somewhat surprisingly, the subsidy system exacerbates inequalities in its impact both before and after liberalization. When in place prior to liberalization, richer groups were well-placed to take advantage of subsidies, relative to the poorest groups. When the subsidies were removed, however, the liberalization generated a much larger negative proportional income effect on poorer groups, since these groups relied more on subsidies as a share of their full income. Thus, given the size of wage increases which accompanied the liberalization and largely benefitted better-off workers in enterprises, the non-poor groups tended to fare relatively better than the poor.

References

Ahmad, E., and N. H. Stern. 1991. *The Theory and Practice of Tax Reform in Developing Countries*. Cambridge: Cambridge University Press.

Braverman, A., J. S. Hammer, and A. Gron. 1987. Multimarket Analysis of Agricultural Pricing Policy: The Case of Cyprus. *World Bank Economic Review* 1: 337–356.

Braverman, A., J. S. Hammer, and J. J. Morduch. 1987. Wheat and Maize Price Policies in Hungary: Tradeoffs between Foreign Exchange and Government Revenue. *Agricultural Economics* 1: 273–290.

Deaton, A. 1984. Issues in the Methodology of Multimarket Analysis of Agricultural Pricing Policies. Princeton University. RPDS Discussion Paper no. 116.

Deaton, A., and J. Muellbauer. 1980. *Economics and Consumer Behavior*. Cambridge: Cambridge University Press.

Hausman, J. A. 1985. Taxes and Labor Supply. In A. Auerbach and M. Feldstein, eds. *Handbook of Public Economics*. Amsterdam: North Holland.

Morduch, J. J., K. M. Brooks, and Y. M. Urinson. 1993. Distributional Consequences of the Russian Price Liberalization. *Economic Development and Cultural Change*. Forthcoming.

Morduch, J. J., and A. M. Taylor. 1992. A Model of Price Liberalization in Russia. Harvard University (January). Photocopy.

Neary, J. P., and K. W. S. Roberts. 1980. The Theory of Household Behavior Under Rationing. *European Economic Review* 13: 25–42.

Taylor, A. M., and J. S. Hammer. 1989. A Multi-Market Model of Tanzania. The World Bank. Photocopy.

4

The Initial Welfare Consequences of Price Liberalization and Stabilization in Poland

Bryan W. Roberts

4.1 Introduction

Polish consumer welfare apparently decreased dramatically after a major stabilization and reform program was initiated in January 1990. The statistically-measured real wage fell by almost 20% in 1990. Estimates of the drop in real private consumption change range from 5% to 16%. Recent stabilization and reform initiatives in Russia have also resulted in a sharp fall in real income and consumption.

However, due to certain characteristics of the pre-transition planned economy and the transition itself, statistical measures of real income are very incomplete measures of overall economic welfare. Price liberalization resulted in the virtual elimination of the queuing and search costs of goods procurement, and import liberalization resulted in a substantial increase in goods variety. Realignment of relative prices is bringing about an end to forced substitution, the overconsumption of some goods and underconsumption of others. After decades of hidden unemployment, open unemployment has emerged. Uncertainty concerning job tenure and income is increasing dramatically as the material and psychological security blanket of east European socialism is torn away. Perverse rigidities in the allocation and remuneration of labor and capital are disappearing, and those with initiative and skills can now take advantage of opportunities that had been previously curtailed. Any account of the total welfare impact of recent reforms must

I thank Richard Excise, Stanley Fischer, Gordon Hanson, Peter Temin, Andy Berg, Revold Entov, Rick Ericson, Herbert Levine, Michael Marrese, Peter Murrell, Kent Osband, Jeffrey Sachs, and participants in the M.I.T. International/Development Seminar and the SSRC Summer Workshop on Soviet and East European Economics for very helpful comments.

consider all of these factors if it is to be complete.[1]

In what follows, I will attempt to measure the change in economic welfare using available statistical data. In particular, the joint impact on welfare of the fall in consumption and the elimination of queuing and search costs will be considered. A representative-agent model is developed that incorporates a fixed-price state market, a free market, and search and queuing costs for goods sold in the state market. Plausible empirical estimates of the net change in consumer welfare due to the elimination of queuing and search costs and the initial fall in real income are calculated using Polish data. The estimates indicate that the welfare gains from eliminating these costs were very significant—and in all likelihood fully offset the welfare impact of the initial fall in real income.

The approach that I take to measuring the welfare costs of searching and queuing develops a formula that directly measures the change in utility resulting from the elimination of these costs.[2] This formula does not require data on how much time is expended in searching and queuing and the value of that time to the consumer. Instead, the free-market/state price differential and the relative volume of purchases at state prices are used to infer the magnitude of deadweight utility loss. This approach contributes to the literature on the empirical evaluation of welfare loss due to rationing (Deacon and Sonstelie 1985; Frech and Lee 1987; Deacon and Sonstelie 1989a). It differs from these previous efforts in that it does not calculate the monetary value of lost welfare due to rationing and thus does not require explicit empirical data on the monetary value of time to consumers. Previous efforts have also focused only on a specific market for one good.[3] This paper investigates the empirical consequences of non-price rationing across all consumer good markets for a national economy.

4.2 A Model of a One-Good Economy with Queuing and Free Markets

The application of neoclassical economic analysis to the consumer goods sector of the pre-transition economies is straightforward. Several researchers have made

---

[1] See Lipton and Sachs 1990 and Berg and Sachs 1992. Anyone who doubts that searching and queuing for goods subtracted significantly from household utility should refer to Wedel 1986 for vivid descriptions of daily life in pre-liberalization Poland. Deadweight utility losses were significant and pervasive.

[2] It is important to note that searching for goods was as important as standing in lines to buy them but was much less visible to the casual observer. Both activities were major drains on time and energy: see Wedel 1986, for example.

[3] In fact, all three papers examine the gasoline market in California in 1980.

important contributions modelling consumer choice under conditions of price disequilibrium (see Stahl and Alexeev 1985; Sah 1987; Weitzman 1991; Polterovich 1991; Boycko 1991; Osband 1991). The following model extends their work by deriving an equation that allows for the empirical measurement of welfare improvement after price liberalization.

Generation of Price Disequilibrium

Consider the consumer goods market under pre-liberalization conditions. A given quantity of a single consumer good is sold to a representative consumer.[4] There is an official state market, with fixed price p_S, and a free market with price p_F.[5] The state price is normalized to 1, so that p_F is the relative free-market price. Price disequilibrium is generated by the assumption that available monetary income for consumption exceeds the value of the consumption good supply at the prevailing state price:

$$x_T < I \ , \tag{1}$$

where x_T is total supply and I is monetary income intended to be spent on consumption.

Because of this disequilibrium, a free market emerges. Some of x_T is sold at p_F, and some at the official price. Denote that part of x_T sold at p_F as x_F, and that part sold at the official price as x_S. The new monetary budget constraint, which will bind in equilibrium, is

$$x_S + p_F x_F = I \ . \tag{2}$$

Consumer Utility Maximization

Household utility depends on both consumption and leisure and can be written as

$$\psi = U(x_S + x_F, L) \ , \tag{3}$$

where U_1, $U_2 > 0$ (the partial derivatives with respect to consumption and leisure, respectively), U_{11}, $U_{22} \leq 0$, and L is leisure. The total amount of time and effort

---

Alternatively, the good is sold to many consumers who have identical utility functions.

[5] There were many different kinds of free markets in pre-transformation Eastern Europe. Some were legal, such as the farmers' markets. Others were illegal but tolerated and involved little risk for sellers. The remaining were illegal and involved substantial risk for buyers and sellers alike.

resources available to the household is T.[6]

Price disequilibrium necessarily generates methods of distributing goods that do not rely on the bidding of monetary resources. The most common method used in Poland, Russia, Romania and perhaps some of the other formerly-planned economies was distribution of goods through a time-bidding process.[7]

Assume that the average amount of time and effort devoted by the household to search and queue for a unit of the consumer good sold at the state price is e, so that total time and effort spent on goods procurement is ex_S. Leisure is therefore equal to $T - ex_S$, and utility is

$$\psi = U(x_S + x_F,\ T - ex_S)\ . \tag{4}$$

The utility maximization problem is:

$$\begin{gathered} \max\ \psi = U(x_S + x_F, T - ex_S) \\ \text{w. r. t.}\ \ x_S,\ x_F \\ \text{s. t.}\ \ x_S + p_F x_F = I\ . \end{gathered} \tag{5}$$

First-order conditions are

$$U_1 - eU_2 = \lambda\ , \tag{6}$$

$$U_1 = \lambda p_F\ , \tag{7}$$

where λ is the marginal utility of income. Substituting (7) into (6) and multiplying by x_S, we obtain

$$\lambda (p_F - 1) x_S = U_2 e\, x_S\ . \tag{8}$$

Thus, *if* utility is linear in leisure, rents obtained on state-market purchases are completely offset in utility terms by procurement costs. The only effect of the fixed state-market price policy is the generation of dead-weight utility loss.

Supply of the Consumer Good to the State and Free Market

It remains to determine how much output is sold on the state market and how much on the free market. If there are no incentives or constraints to force the

---

[6] L should properly be regarded as "effective leisure" and should incorporate a measure of the quality of leisure. The psychic costs of procuring goods affected utility probably as much as the pure time loss incurred.

[7] Another method is "pure rationing," in which goods are distributed according to direct command of the state, and consumers do not have the opportunity to bid for goods with any of their resources.

representative agent to sell some of the good at the official price, then all of x_T would be sold on the free market. This was not the case in reality, because risks and punishments were imposed by the government that kept suppliers from selling everything on the free market, and government officials and enterprise managers had an interest in generating shortage.[8]

For the purposes of this paper, the method according to which the agent determines the magnitudes of x_S and x_F is irrelevant. All that is important is that some positive amount of x_T be sold at the official price. Various approaches could be taken in modelling the behavior of the supplier of x_T. There could be a shopkeeper/pilferer who receives x_T and then allocates it to the state and free market according to the maximization of expected profit on risky free-market sales. There could be some complicated interaction between the supplier and the state. However, changes in modelling the supplier's decision have no impact on the important results of this paper, because the manner in which the supplier makes decisions does not affect the first-order conditions resulting from consumer utility maximization. Note that if the agent chooses the level of x_F by maximizing profits on sales of x_F, one might think that these profits should enter the right-hand side of the budget constraint (2). This is not the case: profits earned on free-market sales are *not* a component of consumer income, and the budget constraint (2) is correctly specified. Because this is a representative-agent model, the supplier and the consumer are the same person. The supplier/consumer receives an amount x_T which it must sell to itself. Given that the agent's income I exceeds the value of x_T at the official price, and given that the state does not permit the agent to sell all of x_T to itself at a market-clearing price, the free market and queuing/searching emerge to bring about equality between supply and demand. The only effect of the free market and its higher price p_F is to reduce the real value of monetary income I so that it equals x_T. Queuing and searching keeps the supplier/consumer from trying to buy all of x_T from itself at the low official price. Profits on free-market sales, $(p_F - 1)x_F$, are transferred from the consumer to the seller, but because they are the same person in this model, there is no distributional effect.

The Ratio of Utility Gains to Utility Losses

The general-equilibrium model of this one-good, representative-agent economy is

[8] See Shleifer and Vishny 1992 for a model of socialist firm behavior in which the firm wants to generate shortage in order to maximize appropriable free-market profits.

fully described by four equations: (2), (6), (7) and an equation that results from the supplier's decision-making.[9] There are four endogenous variables: x_F, p_F, λ and e. Of course, the model is not a general-equilibrium model in the full sense, since labor supply and production are neglected.[10] However, leisure does have a shadow value.[11]

In order to develop an estimation equation for the value of utility lost through state-market goods procurement, substitute (7) into (6) to obtain

$$e\,U_2 = \left(\frac{p_F - 1}{p_F}\right) U_1 \,. \tag{9}$$

This can be rewritten as

$$\left(\frac{p_F - 1}{p_F}\right)\left(U_1 \frac{x_T}{U}\right)\left(\frac{x_S}{x_T}\right) = \left(\frac{U_2}{U}\right) e\,x_S \,. \tag{10}$$

Assuming that real income/consumption x_T does not change, the ratio of post- to pre-price liberalization utilities is

$$\frac{\psi_{POST}}{\psi_{PRE}} = \frac{U(x_T,\, T)}{U(x_T,\, T - ex_S)} \,. \tag{11}$$

$U(x_T, T)$ can be approximated as

$$U(x_T,\, T) \approx U(x_T,\, T - ex_S) + U_2 e x_S \,, \tag{12}$$

where the derivative U_2 is calculated at $L = T - ex_S$. Note that if utility is linear in leisure, (12) holds as an equality. Combining (11) and (12) gives the approximation

$$\frac{\psi_{POST}}{\psi_{PRE}} \approx \frac{U(x_T,\, T - ex_S) + U_2 e x_S}{U(x_T,\, T - ex_S)} = 1 + \left(\frac{U_2}{U}\right) e\,x_S \,. \tag{13}$$

Substituting (10) into (13), the following estimation equation is obtained:

---

[9] The supplier's equation could set x_F equal to some exogenous level, or it could make x_F a function of p_F.

[10] See Appendix C for this extension.

[11] The constraint $L = T - ex_S$, where L is leisure, has been substituted into the utility function. The maximization problem without substitution gives the following formula for the shadow value of time resources: $\mu = (p_F - 1)/e\lambda$. μ is the shadow price of leisure, which equals the value in utility terms of per-unit rent obtained on the state good normalized by the per-unit time cost of the state good.

$$\frac{\psi_{POST}}{\psi_{PRE}} \approx 1 + \left(\frac{p_F - 1}{p_F}\right)\left(U_1\frac{x_T}{U}\right)\left(\frac{x_S}{x_T}\right), \tag{14}$$

or, in percentage terms,

$$\frac{\psi_{POST} - \psi_{PRE}}{\psi_{PRE}} \approx \left(\frac{p_F - 1}{p_F}\right)\left(U_1\frac{x_T}{U}\right)\left(\frac{x_S}{x_T}\right). \tag{15}$$

Thus, the percentage increase in the level of utility due to the elimination of procurement costs equals the product of the free-market price-premium, the elasticity of utility with respect to x_T at the point of actual consumption, and the relative weight of state-market purchases in total purchases. Again note that if utility is linear in leisure, then (14) and (15) hold as equalities.

In the subsequent empirical implementation of the model, the percentage change in utility due to the elimination of state-market procurement costs will not be calculated. Instead, I calculate the ratio of utility gained through the elimination of procurement costs to the utility lost due to the fall in real income in the first year after price liberalization and stabilization.[12] The percentage decline in utility due to a fall in real income can be approximated as

$$\left(U_1\frac{x_T}{U}\right)\left|\frac{\Delta x_T}{x_T}\right|. \tag{16}$$

The ratio of percentage utility gain (15) to percentage utility loss (16) under price liberalization and a fall in real income is therefore approximated by

$$\frac{\left(\frac{p_F - 1}{p_F}\right)\left(U_1\frac{x_T}{U}\right)\left(\frac{x_S}{x_T}\right)}{\left(U_1\frac{x_T}{U}\right)\left|\frac{\Delta x_T}{x_T}\right|} = \frac{\left(\frac{p_F - 1}{p_F}\right)\left(\frac{x_S}{x_T}\right)}{\left|\frac{\Delta x_T}{x_T}\right|}. \tag{17}$$

The ratio defined by (17) will be empirically estimated in the following section. It indicates the degree to which the negative utility consequences of falling real income are offset by the elimination of procurement costs. If the ratio is

[12] This strategy has been adopted due to the fact that in order to make any statement about how much utility increased after the elimination of procurement costs, it would be necessary to specify a particular utility functional form. The technique used here avoids the need to specify a particular functional form: the ratio to be empirically estimated is an approximation to *all* valid utility functions.

greater than 1, then the net welfare change is positive. If the ratio equals 0.5, say, then utility gains offset utility losses by 50%. It is important to note that the ratio of first-order changes in (17) is robust to *any* legitimate specification of the utility function.[13]

If utility is not linear with respect to leisure, then care must be exercised in interpreting empirical results. In particular, if utility is concave with respect to leisure, then the percentage utility gain resulting from procurement-cost elimination is overestimated by the right-hand side of (15). The impact of utility concave in leisure is treated in Appendix A.

Some goods were not distributed through search and queues in eastern European countries. Instead, formal waiting lists were drawn up, and those wishing to obtain the good joined the list and received the good after a significant delay.[14] This method seems to be fundamentally different from the search/queue mechanism in that no deadweight utility loss is generated. Appendix B formally models waiting lists and shows that in fact a deadweight utility loss *is* generated: even though monetary income is available to be spent on the good today, consumption of the good is delayed, and the utility value of consumption is reduced because future utility is discounted. The appendix shows that in the case of utility linear in consumption, the percentage increase in utility due to price liberalization equals the right-hand side of (15).

The model is easily extended to consider issues such as utility nonlinear with respect to leisure, free-market transactions costs, transactions costs in the post-liberalization regime, and labor supply. These modifications and their empirical ramifications are developed in Appendix C.

4.3 Empirical Estimates

Estimates of welfare gain are calculated using 1987 price data. Open Polish price-inflation accelerated over 1988–1989, and a hyperinflation emerged in the last half of 1989. Even as open inflation intensified, repressed inflation accelerated and shortages worsened. However, it is unlikely that a very high level of shortage lasted for more than a brief time. This can be seen in Figure 4.1, which graphs the ratio

[13] Also note that the fact that the utility function is an *ordinal* measure rather than a cardinal measure does not invalidate the approach taken in this paper. I am not estimating the absolute percentage increase in utility, only the degree to which utility gains offset utility losses.

[14] Housing and automobiles were distributed primarily through waiting lists in East European countries.

Figure 4.1
Free-Market/State Food Price Ratio (Parity = 100)

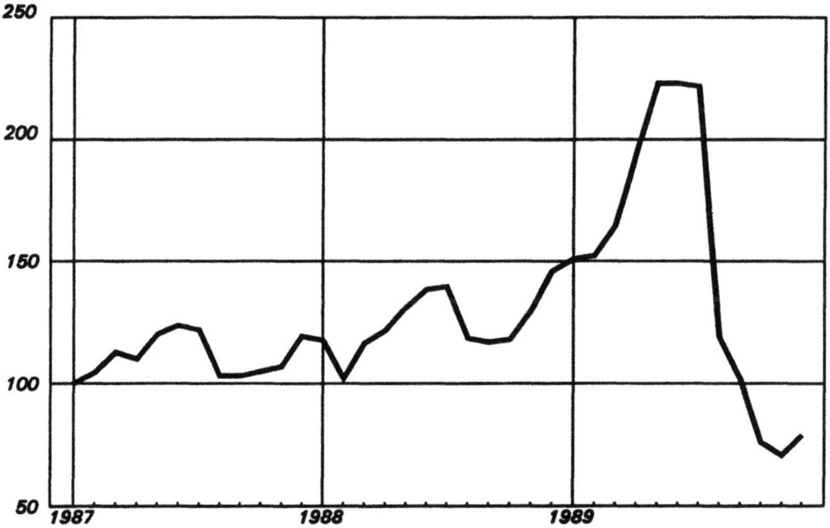

of the free-market food-price to the state food-price. The ratio actually fell slightly during 1983–1986, then slowly rose in 1987 and 1988. There was a brief explosion in mid-1989, which was quickly followed by a spectacular collapse in the second half of 1989 as state food-prices were liberalized. It is more sensible to estimate welfare gain on data from the very stable period 1985–1987 rather than the brief and volatile inflationary period of 1988–1989, as it is much more conceivable that conditions prevailing in the earlier period could have been sustained into the indefinite future. However, it should be kept in mind that if calculations were based on conditions prevailing in 1988 or early 1989, the estimated welfare gain would be significantly higher.

Values for the three terms in equation (26) must be obtained in order to calculate the net welfare gain resulting from the first year after the initiation of the program of price liberalization, stabilization, and reform.

The Free-Market/State-Market Price Ratio

The ratio p_F/p_S has been calculated from a variety of official Polish data on prices

Table 4.1
Polish Free-Market/State Price Ratios

	Aggregate ratio	
	P_F	$(P_F-1)/P_F$
1985–87	1.22	0.181
1987	1.22	0.181

	Ratios by subcategory					
	Food	Alcohol and tobacco	Clothing	Consumer durables	Services	Other
Ratio	1.3	1.3	1.4	1.7	1.9	1.5
% in total	44.2	4.3	14.9	15.5	13.6	6.2
% covered	96.2	64.3	44.0	43.0	24.2	13.9

Notes: % in total is percentage of subcategory in total consumption. % covered is percentage of individual consumption items in subcategory for which there is free-market/state-market price data. Other is energy and fuels (including gasoline), medical and cosmetic items.
Source: Appendix D.

prevailing in state and free markets. Results are given in Table 4.1. The most important source of data is an annual household budget survey which monitors the receipts and expenditures of some 28,000 families. Separate records were kept on purchases in state and free markets, and prices for a large variety of goods were derived from these data.[15] Black-market prices for a limited number of goods were also officially reported, and these were used to construct price ratios for consumer durables.[16] Ratios for individual goods and services were aggregated using consumer expenditure-shares from the household-budget survey and data on the structure of state retail sales. Complete details on the construction of the price ratios are given in Appendix D.

The aggregate p_F/p_S ratio is 1.22 in 1987. The average aggregate ratio for 1985–1987 is also equal to 1.22, indicating that repressed inflationary pressures were constant over this period. The 1987 free-market price premium is 18.1%. It should be noted that this estimate is rather conservative. Price ratios for many individual clothing items, durables, and services are not available. The price ratio is assumed equal to 1 for these items when constructing the aggregate price ratio.

[15] More precisely, records were kept for the socialist and nonsocialist sectors.
[16] Evidently, black market prices were obtained through "market surveys."

However, ratios calculated for clothing, durables, and services *excluding* items for which no price ratio data is available are much higher than 1.22. Full coverage of the consumer basket would substantially increase the aggregate ratio.

Relative Weight of State-Sector Purchases

Evidence on the proportion of consumption goods bought on state markets and free markets were not systematically collected or reported by the statistical authorities. However, enough data exists so that reasonable values of x_S/x_T can be postulated.

It is important to note that x_S should include all purchases on which rents were fully dissipated, and x_F should include all purchases on which rents were not dissipated but were enjoyed by the seller or consumer or both. Goods produced and consumed by the household itself should be treated as part of x_F. x_F should include sales to workers by "special stores" run by enterprises (known as "privileged access" sales), if these sales were at state-market prices and no utility procurement costs were incurred by the workers in procuring these goods. Goods sold under coupon-rationing schemes should also be included in x_F, *if* such schemes eliminated procurement costs. Finally, sales through formal waiting lists did generate deadweight utility losses that were eliminated by price liberalization, and Appendix B shows that for utility linear in consumption, the same empirical estimation equation holds. Thus, waiting-list goods should properly be treated as a component of x_S.

OFFICIAL POLISH DATA

The Polish statistical authorities collected a large amount of statistical data on aggregate consumption that permits the calculation of many of the components of x_S and x_F. The official value of aggregate consumption includes:[17]

(a) Purchase of goods and services at state-market prices in state retail trade stores

(b) Purchase of goods and services at state-market prices in "privileged-access" stores

(c) Purchase of goods and services in the legal private sector at free-market prices

(d) Purchase of goods and services in state-owned hard-currency stores at free-

[17] See the explanatory notes for the section on *spozycie* (consumption) in any *Rocznik Statystyczny* in the 1980s for a description of what the official measure covers.

market prices

(e) The value of agricultural goods produced and consumed by households

(f) Purchase of goods and services at state-market prices through waiting lists

(g) Purchase of goods and services at state-market prices using rationing coupons

(h) Purchase of goods and services at free-market prices at state stores through under-the-counter payments

In this section, values for (c), (d), and (e) are calculated and an estimate of x_S/x_T is obtained. It is important to note that the estimated value of x_S/x_T is an *underestimate* of the true value. The calculated ratio is a ratio of nominal values and equals

$$\frac{p_S x_S}{p_F x_F + p_S x_S} \tag{18}$$

which is less than x_S/x_T.

In most formerly-planned economies, significant amounts of food were purchased on legal "farmers' markets," where goods were priced freely.[18] Other private economic activity, for example production and sale of handicrafts and services, was also tolerated. Data on legal free-market sales of goods and services are shown in Table 4.2. According to this official data, legal free-market sales were rather small, amounting to about 7% of total consumption in 1985–1987. However, the official estimate of the value of these sales are widely acknowledged to be underestimated.[19] Table 4.3 gives new values with legal private sales doubled.[20] In this case, these sales are about 13% of total consumption.

Many formerly-planned economies sold goods for dollars and other hard currencies to domestic citizens through a chain of domestic "export" stores. These

---

[18] In Poland, these were known as *targowiski,* and in the Soviet Union as *kolkhoznye rynki*. Farmers' markets sold fresh food products, including meats, vegetables, fruits, eggs, dairy products, and honey. With the exception of cheese and milk, farmers did not sell processed foods.

[19] Aslund (1985, 7–9) provides a thorough critique of official Polish statistical measurement of the legal private sector, particularly turnover data. He then concludes that "some experts acknowledged that Polish statistics on the turnovers of private enterprises were little more than guesses. The size of biases or their trends cannot be estimated, since it is quite possible that *50 per cent should be added to the GUS estimates of private turnover*" (Aslund 1985, 9; emphasis added). Thus, doubling the official value of private turnover is more than adequate in allowing for undermeasurement of the private sector.

[20] Increasing by 100% seems to be more than enough to take care of underreporting: see footnote 19. Note that the increase in the value of private sales must be added to total household consumption, the denominator.

Table 4.2
Official Polish Data On Household Consumption

	Total household consumption	Private retail sales	Private service sales	Hard-currency sales	Home-produced food
Billion current zloty					
1985	6,370.0	125.0	288.1	254.8	—
1986	7,820.0	150.0	378.5	375.4	—
1987	10,066.0	207.0	507.8	—	775.1
As percentage of total household consumption					
1985	100.0	2.0	4.5	4.0	—
1986	100.0	1.9	4.8	4.8	—
1987	100.0	2.1	5.0	—	7.7

Table 4.3
Polish Household Consumption Data, Private Sales Doubled

	Total household consumption	Private retail sales	Private service sales	Hard-currency sales	Home-produced food
Billion current zloty					
1985	6,783.0	250.0	576.2	254.8	—
1986	8,349.0	300.0	757.0	375.4	—
1987	10,781.0	414.0	1,015.6	—	830.1
As percentage of total household consumption					
1985	100.0	3.7	8.5	3.8	—
1986	100.0	3.6	9.1	4.5	—
1987	100.0	3.8	9.4	—	7.7

Sources: *Rocznik Statystyczny*, 1987; 1988. See also Tables 4.4 and 4.5.

sales of both domestically-produced and imported products were usually made at market-clearing prices. Data on sales through the Polish version of this network, known as Pewex/Polmot, are available for 1982–1986 in total and for a variety of consumption categories and are given as a percentage of consumption in Table 4.4. The relative weight of Pewex purchases averaged around 4.5%–5.0%.

The value of agricultural products produced and consumed by households can be calculated from the household budget survey data. The value of such production and its percentage in total household expenditures for four household types in 1987 are given in Table 4.5. It should be noted that this consumption was

Table 4.4
Ratio Of Hard-Currency Sales To Total Household Consumption

	Total	Food	Alcoholic beverages	Nonfood	Clothing
1982	4.3	1.2	10.4	4.9	13.1
1983	5.0	2.3	7.8	5.8	11.9
1984	4.0	2.2	8.2	4.2	7.9
1985	4.0	2.4	10.1	3.7	6.1
1986	4.8	2.7	11.0	4.7	5.9

Notes: Hard-currency sales are given in millions of US dollars. The dollar values were converted into zloty values through the parallel market exchange rate. Over 1984–1986, imports constituted 70% of hard-currency sales.
Sources: *Rocznik Statystyczny Handlu Wewnetrznego 1980–1986*; *Rocznik Statystyczny*, various issues.

Table 4.5
Home-produced and Consumed Foodstuffs, 1987

Household type	Number of budgets	Estimated expenditures on home-produced foodstuffs	Total household expenditures	Implied budget-share of home-produced foodstuffs (%)
Worker	13,373	378	16,221	2.3
Worker-peasant	3,897	2,631	14,570	18.1
Peasant	3,905	3,796	16,973	22.4
Pensioner	7,647	735	16,304	4.5
Total	28,822	1,240	16,122	7.7

Note: Expenditures are zloty per month.
Source: Household budget-survey data.

valued at free-market prices.[21] Assuming that the survey properly sampled the general population, these shares can be aggregated. The overall percentage of home-produced foodstuffs in total consumption in 1987 was 7.7%.

Summing these four components together, these sales were between 20%–25% of total consumption (see Tables 4.2 and 4.3) in 1987. The ratio x_S/x_T was therefore between 75%–80%. As noted above, because (c), (d), and (e) are valued at free-market prices, this is an underestimate of the true ratio x_S/x_T.

[21] The prices used were state agricultural purchase prices, but for non-obligatory supplies. These purchase prices were generally market-clearing.

Of course, several major components of consumption that should be included in x_F are missing from this calculation, in particular coupon-rationed sales, privileged-access sales, and under-the-counter sales. Also, illegal production of goods and services sold at market-clearing prices that are definitionally not recorded in official statistics are completely neglected.

Coupon-rationed sales were practically nonexistent in Poland in 1987.[22] It is also usually the case that such schemes do not eliminate procurement costs. Even if authorities manage to set the aggregate issue of coupons equal to the aggregate supply of a good, there will be imbalances at the micro level that lead to searching and queuing.[23] For these two reasons, it is assumed that none of the consumption basket was rationed through effective coupon schemes.

No empirical data is available on privileged access sales. Apparently, most of these sales were targeted at particular groups of workers who were considered to be politically important, in particular the coal miners.[24] The elite strata of Polish society also benefitted heavily from these sales, but the size of this elite was very small. It is unlikely that privileged access sales were a very large component of total consumption in 1987. This paper assumes that such sales amounted to 10% of total consumption.

No empirical data from official sources is available on under-the-counter sales, or on illegal private activity not recorded in official statistics. In order to fill in this part of the picture, it is necessary to examine other data sources.

Second Economy Statistical Data

An alternative to these official statistics is attempts to recalculate total household income and expenditures taking into account the items missing from the previous calculation. The Polish state statistical authority estimates that in 1987, private, unregistered economic activity was about 25% of total household income.[25] Combining this with the calculation of the previous section, x_S/x_T in 1987 was about 50%–55% (excluding "privileged-access" sales).

Considerable quantitative evidence on total personal incomes is available for the Soviet Union. If conditions in Poland were reasonably close to those prevailing in the Soviet Union, then a review of this evidence is useful. There is little reason

---

[22] See World Bank 1987: I, 12.

[23] See Deacon and Sonstelie 1989b.

[24] Personal communication from Polish colleague.

[25] Cited in Wedel 1992, 77, footnote 1.

to suspect that the situations in the two countries were dramatically different, given that the institutions used by both countries to distribute consumer goods were remarkably similar and that official statistics on the extent of legal free-market activity for both countries show similar levels.[26]

Data obtained from a survey of emigrants from the Soviet Union in the late 1970s are presented in Table 4.6.[27] This survey sampled roughly 2000 households and acquired detailed data on household incomes and expenditures, both "formal" and "informal." Informal expenditures are defined to be any expenditures associated with the "second" economy and cover almost the entire range of purchases properly included in x_F.[28] The only items of expenditure not covered are privileged-access sales and effective coupon-rationed sales.[29]

The value of x_F/x_T range from 28.7% for working households in Russian cities (excluding Leningrad) to 71.3% for pensioner households in Armenia. For various reasons, the demographic profile of the emigrant sample does not correspond closely to the profile of the Soviet population as a whole. The ratio for the entire USSR is likely to be somewhere between the ratios for households in Russian cities and Belorussia/Moldova/Ukraine, and probably closer to that for Russian cities. Thus, this data suggests that x_S/x_T could be anywhere from 0.6 to 0.7 in the USSR in the late 1970s.[30] Again note that this is an underestimate of the true x_S/x_T, because x_F is valued at p_F.

Various estimates of the total size of the Soviet informal economy have also been made by Russian statisticians. These estimates again include almost all of the purchases that should properly be included in x_F.[31] Using their result that second economy turnover was from 60 billion to 170 billion rubles in the late 1980s and the official 1988 value of personal consumption, 441.2 billion rubles, the ratio x_S/x_T

[26] For example, according to official Soviet statistics, purchases on the farmers' market in the USSR accounted for roughly 5% of total consumer expenditures in the late 1980s.

[27] See Grossman 1989.

[28] Expenditures included free-market purchase of food and nonfood goods, in-kind consumption of foodstuffs and goods stolen from the workplace, private service payments, gifts, bribes, under-the-counter purchases, and purchases made through connections. See Grossman 1989, 165–68.

[29] There was probably very little coupon rationing in the USSR in the late 1970s.

[30] The late 1970s was a period of relatively high repressed inflation in the USSR. The government apparently implemented a stabilization program in the early 1980s which may have slightly increased the value of x_S/x_T through 1985.

[31] The major omitted category that the emigrant survey *does* include is legal purchases of food from free-market sources.

Table 4.6
Informal Expenditures and Personal Incomes, Soviet Emigrant Survey

	Working households				Pensioner households	
	Russia and Baltics		Armenia	Belorus, Moldova and Ukraine	Leningrad	Armenia
	Leningrad	Other cities				
Sample size	294	382	560	558	164	30
Total personal income (rubles/year)	1,943	1,540	3,220	2,174	1,241	2,839
Informal expenditures (rubles/year)	674	442	1,988	880	497	2,023
as % of income	*35*	*29*	*62*	*41*	*40*	*71*

Source: Grossman 1989, 160.

ranges from 72% to 88%.[32] The large difference between the results from the emigre-survey and the Russian calculations may be due to the fact that households in the emigre sample were much more likely to have participated in informal activity than the typical Soviet household.

SUBMARKET EVIDENCE

Finally, it is worthwhile to review evidence on the magnitude of x_F/x_T for several important submarkets, taking advantage of the results of several careful empirical studies.

An extensive research program on the second economy in the former Soviet Union identifies services as one area of intense black-market activity. Calculations based on 1977 data show that at least 80% of consumer services were sold at free-market prices.[33] Studies of the Polish black market also show that most services were sold at free-market prices, although to a lesser extent than in the Soviet

---

[32] These estimates agree that the annual value of black market turnover in the late 1980s was on average equal to 100 billion rubles. The range used here incorporates the lowest and highest endpoints of the various ranges estimated by the Soviet analysts. See Rutgaizer 1992, 62.

[33] See Neuhauser and Gaddy 1989, 15. Their estimate is based on an extensive survey of emigrants from the Soviet Union in the late 1970s and 1980s.

Union.[34] A survey of the Soviet gasoline market found that 50% of the physical quantity of gasoline was sold at illegal black market prices in the late 1970s.[35] These markets were studied precisely because they were ex-ante believed to be sectors of intense black market activity, and the results confirm these beliefs. In contrast, a review of the housing market in Soviet urban areas revealed that only 3% of all urban households rented housing privately in 1989 (Alexeev 1988; 1991, 3, 7).

THE VALUE OF x_S/x_T

Taken together, this body of empirical evidence suggests that a reasonable range for x_S/x_T is 40%–60%. Using the official Polish consumption data, the Polish estimate of unregistered private activity, and a value for privileged-access sales equal to 10% of total consumption gives a range of 45%–50%. The Soviet emigre survey data suggests a value of 50%–60% Anywhere from 5% to 10% should be added to the endpoints due to the underestimation problem resulting from valuing x_F at p_F.[36] The estimated ranges and the correction for underestimation means that the chosen endpoint of 40% is fairly conservative. The true value was probably between 50% and 60%.

Change in Real Consumption in 1990

The change in aggregate Polish real consumption over 1989–1990 is the subject of much dispute. The Polish statistical agency GUS asserts that real private per-capita consumption fell 16%.[37] An alternative estimate of the change in personal consumption using data on the physical consumption of many types of goods obtained from household-expenditure surveys and other sources has been calculated (Berg and Sachs 1992). This estimate indicates that aggregate consumption fell

---

[34] "In some areas, particularly services, the supply was dominated by various forms of unofficial activity. The second sector accounted for between 27 and 76 percent of total supplies of services provided by private and state-owned firms in the repairs of cars, TV sets, household appliances, and so forth, in 1987" (Kaminski 1991, 183–84).

[35] As in the case of services, one would have expected on the basis of a priori information that the black market for gasoline in the Soviet Union was extensive. Automobile production grew more than 20% per year in the early 1970's, but gasoline production increased much more slowly, at 6%–7% per year. Intense shortage inevitably resulted.

[36] Assume that the estimated value of x_S/x_T is 0.5, and the relative free-market price ratio p_F is 1.22. Then it is easily shown that the *true* value of x_S/x_T is 0.55. If p_F equals 1.5, which is more realistic for Poland in 1987 given the very conservative approach taken in estimating p_F in this paper, then the true value is 0.6.

[37] *Rocznik Statystyczny w 1991 roku.*

about 5%.

Another recent effort relies on changes in the food budget share to infer movements in real income.[38] The statistical correlation of growth in the food budget share and growth in the GUS private consumption measure over the period 1981–1989 can be used to forecast private consumption growth in 1990. The point estimate, −0.92%, is far below the −16% value given by GUS, and even makes the Berg-Sachs estimate look rather conservative.

The Berg-Sachs and GUS estimates are assumed to bracket the actual fall in Polish real income. In order to remain consistent with the choice of 1987 as a base year for comparison purposes, the fall in real consumption is calculated over 1987–1990 rather than 1989–1990. The GUS data gives this change as 12%. A corresponding Berg-Sachs estimate is not available, and the 5% value is used. However, if the Berg-Sachs approach was applied to 1987–1990, the fall in real consumption would be less than 5%.

It should be emphasized that there are two serious calculations that show a real income change of 5% or less. Values at the lower end of the range 5%–12% are therefore more plausible as representing the true change in real consumption over 1987–1990. The mid-point of this range of real income change, 8.5%, is also considered in the calculation of the net welfare change ratios.[39]

Estimates of Net Welfare Change

Table 4.7 gives the values of the ratios of welfare increase due to the elimination of procurement costs to the welfare loss brought about by the fall in real consumption. If a ratio is greater than 1, then welfare gain more than offset welfare reduction, and the initial net welfare effect of the reform program was positive.

The welfare gains from price liberalization were very significant. In the case of a fall in real consumption of 5% or 8.5% and x_S/x_T equal to 50%–60%, gains outweighed losses. In the case of a 12% contraction, net welfare change is almost equal to zero if x_S/x_T equals 60%. Even in the unlikely worst-case scenario, gains offset losses by more than 50%. It should be noted that the welfare gains from elimination of forced substitution and an increased variety of consumer goods due

[38] See Roberts 1993.

[39] It is important to note that explaining exactly why output and consumption fell after price liberalization and stabilization is *irrelevant* for the purposes of this paper. In order to assess the welfare consequences of the reform program for the representative consumer, all that is necessary is to determine by how much consumption fell.

Table 4.7
Ratio of Utility Gain to Absolute Value of Utility Loss

	Percentage fall in real consumption		
x_S/x_T	5%	8.5%	12%
0.4	1.45	0.85	0.60
0.5	1.81	1.06	0.75
0.6	2.17	1.28	0.91

Note : Utility is assumed to be linear with respect to leisure.

to import liberalization are not included in these calculations. Their inclusion would significantly increase ratio values. Because the fall in real income was probably closer to 5% than 12%, the value of x_S/x_T closer to 60% than 40%, and other significant welfare gains are not taken into account, the results suggest rather strongly that in the case of Poland, initial welfare gains due to price liberalization exceeded initial welfare losses.

The effects on such empirical results of modifying the model to take into account utility nonlinear in leisure are considered in Appendix A. It is shown that except for very extreme and unlikely degrees of concavity, the ratio values are essentially unaffected. The effects of introducing free-market transaction costs, post-liberalization transaction costs, and labor supply are reviewed in Appendix C.

4.4 Conclusions

Those previously familiar with the east-European economies were aware that substantial welfare gains were to be had from a reform of the highly inefficient distribution system. That the gains were possibly so large, as this paper has shown, is surprising. Given the tenor of the current discussion about reform in eastern Europe and its impact on living standards, few would have expected the initial net welfare-change (as defined in this paper) to be zero or positive.

This empirical finding has general implications for the reform of economies characterized by considerable expenditure of real resources on goods procurement, rent seeking and the like. Thoroughgoing, credible reform efforts can result in *immediate* positive net welfare effects. The received wisdom is that such initiatives generate a welfare "J-curve," in which welfare falls initially and begins to increase only after the positive effects of reform begin to bear fruit. This impression is driven in large part by the empirical fact that a sharp contraction of economic activity in certain sectors often follows major reforms. It has been demonstrated here that the experiences of Poland correspond more to a "gamma-curve."[40] Welfare initially does not change or even rises, and is hopefully followed by significant increases as the benefits of restructuring and greater integration into the world economy are realized.

Of course, the analysis of welfare change made in this paper is incomplete. First, the effect of the reduction of real balances is not considered. The issue of real balance contraction is complex, as a large fraction of accumulated monetary holdings was considered by many to be a monetary overhang. It is not clear that their elimination entailed utility loss.[41]

Second, the assumption that there is a single consumer, so that distributional issues are completely neglected, is clearly open to criticism. Many observers and analysts have focused precisely on distributional effects as one of the most undesirable consequences of price liberalization. Much work needs to be done on the distributional consequences of eastern European reforms.

Third, expansion in product variety and partial elimination of forced substitution is not taken into account. In order to address these issues, a multi-good model is necessary. Both of these changes increase the level of economic welfare.

Finally, as pointed out in the introduction, the analysis does not take into account the significant increase in uncertainty about economic futures. This factor, rather than the supposed contraction in welfare, underlies much of the negative reaction in eastern Europe to the dramatic changes now rapidly unfolding. The populations concerned are aware that economic restructuring is barely underway. Although restructuring does not necessarily result in the lowering of the living standard of a given agent, and will certainly result in an overall increase in welfare, the uncertainty and other costs associated with such fundamental change nonetheless impact on welfare defined in a broad sense.

Appendix A: Utility Nonlinear in Leisure

If utility is not linear with respect to leisure, then care must be exercised in interpreting the empirical results. In particular, if utility is concave with respect to leisure, then the percentage utility gain resulting from procurement-cost elimination will be overestimated. Assume that utility can be written as

If this utility function is concave in leisure, then $h_{11}<0$. The degree of

---

[40] A Γ-curve.

[41] Changes in real balances are only part of the broader question of what is happening to total household assets over the course of transition.

$$\psi = U(x_S+x_F)\, h(T-ex_S) \ . \tag{19}$$

overestimation of utility gains due to concavity for this function is shown graphically in Appendix Figure 4.A.

Another implication of concavity is that rents obtained on state-market purchases are not fully offset by procurement costs. Applying (8) to (19), we obtain

$$\lambda\,(p_F-1)\,x_S = U\,h'ex_S \ . \tag{20}$$

It is clear that rents exceed procurement costs (see Appendix Figure 4.A) since

$$Uh'ex_S > U\ [h(T)-h(T-ex_S)] \ . \tag{21}$$

The following utility function will be used in order to assess the impact of the concavity of utility in leisure on the empirical results derived in the paper:

$$\psi = U(x_S+x_F)\left(\frac{T-ex_S}{T}\right)^{B} , \tag{22}$$

where $B<1$. Rearrangement of first-order conditions of the consumer maximization problem gives

$$\left(\frac{T-ex_S}{T}\right)^{B} = \left[\ 1 + \left(\frac{1}{B}\right)\left(\frac{p_F-1}{p_F}\right)\left(U_1\frac{x_T}{U}\right)\left(\frac{x_S}{x_T}\right)\right]^{-B} . \tag{23}$$

Consider the following sequence of changes in utility. First, prices are liberalized. Denote the pre-price liberalization utility as ψ_{PRE}, and the post-price liberalization utility level as ψ_{POST}. Second, the real income shock hits. The level of utility prior to the fall in real income is ψ_{POST}, and the level of utility after the real income fall is ψ_{REAL}.

The ratio of post- to pre-price liberalization utility is

$$\frac{\psi_{POST}}{\psi_{PRE}} = \frac{U(x_T)}{U(x_T)\left(\frac{T-ex_S}{T}\right)^{B}} = \left(\frac{T-ex_S}{T}\right)^{-B} . \tag{24}$$

Combining (23) and (24), we obtain

Appendix Figure 4.A
Overestimation of Utility Due to Concavity

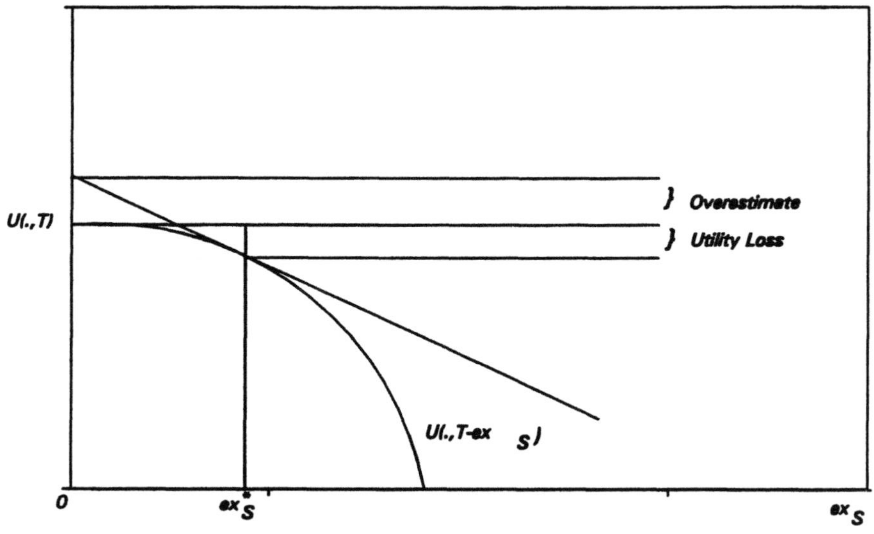

$$\left(\frac{\psi_{POST}}{\psi_{PRE}}\right)^{\frac{1}{B}} - 1 = \left(\frac{1}{B}\right)\left(\frac{p_F - 1}{p_F}\right)\left(U_1\frac{x_T}{U}\right)\left(\frac{x_S}{x_T}\right). \tag{25}$$

The absolute value of percentage change in utility resulting from real income fall can be approximated as

$$\left|\frac{\psi_{REAL}}{\psi_{POST}} - 1\right| = \left(U_x\frac{x_T}{U}\right)\left|\frac{\Delta x_T}{x_T}\right|. \tag{26}$$

Define A to be

$$A = \frac{\left(\frac{1}{B}\right)\left(\frac{p_F - 1}{p_F}\right)\left(\frac{x_S}{x_T}\right)}{\left|\frac{\Delta x_T}{x_T}\right|}. \tag{27}$$

Then it is easily shown that

$$\frac{\psi_{POST}}{\psi_{PRE}} - 1 = \left[A \left| \frac{\psi_{REAL}}{\psi_{POST}} - 1 \right| \right]^{B} - 1 \,. \tag{28}$$

Simulations have been carried out using equation (28) to test the impact of making utility concave in leisure. Assume that the utility of goods consumption function can be written as

$$U(x_S + x_T) = U(x_T) = x_T^{\gamma} \,. \tag{29}$$

Then the elasticity of goods consumption utility with respect to x_T is γ. The value of γ ranges between 0 and 1. The implications for changes in total utility due to changing levels of leisure for different values of B are graphed in Appendix Figure 4.B.

The simulation procedure is as follows. For various values of B, x_S/x_T, and $\Delta x_T/x_T$, the value of A given by (27) is calculated. A range of values for the absolute value of the percentage change in utility level due to the fall in real consumption, $\psi_{REAL}/\psi_{POST}-1$, is postulated: the range is from 1% to 100%. Using the values for A, B, $\psi_{REAL}/\psi_{POST}-1$, and equation (29), the implied values of $\psi_{POST}/\psi_{PRE}-1$ and associated net welfare gain ratio are calculated. The values of $\psi_{REAL}/\psi_{POST}-1$ and $\Delta x_T/x_T$ are used to calculate an implied value of γ. The net welfare ratio associated with $\gamma = 1$ is then obtained: this forms a *lower bound* to the actual ratio. Ratio values greater than this correspond to values of γ less than 1. The ratio values for $\gamma = 1$ are given in Table 4.8 (calculations were made only for $x_S/x_T = 0.5$: using 0.4 or 0.6 makes no difference to the pattern in the results).

Comparing Table 4.8 to Table 4.7, making utility concave in leisure has very little effect on ratio values except in the case where $B = 0.1$, which is a case of extreme concavity: if leisure falls by 99% due to procurement costs, total utility falls by only 37%. This degree of concavity is highly unlikely to have been the case in reality.

The results of this exercise are particular to a specific functional form of the utility function. However, they suggest that the empirical results are generally robust to concavity except for extreme and unlikely cases. The conclusion that procurement cost elimination fully offset the fall in real consumption in utility terms is not substantially affected by concavity of utility with respect to leisure.

Appendix Figure 4.B
Total Utility, Leisure and the Value of *B*

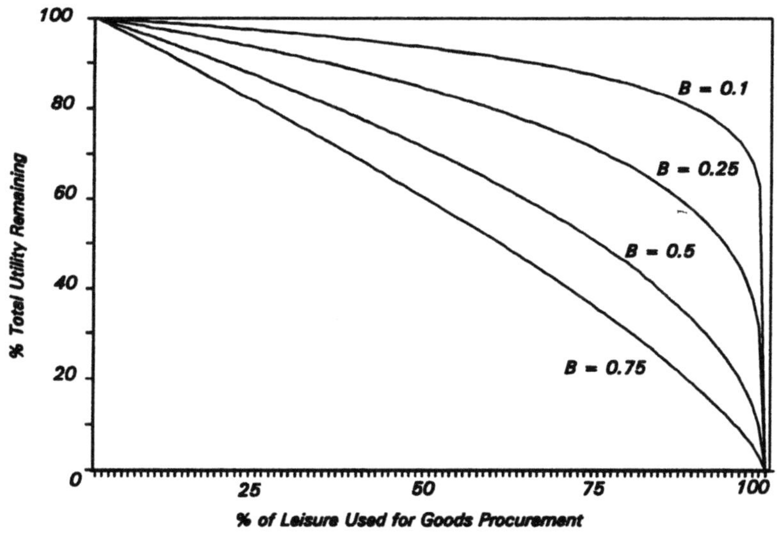

Appendix B: Rationing Through Formal Waiting Lists

Some goods were rationed through formal waiting lists rather than queues in eastern Europe, primarily housing and automobiles. The consumer paid part or all of the official state purchase price and then joined a waiting list which entitled him or her to receive the good after a waiting period, usually measurable in years. Like the queue rationing scheme, waiting lists generate deadweight utility loss. However, these losses are not in the form of lost leisure but of lost utility due to discounting.[42] Of course, the consumer could always purchase the good on a free-market and consume it immediately.

The time path of purchase and consumption under a waiting list regime can be depicted as

[42] For a formal model of rationing through waiting lists, see Lindsay and Feigenbaum 1984. Their model does not incorporate a free market. Excess demand is eliminated not through a higher free-market price, but through uncertainty over the timing of demand.

Table 4.8
Ratio Of Utility Gain To Absolute Value Of Utility Loss

	B = 0.1	B = 0.25	B = 0.50	B = 0.75
x_S/x_T = 0.50 and $\Delta x_T/x_T$ = 0.05	0.94	1.60	1.73	1.77
x_S/x_T = 0.50 and $\Delta x_T/x_T$ = 0.12	0.26	0.67	0.72	0.74

Note: Utility is assumed to be concave in leisure and $\gamma = 1$.

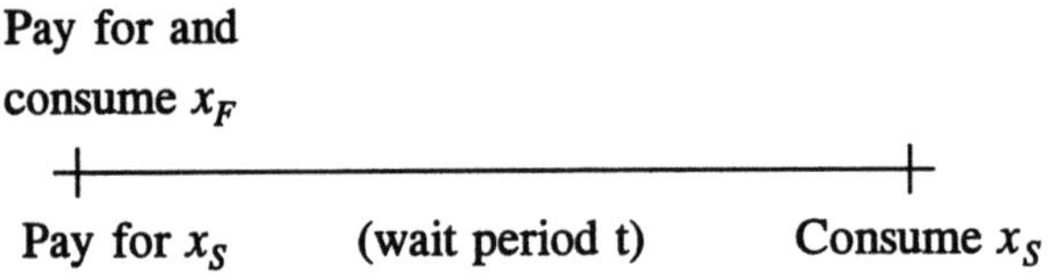

The price of the wait good x_S is normalized to 1, and the relative price of the free-market good which can be consumed immediately is p_F. The consumer maximizes total utility at the time the waiting list is entered,

$$U(x_F) + e^{-gt}U(x_S) , \tag{30}$$

subject to the monetary budget constraint

$$x_S + p_F x_F = I . \tag{31}$$

Note that utility from consuming x_S must be discounted at the time that the right to consume x_S is purchased.

Taking first-order conditions, combining, and rearranging gives

$$p_F = e^{gt} . \tag{32}$$

The relative free-market price is directly related to the degree of utility lost through delay in consuming x_S, a relation analogous to the one between p_F and e in the queue model. Substituting (32) into (30), total pre-liberalization utility is

$$U(x_F) + \frac{1}{p_F}U(x_S) . \tag{33}$$

It is important to note that if the waiting list is to effectively ration demand for x, there *must* be a free-market. Delay in consumption of x_S generates a demand for x_F at a higher price p_F. In each period, total real demand equals x_S+x_F, which equals supply x_T.[43] Monetary income I also equals total expenditures $x_S+p_Fx_F$. Excess demand is eliminated through a higher free-market price.

Price liberalization in this model amounts to elimination of the waiting list and sale of x_T at a freely-set price p_M. Delay in consumption is no longer necessary, and post-liberalization utility is $U(x_T)$. The ratio of post- to pre-liberalization utilities is

$$\frac{U(x_T)}{U(x_F) + \dfrac{1}{p_F}U(x_S)} . \tag{34}$$

If utility is linear in consumption, this can be written as

$$\frac{U(x_T)}{U\left(x_F + \dfrac{1}{p_F}x_S\right)} , \tag{35}$$

or

$$\frac{U(x_T)}{U\left(x_T + \left[\dfrac{1-p_F}{p_F}\right]x_S\right)} . \tag{36}$$

This, in turn, can be rewritten as

$$\frac{U\left(x_T + \left[\dfrac{1-p_F}{p_F}\right]x_S\right) - U'\left[\dfrac{1-p_F}{p_F}\right]x_S}{U\left(x_T + \left[\dfrac{1-p_F}{p_F}\right]x_S\right)} , \tag{37}$$

or

$$1 + \left(\frac{p_F-1}{p_F}\right)\left(U'\frac{x_T}{U}\right)\left(\frac{x_S}{x_T}\right) , \tag{38}$$

which is identical to (14). For small neighborhoods around the point of pre-liberalization consumption, the formulas for calculating deadweight utility losses

---

[43] Implicitly, an overlapping-generations model is assumed in which there is an old consumer and young consumer each period, the young consumer always has the same income level I, and total supply is always x_T.

from queuing and waiting lists are identical.

Appendix C: Extending the Basic Model

The basic model can be modified in order to consider various other factors that might affect welfare over the transition. Three specific cases will be considered in this appendix.

Free-Market Transactions Costs

An important implicit assumption of the basic model is that there are no procurement costs in the free-market. This is unrealistic, as free-market activity was often illegal and inefficient. Free-market transaction costs can be incorporated in the model by rewriting the utility function as

$$\psi = U(x_S+x_F,\ T-e_S x_S-e_F x_F)\ , \tag{39}$$

where e_F is the time cost of procuring a unit of the free-market good. Of course, it must be the case that $e_F < e_S$ if the model is to have an interior solution.

Taking first-order conditions and carrying out manipulations similar to those in the main text, it is easily shown that the difference between the actual percentage increase in utility and the measured increase in utility,

$$\frac{\psi_{POST}-\psi_{PRE}}{\psi_{PRE}} - \left(\frac{p_F-1}{p_F}\right)\left(U_1\frac{x_T}{U}\right)\left(\frac{x_S}{x_T}\right), \tag{40}$$

equals the following expression:

$$\left(\frac{U_2}{U}\right)\left(e_F x_F+\frac{e_F x_S}{p_F}\right). \tag{41}$$

(41) is always positive, and welfare gains from price liberalization are underestimated if there are transaction costs in the pre-reform free-market.[44]

Post-Liberalization Transaction Costs

Another implicit assumption is that there are no transaction costs in procuring goods

[44] The reader might note that this is evidently a system of four equations in five unknowns, so that the model is underidentified. However, this is true only if e_F is an endogenously-determined variable, which is not the case. e_F is determined by arbitrary rules and regulations inhibiting trade and is properly treated as an exogenous variable.

after prices are liberalized.[45] This possibility can be dealt with by rewriting the post-liberalization to pre-liberalization utility ratio as

$$\frac{\psi_{POST}}{\psi_{PRE}} = \frac{U(x_T,\ T - e_M x_T)}{U(x_T,\ T - e x_S)}\ , \tag{42}$$

where e_M is the post-liberalization per-unit procurement transaction cost. Expanding the numerator as in the main text and using results from pre-liberalization utility maximization, it is easy to show that the difference between the actual percentage increase in utility and the measured increase in utility is

$$\frac{\psi_{POST} - \psi_{PRE}}{\psi_{PRE}} - \left(\frac{p_F - 1}{p_F}\right)\left(U_1 \frac{x_T}{U}\right)\left(\frac{x_S}{x_T}\right) = -\frac{U_2\, e_M\, x_T}{U}\ . \tag{43}$$

Because this term is negative, the utility gain from price liberalization is overestimated.

Values of the ratio e/e_M such that net welfare gain is zero for the empirical scenarios for Poland can be derived. If the true value of the ratio is higher, then net welfare gain is positive (and if lower, then negative). See Table 4.9.

The nature of post-liberalization transaction costs requires careful consideration. Immediately after prices are liberalized, significant transaction costs may persist due to a high degree of market fragmentation and price dispersion that results in search for low prices. However, this dispersion should disappear fairly quickly if restrictions on market entry and competition are eliminated. Aside from factors such as search driven by price dispersion, it is not clear that shopping should be considered as a true utility cost to the consumer. In a typical western economy, sellers spend considerable resources in providing services to shoppers in order to maintain market share. Shopping in this case takes on aspects of leisure activity.

Labor Supply

The model can be extended to incorporate a labor-supply decision and thus endogenize the level of total output x_T.[46] Assume that labor supply is L, and output depends only on labor supply and a vector of other variables such as capital

---

[45] I am indebted to Peter Murrell for pointing out the possibility of significant post-liberalization transaction costs.

[46] I am indebted to Michael Marrese for emphasizing the importance of labor supply change over the course of reform.

Table 4.9
Zero Net-Welfare Gain: Implied Values of e/e_M

	e/e_M, for net welfare change = 0	
x_S/x_T	5%	12%
0.50	4.5	—
0.75	2.1	11.5

stock and imported intermediate inputs: $x_T = x_T(L,\beta)$, $\delta x_T/\delta L > 0$, $\delta x_T/\delta\beta_i > 0$, $\delta^2 x_T/\delta L^2 < 0$, $\delta^2 x_T/\delta\beta_i^2 < 0$. Also assume that labor L and procurement costs ex_S are perfect substitutes in leisure, and that the consumer-worker earns an "untied" income I and a "tied" income wL, where the wage rate w is determined exogenously.[47]

The representative agent's problem is now

$$\max \psi = U(x_S+x_F, T-ex_S-L)$$
$$\text{w.r.t. } \{x_S, x_F, L\} \tag{44}$$
$$\text{s.t. } x_S + p_F x_F = I + wL .$$

First-order conditions from this maximization together with the supplier's first-order condition give the equations

$$U_1 - U_2 e = \lambda , \tag{45}$$

$$U_1 = \lambda p_F , \tag{46}$$

$$U_2 = \lambda w , \tag{47}$$

$$x_S + p_F x_F = I + wL , \tag{48}$$

$$x_F = g(p_F) . \tag{49}$$

These five equations determine the five endogenous variables x_F, p_F, e, λ, and L.

The important question is whether labor supply changes over the course of liberalization. The ratio of post- to pre-price liberalization utilities is

---

[47] Endogenizing the wage rate requires explicit description of the decision calculus of the agent who produces x_T. If the agent is a state-owned firm, profit maximization would not be appropriate, and the wage rate is properly treated as being determined exogenously by planners. However, a non-state production sector which does maximize profits could also be incorporated, and in this case the wage rate would be endogenous. As this paper's focus is not on comparative statics given a particular institutional regime, these complications are not relevant.

$$\frac{\psi_{POST}}{\psi_{PRE}} = \frac{U(x_T(L_M, \beta_M), T-L_M)}{U(x_T(L, \beta), T-ex_S-L)}, \tag{50}$$

where the subscript M corresponds to the post-liberalization regime.

Total utility changes over the course of liberalization and reform due to the elimination of procurement costs, changes in labor supply L, and changes in the input vector $\boldsymbol{\beta}$. An increase in L will reduce utility due to falling leisure but increase utility due to rising output x_T. x_T will also change (most likely decrease) due to changes in variables not under the consumer-worker's direct control, which is captured by changes in the vector $\boldsymbol{\beta}$. If the representative agent chooses an optimal level of labor supply before reform, then any change in labor supply over the course of liberalization should reflect the fact that this change increases the agent's welfare level, because otherwise it would not be made.

Distributional issues concerning change in labor supply are probably more important than effects on representative-agent utility levels. For example, employers can now use the threat of unemployment as a device to extract a higher labor supply without increasing the real wage, thus increasing profits. In the representative-agent model, the agent enjoys the increase in real income represented by the increase in profits, and the effect on net welfare is ambiguous (see above). In a multi-agent model, however, some agents clearly gain and some lose.

The emergence of involuntary unemployment is also a distributional issue. In the representative-agent model, involuntary unemployment corresponds to a undesired contraction in the supply of labor and hence consumption x_T. This should be captured in the empirical estimates because the fall in consumption x_T is taken into account. Employment is only a means to obtain consumption. In a multi-agent model which takes into account distributional effects, some agents will enjoy a rise in labor supply and consumption, and others a fall.

Appendix D: The Polish Free-Market/State Price Ratio

A variety of data are available on the state and free-market prices of various Polish consumer goods for the period 1981–1987:[48]

(a) The household budget survey, which monitors some 28,000 household budgets annually, recorded data on purchases in state and free markets

[48] See "Statistical Sources" for references to the statistical publications containing all price data used in this paper.

separately. From this data, the statistical authorities calculated and reported state and free market prices for a wide variety of goods. Almost all food and beverage items were covered, as were most categories of clothing and many consumer durables. However, most services were not covered.

(b) Farmers' market prices for a variety of foodstuffs were collected and reported.

(c) Black market prices were reported quarterly since 1981 for a variety of foodstuffs and consumer durables. The basket of goods covered grew over time (consumer durables were added in the mid-1980s). The methodological notes of the volume in which these prices were published give no details of how these prices were obtained.

(d) Official state list prices and many state transaction prices are available. List prices were determined by state agencies legally charged with setting prices. Transaction prices were calculated by dividing the value of retail sales by quantities sold; the value of retail sales was calculated using actual transaction prices as opposed to list prices.

Most of the price ratios used in this study are calculated from the household budget data. To check the accuracy of these ratios, they can be compared to ratios calculated from farmers' market, black market, and official state price data: see Table 4.10. The correlation of household budget and farmers' market price ratios is quite good. The correlation of household budget and black market price ratios is good in the case of meats, sugar, coffee, and tea. However, in the case of alcoholic beverages and consumer durables, the correlation is poor. The household budget ratios for consumer durables are clearly inaccurate, as they are all less than 1. This is due to the fact that few families purchased a given consumer durable in any given year, even fewer purchased it on the free market, and, most importantly, many (probably most) of the durables sold on the free market were used. The black market price ratios for consumer durables are therefore used as a substitute in the calculation of the aggregate price ratio. All other ratios are derived from household budget survey data.

Individual price ratios were aggregated using weights derived from household budget survey data on consumer expenditures. In some cases, the household budget survey data was not disaggregated enough, and more detailed information on the structure of retail trade sales was used to obtain weights. Household budget weights are from 1987 data, and retail trade weights are from 1985 data. One possibility that could not be corrected for is that goods of higher

Table 4.10
Price Ratio Comparisons

Good	Household-budget ratio	Farmers'-market ratio	Black-market Ratio	State-price type[1]
Potatoes	0.95	1.11	—	CTP
Cabbage	1.12	1.27	—	CTP
Cheese	1.36	1.49	—	CTP
Sour cream	1.83	2.01	—	LP
Eggs	0.97	1.08	—	CTP
Honey	1.09	1.12	—	CTP
Beef	1.39	—	1.31	LP
Veal	1.12	—	1.58	LP
Pork[2]	0.89	—	1.07	LP
Sugar	2.36	—	2.60	LP
Chocolate	1.87	—	4.18	CTP
Cocoa	1.41	—	5.82	LP
Coffee	1.48	—	1.54	CTP
Tea[3]	1.42	—	1.60	CTP
Clear vodka	1.14	—	1.35	LP
Flavored vodka	1.16	—	1.42	LP
Wine	1.35	—	1.51	LP
Beer	1.19	—	1.88	LP
Auto[4]	0.91	—	2.08	LP
Washing machine	0.80	—	1.19	CTP
Black-and-white TV	0.52	—	1.36	CTP
Sewing machine	0.65	—	1.27	CTP

[1] LP = State list price; CTP = Calculated transactions price. [2] For 1983–1984. [3] For 1985–1986.
[4] The black-market and state prices are for the Polski Fiat 126P model.
Sources: See text.

quality were sold on free markets. This problem, if important, would lead to an overstatement of the true value of the price ratio. It is not known to what extent goods sold in state and free markets differed according to quality parameters, nor is it known to what extent those calculating the state and free-market prices from the budget survey data attempted to control for quality differences.

The available evidence does not suggest that quality differences were very important. The price ratio for new automobiles is the ratio of prices for a specific auto model, the Polski Fiat 126P, and there should be no quality difference in this case. In 1987, the ratio was 2.08 (see Table 4.10), a value much higher than those for most other individual items in the consumer basket. Table 4.10 also shows that price ratios calculated from household budget data were very high for sour cream and sugar, goods which did not vary much in quality.

No price ratios are available for most services and some durables and clothing.[49] In these cases, the price ratio is assumed to be 1. It is clearly counterfactual to assume that these ratios equalled 1. For example, the calculated ratio for the services subcategory *excluding* goods for which data was not available is 1.91. This is much higher than the calculated aggregate ratio, 1.22 (see Table 4.1). Because the lower limit on a price ratio is 1, and the price ratios for most goods for which data was not available undoubtedly exceeded 1, the assumption made in this paper is very conservative.

Given that the calculated magnitude of the ratio in 1987, 1.22, is very low, that the correction for state-free market quality differences probably would not make much of a difference, and that the assumption that ratios for goods for which data is not available clearly has a major impact in the other direction, the ratio empirically estimated in this paper should be treated as a *lower bound* to the true value. Correction for quality differences and missing goods would most likely increase the estimated value of the ratio and thus the magnitude of welfare gain due to procurement cost elimination.

Statistical Sources

(a) All price data are obtained from the following publications:
1980–82: Glowny Urzad Statystyczny. Materialy Statystyczne. *Zmiany Cen Detalicznych 1980–1983.*
1983–84: Glowny Urzad Statystyczny. Materialy Statystyczne. *Ceny Detaliczne 1971–1985.*
1985–87: Glowny Urzad Statystyczny. Materialy Statystyczne. *Ceny Detaliczne 1985–1987.*
(b) Household budget data are obtained from:
Glowny Urzad Statystyczny. Materialy Statystyczne. *Budzety Gospodarstw Domowych,* various years.

References

Alexeev, M. 1991. Expenditures on Privately Rented Housing and Imputed Rents in the USSR. Berkeley-Duke Occasional Papers on the Second Economy in the USSR, no 31.

Alexeev, M. 1988. The Underground Market for Gasoline in the USSR. *Comparative*

[49] Price ratios are available for 59% of all consumer goods and services. 35% should be covered but are not due to lack of data. For the remaining 6%, free markets probably did not exist.

Economic Studies 30: 47–68.

Aslund, A. 1985. *Private Enterprise in Eastern Europe*. New York: St. Martin's Press.

Berg, A., and J. D. Sachs 1992. Structural Adjustment and International Trade in Eastern Europe: The Case of Poland. Photocopy.

Boycko, M. 1991. When Higher Incomes Reduce Welfare: Queues, Labor Supply, and Black Markets in Soviet-Type Economies. Photocopy.

Deacon, R., and J. Sonstelie. 1985. Rationing by Waiting and the Value of Time: Results from a Natural Experiment. *Journal of Political Economy* 93: 627–47.

Deacon, R., and J. Sonstelie. 1989a. The Welfare Costs of Rationing by Waiting. *Economic Inquiry* 27: 179–96

Deacon, R., and J. Sonstelie. 1989b. Price Controls and Rent-Seeking Behavior in Developing Countries. *World Development* 17: 1945–54.

French, H., and W. Lee. 1987. The Welfare Cost of Rationing-by-Queuing Across Markets: Theory and Estimates from the U.S. Gasoline Crisis. *Quarterly Journal of Economics* 102: 97–108.

Grossman, G. 1989. Informal Personal Incomes and Outlays of the Soviet Urban Population. In A. Portes, M. Castells, and L. Benton, eds. 1989. *The Informal Economy: Studies in Advanced and Less Developed Countries*. Baltimore: Johns Hopkins University Press.

Kaminski, B. 1991. *The Collapse of State Socialism: The Case of Poland*. Princeton, N.J.: Princeton University Press.

Lindsay, C., and B. Feigenbaum. 1984. Rationing by Waiting Lists. *American Economic Review* 74: 404–17

Lipton, D., and J. Sachs 1990. Creating a Market Economy in Eastern Europe: The Case of Poland. *Brookings Papers on Economic Activity* 1.

Neuhauser, K., and C. Gaddy 1988. Estimating the Size of the Private Service Sector in the USSR. Berkeley-Duke Occasional Papers on the Second Economy in the USSR, no. 15.

Osband, K. 1991. Economic Crisis in a Shortage Economy. IMF Working Paper.

Polterovich, V., Rationing, Queues, and Black Markets. Photocopy.

Roberts, B. W. 1993. Inferring Real Income Change from Change in the Food Budget Share: The Case of Poland, 1990. Photocopy.

Rutgaizer, V. 1992. The Shadow Economy in the USSR. Berkeley-Duke Occasional Papers on the Second Economy in the USSR, no. 34.

Sah, R. 1987. Queues, Rations, and Markets: Comparisons of Outcomes For the Poor and the Rich. *American Economic Review* 77: 69–77.

Shleifer, A., and R. Vishny 1992. Pervasive Shortages Under Socialism. *Rand Journal of Economics* 23: 237–46.

Stahl, D., and M. Alexeev, The Influence of Black Markets on a Queue-Rationed Economy. *Journal of Economic Theory* 35: 234–50.

Wedel, J. 1986. *The Private Poland.* New York: Facts on File.

Wedel, J. 1992. *The Unplanned Society: Poland During and After Communism*. New York: Columbia University Press.

Weitzman, M. 1991. Price Distortion and Shortage Deformation, or What Happened to the Soap? *American Economic Review* 81: 401–14.

World Bank. 1987. *Poland: Reform, Adjustment, and Growth*. World Bank: Washington, D.C.

5 The Sale of Shares to Foreign Companies

Francesca Cornelli

5.1 Introduction

Eastern Europe is now experiencing a very difficult transformation which involves all institutional levels. The creation of a viable private sector seems to be the most important and most complex aspect of such transformation. The debate over the obstacles and problems created by such a task has focused on many aspects, such as the creation of a credit market and of a stock market, the managerial structure and the effects of concentration. The essence of the problem remains, however, how to privatize existing firms. For larger industrial firms the answer is even more difficult, since there is a large number of potential buyers of their shares: current workers in the firms, mutual funds, holding companies, banks, pension funds, citizens, government or foreigners. Foreign companies are very appealing potential buyers, since through ownership they could have an incentive to transfer much-needed technological and managerial skills.

East European (EE hereafter) governments would like to attract the technological and financial capital of Western countries, but they are concerned that foreign companies could gain control over their entire economies. EE populations fear that foreign companies could take advantage of their needy situation and appropriate most of their productive assets. To convince them to accept the sale of shares abroad, EE governments have to show that such sales are worthy to be undertaken. However, this is not an easy task. For example, many experts are afraid that the revenues from such sales could end up being much lower than expected. Political instability may induce foreign companies to impose a high discount on the price for these shares. Given the concerns about the political and

---

I wish to thank Abijit Banerjee for initially suggesting the idea to me and Leonardo Felli and Federica Zagari for useful comments. Errors remain my own responsibility.

economic consequences, an unsuccessful sale could result in a political failure. In particular, as Fischer (1991) mentions, "large scale foreign purchases at low prices could discredit the entire privatization process." On the other hand, the reconstruction of the EE economies—which lack all the infrastructural facilities necessary for domestic firms to develop and compete with foreign production—requires a great amount of capital, certainly much more than the capital presently available internally. Borrowing all the money necessary for the investments would be too great a burden for these countries. As Vishny (1991) notices, "if current consumption standards are to be maintained and essential infrastructure is built... it may make more sense to sell off certain assets to foreigners from the beginning, so that they can start investing immediately."

Others have argued that, in order to be effective, the entry of foreign capital and expertise into eastern Europe cannot take place through a provision of advisory and consulting services. However, as Frydman and Rapaczynski (1990, 13) underline, "the only way in which Western financial institutions can play a truly creative role in the region is if their entry is based on sound business principles, so that they stand to gain or lose by their activities." Some have suggested that foreign ownership could be allowed only in a second phase of the transformation, once the privatization process is well established. However, two difficulties arise. First of all, money is acutely needed now, with the process already started and some infrastructure established. Second, if shares will only be sold to foreigners once decentralization has taken place, it will be impossible for the government to control such a sale in order to use the revenues in the most efficient way (from the point of view of social welfare).

This paper focuses on the issue of the sale of domestic firms' shares to foreign companies. The purpose is to show that, instead of borrowing money, EE governments could do better trying to sell, in the best possible way, some of the shares. Two main ideas are present. The first is that EE governments could ask foreign buyers to pay not in cash, but directly with investments. In fact, they need money to undertake huge investments, especially in infrastructural facilities. It could be argued that the government could sell the shares and then, with the revenues from the privatization process, hire all the experts and buy all the technology necessary for the reconstruction. However, such investments may be less expensive for foreign companies which already have the necessary technology and know-how. Moreover, moral hazard and incentive problems could arise due to the inability of local authorities to judge whether foreign experts are choosing the most profitable solution. Overall, it is much less costly if the foreign companies use their own experts. An additional reason why the government may prefer to be paid in investments is the fact that capital brought in from abroad which does not come in the form of a productive investment will be fed into state treasury:

> Not only is this likely not to be the best use of the money, but also, given the very high external debt of most East European states, large inflows of the proceeds from privatization might result in an intensified pressure for an increase in debt repayment. (Frydman and Rapaczynski 1990, 27)

I focus on investments in infrastructural facilities, and not investments directly useful to the firm whose shares are sold. These latter will increase the future profits of the foreign company: therefore, they may be undertaken spontaneously. But EE countries also need huge investments in infrastructural facilities. For example, foreign companies may be willing to undertake investments in specific human capital, like training employees; but EE countries also have an urgent need for investments in general human capital, which foreign companies will have no incentive to make unless obliged. Another example would be the construction of a network of roads, railways and telecommunications essential for the future development of the economy.

The second idea presented here concerns the fact that political instability may induce foreign companies to impose a high discount on the price for shares, so that the sale of shares to foreign companies could end up a political failure. EE governments usually have a constraint (of a political nature) not to undersell their assets. Given the ongoing debate about whether shares should be sold to foreign companies, and the fact that some groups—for example, workers in Poland—are exerting a strong political pressure to receive the majority of the shares, the government may be able to take a decision to sell some shares abroad only by arguing that this will be very beneficial. I argue that it is not optimal for the government to commit *ex ante* to sell a given number of shares. In fact, the government will be better off if it declares that it will not sell to foreign companies at the beginning of the privatization process unless the sale is "satisfactory." Given the political pressure, such a declaration is likely to be credible.

In this way the government can exploit its weakness to its own advantage. Some foreign companies may desire more than others that an industry is privatized and that they have shares in it. The reason a foreign company may be interested in buying shares may be speculation or the interest to be present in EE markets in view of future developments. Different companies may have different advantages from being in such markets, due, for example, to their proximity, to whether they sell already in nearby markets, or to the good they produce. In particular, many plans in EE countries involve a period of protection for domestic firms from foreign competition. Thus, if a company is present from the beginning, owning shares in a domestic firm, it could obtain a considerable advantage over other foreign companies which will be able to enter the market only years later. Such companies may then be willing to pay a higher price, or undertake a bigger investment, in order to be sure to obtain some shares.[1] Therefore, if the government makes it clear that unless the offer of a foreign company is very appealing it will not sell at all (at least not in the beginning), it could induce the foreign company to pay a higher amount. By trying to sell some shares to foreign companies from the start, the government obtains two advantages: it can use the threat not to go through with the sales in order to obtain a higher payment; and it can directly obtain investments in infrastructural facilities, which are the best "method of payment" from the point of view of the social welfare.

The optimal mechanism described below shows how different firms may be willing to pay different prices in order to obtain the same number of shares. This may be accomplished through a negotiation that will involve the sale of a domestic firm's shares to a foreign company, so that, in the end, every foreign company will have a specific deal with the EE government.

5.2 The Model

Suppose there are N foreign companies, denoted $i = 1,\dots, N$, which want to buy shares of an EE firm. Let q_i be the number of shares bought by company i. Since, in general, the government does not want to sell shares abroad, I impose the constraint that $\Sigma_i q_i \leq Q$, where $Q < \bar{Q}$ and $\bar{Q}$ is the total number of shares: the government will keep some shares or it will distribute them internally. Moreover, the government may wish to limit the maximum amount of shares a company may buy, so I impose also the constraint that $q_i \leq q_0$, for any i, where $q_0 \leq Q$. The government may wish to set such limit, for example, to reduce the concentration in one industry. Notice that if $q_0 = Q$ we obtain the case in which all the shares are

---

[1] I ignore two issues here. The first is whether the number of shares to be sold gives the foreign companies the control of the firm. The second is the fact that, depending on the nature of the interest in the domestic firm, some foreign companies may look more appealing than others to the government. I instead assume here that the government is only interested in the investments offered by companies as payment. Cornelli and Li 1993 examines both issues.

sold to only one company.

The government may be reluctant to sell shares to foreign companies because it may be afraid to give away the little wealth of the country. Such wealth is not represented by the value of the capital of the privatized firm (which is not very high), but rather by the potential profits such a firm may have in the future. In other words, the government is afraid to expropriate the population of their rights over future flows of profits. Let us call

$$\theta_G \bar{Q} = E_G \left[\sum_{t=1}^{\infty} \delta^t \pi_t \right]$$

the present discounted value of the total expected profits. The government wants, in exchange for the shares, a commitment to undertake an investment. Let us call I_i the investment that company i commits to, expressed in monetary terms. The government is *not* indifferent between inducing foreign companies to undertake such investments directly and obtaining the same amount in cash. In principle, the government could sell the shares for cash and spend the money received making the same investments. However, as mentioned in the introduction, foreign companies have trained experts and the necessary know-how, so it is likely that the same amount of money will be more productive if the investment is undertaken directly by a foreign company.

Foreign companies want to buy shares because of the flow of future profits they expect, which is called here θ_i. The parameters θ_i do not represent different expectations over future profits due, for example, to different information. I am concerned, rather, with the fact that different companies have different characteristics—such as proximity, past history, nature of the good produced, and so on—which actually yield (independent of the resolution of the uncertainty) different profits to different firms. The model is not meant to study how firms make speculations on the basis of their different expectations, but, instead, how a government can extract part of the surplus that foreign companies have due to their specificities. One way of explaining this may be to assume that everybody knows θ_G; that is, that everybody has the same expectations about the profits the government obtains if it does not privatize, and the private information concerns the additional benefits each firm expects to obtain as a result of its specificities. Many foreign companies want to buy shares in eastern Europe mainly to be in that market prior to their competitors, to tie alliances, to better-know the market or to discover new business opportunities. All this seems very much in line with the formalization given here.

It could be argued that each θ_i should be made dependent on the investments $I_1,\ldots, I_N$ undertaken by the foreign companies. However, I assume the I_i are investments in infrastructural facilities.[2] For example, investments in general education or in the transportation system should not affect (or they could, but only in a minor way) the interest of the foreign company in having shares in the firm.

In the following pages I consider different issues linked with this situation. First, I focus on the issue of what procedure the government should adopt in selling shares if it prefers to be paid through investments instead of money. Second, I consider explicitly the constraint that a government cannot undersell such shares and the changes this implies for the optimal selling procedure.

Selling Through Investments

In this section I assume that the decision whether to sell shares abroad or not has already been taken, and the government has decided to sell Q shares to foreign companies. I look for the optimal selling procedure when the government wants to be paid in investments. The approach is the standard one of the literature on optimal auctions (Maskin and Riley 1990). The only additional problem is the different method of payment. In the next section I will make the choice of Q endogenous.

As already mentioned, EE governments may prefer to be paid through investments. Given the set of investments the government would like to obtain, this could constrain the offers the buyers can make. In fact, the willingness to pay of a customer could not correspond exactly to the amount necessary to undertake any of the possible investments. Alternatively, two companies could be willing to pay the same amount, but there may be only one investment corresponding to that price. Of course, one could argue that the government can always find a continuum of investments, but in such a case it is likely that most of them are not very urgent, while here I consider a finite set of investments which all have equal priority in the government's agenda.

I assume that no foreign company has an advantage over the others in undertaking the investments; that is, the expenses necessary to make an investment are the same for all companies. Moreover, if I is how much a foreign company has

[2] Alternatively, one could argue that investments with a significant impact on future productivity should affect the profits that each foreign company expects to obtain in the same way. Thus, the common part is dependent on the investment, but not the part specific to the company.

to spend to make an investment, the value to the government of such an investment (that is, the money it should spend if it were to make the investments itself) will be αI, where α is the same for all the investments. In other words, the government selects some investments, which are all necessary and have the same priority. They have to be undertaken in the first stage of the privatization process, either by borrowing money or by inducing foreign companies to undertake them.[3]

Each θ_i is private information of the foreign company i. However, both the government and the foreign companies know that each type θ_i is drawn independently from the same distribution function $F(\cdot)$ over the interval $[0, \bar{\theta}]$, with density $f(\cdot)$. Let $\Theta_i = \{\theta \mid \theta = (\theta_j)_{j \in N}\}$, and $\Theta_{-i} = \{\theta_{-i} \mid \theta_{-i} = (\theta_j)_{j \in N, j \neq i}\}$. It is possible to define

$$G(\theta) \equiv \Pi_{j \in N} F(\theta_j) = [F(\theta_j)]^N ,$$

$$G_{-i}(\theta_{-i}) \equiv \Pi_{j \in N, j \neq i} F(\theta_j) = [F(\theta_j)]^{N-1} ,$$

with corresponding densities $g(\theta)$ and $g_{-i}(\theta_{-i})$.

By the Revelation Principle, it is possible to restrict attention to the direct revelation mechanism where the companies simultaneously announce their valuation to the government and the government determines how many shares each company gets and how much each company has to pay (or, more precisely, which investment it has to undertake) as some function of the announced valuations $(\tilde{\theta}_1, \tilde{\theta}_2, \ldots, \tilde{\theta}_N)$.

Thus, a direct revelation mechanism is described by a pair of outcome functions (q, I) such that, if $\tilde{\theta}$ is the vector of announced valuations, then $q_i(\tilde{\theta})$ is the number of shares that company i obtains and $I_i(\tilde{\theta})$ is the investment that the company i has to make. I look for a Bayesian equilibrium of this mechanism in which companies truthfully reveal their own valuations and I rule out the possibility of collusion among them. Moreover, I assume that both the government and the companies are risk neutral.

The objective of a foreign company is to maximize expected profits obtained from the purchase of shares. A company with valuation θ_i that declares the

[3] The model could be extended to the case in which the government has preferences over the investments by assuming that an investment of type j, which costs I_j to a foreign company, has value $\alpha_j I_j$ to the government.

valuation $\tilde{\theta}_i$ has expected profits:[4]

$$\Pi_i(q,I,\theta_i,\tilde{\theta}_i) = \int_{\Theta_{-i}} [\theta_i \, q_i(\tilde{\theta}_i,\theta_{-i}) - I_i(\tilde{\theta}_i,\theta_{-i})] \, g_{-i}(\theta_{-i}) \, d\theta_{-i} \; . \tag{1}$$

Rescaling everything by α, the objective function of the EE government is

$$\int_{\Theta} \{ \, \Sigma_i I_i(\theta) - \beta \, \theta_G \, [\Sigma_i q_i(\theta)] \, \} \, g(\theta) \, d\theta \; . \tag{2}$$

The expected gain is given by the sum of the values of the investments, minus the expected loss expressed in terms of future profits, where β is a weight representing the preferences of the government between investments and future profits.

The government problem is to maximize (2) subject to the following constraints.

The individual rationality constraint:

$$\Pi_i(q,I,\theta_i,\tilde{\theta}_i) \geq 0 \; ; \tag{3}$$

The incentive compatibility constraint:

$$\Pi_i(q,I,\theta_i,\theta_i) \geq \Pi_i(q,I,\theta_i,\tilde{\theta}_i) \; ; \tag{4}$$

and the additional quantity constraints:

$$\Sigma_i \; q_i(\theta) \leq Q \; ; \tag{5}$$

$$q_i(\theta) \leq q_0 \; . \tag{6}$$

As already explained, the investments have to be chosen among a given set of alternatives the government suggests. This assumption is meant to capture the fact that there are some investments which have priority over all the others, and the government will not accept offers to make different investments. Thus,

$$I_i \in \{I_1,\ldots,I_M\} \; . \tag{7}$$

Following Myerson (1981), the problem can be transformed into the following:

[4] I make here the assumption that the valuation company i has for one share does not change with the number of shares bought. This seems to me to be more adequate than a negatively sloped demand function.

$$\max_q \int_\Theta \sum_i \left[\theta_i - \beta\theta_G - \frac{1-F(\theta_i)}{f(\theta_i)} \right] q_i(\theta)\, dG(\theta) \,, \tag{8}$$

subject to constraints (5) and (6) and

$$\int_{\Theta_{-i}} \frac{\partial q_i(\theta)}{\partial \theta_i} g_{-i}(\theta_{-i})\, d\theta_{-i} \geq 0 \,, \quad \text{for all } i \in N,\ \theta_i \in [0,\bar{\theta}] \,. \tag{9}$$

The expected payment is given by

$$\int_{\Theta_{-i}} I_i(\theta)\, dG(\theta) = \int_{\Theta_{-i}} \left[\theta_i q_i(\theta) - \int_0^{\theta_i} q_i(x,\theta_{-i})\, dx \right] dG_{-i}(\theta_{-i}) \,, \tag{10}$$

where the I_i are given by constraint (7). Notice that although the set of possible investments is discrete, the expected payment is not. This implies that it is possible to overcome the problem of the constrained choice of investments. In fact, it is enough to ask the potential buyers not to offer to pay for one investment but, rather, to quote the different probabilities at which they are willing to undertake each of the investments. The government can compute the expected amount, which is a continuous variable.

Therefore, once we have found the optimal mechanism for the quantities q_i, it is easy to find a mechanism for the investments which satisfies constraint (10). The only limitation is that the expected payment cannot exceed the maximum investment. However, this is not a real problem since the government will always have one investment which is very expensive and very desirable. Hence, it will always be optimal for the government to include this in the set of possible investments and ask the buyers to undertake it with a positive probability. The conclusion is that the government does not lose anything by asking the companies to pay in investments, but makes a gain due to the higher productivity of the foreign companies. To find the optimal selling procedure, let us first impose the following restriction:

Assumption 1 *Let*

$$V(\theta_i) \equiv \theta_i - \frac{1-F(\theta_i)}{f(\theta_i)} \tag{11}$$

be a monotone strictly increasing function of θ_i, *for all* $i \in N$.[5]

We can now characterize the optimal procedure.

Proposition 1 *Define*

$$\theta^* \equiv \max \{\theta_i \,|\, V(\theta_i) = \beta\theta_G\} \tag{12}$$

Then, under Assumption 1, if the government decides to privatize, it will never serve a buyer i with a declared valuation $\tilde{\theta}_i < \theta^*$. *Among the buyers with a declared valuation* $\tilde{\theta}_i \geq \theta^*$, *the government will give* q_0 *shares to the company which declared the highest valuation. Then it will give* min $\{q_0, Q - q_0\}$ *to the company with the second highest valuation, and so on until the shares sold add up to* Q.

Proof The government has to decide whether to sell shares to company *i*, that is, whether to set $p_i = 1$ or 0. The government will find it optimal to set $p_i = 1$ only if its objective function will consequently increase, that is if $V(\theta_i) \geq \beta\theta_G$. Therefore, the government will always choose to serve a buyer if he declares a valuation greater or equal to θ^*. Moreover, the government has a maximum number of shares it can sell, so it is clear from the objective function that it will give priority to the company with the highest $V(\theta_i)$—that is, given Assumption 1, to the company which declares the highest valuation θ_i. Given Assumption 1, the optimal $p_i(\theta_i, \theta_{-i})$ is a non-decreasing function of θ_i, hence it satisfies constraint (9). ■

The presence of asymmetric information implies that the mechanism is *ex post* inefficient, since some buyers, with a valuation higher than the marginal cost $\beta\theta_G$, do not get the good. The government gives all the possible shares to the company offering the most before beginning to sell shares to the second highest bidder. Without constraint (6) (or if $q_0 = Q$) the government would sell all the shares to only one firm. Therefore, in this respect the mechanism is the same mechanism as would be optimal if firms made only cash bids. However, here the bids must needs take a different form.

First, it is important to notice that a traditional auction would not be optimal here. Consider, for example, a first price auction, where everybody makes a bid and the company making the highest bid obtains the good (in this context, it is the

[5] The analysis can be generalized to the case in which Assumption 1 does not hold (Myerson 1981; Maskin and Riley 1990).

one to get the first q_0 shares) and pays its offer. That cannot be optimal if companies are constrained to make bids in terms of investments. In fact, in such a case they cannot bid any amount, but only the one corresponding to one of the available investments (otherwise it cannot pay exactly its bid). This implies that such an auction will not implement the optimal mechanism.

A simple indirect mechanism which implements the above optimal direct mechanism is the following: Each company announces a probability distribution $\{p_1, \ldots, p_M\}$ over the set of investments. The government computes the average investment and then ranks the offers according to the average payment. It then gives q_0 to the highest offer, $\min\{q_0, Q - q_0\}$ to the second highest, and so on, until there are no more units left or no more offers. One interpretation of the mechanism is that each company gives the government a list of preferences and, on that basis, the government decides how many shares each company obtains and which investment it has to undertake. Priority is given to the companies that give higher preference to the more expensive investments.

In this way the government succeeds in making all the offers compatible and at the same time in extracting the highest possible surplus from the foreign companies. The *ex ante* expected revenues of the government would be the same if companies paid in cash. In fact, if there is not an investment which costs exactly the amount a company is willing to pay, then such a company will be asked to undertake with some probability a more expensive investment and with some probability a less expensive investment. Since both government and foreign companies are risk neutral such arrangement is optimal. Moreover, the value to the government of the investments obtained is higher than the amount paid by the companies. Therefore, by obliging foreign companies to offer investments instead of cash a Pareto improvement can be reached.

The Choice of the Quantity

In the previous section, I assumed the government had decided previously not to sell more than Q shares in total. There are many reasons why the government may not want to sell too many shares to foreign companies. Although Western participation in the construction of the infrastructure of the market economy in eastern Europe is seen as a necessary step, the entry of foreign capital also gives rise to special political problems and raises additional questions as to whether the eastern European economy will come to be dominated by foreign capital and whether its economic and political interests will be jeopardized in the privatization process. Therefore, political pressure may be exerted on EE governments not to sell too many shares abroad.[6]

Another important reason is that if the government sells too many shares to foreign companies it may lose control of the economy. It may therefore be that the political cost of selling many shares abroad is too high. It could also be that the cost to sell any share abroad is too high. More generally, we can imagine the government facing a cost of selling shares to foreign companies, due to political pressure, loss of control, and so on. The higher is the fraction of the domestic firm sold abroad, the higher is the political pressure—and therefore the cost. In this section I internalize the choice of the maximum amount of shares the government is willing to sell abroad and take into account these different costs.

One possibility is to assume that selling more than a given percentage of shares implies a cost and that if the benefits of such sale are higher than the costs it will be optimal to sell. However, in this section I show that it is not optimal to commit *ex ante* to a given maximum Q. It is not optimal even to commit to privatize at all. If there is uncertainty about the potential buyers' valuations of the shares, the government will be able to extract a higher surplus from the companies by making it explicit that the decision whether to sell shares at all (and how many shares to sell) will depend on their offer. In particular, the debate about whether to sell shares to foreigners should not be resolved *ex ante*. Rather, the government should make clear that the sale will be finalized only if the results are satisfactory.

To simplify, I assume that these costs can be represented as fixed costs which will be incurred if the government sells shares abroad or if it sells more than a certain number of shares. If the government decides to sell any share abroad, it has a cost M_0; if the government decides to sell more than Q_1 shares, it has to bear an additional cost M_1; if it decides to sell more than Q_2 it has an extra cost M_2, and so on up to the total number of shares.[7]

Notice that M_0 could be zero, which would mean that the government has no problems selling some shares abroad as long as they are not too many. Moreover, the Q_i can be as many as one wishes; in principle, there could be an additional cost for each additional share sold, although it is more likely that costs of this kind remain constant over some interval. Finally, it can be assumed that

[6] To this it may be added the political pressure of special groups, such as workers, to be the main recipients of the shares.

[7] The cost M can be reinterpreted also as the minimum amount of money (or the minimum value of investments) that should be raised in order to justify such sale.

above a certain number of shares the additional cost becomes infinite, which means that it would be impossible to sell more shares abroad.

The EE governments have to decide whether to allow foreign companies to hold an interest in domestic firms and, if so, how many shares to sell in total, to whom, and how much to ask in exchange. As I have shown elsewhere (Cornelli 1993), it is optimal to take all these decisions simultaneously. The reason is that a government does not know how much a foreign company is willing to pay for a share and is trying to extract as much surplus as possible from each of them. If it is clear to foreign companies that the decision whether to sell shares and how many of them has not been taken yet and it depends on their offer, the government may be able to extract a higher surplus from them.

The objective function of the government becomes:

$$\int_{\Theta}\{\Sigma_i I_i(\theta)-\beta\theta_G\Sigma_i q_i(\theta)-M_0 I\{\Sigma_i q_i(\theta)>0\}-M_1 I\{\Sigma_i q_i(\theta)>Q_1\}-...\}g(\theta)\,d\theta, \tag{13}$$

where $I\{\cdot\}$is an indicator function.

The government wants to maximize (13) subject to constraints (3), (4), (5), (6) and (7). The problem can be transformed (as in the previous section) and the objective function becomes:

$$\int_{\Theta}\left\{\Sigma_i\left[\theta_i-\beta\theta_G-\frac{1-F(\theta_i)}{f(\theta_i)}\right]q_i(\theta)-M_0 I\{\Sigma_i q_i(\theta)>0\}-M_1 I\{\Sigma_i q_i(\theta)>Q_1\}-...\right\}dG(\theta). \tag{14}$$

The choice of to whom to sell the shares and of how many to sell is given again by Proposition 1. In addition, the government has to choose whether to privatize or not and how many shares to sell abroad. To find the best selling procedure we proceed in the following way.

For each Q_i there exists an r_i such that $(r_i - 1)q_0 < Q_i \leq r_i q_0$, where r_i is different for each Q_i. Define $J(r_i)$ as the set of the highest r_i valuations declared, if they are all higher than θ^*; otherwise as the set of all the valuations higher than θ^*. Then, if the government decides to sell exactly Q_i shares, these will be sold as in Proposition 1. If there are r_i companies with valuation higher or equal to θ^*, the government will give q_0 shares to the $r_i - 1$ companies with the highest valuations and $\min\{q_0, Q_i - q_0\}$ to the company with the lowest valuation. If less than r_i companies have a valuation higher than θ^*, then the government will give q_0 shares only to these companies.

Given the best way to sell Q_i shares, the government has to decide how many shares to sell. The government will check for all the Q_i (with $Q_0 = 0$), whether

$$\sum_{j \in J(r_i)} [V(\theta_j) - \beta\theta_G] q_j^* \geq M_{i-1} , \tag{15}$$

where the q_j^* are given by Proposition 1. If Q_y is the highest Q_i for which equation (15) is satisfied, then the government will sell a maximum Q_y shares to foreign companies.[8] If, instead, the inequality is never satisfied the government will not sell any share to foreign companies.[9]

The new features in this mechanism are the decisions whether to sell shares at all and how many shares to sell. Such decisions take into account which is the best way to sell such shares if the government actually decides to do so. The decisions depend on the sum of the virtual valuations of all the companies which would receive such shares. In other words, the probability that one company will receive some shares (and, for some, also the number of shares it will eventually receive) is a function not only of its own offers, but also of the offers of all other companies. If one company is willing to undertake a huge investment in order to convince the government to privatize the industry and sell shares abroad, other companies may also benefit. In this way, the government breaks down the competition among companies. Consider, for example, a foreign company which is prepared to pay a high price, or to undertake a very expensive investment, in order to obtain some of the shares. Without the threat not to go through with the privatization (or to sell fewer shares) such a company would like to offer just enough to beat the competition and obtain q_0 shares. However, given the threat, such a company may fear that this may not be enough: the total offers by all companies may not be enough to induce the government to privatize. Such a company may therefore decide to offer more than the minimum necessary to win the competition in order to ensure that (15) is satisfied. Through such a threat the government can extract the highest possible surplus from the foreign companies.

Equation (10) still holds and it gives the expected amount that each firm is willing to pay in order to obtain the shares. It can be shown that the expected

[8] It will sell exactly Q_y if there are r_y valuations higher than θ^*.

[9] The proof that this is actually the optimal mechanism is omitted, but it can be derived easily following the line of the proof of Proposition 1.

investment is an increasing function of how much the foreign company values the shares. Hence, a firm is willing to pay more *ex ante*—that is, before it knows the offers from the other companies—the higher its valuation.[10]

The government should never announce that it is going to sell some shares and then look for the best way to sell them. Instead, it should announce that the decision whether to sell shares abroad and the amount to be sold will depend on the offers it receives. Foreign companies will then offer more in order to be sure that the privatization will actually happen and governments will extract a higher surplus.

5.3 Conclusions

I have derived the optimal procedure for the sale of shares of a domestic firm to foreign companies. Two main features can be underlined. First, foreign companies can make offers in terms of investments. If such companies have better skills for undertaking such investments the result will be an improvement for the EE government without any harm to the foreign companies. Moreover, I have shown that the indivisibilities deriving from the investment can be solved by using an appropriate system of bids. Second, I have shown that the government could exploit to its own advantage one of its weaknesses. EE governments are often subject to political pressure not to sell shares abroad. If the government makes the decision to privatize contingent on whether the offers received are generous enough to overcome the existing political pressure, it transfers the burden of proving that such a sale is advantageous to the foreign companies, and that, in turn, will bring forth higher offers.

References

Calvo, G. A., and J. A. Frenkel. 1991. Obstacles to Transforming Centrally-Planned Economies: The Role of Capital Markets. NBER Working Paper, no. 3776.

Cornelli, F. 1993. Optimal Selling Procedures with Fixed Costs. London School of Economics, Working Paper.

Cornelli, F., and D. Li. 1993. Large Shareholders, Private Benefits of Control and Privatization in Eastern Europe. London School of Economics. Photocopy.

Fischer, S. 1991. Privatization in Eastern Europe Transformation. NBER Working Paper,

[10] A more extensive analysis of this type of effect can be found, in a different context, in Cornelli 1993, which includes some numerical examples.

no. 3703.

Frydman, R., and A. Rapaczynski. 1990. Markets and Institutions in Large Scale Privatizations. New York University, C.V. Starr Working Papers, no. 90-42.

Frydman, R., and S. Wellisz. 1990. The Ownership-Control Structure and the Behaviour of Polish Enterprises during the 1990 Reforms. New York University, C.V. Starr Working Papers, no. 90-50.

Green, J. R., and J.-J. Laffont. 1979. *Incentives in Public Decision Making*. Amsterdam: North-Holland.

Laban, R., and H. C. Wolf. 1991. Wholesale Privatization in Transition Economies. MIT. Photocopy.

Maskin, E. S. 1992. Auctions and Privatization. Harvard Institute of Economic Research, Economic Theory Discussion Paper, no. 6.

Maskin, E. S., and J. Riley. 1990. Optimal Multi-unit Auctions. In F. Hahn, ed. *The Economics of Missing Markets, Information and Games*. Oxford: Oxford University Press.

McAfee, R. P., and J. McMillan. 1987. Auctions and Bidding. *Journal of Economic Literature* 25: 699–738.

Myerson, R. B. 1981. Optimal Auction Design. *Mathematics of Operations Research* 6: 619–32.

Tirole, J. 1991. Privatization in Eastern Europe: Incentives and the Economics of Transition. *NBER Macroeconomics Annual* 7.

Vishny, R. W. 1991. Comment. *NBER Macroeconomics Annual* 7.

6 Foreign Direct Investment and Privatization

Paul J. J. Welfens

6.1 Introduction

After decades of socialism, in which huge state-owned firms produced in accordance with central planning, the countries of central and eastern Europe aim to reestablish a market economy. Systemic transition creates a host of supply-side problems since a long history of central planning and near-autarchy within the Council for Mutual Economic Assistance (CMEA) have to be overcome. The countries of the ex-CMEA area have to open up towards the world economy (which renders a considerable part of the capital stock obsolete), microeconomic adjustments at the level of individual firms have to be achieved, whole industries have to be restructured and the long-neglected service sector has to be expanded.

Given the fact that state monopoly was characteristic of most industries in central and eastern Europe, opening up is necessary not only to enable them to benefit from traditional gains from trade, but also to prevent inefficiencies that would occur in the tradables sector in the presence of monopoly (whether state or private). Not only is demonopolization quite difficult to implement in the face of political resistance, but, moreover, a scarce tradition of private entrepreneurship—beyond the shadow economy with its emphasis on short-term activities—suggests at least a partial replacement of domestic competition by import competition.[1] External support for transformation could come not only from increasing trade, but even more so from rising foreign direct investment (FDI). The ability to attract multinational companies (MNCs) is both a basis for accelerating capital formation and a means to help reduce the entrepreneurial gap. Moreover, in OECD countries

[1] The smaller a country, and the more open it is, the more one may rely on external competition.

a considerable share of international trade is represented by intra-company trade.[2] Hence, allowing FDI inflows would be a step towards catching-up with the internationalization patterns of western economies and FDI could play an important role in systemic transformation in its own right. Moreover, foreign affiliates could influence policies in both the host countries and the source countries of FDI in a pro-market way, increasing and sustaining access to markets.[3] For privatized companies and newly-created companies in the ex-CMEA area this would represent a public good whose provision is likely to improve prospects for privatization.

Accepting FDI in central and eastern European countries which have not been used to MNC production—except for considerable joint ventures in Hungary—could be difficult in terms of, on the one hand, national political policies, and on the other hand, the rivalry quest for FDI from OECD countries and Newly Industrializing Countries (NICs) could weaken regional and international political cooperation in the ex-CMEA area. Rising economic disparities could trigger destabilizing migration—say, from Romania to Hungary or Poland, threatening sustainable transformation policies. Foreign direct investment, maybe unevenly distributed in OECD countries, but at least it is a common two-way factor in all advanced market economies. The fact that firms from the US, France, Germany, Switzerland, Austria or Sweden have invested abroad, probably makes it politically for these countries to accept FDI inflows. Continental-European market economies have, nonetheless, applied restrictions to foreign ownership in many ways: via restrictions on hostile foreign takeovers, explicit regulation, state control of banks or direct state ownership.[4]

The formerly socialist economies will face a more complex acceptance

---

[2] About one third of OECD trade is intra-company trade. Even more important is the high share of intra-company technology trade. See on the increasing role of MNCs in OECD countries UNCTC 1988 and Welfens 1990, 1992c. So far FDI inflows in central and eastern Europe have been significant only in Hungary (Welfens 1992d).

[3] See, for example, Bhagwati 1989 for a view which argues that MNCs' interest in exploiting the advantages of their international production-network induces them to support liberal trade policies. There might, however, be caveats, if one takes into account Latin American examples of inward-oriented policies that aim at reducing import competition and their interplay with foreign MNCs.

[4] However, facing rising Japanese and EC FDI-inflows in the 1980s was not even easy to accept for an experienced foreign investor such as the US (Graham and Krugman 1989). Moreover, it is well known that Japan has become an important source country of FDI, but is not very open nor important as a host country for FDI. In the case of German unification, FDI inflows have played only an insignificant role in the east, largely because of contested premises and unclear property titles, but also because of a rising xenophobia. For Western Germany FDI played a considerable role (Welfens 1992a).

problem. First, because FDI will be quite asymmetric in the first decade. This does not, of course, rule out the possibility that some countries could become major source-countries eventually. The example of a rising number of multinational companies from the NICs in the 1980s is encouraging in the long term. However, potential analogies to successful NICs are uncertain and probably strongly discounted by political decision-makers. Moreover, economic nationalism could fuel anti-MNC sentiments similar to those observed in many developing economies in the 1970s. Second, once state ownership of firms and banks is abolished it will become quite difficult to control foreign investors' inroads into certain industries—this will hold especially for countries which have accepted the principle of free capital-inflows and freedom of establishment, as is the case for all small former-CMEA countries in their association treaties with the EC (Welfens 1993). Third, since private domestic industry is initially non-existent or very weak, there are few natural allies for foreign investors in the business community of the host country. Moreover, many firms may fear competition from foreign multinational companies.

Privatization of firms will enlarge the menu both for foreign acquisitions and joint ventures, but it could also increase the barriers to FDI inflows. The latter holds if domestic firms perceive MNCs as undermining their opportunities for rising output and profits. The more FDI is concentrated in the tradables sector and the more strongly it is targeted on the host countries' export markets, the less conflict-prone FDI will be.

What role could FDI play in systemic transformation and how will privatization and FDI interact? What are the relevant critical points-of-departure in systemic transformation as regards the opportunities for foreign investors? Which microeconomic and macroeconomic effects are crucial for economic development in the transformation process? These and other question will be analyzed in this study.

After five decades of isolation vis-à-vis the (western) world economy, integration into a highly-dynamic international network of trade, investment and finance is an enormous challenge. In addition to the external reorientation there have to be internal adjustments that mean—among other things—not only replacing state ownership with private ownership of the means of production, but also switching from a system of monopoly firms to a system of competition, implying in itself enormous changes in relative prices. These changes are equivalent to an enormous supply-side shock which requires adjustments in product assortments, technologies, regional specialization and international trade. The old socialist institutions have been destroyed, but the new capitalist institutions are not yet in place, so enormous uncertainties are faced by households, investors and firms.

In the socialist system, state monopoly firms produced in the undemanding environment of excess demand in almost all markets for consumer and investment goods. Private firms, however, will have to operate within a competitive environment. The sudden change in both the demand regime and in the supply regime (the switch to competition) renders a large part of the stock physical and human capital obsolete. In addition to the external shock of opening up and converging world prices, there will be a sudden change in ownership and the rules of the game.

For most formerly socialist economies, systemic transformation entailed a fall in real GNP and industrial output that reached 15%–30% during the first three years of transition. Even if we assume that official statistics have not fully covered the rise of private output, the official figures for output and GNP growth suggest serious economic hardship for many—especially for those who have become unemployed or who face the prospect of unemployment. The switch to a capitalist world entails the need to face uncertainty of employment and income for the majority of the population—a price that capitalism requires in return for a higher average standard of living. Moreover, in a market economy, the highest income quintile accounts for roughly 40% of disposable income in OECD economies while the lowest quintile reaches 5%–8% of aggregate income in western market economies. In CMEA countries, the lowest quintile received about 10% of aggregate income. Therefore, the transition to a market economy could entail both a temporary fall of income due to capital obsolescence and adjustment costs and changing income distribution which will disadvantage the lowest income groups.

Since the newly created political and economic institutions will initially enjoy only weak credibility, and since internal competition will be limited for quite some time, one may expect economic agents to fully exploit their growing degrees of freedom; with government authority weakened by the collapse of communism and the disintegration of the old institutions there are prospects for a quickly expanding shadow economy. This holds all the more since privatization and other transition measures create considerable economic rents, which, in turn, could encourage wide-spread rent-seeking and corruption. Thus many (or even most) consumers will at first confront the *ugly face of capitalism*. Since generally-agreed ethical constraints (imposed in most societies by tradition and religion) are weak in many central and eastern European countries, a transitory period of *wild capitalism* is to be anticipated. This, in turn, could create growing political resistance to sustaining the transformation process. From a political-economic point of view, the fall in real income, the rise of uncertainty and the fear of unemployment have to be counterbalanced by credible prospects for high future economic growth. *Achieving a growth-oriented adjustment path is the real challenge of systemic transformation; foreign direct investment and privatization will play a core role in this context as will be shown subsequently.*[5]

The discussion is organized as follows. Section 6.2 takes a look at the difficult supply-side legacy encountered in the ex-CMEA countries and its implications for FDI, asking how FDI can be incorporated into the familiar IS-LM model of an open economy. Section 6.3 analyzes the problem of privatization in an environment of rising international capital mobility. Finally, section 6.4 draws some policy conclusions from the foregoing analysis.

6.2 Overcoming Inefficiency and Stagnation

Supply-Side Perspective

The restructuring of the supply side is crucial for eastern Europe, which has to absorb more than just an oil price shock. Competition should bring a move towards static efficiency, so that producers will adjust output according to the marginal-product rule. In labor markets the marginal-product rule will not hold until privatized firms and foreign firms have reached a critical threshold in industrial output. Privatization and some form of competition policy are important for achieving static efficiency. On the macroeconomic level, the switch to microeconomic efficiency implies a rise of unemployment which reflects the elimination of both socialist overmanning and the occurring structural shifts and shocks. Dynamic efficiency is even more difficult to achieve because it concerns product and process innovations. Product innovations will lead to a transitory violation of the rule of marginal costs equal to market prices because, without a higher (transitory) monopoly price, innovation would not occur in the first place. However, innovations could be strongly promoted by FDI inflows. Both static and dynamic efficiency are important for achieving economic growth, which, in turn, is crucial for successful transformations. Systemic transition to a market economy

[5] On international and national aspects of FDI and privatization see Jasinski and Welfens 1993.

can survive only if economic growth can be restored. The loss in social status, real income and wealth suffered by many groups during the first stage of transition calls for a strong growth in future real income; only then would most individuals be willing to support the transformation process.

I now turn to a formal model. The growth of output Y depends on the development of the production function (with scale factor a and technological-progress rate z) and the increasing availability of improved domestic and foreign inputs:

$$Y = (H+K^*)^\beta L^{(1-\beta)} \exp(z(J,Z,\alpha,X)t) , \tag{1}$$

where H denotes the domestic capital stock, K^* is the stock of foreign direct investment, L is labor input, J the stock of knowledge, Z the ratio of imports plus exports to output Y (a proxy for modernization accruing through relative imports), α the relative scope of market institutions developed (which could be scaled to fall in the 0,1 interval) and X the amount of exports;[6] z is the rate of technological progress, β is the elasticity of real capital output and t is the time index. With profit maximization the growth rate of output g_Y therefore is given by

$$g_Y = (rK/Y)g_K + (1-\beta)g_L + z(J,Z,\alpha,X) . \tag{2}$$

Whether rapid output growth can be achieved will mainly depend on four economic aspects:[7]

- The growth of the capital stock, g_K, in which domestic and foreign capital flows are contained; measured in efficiency units FDI could be more valuable than

---

[6] Exports in the aggregate production function were used in the analysis of Tyler (1981) and Feder (1982) who referred to developing countries. Exports were considered by Sengupta (1991)—focusing on Korea's growth and export dynamics—as driving a quasi-Harrod-neutral technological progress on the one hand; on the other hand, Sengupta assumed that export growth positively influenced output growth in the nontradables sector. Sengupta found positive significant externality-effects of exports on growth for Korea, Taiwan, Belgium and Germany for the period 1967-86, but not for Japan and the Phillipines. To argue that cumulated exports influence technological progress is, of course, to be distinguished from the standard argument that current exports positively influence output.

[7] In the traditional neoclassical model with exogenous growth of labor, the growth rate of labor, n, determines long term economic growth, while the savings rate s and the level of the per capita capital stock k determine the level of per capita consumption $(1-s)y(k^*)$, where k^* is the steady state k to which the economy will converge according to $sf(k^*)-jk^* = 0$, where $j=n+h$. Savings, being proportional to output, must be equal to gross investment: $sY(K, NL)= dK/dt + hK$, where N represents the level of knowledge, n the exogenous growth rate of N, dK/dt is net investment, h is the capital depreciation rate and y is per capita income. New growth approaches have endogenized n by linking it to human capital formation (Lucas 1988) or R&D activities (Aghion and Howitt 1992; Grossman and Helpman 1991; Romer 1990).

domestic capital formation provided that indigenous firms cannot quickly harvest free technology-spillover effects via learning from foreign investors. The greater the size of the economy the greater the required absolute number of foreign investors and amount of inward FDI for economy-wide technology spillovers.

- The efficiency of investment decisions which ensures that the marginal product of capital will be equal to the real interest rate r. The implicit assumption of profit maximization under competition (which will yield $rK/Y=\beta$) is probably not met in the early transition stage because competition in factor markets and goods markets has yet to be established.
- The growth of labor in efficiency units, g_L, which will be negative in the first stage of transformation because high participation rates are likely to fall, established teams in factories will disband, and some skilled labor might move from eastern Europe to OECD countries. Only higher work efficiency and retraining, as well as superior work organization (some of which could be undertaken by foreign investors) Leads to one expect that labor will contribute to economic growth in the medium term.
- The rate of technological progress, z. It is assumed here that know-how J (or human capital), the benefit from exposure to world markets as proxied by T, the relative scope of market institutions (acting as the basis for the propagation of technological information) and the cumulated amount of exports positively influence the rate of technological progress. Cumulated export output and, hence, the cumulated competitive experience from successful business in world markets will be more important for raising the rate of technological progress the greater the role of dynamic economies of scale. A growing presence of MNCs is likely to positively influence all determinants of z.

The Communist Legacy

Several problems represent a difficult supply-side legacy in central and eastern Europe. Socialist firms were oversized by western standards, not least because central planners emphasized static economies of scale and found planning easier in an environment of not more than several hundred big companies; firms have been inefficient not only because of disincentives to innovate (Balcerowicz and Welfens 1988), but also because of oversized plants. In Poland, not more than 3,300 firms constituted the manufacturing sector and big firms dominated output and employment (Lipton and Sachs 1990). Bold plans for quick privatization—envisaged under the Mazowiecki government in 1990—quickly turned out to be unrealistic:

by mid-1993, 50% of industrial output was expected to come from the private sector, but less than half the goal could be reached in reality. A major reason for slow privatization in Poland was the entrenched resistance of big firms with well-organized labor.

While in West Germany in the late 1980s, 18% of all the employed worked in firms with up to 100 employees, only 1.0% and 1.4% of all employees in the GDR (former East Germany) and Poland, respectively, were working in such small firms. Hence, privatization entails not only finding new owners, but also unbundling industrial assets so as to realize optimal plant sizes. Few capitalist economies were ever up to the task of dismembering big firms: it is doubtful that the post-World War Two dismemberment of huge firms in Western Germany and Japan could have been achieved if the US forces of occupation had not intervened.

In terms of property rights, privatization ultimately means the transfer of ownership rights to private citizens and, thus, the creation—via coupons, vouchers or stocks—of other financial assets besides domestic money and foreign currency. It is clear that privatization will not just affect allocation and generate indirect wealth effects—for example via exchange rate effects and real interest rate effects; there will be direct wealth effects equivalent to discretionary changes in initial wealth positions that will largely depend on the type of ownership-transfer chosen. Individual wealth positions are, in turn, relevant in the savings function and the labor-supply function.

In countries in which no free allocation of vouchers or stocks occurs, and in which employee share ownership programs (ESOPs) with preferential stock sales to employees are of minor importance, privatization is likely to create a very uneven distribution of wealth and income—an uneven distribution would develop over time in any case, but comparing Latin American income-distribution figures with those of OECD countries clearly points to the importance of politico-economic problems related to a thin middle-income group in industrializing economies. Low savings ratios of 2%–7% of disposable income in ex-CMEA countries point to the problem that people lack the funds to acquire industrial assets on a broad scale. west European ratios of the value of real assets to national income is about 3. On the one hand, hyperinflation in some formerly socialist countries is likely to drive up real prices of tangible industrial assets and land. On the other hand, price liberalization with modest inflation, foreign economic liberalization and the collapse of CMEA trade could depress industrial asset values. With high transformation transaction-costs in capital markets, the net price of many industrial assets could be zero, or and below scrap value. Transaction costs are equivalent to a tax and drive a wedge between the marginal willingness to pay on the part of investors and the price obtained by the present owner of the asset. The *natural market asset-value* of industrial assets is, however, the price of real capital which is obtained in a functional market economy with low transaction costs—that is, in an environment in which the transformation process has been completed. Foreign investors' demand for capital goods and firms, respectively, will raise the value of industrial assets. With depressed real-wages rates and real devaluations in the host country, foreign investors' reservation price for industrial firms will be relatively, high provided that many foreign firms compete in the acquisition process. This phenomenon has induced the ex-CSFR and other countries of the ex-CMEA area to allow bidding by foreign investors officially only after at least one privatization round in which only domestic residents are eligible.

In quantitative terms, FDI can naturally play only a limited role in the restructuring and modernization of east European economies; even very attractive host countries in western Europe or East Asia have only 10%-20% of capital formation undertaken by foreign investors. However, the typical focus of MNCs on tradables (and sometimes on technology-intensive industries) suggests that the areas that are most important for economic growth could be promoted by FDI. The new growth theory (Romer 1990) emphasizes positive technology spillovers from the tradables sector, as well as dynamic economies of scale which often can be realized only if firms export to the world market.[8]

The Economic and Political Role of Foreign Investment

In the 1970s and the 1980s FDI played a very import role as an engine of growth in developed and developing countries. There are various caveats as regards suggesting analogies between NICs' economic catching-up and potential catching-up in transforming economies of the ex-CMEA area; but one may try to draw at least some tentative conclusions from the contrast between inward-oriented Latin American development strategies (which were all outright failures as regards technological modernization) and the success of outward-oriented Asian NICs.[9] Asian NICs benefitted greatly from FDI inflows which accounted for 5%–10% of

---

[8] From this perspective firms in Russia might be an exception since they could rely on a huge domestic market in some fields, similar to the case of the United States.

[9] For some estimates of the effects of integrating the ex-CMEA into the world economy see Collins and Rodrick 1991.

Table 6.1
FDI in Selected NICs

Country	Foreign-owned share (%) in					
	GDCF[a]	Private fixed investment	Assets[a]	Manufacturing investment	Assets in manufacturing[b]	Service Assets[b]
Hong Kong	19	n.a.	18	n.a.	n.a.	n.a.
South Korea	2	n.a.	n.a.	19–31[c]	n.a.	n.a.
Malaysia	10	5–10[c]	19[c]	n.a.	n.a.	n.a.
Mexico	9	n.a.	n.a	n.a.	76[c]	34
Philippines	9	n.a.	19[c]	n.a.	32[c]	21
Taiwan	4	4[c]	n.a.	6	n.a.	n.a.
Thailand	5	4–10	16	n.a.	83	43

[a] 1986
[b] 1986–88
[c] 1984–86 (Malaysia: 1988; Philippines: 1987; Taiwan: 1987–88; Thailand: 1986–88)
Source: UNCTC 1992; Lee and Ramstetter 1991; Schive and Tu 1991.

gross capital formation in selected NICs (Table 6.1). Hong Kong, with a foreign share of 20% and South Korea, with a share of 2%, represent two polar cases (where the South Korea case probably understates the role of foreign capital because weak forms of foreign ownership—especially subcontracting—are not taken into account). About 20% of assets were owned by foreign MNCs which were important for both service and manufacturing sectors. MNCs' impact on productivity growth, rising export proceeds and competitive pressure can be much stronger than suggested by the foreign share in gross capital formation: this holds because MNCs are typically active in technology-intensive industries and are embedded in international production-networks which are conducive to trade and international technology flows.

A study on the role of FDI in South Korea argues that during the second half of the 1970s the share of the growth of value-added accounted for by foreign production ranged from 5% to 10%, while the foreign share of the growth of value-added in manufacturing was between 16% and 45% (Koo 1985). A recent study on Korea concludes that foreign firms contributed almost half the new capital in the period 1984-86 in those industries—electrical machinery and transportation equipment— which were particularly important for Korea's rapid export-led growth (Lee and Ramstetter 1991; Lim and Fong 1991). As regards economic growth and exports, it is obviously important that firms with significant export orientation and strong technology spillovers are attracted. Economic policy in Korea was not outward-oriented in the sense of encouraging the expansion of the tradables sector, but rather in supporting technological catching-up with state R & D programs, preferential credit-allocation by state-controlled banks and massive investment in higher education (Son 1991). Similar approaches and a mix of export support and import protection were employed in Taiwan which, like Korea, benefitted from US aid, while Singapore combined free-trade policies and FDI promotion successfully (Pascha 1990). The UN reports for Taiwan for the period 1960–1990 give the following regression result (UNCTC 1992, 250):

$$g^{Yt} = 4 + 0.0556(I/Y)_{t-1} + 1.5137(\mathrm{FDI}/Y)_{t-1} + 1.3430g_{Lt} + 1.1123E_t + 0.0788T_t,$$

$$R^2 = 0.48;\ \text{adj. } R^2 = 0.34;\ \text{SEE} = 2.4;\ \text{DW} = 2.09;\ N = 27.$$

Except for the ratio (I/Y) of domestic investment to output all variables were significant at either the 1% or 5% levels of significance. An increase in the FDI/Y ratio by one percentage point would increase economic growth by more than one percentage point. Similar results were found for a cross-section sample of 69 non-oil-producing developing countries by Blomstrom, Lipsey and Zejan (1992) for the period 1965–85: FDI inflows averaged over the period from 1965 to 1985 had a positive significant impact on real GDP per capita for middle-income countries. In the single-equation approach, secondary-education enrollment also showed a positive and significant sign.

The 1980s witnessed an increasing role for FDI worldwide and some recontraction of FDI flows on intra-OECD capital flows. In 1990 global FDI outflows reached \$225 billion—with an outward stock of \$1.7 trillion—where Japan, the US, the UK, Germany and France accounted for outflows of \$48, \$21, \$35, \$23 and \$35 billion, respectively (UNCTC 1992, 16). MNCs, which were considered with mistrust in the 1970s by many host countries, have become important and welcome catalyst for modernization, tax receipts, jobs and exports (UNCTC 1992).

FDI increased three times as fast as world trade and four times as fast as world output in the period 1983–90, and in 1991 the largest 100 MNCs (excluding banking and finance) represented $3.1 trillion of worldwide assets, where $1.2 trillion was outside firms' respective home countries (*Economist* 1993). Some 35,000 MNCs were recorded in 1990, when the US, Japan, Germany and Switzerland accounted for about half of all MNCs worldwide (for comparison, in 1970 the UN only some 7,000 MNCs worldwide. 35,000 MNCs had some 150,000 foreign affiliates in 1990. In 1991 central and eastern Europe accounted for 10,900 affiliates, with Hungary, Poland and the CIS each representing 2,200 affiliates. Romania recorded the highest number with 3,527, while the Czechoslovakia and Bulgaria recorded only 592 and 117, respectively. All these figures will quickly change over time and, certainly, the number of affiliates should not be confused with the significance of FDI amounts; high Polish and Romanian numbers of MNC affiliates go along with FDI inflows smaller than those in Hungary, and this points to a strong role of small foreign companies as investors and the absence of major MNCs. Reversing decades of investment autarchy, central and eastern European countries have started to welcome and support FDI inflows. In early 1992, foreign investment registrations in Hungary reached 11,000 and foreign equity capital amounted to $2.1 billion. In the CIS, the number of registered foreign investments was 5,400 which represented some $6 billion. All other ex-CMEA countries were under $1 billion cumulated FDI in 1992 (UNCTC 1992, 30).

The successful NICs have inspired the transforming economies of the former CMEA area, especially Asian NICs, which relied on FDI inflows (including weak forms such as long-term subcontracting) and have gradually increased export-GNP shares, improved product quality and raised their market shares in OECD countries at the expense of CMEA countries (Hoen and van Leeuwen 1991; Poznanski 1987). Outward-oriented policies were successfully coupled with technological modernization in Asian NICs. A prominent case was Korea which relied on a refined infant-industry protection scheme, exposing industry to world-market pressure via a strong export orientation. Korea also protected home markets, allowing high profits as a sound basis for investment, R&D and modernization (UNIDO 1987, 28). In Taiwan and Korea governments strongly encouraged firms to move up the technological ladder by both indigenous R & D efforts and by encouraging learning efforts of domestic firms facing competing foreign MNCs; a technologically-receptive economic environment that encourages international technology transfer through FDI and stimulates positive technology-spillovers through reduced learning costs is important for technological and economic catching-up (Blomstrom 1989; Wang and Blomstrom 1992).[10]

Capital became more mobile and telecommunication and computer technologies facilitated the spatial organization of international firms whose subsidiaries nevertheless enjoyed considerable autonomy in decision-making. In modern capitalism firms have become bigger than ever, but the degree of decentralization has not necessarily reduced if one takes into account the high degree of internal flexibility and autonomy in many modern firms.

The shortage of capital and entrepreneurship in the formerly socialist countries of the CMEA area makes it important for these countries to attract foreign capital. In the course of Russian, Hungarian and Czechoslovakian industrialization foreign capital had played an important role, and this historical precedent leads one to expect that for Russia, Hungary and Czechoslovakia it might not be too difficult to accept a considerable amount of foreign investment—at least as long as sustained economic growth is achieved. Compared to the nineteenth century and the interwar period there is nowadays one additional important source country, namely Japan, whose capital outflows were the highest worldwide in 1990 and 1991. While Japanese investors have been reluctant to invest in central and eastern Europe in the first stage of transformation (although Japanese MNCs are active in China) investments from MNCs from some Asian NICs have been more forthcoming, so that the traditional source-countries of the OECD area are no longer exclusive sources of FDI. Since about one third of OECD trade is organized as intra-company flows within the network of multinational companies and their respective subsidiaries, the expansion of trade both in the former CMEA area and in the east-west context could be stimulated by FDI.

As regards balance of payments effects, one may note that FDI inflows typically contribute to a trade-balance deficit in the medium term, because subsidiaries tend to import modern equipment from industrialized western countries in the first expansion stage. In the long term, however, the rising output of subsidiaries will increasingly be exported (under an adequate policy framework) to the country of the parent company or to third countries; this at least is the pattern suggested by the Korean example (Inotai 1991). If eastern Europe were to follow the Asian and Pacific pattern of FDI inflows, balance of payments problems will be reduced by the presence of MNCs' affiliates. The US affiliates' export

---

[10] Developing countries which applied restrictions to foreign investment and refused to comply with international patent conventions suffered from long delays in MNCs' intra-company technology transfers; for the case of US subsidiaries see Mansfield and Romeo 1980.

propensity—defined as the proportion of export sales in total sales by affiliates—reached 56.2% in developing countries in Asia and the Pacific in 1989, but export propensity in Latin America and the Caribbean reached only 21.4% (UNCTC 1992, 201). Similarly divergent patterns can be observed for Japanese affiliates in Asia, Africa and Latin America where the export propensities reached 40.2%, 15.2% and 23.9%, respectively. This suggests that policy orientation in the respective regions played a crucial role for the orientation of MNCs' affiliates. Should the ex-CMEA countries adopt inward-oriented policies the contribution of MNCs to export expansion and economic growth will remain limited and could be concurrently reduced by balance-of-payments problems. Balance-of-payments crises could create tendencies to suspend convertibility, to reinforce protectionism and to slow down the process of liberalizing capital flows.

An important question concerns potential restrictions on foreign investors in central and eastern Europe, where all countries have made it difficult for foreigners to acquire land. Hungary had the most liberal FDI laws early on, while, for example, Poland and Bulgaria adopted liberal legislation only reluctantly. Many countries in the former-CMEA area are afraid—for historical reasons—of German dominance in direct investment inflows (the German share in Poland is about 30%) which raises major political concerns, not least because the united Germany also is the most important export market. Whether foreign firms should be favored over domestic firms is an open question, but as long as state firms dominate one must anticipate that a neutral tax and commercial policy would indeed discriminate against foreign investors (Inotai 1992).

FDI inflows will increase production potential and thereby have effects on the supply side. Since a rising presence of foreign investors could change the propensity to import or export there will be supply-side and demand-side effects on the goods-market equilibrium. Privatization will also have macroeconomic effects, where increasing supply elasticities, as well as demonopolization effects—influencing the price level and relative prices—could be important. Privatization and FDI will affect all macro markets of the economy, especially the labor market and the foreign-exchange market; exchange-rate movements will influence the net wealth position of countries with high foreign debt, the development of the trade balance, the share of the tradables sector and foreigners' propensity to invest. If some groups of domestic residents hold foreign exchange there will also be changes in the distribution of wealth within the country. There could indeed be considerable distribution effects that should not be overlooked in a debate which typically is centered on allocation aspects.

Privatization of socialist firms in the sense of transferring well-defined ownership rights to domestic residents and encouraging entrepreneurs to launch their own businesses is a major challenge for systemic transformation and raises in itself various theoretical issues: for example, which firms and industries should be privatized first? how should privatization be organized? which forms of privatization are suitable? and which politico-economic impediments to a comprehensive and sustainable privatization are relevant? Moreover, to what extent does privatization change the macroeconomic effects of economic policy, especially innovation policy, fiscal policy and monetary policy?

Basic Theoretical Aspects of Foreign Direct Investment

A host of issues are important for the assessment of the role of FDI in systemic transformation. Since the late 1980s, FDI has grown faster than trade world wide, but FDI has also become more regionally concentrated—especially in the Third World—than it was in the 1960s and 1970s (UNCTC 1992). Clearly, FDI is taking place in a world economy in which the mobility of real capital has increased. A better theoretical understanding of some aspects of FDI seems important for growth-oriented transformation programs in central and eastern Europe.

THE MODERN OLI APPROACH

It is clear that foreign investors will require that some basic form of currency convertibility be established quickly. Without safe prospects for the repatriation of profits, future profits in the host countries would be strongly discounted—reducing the sales proceeds from selling industrial assets to foreign companies. The basic problems of establishing convertibility are well known (Williamson 1991; Kornai 1990) and will certainly entail some form of capital account liberalization—even if the IMF statutes traditionally emphasize current account convertibility. External convertibility is a prerequisite for bringing locational advantages to the attention of foreign investors, but, at the same time, it is true that foreign investments can help to achieve convertibility. Creating positive economic expectations, thereby supporting political stability, which, in turn, should reduce the risk premium in international capital markets—thus encouraging portfolio-capital inflows—is one possible avenue.

Various economic approaches have been proposed in the literature to explain FDI (see, for example, Caves 1982; Welfens 1990). Given the specific problems in the ex-CMEA area, a closer look at Dunning's approach seems to be particularly relevant. Locational conditions, ownership-specific characteristics of firms in potential FDI source countries, as well as transaction costs for intra-company trade as compared to using anonymous markets all play a crucial role in this context.

FDI can be viewed as an alternative to exports and contractual resource transfers, and only under certain conditions will firms consider production abroad as a viable alternative to exports or licensing. This is a basic idea in Dunning's Ownership-Location-Internalization (OLI) approach. In Dunning's eclectic theory, multinationals are assumed to have some owner-specific advantages—for example, patents—that allow the potential foreign investor to successfully compete with true indigenous producers abroad who enjoy certain natural advantages—for example, familiarity with the domestic economic and political system. If only O-advantages of the MNC are present, licensing could be a suitable strategy to serve a foreign market indirectly. However, the implicit assumption that private partner firms already exist and enjoy sufficient technological and organizational competence to produce the products envisaged typically is not fulfilled in ex-CMEA countries. Licensing also entails the risk for the foreign firm that the licensee could soon invade the traditional markets of the firm. EC firms will be particularly reluctant to grant licenses to firms in the former Czechoslovakian area if full access to EC markets has to be anticipated in the near future—as in the case of Hungary, the ex-CSFR and Poland.

If the firm also enjoys internalization advantages—in the sense that specific organization skills or peculiarities of the sector or the product allow a profitable substitution of pure market-transactions by intra-firm transactions—then exports are the best way to serve the foreign market, unless there are particular locational advantages relevant to local production. In transforming economies in which tradable goods-markets often are characterized by high transaction costs, firms with sufficient knowledge of organizing international production networks can be expected to strongly consider setting up a foreign affiliate. In the case of close geographical proximity and industry characteristics that allow them to separate certain stages of the value-adding process across countries—for example disconnecting R&D activities from the assembly process—the creation of new affiliates is a particular attractive option. However, this holds only if the existing MNC production network does not suffer from capacity underutilization. The recession in western Europe and Japan in 1992–93 leads one to expect that OECD countries' FDI outflows will remain limited by overcapacity problems in existing firms for some time. Part of the FDI inflows in the ex-CMEA area in the first transition stage probably reflect MNCs' catching-up with investment opportunities that were not feasible because of the investment autarchy of socialist command economies. Once *normal* politico-economic conditions characterize eastern Europe, it remains to be seen whether locational advantages in the ex-CMEA area are strong enough to attract high FDI inflows.

If, in addition to ownership and internalization advantages, there are attractive conditions in host countries then the firm would establish production abroad and serve both local and third-country markets (possibly including at some date the home market of the parent company). Eastern European economies have to develop locational advantages in order to attract foreign direct investment. Locational advantages can consist of low energy prices and real wages, a well-developed infrastructure, skills in adopting foreign technologies and a broad range of competitive supplier firms. Given the fact that infrastructure in the ex-CMEA was relatively poor by Western standards, high FDI inflows are likely to create bottleneck problems: as soon as many foreign investments occur, ex-CMEA countries will face infrastructure bottlenecks that need to be anticipated by economic policymakers if continuing inflows are to be maintained.

A receptive policy for foreign investors is only visible in Hungary. The government introduced external convertibility, reduced tariffs (especially for intermediate inputs) maintained a firm commitment to progressive liberalization and rarely was reluctant to sell major state-owned firms ("crown jewels") to foreign investors. This held at least until late 1992, when the public called for a stronger role for Hungarian investors in the privatization process, which until then had been characterized by the fact that about three-fourths of the privatization proceeds came from foreign investors. Former Czechoslovakia also welcomed FDI inflows explicitly, where the Czech republic recorded more than 80% of all inflows. Poland, at first, only reluctantly admitted foreign investors, then changed course towards a more receptive policy stance in 1991. However, in Poland as in other ex-CMEA countries the general population and influential political parties display strong resistance to foreign investors. People are afraid that foreign firms could buy assets at below long-term market prices, that foreign owners will be less willing to save jobs in outdated factories and will be able to keep wages relatively low for many years. From a microeconomic point of view, that is, in the case of an individual firm, these reservations might, in some cases, be substantiated. Macroeconomic aspects and evolutionary dynamics are totally neglected in such a view: if a high amount of FDI can be attracted economy-wide one would expect that capital intensity, the marginal product of labor and, thus, real wages will increase.

Foreign investors' willingness to pay relatively high prices for acquiring firms in former CMEA countries depends on the expected profitability, the perceived uncertainty of investment conditions and the degree of political risk. Profitability will be increased if there is local private industry with firms that can supply intermediate products and specific inputs for production. Here privatization is important for successful foreign investment policies. Employee share-ownership participation (ESOP) could be specifically encouraged for firms in which foreign investors have a high stake. The introduction of a moderate capital gains tax could also be considered which would split the gains from transformation between firms and society.

The infrastructure and hostile bureaucratic attitudes vis-à-vis foreign investors are still an impediment to foreign investment inflows in most ex-CMEA countries. Only if a critical mass of FDI can be mobilized would people in the host country become more aware of the positive economic impact of MNCs. Finally, the new private firms of central and eastern Europe will have to learn themselves that exports, local production abroad or contractual services are alternatives that should be considered in a long term business strategy. International investment could be as much an engine of economic growth as international trade has been for such a long time.

FDI in the Open Economy Model

Foreign investors are expected to augment capital stocks, introduce less costly technologies and contribute to higher product quality. At first sight, these are mainly supply-side effects, and—as is well-known—the supply side is not well covered in the familiar Keynesian IS-LM model. The situation in central and eastern Europe, however, makes a modified IS-LM-ZZ model of an open economy with underemployment still relevant. Inflation can be incorporated by distinguishing the nominal interest rate i (relevant for the money market equilibrium line LM) and the real interest rate r (one of the important factors shaping the goods demand curve IS via the influence of r on investment)—and even the supply-side can be incorporated (Welfens 1992b). The expected rate of inflation will be the difference between i and r.

A major transformation aspect associated with the slope of the balance of payments curve (ZZ) that portrays equilibrium in the foreign-exchange market is that both privatization and FDI will tend to increase the elasticity of net capital inflows Q which depend on the difference between the domestic and foreign interest rates $(i-i^*)$, the expected devaluation rate a, and—as regards FDI—the real interest rate differential $r-r^*$; under perfect capital mobility (and if domestic and foreign bonds were perfect substitutes) one could assume interest parity $i-i^*=a$; but since political risk R can be expected to play an important role we will use modified interest parity in the form $i-i^*= a+R$. If modified purchasing power-parity held (in the sense that the devaluation rate is equal to the inflation differential) the nominal interest rate parity would be equivalent to real interest rate parity in this model.

As suggested by Froot and Stein (1992), part of capital inflows (namely, FDI) depends upon the real exchange rate $q=eP^*/P$, where e denotes the nominal exchange rate, P^* the foreign and P the domestic price level. Note here that if the devaluation rate a reflected modified purchasing power parity $(a=\pi-\pi^*)$, net capital inflows Q could be written as $Q'(r-r^*, q, R, W)$; the variable W, negatively affecting capital inflows, is a crucial exogenous variable here and measures the degree of doubt—as perceived by market participants—that convertibility could be maintained. In the short term one cannot, of course, assume that modified PPP will hold. As in the long term, net imports can be written as $Q'(\ldots)$ and, as soon as expectations are forward-looking, one would have to consider, even within a short-term analysis, the implied long-term equilibrium values for Y and r. For the foreign exchange market to clear equation (5) must hold, namely that the net import of goods and service $-T$ (T is therefore net exports) will be equal to net capital inflows $Q(\ldots)$. Net exports are conventionally assumed to be a positive function of real income abroad Y^*, a negative function of domestic income Y and a positive function of the real exchange rate q. In addition we also assume that net exports are a positive function of K^*, the stock of FDI. One could argue that the higher is K^*, the better will be product quality, such that imports will reduce and exports likely increase. The intensity of competition v is also assumed to stimulate net exports; the latter could be proxied by the share of output produced in the private sector, and one could take into account the effective import tariff as a negative determinant of v. A specific element of the net export function $T(\ldots)$ is, therefore, that a change of the supply potential as well as competition are taken into account in a straightforward formulation yielding the ZZ curve:
Under competitive profit maximization, and assuming a Cobb-Douglas function, the

$$-T(q,Y,Y^*,K^*,v) = Q(...) \, . \tag{3}$$

supply side of the economy is given by the production function $Y = K^{\beta}L^{(1-\beta)}$, which implies that $Y = rK + (1\text{-}\beta)Y$. K includes the domestic capital stock, H, plus the stock of inward FDI, K^* and $K=H+K^*$. Hence the goods-market equilibrium condition is given by equation (4), in which C represents private consumption, I investment demand, G government consumption and T net exports. Investment is assumed to depend not only upon the real interest rates r at home and abroad (r *and* r^*), but also on the terms of trade (Froot and Stein 1992). This formulation of the investment function implicitly considers FDI inflows as greenfield investments. In reality, foreigners acquire part of the existing capital stock, but they also add to it. C is assumed to positively depend on real income Y, government net transfers N, and wealth $A=M/P+B/P+H-qF^*$, where M/P denotes the real money stock, B/P the real value of the stock of (short-term) domestic bonds, H the domestically owned capital stock and F^* the stock of (indexed) foreign debt. Increasing competition through privatization will improve product quality and therefore shift both the IS curve and the ZZ curve to the right; a special assumption could be that the production potential would positively influence the exports of goods and services. We thus derive IS curve:

$$rK + (1-\beta)Y = C(Y,A,N) + I(r,r^*,q) + G + T(...). \tag{4}$$

If we integrate the supply side as suggested here (Welfens 1992b), it immediately becomes apparent that the supply-augmented goods market equilibrium curve IS is less steep than suggested by the traditional IS curve in the pure demand setting. An exogenous increase in the capital stock K—regardless of whether it stems from H or K^*—will reduce the slope of the IS curve such that the new intersection point with the LM curve would indicate a higher real income (GNP) Y. Capital formation will thereby lead to a higher output. Finally, note that if cumulated exports are an argument of the production function a rising foreign GNP would stimulate exports which, in turn, would raise GNP and, hence, foreign exports.[11]

The demand for money can conveniently be written as follows:

[11] The growth effect of cumulated exports may be assumed to fall over time as the disembodied learning effects from exporting will depreciate over time in the sense that the associated know-how and knowledge gradually will become obsolete (it could become obsolete over night if a regional trade system, such as the CMEA, is collapsing).

$$M/P = Y\exp(-\sigma i)\ , \qquad (5)$$

from which we can derive the LM curve:

$$\ln\left(\frac{M/P}{Y}\right) = -\sigma i\ , \qquad (6)$$

where i= nominal interest rate, and $i = r + E(\pi)$ (the expected inflation rate $E(\pi)$ can be treated as exogenous in the short run—a monetarist view would suggest that actual inflation π is determined by the difference between the growth rate of the money supply and the growth rate of the productive potential) and where σ= semi interest-elasticity, and where the elasticity of the real demand for money is assumed, for simplicity, to be unity.

As is well known from standard analysis, a rising degree of capital mobility means that the ZZ curve will become flatter. Its slope is $di/dY = j^*/(\delta Q/\delta r - r^*)$, where j^* is the marginal propensity to import and $\delta Q/\delta r - r^*$ denotes the marginal reaction of Q with respect to the net interest rate differential. Progress in privatization and a rising stock of FDI inflows will not only increase $\delta Q/\delta r - r^*$, but will also raise j^*. If the government deliberately interferes with the switch to rising capital mobility the rise of j^* could dominate in the medium term, so that the ZZ curve will remain steeper than the LM curve. If privatization helps to reduce the budget deficit, and thereby facilitates anti-inflationary policies, it might be expected that capital mobility would be indirectly reduced. It is well known from Western countries that the higher the inflation rate the lower the average maturity of bonds; to put it differently, with a low inflation rate more financial investments will be long term, which should reduce the average responsiveness of capital flows to changing international interest rate differentials.

If the LM curve is less steep than the ZZ curve (here ZZ_1) an expansive fiscal policy or an exogenous increase in exports of goods and services will establish IS-LM equilibrium at point B in Figure 6.1; from the initial general equilibrium in A, the economy would move towards B, where real income is higher than before.[12] Since point B is below the ZZ_1 curve B reflects a trade-balance deficit (a ZZ disequilibrium). In the case of fixed exchange rates, the excess demand in the foreign-exchange market would force the central bank to sell reserves in order to maintain the parity. This implies, of course, that the LM curve will shift

[12] We disregard dynamics here. The traditional view is that stability requires the ZZ curve to be less steep than the LM curve.

Figure 6.1
Systemic Transformation in the Supply-Augmented Macro Model

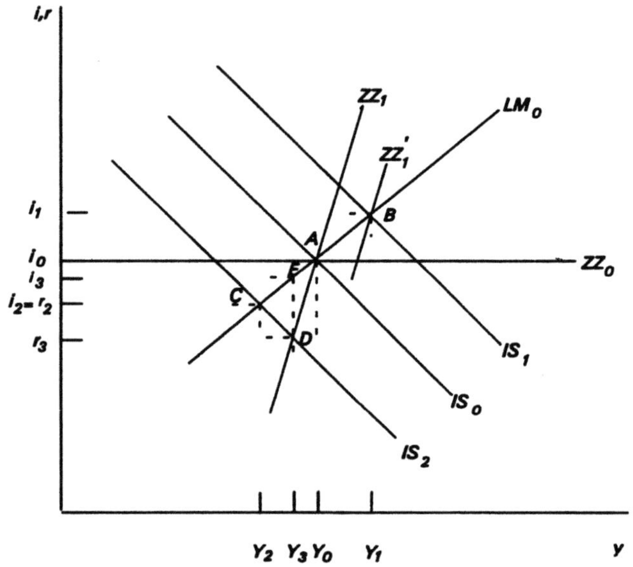

to the left, meeting the intersection of IS_1 and ZZ_1. In the case of zero capital mobility and hence a vertical ZZ line, the economy would return to the initial income level. If the government were to increase capital mobility through liberalization policies, the markets' anticipation of problems in financing an expansionary government policy (and, hence, a rising budget deficit) will lead to massive portfolio-capital outflows, which would reinforce the excess demand in the foreign exchange-market and force the government to reimpose foreign-exchange controls or else to suspend convertibility—both measures likely to reduce future FDI inflows. To the extent that FDI inflows effectively increase capital mobility (for example, by improving market transparency, reducing transaction costs and raising capital-control costs for government authorities) foreign investment contains the promise of successful expansion, but also the risk of a self-reversing economic expansion: FDI makes the ZZ curve less steep so that point B could even entail an excess supply in the foreign exchange market (if the ZZ curve is flatter than the LM curve). However, fear that transitional excess demand in the foreign exchange market could force the central bank to run down reserves and to suspend convertibility might trigger speculative attacks and massive capital outflows, so that a sustained increase of Y is not feasible. Fear of such a problem can prevent the expansionary effects in the first place. In a two country model FDI plays an ambiguous role in the following sense. If eastern Europe (country I) could attract FDI inflows from western Europe (country II) positive competition-effects in the host countries, the increase of the real capital stock and the production potential and higher expected long-term income in eastern Europe would increase consumption demand and shift the IS curve to the right such that *Y* would increase, this would imply a balance-of-payments deficit—as long as the ZZ curve is steeper than the LM curve—and, via interventions in the foreign-exchange markets, a leftward shift of the LM curve. The increase of real income in eastern Europe will raise the net exports of western Europe and, thus, increase EC real output; this, in turn, will raise the level of imports from eastern Europe.

If one assumes that FDI in eastern Europe is of the *substitution type*—in the sense that MNCs global production capacity is maintained via offsetting disinvestments in western Europe—FDI flows from the EC to eastern Europe could indeed mean that output in transforming economies will increase and the IS curve moves to the right in the first stage; but, as a consequence of a reduced production potential and falling real income as well as employment in the EC, east European net exports will reduce such that the IS curve and the ZZ curve for eastern Europe will shift to the left again. Positive all-European income effects of FDI flows can be expected only if firms in the EC envisage at least some FDI projects in eastern Europe as a means to improve international competitiveness vis-à-vis the US, Japan and the rest of the world. Similarly, if there is a strong role of positive technology spillovers of FDI in eastern Europe one would expect the aggregate technology level in the whole of Europe to increase and European real output in both parts of Europe could increase at the same time.

In the case of flexible exchange rates point B would entail a real depreciation of the currency, which would improve the balance of payments if the Marshall Lerner condition holds. In that case the IS curve and the ZZ_1 curve would shift further to the right. The real devaluation would stimulate FDI inflows in accordance with the Froot-Stein argument, and a favorable impact on Y follows. There is, however, a caveat—namely, that (under flexible exchange-rates) exchange-rate volatility could negatively affect portfolio-capital inflows and even the volume of trade. If the volume of trade—the actual or the cumulated volume—influences the production potential, the latter effect would imply that with a given increase in aggregate demand the likelihood of ending up with an excess demand is increased such that inflationary expectations could develop, which, in turn, could encourage capital outflows, currency substitution and a more general credibility problem.

If capital flight occurs the terms of trade will fall, be it via a fall of the domestic price level P (deflation) or an increase of the exchange rate e (depreciation). Net wealth will be reduced. This will tend to reduce domestic per capita wealth A, so that the IS curve will shift back towards its original position, IS_0 in figure 6.1. If, however, the trade deficit goes along with a corresponding net FDI inflow the long term result will be an improved quality of export goods. In the case of a small country—facing no restrictions on exports to the rest of the world—this implies that both the IS curve and the ZZ curve will shift to the right, such that B could indeed be a long-term solution of the model (intersection of ZZ_1' and LM_0 and IS_1).[13]

In the very first stage of systemic transformation employment and the number of firms is reduced, wealth is falling and government consumption is typically reduced (partly under external pressure, for example, from the IMF). Point C in Figure 6.1 will be realized as an IS-LM equilibrium, so that the real interest rate and output are falling (IS_0 shifts to IS_2. Assuming a steep ZZ curve (ZZ_1) there will be a trade-balance surplus. This was indeed the situation observed in Hungary, Poland and the Czechoslovakia in 1990–91.

So far we have disregarded inflation. One could easily take inflation into account if one assumes (for simplicity) that purchasing-power parity holds. Consider the early stage of transformation with a shift from IS_0 to IS_2. The equilibrium real interest rate r_3 is determined by the intersection of the IS_2 curve and the ZZ_1 curve (point D): The nominal interest rate i_3 is determined on the LM curve, as is real income Y_3 (point E). The real interest rate is lower than in a situation of zero inflation ($r_3 < r_2$); output is higher ($Y_3 > Y_2$). The distance DE would reflect the expected inflation rate.[14] We disregard here currency substitution, which could become increasingly important in the presence of MNCs. One may note, however, that if currency substitution can be reversed the demand for real domestic money balances will increase such that a given government deficit-GNP ratio could be financed by a lower level of seignorage—that is, a lower inflation rate could result,

[13] In the very long-term, in which the ZZ curve is assumed to be rather flat (ZZ_0 is shown as an extreme case), point B would indicate a current account surplus and an excess supply in the foreign exchange-market, which would force the central bank to intervene in the case of fixed exchange rates; if exchange rates were flexible there will be a currency appreciation. If, however, the ZZ curve were steeper than the LM curve, one would witness currency depreciation.

[14] In a more elaborate analysis, non-neutrality of inflation could also occur via inflation-induced shifts of the IS and ZZ curves.

encouraging FDI.

Capital Markets in Systemic Transition

Foreign investors will play an important role in macroeconomic outcomes, but they are crucial to systemic transformation itself because they will affect industrial production as well as the financial systems of host countries. FDI in banking and insurance could be important catalysts for improving the efficiency of capital markets in ex-CMEA countries where credit allocation through state banks still was dominant in 1991–92. Market price signals induce efficient investment patterns only if competition in goods markets and competition in financial markets—the latter leading to hard budget constraints—interact.

In the presence of growing FDI one may assume that: (i) capital mobility will increase because the presence of MNCs means that information about international financial markets as well as access to these markets is increasing; (ii) it will become technically more difficult to control capital outflows if domestic firms have the option to form joint ventures with a growing pool of foreign investors; (iii) foreign investors will build up political pressure for capital import liberalization because they are familiar with used to and interested in taking loans wherever the costs of borrowing are lowest. Moreover, domestic firms will argue that MNCs' subsidiaries enjoy an unfair advantage even in the presence of official restrictions, if they can effectively borrow in international markets (for example, through the parent company), while local competitors are not allowed to use the cheapest sources of capital.

The capital market necessarily played an important role in achieving economic efficiency in the CMEA economies in the 1960s and 1970s. Investment-GNP ratios of socialist economies were much above those of western Europe. The economic stagnation of the 1980s suggests that the marginal product of capital must have been close to zero and that the investment selection process in the (reforming) planned economies was very inefficient. Inventory-turnover ratios exceeded those of western market economies.[15] A competitive banking system and a viable stock exchange are needed as an effective means of pricing investment decisions and valuing firms. Foreign banks and investment firms are, of course, particularly important for bringing about competition and efficiency in the capital market. It

---

[15] Total inventories in months of turnover were 1.81 in Polish manufacturing, compared to 1.48 and 1.52 in the U.S. and Canada, respectively. See Berg and Sachs 1992.

may be that banks or investment firms that have acquired a formerly state-owned firm will realize large capital gains if the stock acquired can be resold in the international market under favorable conditions. For example, citizens in Hungary watched with some unease as Austrian banks acquired Hungarian firms and very quickly sold the investment for considerable profit; nationalist sentiments can then, of course, be exploited by extreme political parties—especially if the general economic situation of the country is stagnant.

As long as most banks are still state-owned and competition is limited in the financial services industry, one cannot assume that the pricing of investment projects and investment risks will be optimal. Indeed, it will be distorted in favor of state firms, and many projects by privatized firms and would-be newcomers will be crowded out by investment credits that are biased in favor of state industries. Therefore the privatization of the banking industry under competitive conditions is important.

Finally, it is important that macroeconomic policies ensure a positive real interest rate (which might not be the case in countries with very high inflation); otherwise firms would be stimulated to make investments where the typical marginal product of capital is negative and typical long-term economic profitability quite dubious.[16]

The Interdependency of FDI Privatization

Foreign direct investment can help the economies of central and eastern Europe to achieve a net resource transfer which is necessary to really improve the supply-side and avert a drastic fall in the standard of living. In contrast to portfolio inflows, FDI inflows are typically long term and include—at least in the case of big multinationals' investments—a transfer of technology and know-how. Improving technologies will contribute to cutting costs and improving the price competitiveness in world markets. With better access to modern intermediate products and advanced technologies, there are also prospects to improve the terms of trade by raising the quality of products exported and moving into new sectors with high value-added products. The former socialist duality of poor-quality goods sold at home and

---

[16] Taking into account the experience of Korea (Collins 1990) and other NICs, growth-oriented investment policies require that real interest rates be positive. The East-Asian experience of positive real interest rates is in stark contrast to Latin America's slow growth under negative real interest rates. The yardstick for evaluating competing investment projects in East Asian countries have been positive real interest rates and world market prices (an outward-oriented policy framework). On some other important lessons from Asian NICs see Krueger 1990, 1992.

superior-quality goods shipped to foreign markets will largely collapse, and, in general, the population is likely to benefit from improved access to high-quality goods. If the terms of trade can be improved the real burden of foreign debt will be reduced.

Provided that a critical minimum of FDI inflows can be attracted, the prospects for an expansion of domestic firms will improve in the medium term. This could ease the problem of privatization which generally will be easier in an environment of sustaining economic growth. High FDI inflows will particularly benefit part of the nontradables sector: foreign firms will contribute to an increasing demand for infrastructure so that construction firms, power generation and service providers face favorable business prospects.

Given the increasing role of intra-company trade, international technology flows, and international R & D cooperation in the 1980s (UNCTC 1988; Klein and Welfens 1990) one should also emphasize that foreign direct investment is an engine of economic growth. Murrell (1990, 1991) argued that the absence of FDI largely explains the distorted trade patterns and slow economic growth in socialist economies, and that rebuilding the institutional network under new political and economic rules is a time-consuming task which should not be solved by a shock therapy. If one adopts this view, the conclusion is that eastern Europe needs not only institutional liberalization, but positive incentives for exports and FDI.

In 1990 the highest inflows in eastern Europe were recorded in Hungary, Czechoslovakia and Poland with $1 billion, $600 million, and some $500 million, respectively. Figures for 1992–93 will be slightly higher, but so far only Hungary has an impressive FDI inflow; and Hungarian firms—sometimes building on expatriate communities abroad—could also become the first significant source country for long-term capital outflows (a position which in central and eastern Europe was held only by the Czechoslovakia in the interwar period).

Foreign direct investment flows reached some $200 billion worldwide in 1990–91, up from average annual values of $42.4 billion in the period 1980–84 and $134.9 billion in the period 1985–89 (BIS 1992). The group of source countries is highly concentrated and so is the group of recipient countries. Considerable equity inflows—as part of portfolio investment—have reinforced the international inflow of risk capital in the industrial countries. Average annual equity inflow values reached $31.4 billion in the period 1985–90, and in 1991 there was a record flow of $90.1 billion, equivalent to one-third of total portfolio outflows. The EC recorded annual inflows of $22.7 billion annually in the period 1985–89, up from roughly $2 billion annually in 1975–1984.

Given the increasing outflow of foreign capital and the amount of equity investments worldwide, there is considerable potential that could be tapped by transforming countries in the former-CMEA area. The increasing mobility of real capital is also raising specific problems, however: potential host countries face more fierce competition for foreign capital and a period of high real interest rates in Europe—partly caused by the need to finance high investments in the ex-CMEA area.[17]

Empirical evidence and historical experience hold two lessons for countries eager to attract foreign capital inflows: (i) Portfolio-investment flows are highly mobile and sensitive to nominal and real exchange-rate fluctuations which imply a risk premium on investment (Tilly 1992); but (ii) there is little evidence—except for the case of developing countries—that FDI flows are influenced by exchange-rate volatility (Bailey and Tavlas 1991).[18]

In 1991, equity inflows in industrial countries reached a very high level of almost 60% of FDI inflows, but the more traditional share of about 25% would also be impressive. This suggests that portfolio investment flows could play a significant role also in eastern Europe. EC countries and the United States might support such developments by introducing tax exemptions for investment funds investing in the transforming ex-CMEA countries.

In order to assess the possible impact of FDI inflows in eastern Europe one may analyze the effect of EC FDI inflows. $60 billion of total annual FDI inflows into the EC plus another $30 billion of equity inflows should generate additional value-added of some $150 billion in the EC, if one assumes that the capital output ratio is 4 to 1 and that output is generated over a ten year period. The direct value-adding effect of these capital flows could reach more than 10% of total EC exports (in 1988: 907 billion ecus); if one could include technology-spillover effects and take into account the fact that part of EC trade is generated by multinational companies, the economic significance of FDI inflows and equity inflows in the EC is even higher. Eastern Europe could hope to attract at least part of the worldwide

[17] The surge in real interest rates is partly due to German unification; see on German unification Welfens 1992b.

[18] FDI flows could, of course, be influenced by long-term real exchange-rate changes that lead to capital gains or losses. A real appreciation of the currency of major source countries will encourage FDI inflows into transforming economies because real assets then become cheaper in terms of the investor's domestic prices. In industrial countries, equity inflows amounted to about one-fifths of all portfolio inflows which, of course, are more volatile than FDI flows (BIS 1992).

FDI flows and equity inflows. FDI inflows into eastern Europe jumped from an annual value of $0.1 billion in 1989 to $0.5 billion and $2.3 billion in 1990 and 1991, respectively; however, almost half the inflows were recorded by Hungary, where the stock of FDI at end-1992 will reach some $5 billion. Foreign investment flows could indeed contribute to some 10% of gross capital formation in the 1990s, and would thereby match the high values Taiwan recorded in the 1960s.

While Asian NICs always enjoyed the advantage of almost unrestricted access to the huge United States market, east European economies are less well positioned with respect to western Europe. The EC has been reluctant to fully liberalize imports in the association treaties signed with the Czechoslovakia, Poland and Hungary in November 1991. Textiles and agriculture are potential fields for high export growth within transforming economies, but the EC has remained quite protectionist in these areas. Export growth and the expansion of the service industry would have to be exceptionally high if massive unemployment problems are to be avoided given the huge productivity gap between western Europe and eastern Europe, the potential for a broad west-east technology transfer in the long-term and the high shares of industry and agriculture in the ex-CMEA area.[19]

Foreign investors will, of course, be quite reluctant to invest much in all the industries of central and east European countries where EC import barriers are existent or looming. For the smaller ex-CMEA countries it could be important to target not only EC markets but other markets in industrial countries, the NICs and the developing countries; and to try to establish free trade within a wider group of transforming economies. The arguments in some of the smaller countries that local production could serve both a growing domestic market and a huge Soviet market have become invalid and probably never were sound. Foreign investors often will invest in the new republics and states of the former Soviet Union (FSU). Furthermore, huge potential markets such as those in the FSU could also be covered by subsidiaries located in other low-wage countries, for example, in South-East Asia.

Whether competition and growth can be achieved will depend not only on FDI inflows but, of course, largely on progress in the task of privatization. Only privatization can create an economic system with flexible industrial structures and

---

[19] Except for Hungary and the Czech republic. Hungary enjoys the advantage of a long history of internal and external reforms as well as having been a leader in joint ventures in the ex-CMEA, while the CSFR was a modern industrial country before 1939 and does not face the problem of high employment shares in agriculture.

an efficient allocation of production factors. To attract FDI to a significant degree clearly requires locational advantages, modern infrastructure and an outward-oriented policy program; it above all requires to establish political stability; yet a coincidence of economic stagnation, uncertainty and political instability would exclude significant FDI inflows in central and eastern Europe. The contrasting cases of Hungary and Poland (with 29 parties in Parliament in 1992) are significant in this respects, and the divergent experiences of the FSU and China are equally interesting.

6.3 Privatization

Privatization in formerly socialist economies is radically different from privatization in existing market economies, where the privatization of a few state firms hardly changes macroeconomic structure at the margin. One may envisage privatization of whole industries as a positive sum game in which positive external effects in the form of network externalities play an important role. Therefore, one cannot correctly price real assets if privatization occurs in a step-by-step manner. For practical purposes, this is unavoidable and government should not hesitate to quickly advance small privatization and the privatization of the tradables industry. The rents from economy-wide privatization that will accrue to private investors could be partly captured by government through a capital-gains tax (probably even through a regressive capital-gains tax). A capital-gains tax—which later may be phased out—can, however, be only one part of a functional tax system whose aim is not least to ensure that a stability-oriented monetary policy remains feasible. Clearly, a capital-gains tax would reduce future budget deficits and could thereby restrict upward pressures on real interest rates which will adversely affect investment. One may also note that monetary stability and political stability are important for attracting foreign investors.

Private firms—whether owned by foreign or domestic investors—will be more responsive to real-exchange rate changes than state firms. To the extent that this is true, exchange-rate policies could become a preferred instrument in the adjustment process of transforming economies. Privatization can contribute to balance-of-payments problems because the state can no longer directly control imports. An important policy question is which exchange-rate regime is chosen. By all standard criteria discussed in the optimum currency-area literature, there is no reason to support fixed exchange rates. However, the policy credibility problem might prompt the new central banks in the ex-CMEA area to opt for fixed exchange-rate regimes (after hyperinflation has been eradicated) in order to borrow policy credibility from abroad. This would mean not allowing market forces to determine the equilibrium exchange-rate in a period of sustaining and thorough real and monetary adjustments. This does not seem to be a prudent policy strategy of macroeconomic adjustment.

With a flexible exchange-rate regime, the establishment of current-account convertibility and internal convertibility is probably easier to achieve and to maintain than with a fixed exchange-rate approach. Import demand in a privatized economy will be quite elastic so that the Marshall-Lerner condition is more likely to hold than in the case of state-run firms. Of special interest here is the Robinson condition because it contains the supply elasticities (E, $E^* > 0$) and demand elasticities (D; * for foreign country; X=exports, X^*= imports). Most crucial is the supply elasticity in the case of a large country, for example Ukraine and Russia. Big countries face a considerable risk that their terms of trade will fall when they expand exports significantly.

Transformation to a market economy will raise the import-demand elasticity (D) and the export-supply elasticity (E).[20] For all ex-CMEA countries—except for the FSU—one may assume that the foreign supply elasticity is infinity and that the demand elasticity abroad is minus infinity (small country assumption for the transforming economies). The corresponding Robinson condition is then $X(1+E_X) > X^*(1+D_{X*})$, so that—following a devaluation—the trade balance will improve the higher the export supply and import demand elasticities. To the extent that privatization and FDI inflows make the supply side economies more responsive, the usefulness of the exchange-rate instrument for current-account policies strongly depends on progress in the privatization process and sustaining FDI inflows. In the short term, FDI inflows could reduce the demand elasticity because subsidiaries will probably import machinery, equipment and intermediate products without reacting very strongly to exchange-rate changes.

Both privatization and FDI could create some common problems. Clearly, one has to expect a short term increase in unemployment: overmanning in socialist firms was typical and private owners guided by the pursuit of profits will reduce

---

[20] The Robinson condition requires for a normal reaction of the trade balance that

$$D_{X*} D_X\left(E_{X*} + \frac{X}{X*}E_X + \frac{X}{X*}\right) + E_{X*} D_X\left(1 - \frac{X}{X*}\right) > E_X E_{X*}\left[\frac{X}{X*}\mathrm{A}\right];$$

$$\text{with } \mathrm{A} = D_X + \frac{X*}{X}D_X + \frac{X*}{X}.$$

overmanning and raise labor productivity by investment. Moreover, efficiency gains often can be only reaped if outsourcing is considered as a means to cut production costs and if new opportunities for imports from world markets are exploited. Privatization could reduce tax revenues because private entrepreneurs engage in shadow economic activities, while foreign investors typically use transfer pricing to reduce tax payments in host countries; even in the US, with its effective Internal Revenue Service and established tax systems, the share of foreign firms that pays no taxes is much higher than that of US firms.

If a critical minimum of foreign investors can be mobilized this could have a positive effect on growth, exports and future tax receipts, which, in turn, could help to create political stability and to accelerate the costly process of privatization, the restructuring of firms and the retraining of labor and management. Substantial progress in privatization itself could become a starting point for rising capital inflows and an appreciation of the currency, because, with a competitive private industry, foreign firms could become more interested in acquiring assets and investing in greenfield projects. Equally, if privatization fails, FDI flows will be sluggish. If FDI flows can never be mobilized significantly, the private sector might never be able to achieve economic parity with the OECD countries, where most technology flows are represented by intra-company flows and cross-licensing among multinational companies (UNCTC 1988). As much as there might be a potential for a virtuous cycle of privatization and FDI, there could also be a vicious cycle of protracted state ownership and lack of FDI. In major EC countries and the US foreign ownership represents between 2% and 10% of the capital stock; shares of between 4% and 45% (Belgium) in industrial output or sales; and about one-third of OECD exports is intra-company trade within the network of multinational companies. MNCs are typically in the tradables sector and services, provided that such activities are allowed by host countries and not reserved for state providers or domestic firms. Therefore, MNCs are important for the expansion of the tradables sector in general and might be crucial in accelerating the move to modern economic structures characterized by a rapid growth of the service industry. Figure 6.2 summarizes the major effects of privatization and FDI inflows.

6.4 Summary and Normative Conclusions

It has been shown that FDI has been relevant for NIC's economic growth, and that transforming economies could also gain from FDI inflows. Such inflows are, however, only to be expected if privatization can be organized as a sustainable and

Figure 6.2
Effects of Privatization and FDI in Systemic Transformation

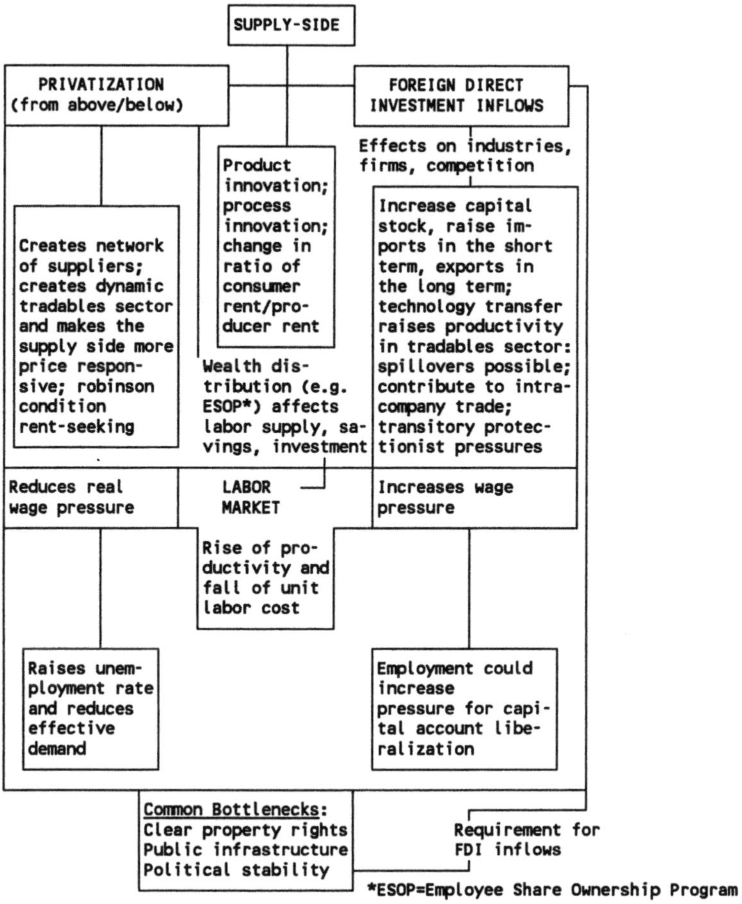

efficient process. FDI and privatization will fundamentally affect the supply side of the economy and directly contribute to the transformation of economic systems. These desired characteristics, at the same time, create problems because the transmission process of policy impulses will change as supply elasticities and price-setting behavior change. There are some new macroeconomic aspects of FDI which are mainly related to the fact that it increases the production potential and affects export performance and economic growth in various ways. Labor markets and foreign-exchange markets will be strongly affected by high FDI inflows and comprehensive privatization.

Privatization represents a complex adjustment problem in the transforming economies. It is tempting for many of these countries to simply imitate the private-public sector mix of west European economies. The energy sector, transportation and telecommunication would then remain regulated state monopolies. One may, however, doubt that a traditional (European) private-public mix is consistent with a growth-oriented strategy. The provision of telecommunication services, mass transportation and energy can contribute greatly to widening markets and the reduction of costs for many industries which rely on inputs from those industries.

It might be that an optimal privatization strategy would actually start with privatizing telecommunication and public utilities on a competitive basis; small countries might consider joining neighboring countries in order to create markets sufficiently big to allow competitive provision of services. Even major infrastructure projects such as building new highways could be organized within the private sector. If new highways are administrated by government one might at least consider a toll system which allows for the introduction of a pay-as-you-use financing scheme. Tolls differentiated according to rush hours and non-rush hours could help to optimally utilize scarce infrastructure capital and encourage firms to organize shifts and choose production locations in accordance with crowding problems. Systemic transformation indeed offers some unique options and opportunities here. So far, Hungary is the only country in the ex-CMEA area which has envisaged some innovative schemes in the provision of infrastructure services. Former CMEA countries willing to join the EC might particularly benefit from anticipating the continuing process of deregulation and privatization in western Europe. The demise of the state as an entrepreneur has begun in western Europe, where institutional and economic integration encourage a new kind of handshake between the visible hand of the national or multinational firm and the invisible hand of market forces (Welfens 1992d).

The *big privatization*—focusing on big state firms—should be embedded in a long-term program of growth policies, because removing obstacles to economic growth and actively encouraging economic actors to take a long view in investment and savings is success-promising. These policies should be combined with an outward-oriented strategy that helps focus decisions concerning investment and human capital formation. Without rapid economic growth it will not be possible to attract considerable FDI inflows nor catch up with western Europe. The paradox problem is that without massive FDI inflows prospects for rapid economic growth are poor. Given the importance of political risk in FDI decisions, strictly avoiding political instabilities is vital for creating FDI inflows in eastern Europe.

Unfortunately, for geopolitical, economic, ethnic and historical reasons, instability in one major part of the ex-CMEA area might destabilize the whole region.

Privatization from below—that is, the active promotion of new business establishments, is a much neglected element in most privatization programs in eastern Europe. The move to a dominant private-business sector will bring greater income inequalities and a greater need for adjustment at the micro level; this characteristic of capitalism will not be easily accepted in the formerly socialist economies where people often associate market economies simply with a higher standard of living. Privatization cannot be organized without regard for unemployment consequences. While transitory unemployment cannot be avoided, however, market-clearing mechanisms can be improved in various ways. Reducing housing shortages and providing tax incentives for greater mobility are two possible steps. There are many more aspects of privatization that require a more comprehensive analysis.

The fact that sales proceeds from privatization have been lower than initially expected in various transforming countries is a budget problem only from a short-term perspective; and the only to the extent that one overlooks the fact that state firms in western Europe typically operate at a loss.[21] If privatization means rising output and rising exports, the rise of *future* wages, profits and tax receipts should be of greater interest than short-term impacts.

The case of Hungary, which had a share of FDI of 15% in capital formation in 1991-92 and seems ready to accept figures even around 30%—similar to those in Austria—has shown foreign investment can play a crucial role in systemic transformation. However, low FDI inflows into Slovakia, Poland, Romania, Bulgaria and the CIS indicate that the ex-CMEA countries have not exploited their potential for attracting foreign investors. If progress in FDI is rapid, privatization can proceed more slowly, although it might be politically wise to use the momentum from FDI inflows to privatize at least the tradables sector quickly. If neither FDI nor privatization gain momentum, the transformation could fail both economically and politically. High FDI inflows are required for rapid modernization in eastern Europe. Larger markets in host countries and access to larger oversees markets—such as the EC—could indeed attract considerable FDI inflows provided

---

21 This might be economically efficient in certain cases: (a) if there are positive external effects exceeding those under private ownership; (b) if there are falling marginal costs which would not allow profitable private production under the efficiency rule that the marginal willingness to pay (prices) should be equal to marginal productions costs.

that political stability can be maintained. Larger markets in the ex-CMEA countries could be created by free-trade areas; the disintegration of Czechoslovakia and of the Soviet Union points, into the opposite direction, however, and the rising political instability in the area also reduces the scope for high FDI inflows. Access to EC markets can probably be expected in the long term only by Hungary, former Czechoslovakia and Poland in the long term.

Privatization raises a series of problems in systemic transformation, and the pace of privatization has been very slow in all ex-CMEA countries except for the special case of eastern Germany. Momentum in the privatization process is important if a sustainable trajectory for transformation is to be established. From a political point of view one should start with privatization, where resistance is weakest. From an economic point of view one should focus on whole industries, in order to generate gains from competition, and first on those which are important for technological progress, economic growth and export growth. Given the problem of foreign indebtedness, the latter would help prevent the foreign-exchange constraint from binding for maximizing economic growth.

Combining privatization and FDI inflows in a meaningful way is important. Without a competitive-supplier, industry few MNCs will consider major investment in central and eastern Europe. This holds especially because the locational advantages of host countries are few and because economic growth in these countries is moderate at best. Foreign indebtedness need not be a major impediment to mobilizing FDI inflows as the Hungarian case shows, but monetary instability, complex regulations and bureaucratic inflexibility can prevent FDI inflows.

We have shown that it is possible to identify certain criteria that suggest where and when privatization should be accelerated. FDI should generate positive external effects, but conflict over profit income in transforming economies might make it difficult to fully accept FDI inflows. Policies that encourage parallel inflows and thereby create competition, while possibly broadening the group of source countries, could be useful on the one hand; this could require an opening up of industries with international oligopolistic structures first to FDI inflows, because in oligopolistic industries FDI often occurs in clusters—rivals from various home countries will follow each other. Thus, both the amount of FDI attracted and the regional diversity of source countries could be greater in the first critical stage than if non-oligopolistic industries were opened up for FDI inflows in the beginning of the transformation process. Some ex-CMEA countries might consider special tax preferences for foreign investors, and could try to convice governments of major

FDI source countries to stimulate FDI outflows to eastern Europe by various means. On the other hand, industries in which the ratio of the elasticity of demand to that of supply is high could be opened up to foreign investment first (Welfens 1992b).

The main prospective sources of capital are the EC countries, Switzerland, Japan and the United States. Non-European FDI inflows are dominant in Hungary, while former Czechoslovakia and Poland are dominated by European investment inflows, mostly from Germany. Governments in the West might have to actively support FDI outflows if systemic transformation is to be completed successfully. In western Europe a major motive for such a policy stance could be an interest in avoiding rising immigration pressure from eastern Europe.

Given the enormous role of political risk in eastern Europe, capital is not very likely to flow from western Europe to eastern Europe. Lucas (1990) emphasized the political problem in the North-South context, and indeed this problem might be even more crucial within Europe in a West-East context. Moreover, the role of skilled human capital for economic growth also emphasized by Lucas could be crucial with respect to migration in Europe. If skilled and young people move massively to western Europe, prospects for raising per capita income in eastern Europe would be strongly reduced, while opportunities to increase per capita income in western Europe would hardly increase. The serious lack of skilled management personnel in the ex-CMEA area is already a crucial bottleneck factor. Without sufficient economic growth the transformation process probably cannot be sustained politically. A sober analysis of the extremely difficult problems in central and eastern Europe is required, and modest expectations on the side of politicians and the public could be a vital element in solving the transition problems. From the perspective of the rich OECD countries support for privatization and FDI are crucial. Probably, the strongest support would be to open up OECD markets in a gradual and credible manner; governments in OECD countries, as well as the business community, would have to envisage the challenges of enormous structural adjustments that are required if central and eastern Europe is to become a major exporter to OECD markets. However, it was difficult for OECD countries to accept the *invasion* from Asian NICs, and there is little reason to believe that the challenge from the ex-CMEA area—with real wages below some NIC countries and technological potentials sometimes higher—would be easier to cope with. Instead of overambitious goals and unrealistic promises in western Europe, a gradual and credible liberalization in trade policies would probably be most helpful.

References

Aghion, P. M., and P. Howitt. 1992. A Model of Growth Through Creative Destruction. *Econometrica* 60: 323–51.

Bailey, M. J., and G. S. Tavlas. 1991. Exchange Rate Variability and Direct Investment. *Annals of the American Academy of Political and Social Science* 516 (July): 106–16.

Balcerowicz, L., and P. J. J. Welfens, eds. 1988. *Innovationsdynamik im Systemvergleich*. Heidelberg: Physica Verlag.

Bhagwati, J. N. 1989. *Protectionism*. Cambridge: MIT Press.

Blankart, C. B., and G. Knieps. 1992. Network Evolution. In H. Wagener, ed. *On the Theory and Policy of Systemic Change*. Heidelberg: Physica Verlag.

Blomstrom, M. 1989. *Foreign Investment and Spillovers*. London: Routledge.

Blomstrom, M., R. E. Lipsey, and M. Zejan. 1992. A Cross-Country Study of Growth in Developing Countries. Paper prepared for conference, Historical Perspectives on the International Convergence of Productivity, New York University, 23–24 April.

Berg, A., and J. D. Sachs. 1992. Structural Adjustment and International Trade in Eastern Europe: The Case of Poland. *Economic Policy* 14 (April): 118–73.

BIS (Bank of International Settlements). 1992. *Annual Report* 62. Basel: BIS.

Caves, R. E. 1982. *Multinational Enterprise and Economic Analysis*. Cambridge: MIT Press.

Chung, H. L., and E. D. Ramstetter. 1991. Direct Investment and Structural Change in Korean Manufacturing. In E. D. Ramstetter, ed. *Direct Foreign Investment in Asia's Developing Economies and Structural Change in the Asia-Pacific Region*. Boulder, Colo.: Westview Press.

Collins, S. M.. 1990. Lessons from Korean Economic Growth. *American Economic Review, Papers and Proceedings* 80: 104–7.

Collins, S. M., and D. Rodrik. 1991. *Eastern Europe and the Soviet Union in the World Economy*. Washington, D.C.: Institute for International Economics.

Dunning, J. H. 1981. *International Production and the Multinational Enterprise*. London: Allen & Unwin.

Economist. 1993. A Survey of Multinationals, 27 March.

Feder, G. 1982. On Exports and Economic Growth. *Journal of Development Economics* 12: 59–73.

Graham, E. M., and P. R. Krugman. 1989. *Foreign Direct Investment in the United States*. Washington, D.C.: Institute for International Economics.

Grossman, G. M., and E. Helpman. 1991. *Innovation and Growth in the Global Economy*. Cambridge: MIT Press.

Hoen, H. W., and E. H. van Leeuwen. 1991. Upgrading and Relative Competitiveness in Manufacturing Trade: Eastern Europe versus the Newly Industrializing Economies. *Weltwirtschaftliches Archiv* 127: 368–79.

Inotai, A. 1991. Liberalization and Foreign Direct Investment. In A. Köves and P. Marer, eds. *Foreign Economic Liberalization*. Boulder, Colo.: Westview Press.

Inotai, A. 1992. Foreign Direct Investments in Reforming CMEA Countries: Facts, Lessons and Perspectives. In M. W. Klein and P. J. J. Welfens, eds. *Multinationals in the New Europe and Global Trade*. Berlin: Springer Verlag.

Jasinski, P. 1990. *Two Models of Privatization in Poland: A Critical Assessment*. Vol. 3, *Communist Economies*.

Jasinski, P., and P. J. J. Welfens. 1993. *Privatization and Foreign Direct Investment in Transforming Economies*. Forthcoming.

Koo, B. Y. 1985. The Role of Foreign Direct Investment in Korea's Recent Economic Growth. In W. Galenson, ed. *Foreign Trade and Investment: Economic Growth in the Newly Industrializing Asian Countries*. Madison, Wis.: University of Wisconsin Press.

Krueger, A. O. 1990. Asian Trade and Growth Lessons. *American Economic Review, Papers and Proceedings* 80: 108–12.

Krueger, A. O. 1992. Capital flows and Trade in a Dynamic Perspective. In H. Siebert, ed. *Capital Flows in the World Economy*. Tübingen: Mohr.

Klein, M., and P. J. J. Welfens, eds. 1992. *Multinationals in the New Europe and Global Trade*. Berlin: Springer Verlag.

Kornai, J. 1990. *The Road to a Free Economy*. New York: Norton.

Lee, C. H. and E. D. Ramstetter 1991. Direct Investment and Industrialization in Korean Manufacturing. In E. D. Ramstetter, ed. *Direct Foreign Investment in Asia's Developing Economies and Structural Change in the Asia-Pacific Region*. Boulder, Colo.: Westview Press.

Lim, L. Y. C., and P. E. Fong. 1991. *Foreign Direct Investment and Industrialization in Malaysia, Singapore, Taiwan and Thailand*. Paris: OECD.

Lipton D., and J. D. Sachs. 1990. Privatization in Eastern Europe: The Case of Poland. *Brookings Papers on Economic Activity* 2: 293–341.

Lucas, R. E. 1988. On the Mechanics of Economic Development. *Journal of Monetary Economics* 22: 3–42.

Lucas, R. E. 1990. Why Doesn't Capital Flow from Rich to Poor Countries. *American Economic Review, Papers and Proceedings* 80: 92–96.

Mansfield, E., and A. Romeo. 1980. Technology Transfer to Overseas Subsidiaries by U.S.-based Firms. *Quarterly Journal of Economics* 95: 737–50.

Murrell, P. 1990. *The Nature of Socialist Economies*. Princeton, N.J.: Princeton University Press.

Murrell, P. 1991. Evolution in Economics and in the Economic Reform of the Centrally Planned Economies. University of Maryland (May). Photocopy.

Pascha, W. 1990. Dritte Welt im Aufbruch: Ostasiatische Schwellenländer als neue weltwirtschaftliche Entwicklungspole? In D. Cassel, ed. *Wirtschaftssysteme im Umbruch*. Munich: Vahlen.

Romer, P. M. 1990. Endogenous Technological Change. *Journal of Political Economy* 98: 71–102.

Schive C. and J.-H. Tu. 1991. Foreign Firms and Structural Change in Taiwan. In E. Ramstetter, ed. *Direct Foreign Investment in Asia's Developing Economies and Structural Change in the Asia-Pacific Region*. Boulder, Colo.: Westview Press.

Sengupta, J. K. 1991. Rapid Growth in the NICs in Asia: Test of the New Growth Theory for Korea. *Kyklos* 44: 561–80.

Song, B. 1991. *The Rise of the Korean Economy*. Oxford: Oxford University Press.

Tilly, R. H. 1992. German Banks and Foreign Investment in Eastern and Central Europe Before 1939. Paper prepared for conference, The Economic Future of Central Europe, University of Minneapolis, 16–18 April.

Tyler, W. G. 1981. Growth and Export Expansion in Developing Countries: Some Empirical Evidence. *Journal of Development Economics* 9: 121–30.

UNECE (United Nations Economic Commission for Europe). 1992. *Economic Survey of Europe in 1991–1992*. New York: UNECE.

UNCTC (United Nations Center on Transnational Corporations). 1988. *Transnational Corporations in World Development*. New York: UNCTC.

UNCTC. 1992. *World Investment Report 1992: Transnational Corporations as Engines of Growth*. New York: UNCTC.

UNIDO (United Nations Industrial Development Organization). 1987. *The Republic of*

Korea. Industrial Development Review Series. Vienna: UNIDO.

Wang, J.-Y., and M. Blomstrom. 1992. Foreign Investment and Technology Transfer. *European Economic Review* 36: 137–55.

Welfens, P. J. J. 1985. *Theorie und Praxis angebotsorientierter Stabilitätspolitik*. Baden-Baden: Nomos.

Welfens, P. J. J. 1990. *Internationalisierung von Wirtschaft und Wirtschaftspolitik*. Berlin: Springer Verlag.

Welfens, P. J. J., ed. 1992a. *Economic Aspects of German Unification*. Berlin: Springer Verlag.

Welfens, P. J. J. 1992b. *Market-Oriented Systemic Transformations in Eastern Europe*. Berlin: Springer Verlag.

Welfens, P. J. J. 1992c. Privatization, M & As, and Interfirm Cooperation in the EC: Improved Prospects for Innovation? In F. M. Scherer and M. Perlman eds. *Entrepreneurship, Technological Innovation, and Economic Growth: Studies in the Schumpeterian Tradition*. Ann Arbor, Mich.: University of Michigan Press.

Welfens, P. J. J. 1992d. Foreign Investment in the East European Transition. *Management International Review* 32: 199–218.

Welfens, P. J. J. 1993. *The Single Market and the Eastern Enlargement of the EC*. Heidelberg: Springer Verlag. Forthcoming.

Williamson, J., ed. 1991. *Currency Convertibility in Eastern Europe*. Washington, D.C.: Institute for International Economics.

7 The Political Economy of Privatization

Alfred Schipke

7.1 Introduction

Until recently, research on privatization has focused almost exclusively on whether, and under what circumstances, a change in ownership leads to gains in efficiency and increases in social welfare. One of the fundamental questions has been whether ownership or competition is the key variable. With an emphasis on allocative efficiency, the focus has been on how to increase competition, especially in industries having the characteristics of natural monopolies, externalities and public goods. In these cases measures of regulation and deregulation seem to be more crucial than ownership.[1]

However, Leibenstein (1966) has already demonstrated empirically how important it is to overcome "x-inefficiencies" which are the result of failures internal to the company. Depending on the organizational form of a company and the institutional framework in which it operates, managers are able to shirk and often lack incentives to employ resources in the most efficient way. A whole range of literature has focused on these internal failures and how to overcome them.[2] The mere existence of a market for corporate control, and, hence, the potential threat of takeovers, seems to assure that the separation of ownership and management in the case of private corporations will keep the interests of the principal and the agent aligned. The absence of such a market for corporate control is considered to be one of the major reasons why state-owned enterprises (SOEs) are internally less efficient than their private counterparts.

I am thankful to Thomas Apolte and Dieter Cassel for their comments.

[1] For an overview of the relationship between deregulation, privatization and efficiency see Pera 1989. Vining and Boardman (1992) present a taxonomy of empirical findings.

[2] For a general treatment of the issue see Hart and Holmström 1987.

Another area of research has focused on the process of privatization, that is, how SOEs can be transferred to the private sector in the most efficient manner. In the search for an optimal privatization method various auction models have been adopted (Maskin 1992)[3]. Yet, the political side of privatization has been almost completely neglected so far. Ultimately, privatization decisions are being made by politicians who are maximizing their own welfare rather than that of society at large. Economic theory suggests that private ownership is preferable to public if it makes society better off; hence, the ultimate rationale for the transfer of ownership should be efficiency. Nevertheless, past experiences reveal that privatization takes place regardless of efficiency considerations and that, frequently, the chosen and implemented privatization methods are certainly not—at least from a normative point of view—optimal. The reason why, is, of course, fairly simple: privatization is highly political since it affects the distribution of wealth and income.

If the assumption is made that the utility of the political representatives in office is higher than those out of office and, hence, that politicians are likely to maximize the probability of being (re-)elected, one could argue that a representative democracy is a political system that leads to Pareto-optimal outcomes. In such a system, political officials privatize state companies if doing so would improve social welfare. Such a perfect political market does not exist. First, it is simplistic to assume that public interest can be captured in a well-defined objective function and that government has an interest in maximizing such a utility function. Second, informational asymmetries between elected politicians and voters make monitoring a costly endeavor. Since the public votes once every few years and is concerned about numerous issues, the voter's probability of influencing the outcome is close to zero; there is no incentive for him or her to acquire costly information. Lastly, the costs and benefits of re-distributing the assets are not likely to be distributed equally. Those groups that tend to lose from privatization will have higher incentives to monitor the behavior of politicians than the average voter. The potential magnitude of the redistribution of income and wealth is especially high in Former Socialist Countries (FSCs) since the majority of all productive assets are in the hand of the state. Those who are likely to lose out in the process of privatization have large incentives to participate in the political decision-making process in order to defend the *status quo* and actively influence the process of

---

[3] Rees (1985) develops a theoretical model which focuses on the process of privatization. See also Bös 1987.

redistribution.

This chapter will shed some light on the political dimensions of privatization. It starts out in section 7.2 with an analysis of the role of the politics of privatization in market economies. Section 7.3 assesses the circumstances of political and economic transformation and how conditions in FSCs differ from those in western economies. In section 7.4, the public choice rationale is applied to privatization. Based on these arguments, section 7.5 makes recommendations on how to overcome potential political opposition. An outline of an optimal privatization program from a political-economy viewpoint is given in section 7.6, and two quite different FSCs are used to assess privatization strategies and identify potential shortcomings. Some general conclusions are drawn in section 7.7.

7.2 The Politics of Privatization in Market Economies

Countries as different as the United Kingdom and Argentina, for example, demonstrate that economic efficiency is at most an accidental, if positive, side-effect of privatization. Privatization has just become another instrument for policymakers to use to maximize their own welfare irrespective of whether this leads to an increase in the welfare of society at large. In the case of the UK, Heald (1989) argues that

> the rationale for the (privatization) programme was invented after the event. In particular, economists have attempted to adopt and redirect the programme, highlighting the efficiency rationale, with limited, but variable, success. Much of the telling criticism has (at least implicitly) come from a market-oriented perspective, namely that the government was not taking its own efficiency objectives seriously enough.

For almost a decade, the UK engaged in privatization methods that were concerned with maximizing political support, and numerous measures were undertaken to ensure that the Conservative government under Thatcher would seize the traditional Labour voter and that the general population would perceive privatization as a success story. In order to reach the first goal, the government pursued a strategy of widespread ownership (dubbed "people's capitalism") by underpricing shares and rationing the number of shares sold to each individual buyer. In addition, it provided financial incentives to the new stockholders to hold on to their financial assets and discourage immediate resale. Employee ownership was encouraged as well (Vickers and Yarrow 1988). The resulting (and unsustainable) spread-of-ownership undermined effective ownership control which would have required a certain degree of ownership concentration. In order to build popular support for the program, the government practically guaranteed the commercial viability of the companies by continuing to protect the respective industries from foreign competition, neglecting to de-monopolize and failing to set-up an adequate regulatory framework. Hence, privatization in Britain, while politically successful failed to channel scarce resources to their most productive use. Polls that were taken after the first companies had been sold via initial public offerings (IPOs) to employees and a large number of citizens demonstrated that 57% of the people who bought stock in one of the privatized companies—including factory laborers, the hard core of Labour's historic base—planned to vote Conservative in the June 1987 election. Exit polls in that election indicated that indeed 6 out of 10 people who owned shares voted Tory (HBS 1988, 12). The political rationale behind such public policies is, of course, that the *lucky* investors enjoying windfall profits as a result of the difference between the low offering price (undervaluation) and the opening price on the day of quotation—are aware of their gain, whereas the taxpayer—being the loser in this transfer game—is more likely to be indifferent because of his or her marginal stake.

Short-term political objectives as the *ultima ratio* for privatization are also fairly common in developing countries. Huge budget deficits and the associated tendency to hyperinflation have motivated numerous governments to cash in their state assets in order to find a quick budget fix and claim political victory shortly thereafter. Since efficiency improvements would often go beyond the scope of a political voting cycle, they are low on the list of public-policy measures. Indeed, governments are often willing to sacrifice economic efficiency in order to maximize sales proceeds by granting monopoly power via exclusive licenses and promising to keep national industries protected for a certain period of time.

7.3 Economies in Transition

In the case of FSCs, there seems to be general agreement that the introduction of a market economy based on decentralized decision-making and private property is a prerequisite for economic growth and higher standards of living. The discussion about efficiency in market economies focuses on market and organizational failures. It also considers whether public ownership is the right response or whether private ownership with other forms of government intervention, such as anti-trust legislation or regulation, would lead to a more efficient allocation of resources. If natural-monopoly arguments originally justified state ownership, the question arises whether technological innovations have changed the nature of the industry such that industries with formerly high sunk costs have lower barriers to entry today. The existence of public ownership, especially in protected industries with public monopolies can be questioned. Telecommunication serves as a good example, where technological breakthroughs such as satellite technology have led to close substitutes for traditional telephone services. In western market economies, the efficiency argument has become the focus of economic research devoted to finding an optimal mix of private and public ownership in combination with other forms of government intervention to overcome market failure. The question can largely be ignored, at least at this stage, in transforming FSCs. The discussion about whether certain companies should stay public is marginal, since the number of socialist enterprises in industries without market failures is extremely large. This is because the creation of competition was not part of the political and economic rationale of socialist decision-makers and companies in traditional industries were established as domestic monopolies.

Another central difference between FSCs and western economies is that the objectives of the governments in FSCs, at least at the beginning of the reform program (t_0), seem to be more in line with those of normative economics. The economic collapse of the socialist system gives the newly-elected governments a broadly based mandate to create an efficient market economy based on decentralized decision-making and private ownership. Since this is probably also the perception of the government, one can argue that, at t_0, we basically have the unique circumstance of a benevolent government aiming at implementing an efficient market system. In other words, governments at t_0 are actually seeking to achieve a Pareto-optimal outcome. By doing so, the government expects to maximize the probability of getting re-elected. In this initial period, both social objectives and political objectives coincide. It is not surprising that the first democratically-elected governments perceived their mandate in exactly that way. In this respect, the economic reform programs of Leszek Balcerowicz in Poland, Vaclav Klaus in Czechoslovakia or Yegor Gaidar in Russia are almost identical. The situation differs from the one in established market economies because elections in western economies are concerned with a wide variety of conflicting issues. The political market is less likely to lead to a Pareto-optimal outcome. A political-economy approach would help to explain why countries such as the United Kingdom pursue certain objectives such as privatization. Since in FSCs the objectives are given as a result of the systemic change, a political-economy framework can help to determine how political constraints can be overcome to successfully implement certain policies such as privatization.

7.4 Firm Behavior in the Transition and Efficiency Gains from Privatization: The Public Choice Rationale

Although concepts of standard microeconomic theory and industrial organization cannot readily be applied to explain the behavior of socialist enterprises in centrally-planned economies, they help explain the behavior of state-owned enterprises during the transition period. One of the major caveats for the application of standard economic theory to socialist enterprises is the way decisions are being made concerning both output and prices. This limitation, however, has almost completely been eliminated because of the decentralization of decision making—a phenomenon which was already initiated with reform socialism, and the liberalization of prices. Prices have been liberated in almost all eastern European countries as a part of the initial stabilization programs. Due to a change in property rights—which is discussed below—managers of state-owned companies today have almost complete control over outputs and prices. One of the legacies of socialism, however, still prevails: the degree of industrial concentration and the relative size of the firms. Newbery and Kattuman (1992) calculate that socialist enterprises are more than ten times the average size of those in Western market economies, and that small- and medium-sized enterprises are rare. During economic transformation it can be expected that a large number of state-owned enterprise will enjoy monopoly power. The only countervailing forces are trade liberalization and the development of a dynamic private sector. The potential competitive threat of such forces will be limited. First, trade barriers will only slowly be reduced; moreover, the process will also depend on the policies of other trading blocks or nations, such as the EC.[4] Furthermore, trade liberalization has an impact only on the tradable sector of the economy. Second, the lack of credibility of private institutions (such as corporate and foreign investment laws) and the absence of developed capital markets will limit competition from new private entrants. Such competition is most likely to be confined to less capital-intensive industries and the service sector. Therefore, the potential gains from privatization can be analyzed within the simple framework of a partial equilibrium model of monopoly.

---

[4] In countries such as Poland, where trade barriers were almost completely eliminated at the beginning of the reform program, tariffs have lately been raised again.

For the following analysis it will be assumed that socialist enterprises enjoy monopoly power during the transition process and that the mere transfer of ownership to the private sector does not change the level of industry concentration.[5] The positive effects of privatization are hence limited to the effects of instilling the profit motive. By defining real owners and creating a market for corporate control, some of the typical internal failures of public enterprises will be overcome and the companies will become more x-efficient. In the case of eastern Europe, labor productivity will increase dramatically as a result of privatization, since socialist enterprises suffer from overmanning. The effect is presented in figure 7.1. Demand is linear $q_d = q(p)$ with $dp/dq < 0$ and marginal costs (MC) are assumed to be constant. Since privatization does not have an immediate effect on monopoly power, the monopoly price and quantity is set irrespective of ownership status. As profit maximizers, the new owners have an incentive to minimize the costs of employing and combining labor, capital, and other factors of production in the most efficient way. Even with continued monopoly power, society is better off by an amount:

$$\Delta w = \int_{p^p}^{p^s} q_d(p)\, dp, \tag{1}$$

with $p^s > p^p$, the prices before and after privatization, respectively. Instilling the profit motive in eastern Europe will certainly improve efficiency and benefit consumers. In addition to static increases in efficiency, it can be expected that FSCs will also experience large dynamic efficiency improvements.

However, the per-capita gain of consumers is only marginal. Hence, their willingness to articulate politically their preferences in favor of privatization will be limited since the associated costs of doing so would, almost certainly, outweigh any benefits. This is in sharp contrast to those groups who are to lose from privatization and the reallocation of resources. The per-capita stake of ministerial bureaucrats, workers, and directors of the socialist enterprises is quite high. The absence of real owners and the drive for cost minimization allowed them to reap non-pecuniary benefits such as special privileges, access to rationed goods or job

[5] As Lipton and Sachs (1990) point out, the danger that industrial monopolies will survive is rather small. On the one hand, a large number of monopolies are so specific that deregulation and the development of a private sector will undermine these artificial monopolies through the production of close substitutes. On the other hand, trade liberalization will lead to increases in allocative efficiency, at least in the tradable sector.

Figure 7.1
Efficiency and the Public Choice Rationale

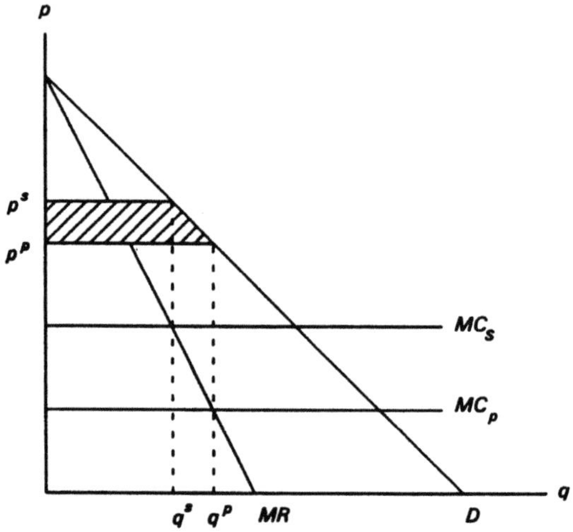

security. Certainly, they have an incentive to fend off any measure which would threaten their *status quo*. As long as the cost of maintaining the *status quo* is less than or equal to Δw, these groups are likely oppose privatization.

7.5 Overcoming Obstacles to Privatization

Drastic regime changes create a political void and undermine the functioning of existing institutions. The collapse of socialism weakened or eliminated, for example, the all-encompassing power of communist institutions. The weakening of political institutions strengthens the power of individual political leaders and enables them to implement reform measures even if they are associated with high social costs and a massive redistribution of income and wealth. Economic austerity measures implemented immediately after the rise of new regimes both in developing countries and in eastern Europe were widely accepted or, at least, did not face organized political opposition. After such a regime change, the population at large seems to be willing to accept short-term sacrifices (in terms of lower real income) if the government measures are credible and promise to result in higher standards of living in the medium run. Over time, however, political interest groups begin to regain strength and start building new coalitions. Hence, the political power of opposing interest groups is a function of time. *Ceteris paribus*, the cost of overcoming opposition increases over time as well. At the same time, the government's general mandate to go ahead with drastic reform measures diminishes as the negative effects of these measures in the form of high unemployment and lower levels of real income becomes tangible (Przeworksi 1991).

If the drastic measures of a comprehensive privatization program are not designed and implemented immediately after the collapse of old institutions, new alliances ranged against the redistribution of wealth will emerge which could paralyze the reform process. In this case, it becomes crucial to design privatization programs which may depart from first-best solutions based purely on efficiency considerations but which take political constraints into consideration.

Based on the public-choice rationale mentioned above, two strategies could be pursued either separately or jointly: (a) reduce the transaction costs for those favoring privatization and (b) buy out those groups who will be stripped off their privileges. With respect to the first, those who stand to gain from privatization, such as consumers and taxpayers, are facing prohibitive high marginal costs to voice their preferences explicitly and in an organized manner compared to their potential marginal gains in form of better and cheaper goods and services. Since the efficiency gains would be spread over the entire population, they would be infinitesimal (Hanke and Walters 1990). A transition government which advocates privatization should then design a program which allows pro-privatization interest groups to coalesce and voice their preferences. Some of the political power of the opposing interest groups could thus be offset. The pro-privatization government can reduce the information costs to the individual by running large advertizing campaigns, thus spreading information costs among all taxpayers. The fact that most of the governments in FSCs have refrained from large campaigns seems to indicate a naïve assumption that the population at large understood the importance of privatization as a prerequisite for future economic growth and prosperity and that they would be a sufficient pressure group to counterbalance any opposition to privatization.

Although any transition government is in a position to reduce the information cost, it is more problematic to institute a system which would allow pro-privatization citizens to voice their opinion at a low per capita cost. The remaining alternative is for the government to compensate opposing interest groups for their expected losses from privatization. Unlike in western market economies, such compensation would have to exceed the discounted value of expected future incomes and include non-pecuniary forms of compensation. This is because a large part of the manager's income in socialist enterprises derived from having access to non-traded goods in official markets (or if they were traded, they had access to higher quality products including imports from the west), being able to avoid queuing, and even less tangible advantages such as being part of the political elite, and so on. The same applies to other vested interest groups such as ministerial bureaucrats.[6] Since there is no market for non-pecuniary goods, it will initially be difficult for the government to assess the potential costs of buying out. Since the efficiency gains from privatization are expected to be high in eastern Europe, it can be assumed that the social savings from privatization will be greater than the cost associated with buying out.

Objections to buying out interest groups in former socialist countries can be raised on ethical grounds. To accept the notion that powerful interest groups can paralyze privatization by transferring part of the resultant social savings to them implies acknowledging that their property-right claims are valid and justified. To compensate workers and workers' councils of socialist enterprises might be less problematic; however, this is not so in the case of directors and old bureaucrats who often represented the old *nomenklatura* and profited from and supported the socialist system in the first place. Buying them out not only gives them a headstart in the new system, creating an uneven playing-field right from the outset, but also solidifies their property-right claims. The initial distribution of wealth would continue to reflect old injustices. However, with the exception of cases where criminal charges can be brought, political reality might suggest that a buy-out strategy is an acceptable second-best solution. This is especially true if these groups are powerful enough to paralyze privatization and hence, to undermine any stabilization effort due the continuation of the soft budget constraint, endangering both the entire economic reform program and political stability at large.[7] A first-best program which focuses on the maximization of efficiency is bound to fail whenever interest groups are organized and powerful and stand to lose from privatization. In FSCs this appears to be both a function of (a) the initial distribution and degree of attenuation of property rights, and (b) the time that elapses between the collapse of the old system, the initiation of economic reform measures and the beginning of the privatization program. The more time passes by,

---

[6] On political constraints see Bienen and Waterbury 1989.

[7] For a discussion of the soft budget constraint of socialist enterprises see Kornai 1986.

the more costly it becomes to buy out an increasingly better-organized group of privatization opponents.

The above analysis suggests that to minimize the political cost of privatization,

- privatization should be part of the initial reform program;
- privatization should begin immediately;
- privatization should be implemented rapidly; and
- political constraints should be taken into consideration right from the outset.

Standard privatization methods, that is, those which have been applied widely in industrialized and developing countries (such as IPOs and public tenders) fulfill these conditions only partially. The most severe disadvantage of these methods is that they are extremely time consuming and require institutions and information which are the very outcome of the transition to a market economy and hence cannot be a precondition for privatization. Among the more recent and innovative privatization methods, the voucher or coupon scheme is more effective in dealing with the political constraints. Whether the vouchers are being distributed for free or sold at a token price, whether they serve as a means to purchase company shares directly or via financial intermediaries, they assure that ownership rights are defined rapidly—at least legally—hence providing the foundation for increases in efficiency.[8] Although they meet the condition of speed, vouchers are viable only as long as interest groups are weak and unorganized. Once these groups have enough time to establish themselves and begin to engage in negotiations with the government over their claims of ownership rights, voucher privatization has to be accompanied by specific concessions to managers, workers and other vested interest groups. To assure the success of the program at a later point in time (t_1), a certain part of the shares has to be earmarked for these vetoing interest groups. Again, the price tag is likely to depend on the amount of time between the initiation of economic transformation at t_0 and mass privatization. Conceptually, at point t_2, the cost of buying them out would equal the potential gains from doing so. After this point, the only viable alternative for the development of an efficient economy is through the establishment of new private businesses.

7.6 Experiences from Eastern Europe

At this point in time, an analysis of eastern European privatization strategies has

[8] Borensztein and Kumar (1991) provide an overview of different mass-privatization schemes.

to be speculative and inconclusive. Nevertheless, certain patterns have become obvious. In the following part, two quite different cases will be analyzed: the case of Poland, which was one of the first eastern European countries to embark upon a comprehensive transformation program; and the case of Russia, which began the transition from reform socialism to a fully fledged market economy only at the beginning of 1992.

POLAND

Poland began its transformation process at the beginning of 1990. Bold measures were taken to free domestic prices from state control, eliminate trade barriers, and implement measures (both institutionally and via policy) to stabilize the domestic economy. The government was able to implement austerity measures since a large part of the population was willing to make short-term sacrifices in order to reach high standards of living comparable to those of its west European neighbors and the United States. The overwhelming majority of the population was convinced that this could be achieved only through the implementation of a market economy and the integration of Poland into world markets. Indeed, the Polish case reveals how the collapse of socialism resulted in a weakening of traditional institutions, allowing a handful of key figures in the new government to implement drastic reform measures with little political resistance.[9]

Although from the outset the government identified the creation of a private sector as being crucial for a functioning market economy, privatization did not receive the same priority as did other reform measures—Poland's shock therapy did not include the needed privatization medicine. However, by delaying the process of ownership transformation, the government lost its initial advantage of muted political opposition. Instead of promoting a strategy assuring rapid privatization, the government was undecided about what method to choose. The ensuing political discussion about the pros and cons of different privatization methods turned into a battle of interest groups over their respective property-right claims. It quickly

[9] Drastic reform measures are less likely to occur in the case of powerful institutions. In order to please all relevant interest groups, reform measures are watered down. However, when institutions are weak, as, for example, after major political and economic crises, individuals are able to make major decisions. In Poland, economic transformation can be associated with a single person, the then Finance Minister Leszek Balcerowicz. There are ample examples of this in other countries as well, ranging from countries such as Czechoslovakia, whose economic policy was mostly determined by Vaclav Klaus in 1989, to Argentina and its current Minister for Economic Affairs, Domingo Cavallo.

became clear that any broad-based piece of legislation would have to fulfill the demands of all vested groups, with the average citizen having to bear the cost in the form of suboptimal solutions and a redistribution of wealth at their expense.

The danger of not capitalizing on the initial public support for drastic reform measures at t_0 is that interest groups and property-right claimants gain political influence as they become better organized. In Poland, the potential for groups opposing privatization was laid in the early 1980s, when the then-socialist government decentralized economic decision-making and granted a certain degree of autonomy to socialist enterprises. During this period of reform socialism, control rights were *de facto* transferred to the workers and directors of the companies.[10] The demise of socialism in 1989, and, with it, the system of central economic planning, reinforced the ownership rights of the workers and managers. At present, Polish state enterprises enjoy the status of "independent, self-governing, and self-financing economic units with their own legal personality" (Frydman, Rapaczynski, Earle, et al. 1993, 160). Although the state, via its founding organs such as branch ministries, initially provided the assets and determined the charter of the company, the current legal framework requires the consent of workers and management. As a matter of fact, the government has even lost the power to dismiss directors of state companies—all these rights are currently controlled by workers.

A pragmatic solution to the attenuation of property rights in Poland would have been for the state to reclaim those rights; opposition would have been minimal at the beginning of the reform process. Through *corporatization*, that is, through the conversion of socialist enterprises into legal entities such as joint stock or limited liability companies—the state or the state treasury would have become the sole stockholder again. Since, at the beginning of 1990, the Polish government focused more on stabilization than on privatization, a general privatization debate broke out which is still ongoing. A compromise privatization law was adopted in the summer of 1990, but this leaves open both property-right issues and the question of what privatization method to apply. As a matter of fact, all vested interest groups ranging from the old bureaucracy at the state and local level to the

[10] In a purely legal sense, the central government continues to be the sole owner. Furthermore, the Law on State Enterprises distinguishes between public utilities and other state companies. With respect to the former, the government has retained almost all control rights since it continues to have the right to dismiss management at its discretion.

enterprise workers and managers gained actual veto power.[11]

These groups have paralyzed mass privatization thus far. Three years after the initiation of systemic change in Poland, privatization is almost exclusively restricted to small- and medium-sized companies. The cost to society of embarking on a mass-privatization scheme through the distribution of vouchers is continuously rising. Powerful interest groups are more entrenched than ever. The mass-privatization bill which was passed in May 1993 caters specifically to strong political groups by earmarking, for example, shares of approximately 200 companies in 10 investment funds to buy out 3.6 million civil servants (*Financial Times*, 1–2 May 1993, 2). Poland might have reached a point where the cost of buying out opposing interest groups to secure their support outweighs the benefits, and a less costly option would be to focus on privatization from the bottom. Such a scenario would oblige the government to channel its scarce resources into the establishment of an institutional framework which would foster the creation of private enterprises and lead to an inflow of foreign capital.

While interest groups opposing privatization are better organized today than they were at the outset of the reform program in 1990, the government is losing its initial mandate to pursue privatization. Public opinion polls show that public support for privatization is declining steadily. Already in the fall of 1991, the majority of citizens interviewed believed that large state enterprises should remain in the hands of the state.[12] Therefore, a government trying to maximize votes will be less likely to push for privatization.

Russia

In Russia, the political and economic conditions under which privatization is supposed to take place are even more unstable and uncertain than those in most other regions of eastern Europe. In addition to the obstacles so commonly found in FSCs, Russia faces the threat of regional and local decentralization and separatism and, on the national level, a constant struggle between a pro-reform executive branch and a parliament which favors the *status quo*. In Russia, more so than anywhere else, the success of economic reforms will ultimately depend on whether

---

[11] The privatization law grants the Prime Minister the authority to initiate privatization measures without having to get the consent of the respective parties. However, it is understood that these powers are limited to extreme cases and are meant to be the exception rather than the rule.

[12] The polls were taken on 2 and 9 October 1991 by the Center for Public Opinion Research in Warsaw and the results are cited in Frydman, Rapaczynski, and Earle, et al. 1993, 177–178.

the political opposition to reforming and privatizing the economy can be overcome.

At the beginning of 1992—two years after Poland began the process of economic transformation—Russia embarked on a path of drastic economic reform measures which included price liberalization, the convertibility of the Russian ruble and the privatization of state enterprises. Until the mid-1980s, the Former Soviet Union (FSU) was centrally administered and abstained from granting independence to enterprises. This changed, however, with Gorbachev's policy of *perestroika* and the reform of the Russian economy. Like Hungary and Poland, Russia began to grant more and more independence to the "insiders" of enterprises, hoping to reduce the shortcomings and inefficiencies of central planning. That tendency gained even more momentum after the demise of the Soviet Union and the abolition of the communist party—effectively undermining the control structures of the government.

Uncertain external conditions and political instability forced the Russian government to design a privatization program which, because it stresses political constraints, might actually be an example of how to deal with an environment of political uncertainty and extremely powerful opposition groups. It was quite clear from the outset that a first-best method focusing exclusively on efficiency would have been certain to fail. In contrast to Poland's optimistic approach, the Russian government was quite pragmatic right from the outset. The Russian government had the advantage of being able to draw from the experiences of other eastern European countries. Not surprisingly, Russia adopted a program that is more in line with that of Czechoslovakia—which has proven rather effective—than with those of Poland and Hungary.

In addition to the distribution of privatization vouchers to the general populace, Russia's program also addresses the potential resistance of influential interest groups. Within a few months of the beginning of economic reforms, privatization vouchers were distributed free of charge to the general populace (Djelic 1992). Although the mere distribution of vouchers does not automatically secure privatization it suits two purposes: (a) it increases the interest of the population in privatization and (b) it lays the groundwork for speedy ownership changes. As was mentioned above, although the mere distribution of vouchers does not lead to a large per-capita stake of Russian citizens, and although the cost of politically defending the per-capita stake still outweighs the loss of entrenched interest groups, vouchers in hand make privatization a tangible experience. This is certainly preferable to some of the less tangible gains from privatization, for example, tax savings. Since Russians do not have a history of personal income taxes, a potentially lower tax burden in the future is not likely to affect their behavior today. Furthermore, the program allows the trading of vouchers right from the outset. A voucher market can hence lead to the accumulation of vouchers, for example, through private mutual funds. In the Czech case, about 10% of the vouchers ended up in a single private investment fund. Overall, the Russian program converts the public into a forceful lobbying group for privatization. It can be expected that the public might even be willing to voice their preference politically in public rallies. In particular, the pressure on local politician is expected to be high.

Russia faces even more risk of political opposition to privatization than do other FSCs. Regional ethnic differences and a latent tendency toward independence movements and regional separation continue to force the government to transfer the control rights of former SOEs to local governments. The political bargaining power of the different regional governments remains strong even today. Without the support of the local governments, as Boycko and Shleifer (1992) point out, privatization is doomed to fail. The Russian program specifically addresses these property-right claims.

The current property-right situation reflects the fact that the government *de facto* lost the right and authority to privatize from above, which means that privatization has to be initiated by one of the "insider groups" without veto by the remaining groups (Heinrich 1993). Hence, the success of Russia's privatization will depend on whether the government can effectively coerce the respective opposition groups (local governments, enterprise insiders and ministerial officials) into privatization. This cannot be done without compensating them for their potential loss in control rights. The current legislation provides a variety of incentives to the various property-right claimants.[13] Before the enterprises can be sold, they are to be converted into corporate form: for example, a joint stock company with the respective government (municipal, regional, central) becoming the sole shareholder. *Corporatization* is, of course, only a prerequisite for the privatization of the company at a later stage—for example, through the voucher method. Corporatization, however, means that workers and management lose their control rights, since these rights are back in government hands. Depending on the option chosen, workers are, for example, entitled to 25% of the company shares. In order

[13] See Evers 1992 for a detailed treatment of the legal framework in Russia.

to entice them to opt not only for corporatization but also for privatization, they are granted 10% of the privatization proceeds. Provisions for company managers are equally accommodating.

7.7 Conclusion

It has been argued that the focus of the current privatization debate has to be redirected. For too long, debate was restricted to technical aspects: under what circumstances are private companies superior to their public counterparts and, once a decision is made in favor of privatization, what method is most efficient? Although the ultimate goal of privatization continues to be the maximization of social welfare, the key question will be whether the programs are designed so as to find political acceptance. Textbook privatization strategies are doomed to fail if political constraints are neglected. As a matter of fact, western privatization experiences reveal that political objectives are paramount, and it is not unusual to find cases where the transfer of ownership to the private sector was accompanied by protectionism aimed at making privatization politically acceptable, a procedure which is clearly at odds with any efficiency objective.

The magnitude of the current economic reforms in eastern Europe—and the corresponding redistribution of wealth and income—make privatization a highly political endeavor. Although society at large is expected to be better off at the end of the day, certain groups stand to lose in the process. The groups that will be net losers will oppose privatization and defend the *status quo*. Since their per-capita stake is higher than that of those likely to profit from economic reform, they will have an incentive to voice their preference politically. Eastern European governments that neglect to address these obstacles adequately might jeopardize not only privatization but the entire transition process and, ultimately, the process of democratization. Under these circumstances political backlashes are quite probable.

The old *nomenklatura*, that is, ministerial bureaucrats, enterprise directors, workers and (in certain cases) local governments, are especially likely to oppose privatization. Their current claims are partly the result of the continuing deterioration of property rights which began during the final years of socialism. Today, "insiders" enjoy almost complete control over state enterprises. The relative power of these interest groups is, of course, weakest at the beginning of the transition process, when old institutions lose their legitimacy and new ones are still not in place.

Therefore, a privatization program that is politically viable and which minimizes social costs requires that privatization is initiated at t_0, that is, as part of the first economic reforms. By engaging in mass-privatization schemes, the government can "kill two birds with one stone." On the one hand, the government provides the general populace with a tangible stake in privatization, giving them an incentive to voice their preference politically. On the other hand, it speeds up the process of transferring large parts of state assets into private hands, giving opposing interest groups less time to organize themselves, hence minimizing the compensation payments such groups can expect to receive.

Nevertheless, eastern European governments need to realize that privatization will only be successful if interest groups with vetoing power are compensated right from the outset. The two cases, one taking political constraints into consideration and the other neglecting them, appear to support the central hypothesis: A second-best privatization program is still superior to the *status quo*.

References

Bös, D. 1987. Privatization of Public Enterprises. *European Economic Review* 31: 352–60.

Borensztein, E., and M. S. Kumar. 1991. Proposals for Privatization: Some Notes on the Debate. *IMF Staff Papers* 38 (June): 487–504.

Boycko, M., and A. Shleifer. 1992. The Russian Privatization Program. Harvard University. Photocopy.

Djelic, B. 1992. Mass Privatization in Russia: The Role of Vouchers. *RFE/RL Research Report* 1.41 (16 October 1992): 40–44.

Evers, E. 1992. Privatisierung in Rußland. *Recht in Ost und West* 36 (December): 357–75.

Frydman, R., A. Rapaczynski, J. S. Earle, et al. 1993. *The Privatization Process in Central Europe*. Budapest: Central European University Press.

Hanke, S. H., and S. J. K. Walters. 1990. Privatization and Public Choice: Lessons for the LDCs. In D. Gayle and J. N. Goodrich, eds. *Privatization and Deregulation in Global Perspective*. New York: Quorum Books.

Hart, O., and B. Holmström. 1987. The Theory of Contracts. In T.F. Bewley, ed. *Advances in Economic Theory*. Cambridge: Cambridge University Press.

Heald, D. 1989. The United Kingdom: Privatization and its Political Context. In J. Vickers and V. Wright, eds. *The Politics of Privatization in Western Europe*. London: Frank Cass.

HBS. 1988. Harvard Business School Case no. 9-389-036 (revised 10/89). Harvard College.

Heinrich, R. 1993. The Merits of Insider Privatization: What Russia Can Learn from Eastern Europe. Kiel Institute of World Economics, Discussion Paper, no. 201.

Kornai, J. 1986. The Soft Budget Constraint. *Kyklos* 39.39: 3-30.

Leibenstein, H. 1966. Allocative Efficiency versus 'X-Efficiency'. *American Economic Review* 56: 392-415.

Lipton, D., and J. D. Sachs. 1990. Privatization in Eastern Europe: The Case of Poland. *Brookings Papers on Economic Activity* 2: 293-333.

Maskin, E. S. 1992. Auctions and Privatization. H. Siebert, ed. *Privatization*. Tübingen: Mohr.

Newbery, D. M., and P. Kattuman. 1992. Market Concentration and Competition in Eastern Europe. *World Economy* 15 (May): 315-33.

Pera, A. 1989. Deregulation and Privatization in an Economy-Wide Context. *OECD Economic Studies* 12 (Spring): 159-204.

Przeworski, A. 1991. *Democracy and the Market*. Cambridge: Cambridge University.

Rees, R. 1985. The Theory of the Principal and Agent. *Bulletin of Economic Research* 37 (January): 3-26; (May): 75-95.

Vickers, J., and G. Yarrow. 1988. *Privatization: An Economic Analysis*. Cambridge: MIT Press.

Vining, A. R., and A. E. Boardman. 1992. Ownership Versus Competition: Efficiency in Public Enterprise. *Public Choice* 73: 205-239.

Waterbury, J., and H. Bienen. 1989. The Political Economy of Privatization in Developing Countries. *World Development* 5: 617-33.

8 European Integration: Lessons from the South and Prospects for the East

Oliver Fratzscher

8.1 Introduction

Montesquieu, an influential French philosopher of the eighteenth century, inspired by his experience in Britain, thought that trade between two nations was always mutually beneficial and naturally created peace:

> Peace is the natural effect of trade. Two nations who traffic with each other become reciprocally dependent; for if one has an interest in buying, the other one has an interest in selling; and thus their union is founded on their mutual necessities. (de Montesquieu 1748)

Hirschman, a respected economist of the twentieth century, called this component the *supply effect* of foreign trade. But he also recognized another component, which leads to dependence and influence between trading nations, and he called it the *influence effect*:

> Among the economic determinants of power, foreign trade plays an important part.... Commerce, considered as a means of obtaining a share in the wealth of another country, can supersede war.... The internationalization of power over external economic relations would go far toward the goal of a peaceful world. (Hirschman 1945)

When a large state directs its trade away from large and toward small trading states, it gains more influence because of its power to interrupt the commerce with the dependent small states. One example was the German-Bulgarian

---

The first version of this paper was completed while the author was working with the International Monetary Fund in September 1992. The author is indebted to George Anayiotos, Gérard Bélanger, Andrew Berg, Ulrich Blum, Liam Ebrill, Grzegorz Ekiert, Michel Galy, Dale Jorgenson, Thomas Krüger, Anton OpdeBeke, Jeffrey Sachs, and Peter Timmer for insightful discussions and comments. Financial support from the German National Science Foundation is gratefully acknowledged.

trade in 1938, where Germany deliberately built up a position to control more than half of Bulgaria's exports and imports. More recently, the Soviet Union built a position of substantial power within the trading bloc of members of the Council for Mutual Economic Assistance (CMEA). Small countries such as the central European states, want to enjoy the supply effect and minimize their dependency on foreign trade. This was one consideration which led to the demise of the CMEA system and to the reorientation of trade with neighboring, friendly countries such as members of the European Community (EC), allowing substantial benefits from the supply effects of trade. Forty-five years earlier, the Marshall Plan had a similar objective: to create a system of mutual dependencies, where western European countries would integrate as a region, reduce the risk of potential hostilities, and enjoy the benefits from free trade. The eastern European transition led to the demise of the CMEA system, which was characterized by large one-sided dependencies and only limited economic effects of foreign trade. The integration of eastern European countries into a larger European Community is expected to further increase mutually beneficial economic effects and to reduce remaining political effects of foreign trade.

European integration has increased trade among its member countries, which accounted for the main benefits from integration, improving both allocative and production efficiency. The supply effect of foreign trade can more generally be called the *economic effect*. On the other hand, the influence effect is often called the *political effect*, which was reduced during the process of European integration by internationalizing the power over external economic relations. Economists usually focus on the economic effect of foreign trade and integration, since the political effect is hard to model. Certainly, the economic effect has been dominant in the process of western European integration and during the accession of southern European economies. With a perspective on a future pan-European Community, our analysis focuses on this economic effect of foreign trade. The purpose of this paper is to study the process of the central and eastern European transformation within a larger perspective of European integration. The first objective is to draw some parallels between the southern and eastern transitions, and the second is to explore the prospects for the envisaged pan-European integration by analyzing the evolving trade and industrial structures in central European countries (CECs). Therefore, two main questions are the focus of our analysis: What are the lessons from the southern enlargement of the European Community in the 1980s for the envisaged eastern enlargement? Which trade patterns and which industrial structures are expected to evolve in central European economies during the integration process?

The analysis of the southern European transformation will focus on three recent integration experiences in the European Community, namely the accessions of Greece in 1981, and those of Portugal and Spain in 1986.[1] The results reveal a distinct contrast, with a much more successful transformation in the cases of Portugal and Spain than in the case of Greece. All three southern European countries experienced structural changes in political and economic systems during the 1970s, and initially had economic structures similar to those in central and eastern Europe today.

The study of the eastern European transformation will focus on the most advanced economies: Czechoslovakia (the Czech and Slovak Republics), Hungary and Poland.[2] We will call these countries *central Europe*, and consider them as a distinct region within the larger environment of *eastern Europe*. In February 1991, these three central European countries concluded the Visegrad cooperation agreements, and signed a free-trade pact in Cracow in December 1992, forging the central European Free Trade Area (CEFTA). It is designed to gradually eliminate tariff barriers by the end of this century and ensure legislative compatibility with the European Free Trade Association (EFTA) and the European Community. By concluding association agreements with the European Community in December 1991, these countries also built "a bridge toward a unifying western Europe."[3]

In Section 8.2 the Spanish, Portuguese and Greek transitions are studied, static and dynamic growth effects of integration are distinguished, and the distribution of benefits among member states and across industries are analyzed. Some parallels are then drawn between southern and eastern transformations. Section 8.3 then reviews the progress of the central European transition, examining the trade structure of central European economies and the reorientation of trade from the East towards the West. During 1989–92, trade with western Europe doubled in volume, the quality and product differentiation of exports increased, and the composition shifted towards labor-intensive products using substantial human capital. The competitiveness of central European industries is analyzed, the degree of complementarity estimated, and the potential for intra-regional trade evaluated.

---

[1] A comprehensive review of the Southern European transition, as well as a theoretical review of the literature on costs and benefits of European integration art part of my more extensive working paper, Fratzscher 1993.

[2] The Czech and Slovak Republics became sovereign states in January 1993.

[3] Statement by Karol Szwarc, Deputy President, Polish Planning Office (Palankai 1991).

Regional integration should be facilitated by a largely complementary industrial structure, which could also become a catalyst for EC integration.

8.2 Lessons from the South

Historical Background

It is a formidable task to compare economic developments in three so different regions as western, southern, and eastern Europe. This part will focus on three southern European states: Spain, Portugal and Greece. Although comparisons with eastern Europe will always be simplified abstractions, they might help us to recognize some similarities and differences in the ongoing processes of transformation. However, I believe the course of history can reveal some valuable insights.

The three southern European economies industrialized rather late and became integrated in international markets during the second half of the nineteenth century. In a reversal of the sequence observed in western Europe, the liberalization of the political system and the introduction of parliamentary institutions in southern Europe occurred before industrialization, and initially was not accompanied by intense social struggles, since a weak bourgeoisie was temporarily able to exclude the working class from political participation. The resulting social cleavages led to a long history of competitive politics and authoritarian rule.[4]

An important characteristic in southern European states was the presence of an overinflated, cumbersome, and weak state that has traditionally played a key role in their economies, either through the public sector or the network of publicly controlled enterprises. The state became highly centralized, autarchic aspirations guided the development of the state sector and civil society remained heterogeneous and fragmented. The evolving social structure was characterized by a long urban tradition and heightened urban-rural cleavages, quite different from the structure in eastern Europe. Urbanization in southern Europe was higher, whereas the rural sector was characterized by landlessness and minifundism until the recent past.

A long period of authoritarian rule, lasting from the interwar period to the mid 1970s, set up the structures for ending a vicious circle of democratic breakdowns and authoritarian takeovers in southern Europe. The intense social and

[4] Diamandouros 1986 gives a more detailed analysis of the political factors in the southern European transformation.

economic transformation of the three countries during the past three decades resulted in high rates of growth, but an uneven distribution impeded social reconciliation. During the 1970s, democratic governments from the left took over from authoritarian regimes in Portugal and Spain, and gradually achieved social pacts designed to contain potential dangers to the maintenance of democratic order. Spain's system of "pactismo" became particularly well known after the conclusion of the Moncloa Agreements in late 1977, which restored social peace and built the foundation for sustainable economic reform.

When the southern European countries returned to democracy in the 1970s, they went through a process of political and economic transformation. Predominant initial structures were a centralized state, a large public sector, a high level of protection and isolation, and a low level of productivity. Two external shocks coincided with these domestic transformations. The two oil-price shocks in the 1970s required substantial economic adjustment to cope with an 800% increase in the price of the primary energy source. Then, in the 1980s, the process of integration into the European Community presented the southern European countries with increased international competition.

In their response, southern European governments combined a set of policies designed to foster modernization and competition with new social and welfare policies and regional integration on the Iberian peninsula has been a successful catalyst promoting integration into the European Community.

Costs and Benefits

None of the three southern European economies succeeded in the way their adjustment programs had predicted. Repeated slippage and political disputes occurred. However, the wide social consensus that evolved in Spain after the Moncloa Agreements built the foundation for the most successful transformation. Although Spain achieved a successful opening up and restructuring of its economy and the highest investment-led growth in OECD countries during the past six years, the cost was significant: unemployment has remained above 15% since 1984, real interest rates were among the highest in Europe during the 1980s, and fiscal deficits of between 3% and 6% of GDP were quite burdensome.

The Portuguese transition can be called a moderate success. Portuguese GDP per capita, in terms of purchasing power parity, climbed to 56% of the EC average. However, after growth rates of 4.3% in the second half of the 1980s, growth has not been equally distributed and the bottom third of the population remains the poorest in the EC. Legal reforms have been implemented with some delay, most remarkably the amendment to the constitution in 1986 to enable privatization, and the tax reform bill in 1989. Unemployment has remained below 5% since 1989, but nominal convergence has been problematic. Budget deficits of 6%, inflation above 11%, and interest rates above 17% demand further adjustment in order to meet the criteria for integration into the European Monetary Union (EMU).

The Greek transition has been disappointing overall. Several attempts at adjustment have failed in political turmoil, leaving the Greek economy in the weakest position with a GDP per capita only 52% of the EC average. Assistance from the EC has been of at least the same magnitude as to Portugal, but domestic mismanagement, misguided industrial policies, and excessive social and welfare policies produced poor results. After three years of growth below 1%, the government deficit surpassed 15% of GDP in 1992, public sector debt reached 116% of GDP, the trade balance revealed a deficit of 18% of GDP, inflation stood above 18%, and interest rates further rose to 27%. Expansionary macroeconomic policies, an excessive public sector deficit, a largely uncompetitive industry, and an inadequate functioning of markets do not provide much optimism concerning convergence and European integration in the near future.

An evaluation of the southern European integration must, therefore, be well differentiated. Nonetheless, some broad conclusions emerge. Despite substantial changes in the external environment and considerable financial support from the EC, national political will and macroeconomic policies have remained the major decisive variables for a successful transformation. Sustained social consensus and a decisive strong government seem to be crucial conditions for success.

The costs of liberalization have often been underestimated. The increasing openness of economies led to persistent large trade deficits and did not achieve the expected nominal convergence of prices. Trade deficits increased by 4% of GDP in the case of Spain and Portugal, and by 5% in the case of Greece after the beginning of their integration process, have recently further widened, and reached 6% in Spain, 11% in Portugal, and 18% in Greece. Whereas large appreciations of the Spanish and Portuguese currencies led to a worsening in their terms of trade and made exports less competitive, the Greek devaluation did not improve the trade balance either, because the expected benefits were offset by large fiscal deficits, continued high inflation, and lacking structural reforms. Tourism revenues of between 3% and 6% of GDP, as well as EC gross transfers of up to 3.5% of GDP only partially financed those large external imbalances.

The burden on fiscal policies was higher than expected. Large public sectors, slow progress on restructuring and privatizing public enterprises, and the vigor of international competition implied large subsidies, straining a fiscal balance already under pressure from decreased tariff revenues. Capital liberalization and integration into the European Monetary System limited the leverage on monetary policy and put the emphasis on fiscal adjustment. Fiscal reforms have been key elements in the southern European transformation, including measures for improved tax collection, the introduction of value-added taxes (VATs), and comprehensive tax reforms. Structural reforms were both controversial and expensive, for example the cost of the Spanish reconversion program from 1984-86 involving only 10% of the industrial sector was estimated at over 4% of GDP.

Capital liberalization attracted large inflows of foreign investment, when liberalization was combined with sound macroeconomic policies. Net foreign investment accounted for between 3% and 6% of GDP in Spain and Portugal, which limited the necessary debt financing of fiscal deficits. However, macroeconomic imbalances in Greece did not attract foreign investment, which accounted for less than 2% of GDP. Instead, huge budget deficits led to both monetary expansion, pushing interest rates up to 25%, as well as to excessive debt financing with public sector debt rising above 100% of GDP.

Decisive structural reforms, in particular modernization of private firms as well as restructuring and privatization of public enterprises, proved to be crucial in adjusting to vigorous international competition and reducing large fiscal deficits. Structural funds from the EC have been substantial in size and have recently been doubled, today accounting for about 3% of GDP in Portugal and Greece, and 0.6% of GDP in Spain. However, their efficiency is debatable, since they represent simply budgetary and balance-of-payments support, if the targeted projects would have been developed anyway. On the other hand, if they require matching funds by national governments, those funds may not be available, as in Greece, which then results in non-disbursement and hence no efficiency at all. Nevertheless, their impact on the growth of southern European economies has been estimated at between 0.5% and 0.7% per year, and in 1992 they are estimated to account for between 7% and 11% of total investment.

The duration of adjustment periods has been largely underestimated. Given the domestic political cycle, radical reforms have usually taken less than one electoral period to be implemented; but, in order to be sustainable, there had to be a set of preconditions in place. Spain's adjustment started early in the 1970s, although the final legislation for industrial restructuring (*reconversación*) was only passed in 1984. The transitional periods which were specified in the accession treaties have been lengthened, and while they were five years for Greece, they were extended up to ten years for Portugal.

Benefits from European integration have come in two steps: small benefits in the short term through increased efficiency, competition, and reduced trade costs, and larger benefits in the medium term through the integration of markets and economies of scale. Moreover, long-term benefits may result from increased capital accumulation and rising long-term growth rates. Estimates of the total economic gains from completing the internal EC market range from 4.3% to 6.4% in the short term (according to Cecchini 1988), with an additional 11.5% to 35% in the medium and long term (according to Baldwin 1989).

The distribution of costs and benefits from European integration among EC member countries has not been equal. They depend on the structure of trade, which is quite different among northern and southern European economies. The South, especially Greece and Portugal, have a high share of inter-industry trade, motivated by comparative advantage based on different initial factor endowments. The North, and to some degree also Spain, show a high proportion of intra-industry trade, driven by scale economies and consumer preferences for differentiated products. The main beneficiaries of increased inter-industry trade seem to be the southern European economies Greece, Portugal, and to some degree Spain, which have a comparative advantage in labor-intensive industries.

On the other hand, increased intra-industry trade benefits most those economies which have not yet exhausted their economies of scale. Under the supposition of a successful structural adjustment, the main beneficiaries may again be the southern European economies. A recent study based on a computable general-equilibrium model estimated that under integrated markets with free entry of firms, the southern European economies would gain more than 2% of GDP; northern European gains would also be positive, but only about 1% of GDP.[5]

The envisaged monetary union (EMU) requires further adjustment, which

[5] The impact of European integration on different industries also varies widely. The North is expected to gain mainly in skill-intensive industries, in particular in office machinery and transport industries. Gains in the South are expected largely in labor-intensive industries, especially in textiles, timber, and plastics. Differences will also occur among locations of the same industries, for instance production in the office machinery industry is expected to increase by 46% in Great Britain, but to decline by 7% in Italy. However, research on these questions is just starting, and more disaggregated general-equilibrium models incorporating features of endogenous growth have yet to be developed.

will result in improved long-term prospects for growth, but also implies short-term costs of adjustment which will not be equally distributed. The highest costs will arise in countries with large macroeconomic imbalances, and the overall level of costs will depend on the credibility of reducing interest-rate differentials. The estimated range of costs for an average European economy lies between one half and one percentage point of GDP, for a period of convergence lasting at least two to three years.

Parallels Between South and East

The transition from a command economy to a market economy now taking place in eastern Europe is a process unique in history—there exists neither a theoretical foundation nor sufficient practical experience concerning such a profound systemic, political and economic transition. Lacking an adequate model, the experience of other countries with similar problems in a different context may provide some new ideas, a set of options and a list of warnings to help prevent failures in the transformation of central and eastern European countries. The following remarks should, however, be taken with considerable caution, since a comparison between different systems and different geographic regions must always be somehow anecdotal.

It is largely agreed that price liberalization, stabilization, privatization, modernization, industrial restructuring, and integration in the world economy are important steps in the eastern European process of transformation. Most of these elements had some significance in the southern European transformation as well. Therefore, some parallels between these two transitions can be drawn, although the magnitude of change has been quite different. In the following, starting conditions, objectives, the nature of external shocks, levels of external financial support, and characteristics of liberalization programs will be presented for both southern and central European countries.

The objective of both southern and central European countries has been their integration into the European Community. In contrast to membership in the European Free Trade Association, the EC clearly has a political basis among its member countries, which is founded on democratic values. Applications for accession by new countries have only been considered after their transitions to democracy had been firmly established. Although Greece signed an association agreement with the EC in 1961, it was twenty years later that Greece finally reached accession to the EC after authoritarian rule was firmly rejected.

The starting positions among two countries are, by definition, always different, although there are some similarities in the southern and central European cases: structural changes in the political and economic systems occurred at the same time; the public sector had a predominant importance; public enterprises were highly uncompetitive; the economy was largely isolated and protected from international competition; the political structure was highly centralized; and the institutional structure was underdeveloped. The main difference between southern and central Europe has been the magnitude of change: while Spain restructured 10% of its industry, Slovakia may have to restructure more than 80%.

Integration evolved over decades and was usually preceded by periods of increasing cooperation: Spain and Portugal entered into free trade agreements with the EFTA countries; Greece concluded an association agreement with the EC. The four central European countries recently concluded association agreements with the EC, cooperation agreements with EFTA countries, and a free trade agreement among CEFTA countries.

External shocks hit southern European economies with the 800% increase in oil prices in the 1970s and then the vigorous international competition in the 1980s after their liberalization programs had been implemented. Those shocks are similar for central European countries today, although of quite different magnitude: full-scale price reform, prices for Soviet oil reaching world-market levels, huge adverse terms-of-trade shocks, collapse of trade within the former CMEA, radical liberalization, and increasing international competition.

These descriptions should not sound like generalizations. Certainly, southern European countries have had very different experiences, and those differences tend to be even larger within central Europe. The European Community treated the Portuguese and Spanish application *en bloc,* requiring a bilateral agreement between the two Iberian countries prior to their accession to the EC. The successful implementation of the Iberian common market may represent a good example for regional cooperation and integration in central Europe, although this would now include four nations after the split of Czechoslovakia. Moreover, the EC is continuing to emphasize the regional dimension, negotiating with the central European states as a bloc, as practiced in the Association Agreements in December 1991.

The length of the transformation and adjustment periods in central Europe will be longer than commonly expected. Spain and Portugal started their transformation in 1974 and gained accession to the EC in 1986, after the implementation of several adjustment programs and nearly nine years after their applications. Transition periods were up to ten years for the Portuguese adjustment, and may be expected to be at least as long for central European states. In strategic sectors such as agriculture, steel and textiles, the length of transition agreements may be even longer.

The level of EC assistance to central Europe will depend mainly on three factors: the size of the economy, the degree of structural problems in the economy, and most importantly, the political bargaining process within the EC. Given the size of the central European economies (GDP of US$26.5 billion for the Czech Republic, US$35.5 billion for Hungary, US$72.6 billion for Poland, and US$9.6 billion for Slovakia, according to World Bank estimates), they are of about the same size as the Greek and Portuguese economies (GDP of US$64 billion and US$60 billion respectively), but not comparable to the much larger Spanish economy (GDP of US$527 billion). However, the level of GDP per capita is around US$3,000 in all three central European economies, about half the level of Portuguese and Greek GDP per capita. Assuming that central European countries obtain the same level of structural assistance as southern European countries, net transfers to central Europe may barely exceed 3% to 4% of their GDP, and even then only after their accession to the EC.

The sequencing of stabilization and adjustment policies reveals an obvious lesson from southern Europe: until stabilization is fully achieved, adjustment and full liberalization cannot be successful. The experience of Greece is illustrative. Repeated devaluations and adjustment efforts failed to achieve their expected benefits, because a lack of fiscal discipline and expansionary macroeconomic policies did not provide a solid foundation. Under a successful liberalization and sound macroeconomic policies, the initial exchange rate should be rather undervalued, since the Portuguese and Spanish case have shown that large inflows of capital later may exert an upward pressure on exchange rates, a phenomenon also experienced in Latin American adjustments.

Trade expansion and reorientation have been key elements in all cases. The overall level of trade has usually been increasing (trade creation), although a certain bias towards higher rates of increase within the integrating bloc has been recognized (trade diversion). In the context of southern European integration, trade liberalization has often widened trade deficits. In the Portuguese case, trade deficits of about 10% have only been sustainable because the country experienced large invisible surpluses of tourism revenues and emigrants' remittances. Regional trade between Portugal and Spain grew, albeit from low levels, by 750% from 1985 to 1991, with large Portuguese trade deficits in the range of 40%. In contrast, central European regional trade has dropped since 1990, admittedly from initially high levels.

Initial strains on the government budgets are large. In the Portuguese case the budget deficit gradually decreased from over 10% of GDP to about 5% of GDP. Still, the target for the envisaged EMU is a maximum government deficit of 3% of GDP. The magnitude of subsidies to public enterprises in central Europe is much larger, and recent slippage in Hungary revealed that budget deficits rose dramatically from an expected 2% to over 7% of GDP in 1992. Taking account of southern European experience, those initial strains on the budget should be expected, although they must be gradually decreased, aiming to eventually achieve the EMU criterion of a maximum level of 3%. Fiscal and structural reforms are key elements in each stage of adjustment and will prove to be of crucial importance in central Europe. Eroding fiscal revenues from declining tariff revenues, wild privatization, and a growing informal sector, must be balanced by a comprehensive tax reform and possibly higher tariffs during a transitional period.

Central European countries have also started to open their capital markets, but only Hungary has so far been successful in attracting large inflows of foreign investment. The early implementation of capital market liberalizations in Spain and Portugal have been attracting large amounts of foreign investment, totalling up to 5% of GDP. On the other hand, Greece was forced to proceed more slowly, maintained controls on capital flows for an extended period, did not succeed to implement sound macroeconomic policies, and had accumulated public debt of 116% of GDP in 1991, compared to 66% of GDP in Portugal. The external debt situation in central Europe was most problematic for Poland, until an agreement in April 1991 wrote off US$17 billion of its debt, leaving it with a similar debt ratio to Portugal. The Czech debt to GDP ratio was 33% in 1991, relatively low compared to Hungary's ratio of 80%. Continued progress on capital liberalization combined with sound macroeconomic policies, rising productivity, and a restructuring of internal and external debt, should attract further foreign investment to central Europe, which should help to accelerate the transfer of knowledge and technologies and avoid excessive foreign-debt financing. Regarding the international environment, the restructuring of the industrial sector in central Europe can barely be successful without the opening up of markets in strategic sectors like agriculture, steel, and textiles in the European Community and without substantial external financial assistance during the transitional period.

Therefore, four necessary elements form the basis for a successful transformation: a stable domestic political economy with strong social consensus; sound domestic macroeconomic policies with progress on structural adjustment; trade and capital liberalization with increasing export market shares; and substantial external financial assistance.

How could the future structure and composition of trade for the central European economies evolve and how may costs and benefits be distributed? It seems that central Europe may follow two different paths. On the one hand, it may take the southern European path, like Portugal, developing a structure of inter-industry trade with comparative advantage in labor-intensive industries. On the other hand, it may take a northern European path like the EFTA countries, specializing in skill-intensive industries with differentiated products and intra-industry trade. Human capital statistics in all central European countries are higher than those in southern European countries. This would suggest a higher probability for the latter path, a path which may also be more promising, since the prevailing academic view indicates that the costs of adjustment are smaller in the case of intra-industry division of labor, than in that of inter-industry specialization.[6]

8.3 Prospects for the East

The revolutions in central and eastern Europe in 1989 started a progressive and irreversible move towards political pluralism and parliamentary democracy, as well as a transformation of centrally planned economies towards market economies. The systemic change has been accompanied by macroeconomic stabilization programs and a process of integration into the world economy. In general, stabilization has been relatively fast and successful, but the transformation has been slower and more painful than expected, and restructuring is still in early stages.

The initial results of stabilization programs have been encouraging, although the initial price shock was larger than expected and has led to persistent inflationary pressure. Balance-of-payments improvements should be seen as a temporary success, which is not likely to remain permanently. Surprisingly, the response of the productive system to the new price and incentive signals has been rather sluggish. The four countries suffered serious and protracted recessions, as witnessed

[6] It is argued that it is easier to reallocate factors of production within industries than among different industries. For a discussion, see Balassa 1986; Hine 1989; and Krugman 1987.

by rapid declines of national income, industrial output, investment, living standards, and large scale unemployment. The decline in industrial production is estimated at 40% for Czechoslovakia, 32% for Hungary, and 34% for Poland during the period 1990–92. Unemployment rapidly climbed and exceeded 14% in most areas, and is expected to reach 20% in Hungary during 1993.

The causes of this savage fall in output were complex. About one third of the decline was probably linked to the terms of trade shocks after oil prices were liberalized and to the collapse of the CMEA system, which ended in September 1991, and which had previously absorbed more than 50% of CECs' exports. Moreover, domestic demand and supply factors contributed their share, since output of the large state-owned enterprises sharply declined. Other specific factors also had their impact, especially the slow speed of structural adjustment, the delays in privatization, the initial overshooting of monetary and credit squeezes, initial under- and over-valuation of the exchange rate, and the unexpectedly high costs of liberalization. However, the decline in output was also partly overemphasized by the statistical procedures and the underrecording of private sector growth.

Fortunately, it seems that the recession has stopped by the end of 1992—GDP stabilized in all CECs, and, with the exception of Slovakia, the economies are expected to grow by up to 3% during 1993. The private sector is estimated to account for already more than 40% of GDP in Poland and Hungary, and close to 20% of GDP in Slovakia and the Czech republic. Inflation has declined significantly, but still has to come down a long way. Foreign direct investment during 1991–92 exceeded US$4 billion in Hungary and US$2 billion in the Czech republic, close to 5% of their GDP.

Despite such encouraging news, some problems still remain. Besides domestic political difficulties after the separation of the Czech and Slovak republics, there are three main economic problems to be addressed. First, a fiscal crisis has emerged after the tax base of enterprise profits eroded, and expenditures increased under social pressure; there is a need to modernize tax systems and administrations, and to achieve budgetary discipline. Second, inter-enterprise debts have accumulated, many of which are bad loans which threaten financial stability. Third, progress on privatization has been slow, hindering both structural reforms and inflow of foreign capital. A social pact seems necessary to cope with inflation and budgetary problems and to advance privatization and structural reforms.

Recent Developments

CZECHOSLOVAKIA

The reforms in Czechoslovakia are generally called successful, resulting from favorable initial macroeconomic conditions, comprehensive and rapid economic reforms, and good macroeconomic management. However, this success was overshadowed by political developments, which halted most legislation during 1992 and led to the dissolution into two separate states in January 1993. The economic impact of this divorce seems to be surprisingly mild. Cooperation between the two states continues within a customs union, but economic hardships will probably continue in Slovakia.

The country embarked on the transition to a market economy in early 1991 under better macroeconomic conditions than other eastern European countries. Inflation had never emerged as a problem, the monetary overhang was small, external debt was less than 16% of GDP in 1989, and the country was well endowed with human capital. However, the country also had its problems with regard to the structure of the economy (no private sector, all prices controlled, large-scale industries, heavy trade with CMEA), its legal framework, and basic institutions.

Cornerstones of the reforms were a "big bang" liberalization of prices and external trade, large-scale privatization, and a rigorous macroeconomic stabilization policy. The first phase has been successfully implemented, with prices stabilized and balance-of-payments pressures contained. However, output fell sharply and structural reform has proven more difficult than expected. Altogether, industrial output declined by 40% in 1990–92 and GDP declined by 16% in 1991 alone. Public consumption stagnated, personal consumption was reduced by one third, net investment became negative. Exports have been redirected away from CMEA and towards EC markets, and the trade balance has come into surplus.

Privatization seems to be well under way. Small-scale privatization got off to a quick start in 1991, and large-scale privatization started in May 1992. The coupon scheme was a success, transferring ownership of firms to citizens and investment funds. Still, major structural adjustment has been slow, and significant repercussions are expected in the labor market and on enterprises' balance sheets. The "velvet" divorce left Slovakia with much larger problems, with unemployment of four times that of the Czech republic and an obsolete arms industry to restructure. Given the sluggish pace of reforms in Slovakia, coordinating macroeconomic policies may prove harder than expected and independent currencies may be required.

HUNGARY

Hungary was the first centrally-planned economy to introduce a broad market-oriented reform, in 1968. Yet in 1990 the country still had an overly centralized economy with low external reserves and the highest per capita debt in eastern Europe. The country was in a better macroeconomic position than Poland, and rejected radical reform in favor of more gradualist policies leading to price and trade liberalization. Declining inflation and a positive current account are the favorable results of the Hungarian stabilization, combined with a nearly completed legal and institutional reform.

However, the predicted recovery failed to materialize in 1992. Industrial production continued to decline by 11% in 1992, and GDP fell by 6%. Unemployment was rapidly rising to 14% by the end of the year and is expected to reach 20% in 1993. The fall in private consumption became the main driving force in the recession. Official statistics overestimated the extend of the recession, not fully accounting for growth in the private sector, which is estimated to account for nearly 40% of Hungary's GDP. By the end of 1992, the decline halted, and estimates predict the economy should grow by 2% in 1993.

Inflation declined to 22% in 1992, down from 35% in 1991, and industrial producer-prices rose only by half the rate of consumer prices. The positive external performance was unexpected, with a current-account surplus in 1991, and a balanced current account in 1992, although balance-of-payments data and customs data show some disparities. International reserves expanded to the value of about six months' imports, and external debt has been stabilizing at US$22 billion. Hungary's position as a center for foreign investment from the West has been reinforced, with more than US$4 billion of foreign direct investment (FDI) flowing into the country in 1991–92.

Two major problems appeared during 1992: an overshooting of the budget deficit, which halted IMF supports, and problems in the privatization program. The private sector growth had been largely due to the rapid expansion of new enterprises and the inflow of foreign capital, with little help from the privatization of state-owned companies. Multinational firms had taken over the most promising enterprises, but left about one thousand smaller and less attractive firms on the government's books. Fiscal revenues fell significantly and caused the budget crisis.

Besides controversies on the design of mass privatization and fiscal problems, Hungary faced tensions with its minority population of more than 600,000 and externally strained relations, especially with Slovakia.

POLAND

Poland's government chose to implement radical stabilization measures in January 1990, aiming for full price liberalization, an end to subsidies, currency devaluation, full convertibility, wage controls and a reduction of the budget deficit. This stabilization program helped to reduce hyper-inflation from 640% in 1989 to less than 40% in 1992. However, Poland also experienced a deep recession with output declining by more than 34% in 1990–92 and unemployment rising above 14% on average and to over 20% in the northern regions. By the second half of 1992, macroeconomic indicators signaled considerable improvement and an end to the recession. Poland's economic performance in 1992 was considered the best in the region.

The industrial sector is now showing signs of recovery, but agricultural production fell by over 10% due to the drought in 1992, so that GDP is only expected to grow now in 1993. The turnaround has been driven primarily by the country's strong export performance. Poland's exports to the EC rose from 32% of total exports in 1989 to 56% in 1991, and the performance on the current account has been more favorable than expected. Parts of this improvement are also attributed to gains in efficiency resulting from structural reforms. The private sector accounted for more than 40% of GDP in 1992 and now employs more than half of Poland's labor-force.

The fiscal accounts have shown signs of severe strain. In the first half of 1992, the budget deficit exceeded 5% of GDP, and revenues continued to fall, requiring a severe cut in expenditures. By March 1993, the parliament had approved a new budget, which met IMF requirements. IMF support had been suspended in June 1991, since the government failed to meet criteria for the budget deficit, the inflation rate, and the level of foreign reserves. Poland achieved a remarkable restructuring of its foreign debt, which stood at US$49 billion in 1991. In March 1991, government creditors of the Paris club agreed to reduce Poland's debt by US$17 billion, and negotiations with the London club of creditor banks are continuing with the budget impasse now resolved.

Poland's political scene was full of confusion in 1992: popular support for the reform program weakened, a wave of strikes tried to stop the decline of real wages, a legislative stalemate occurred, and, within twelve months, Poland had its third prime minister. The *Sejm* again rejected the government's privatization plan in March 1993. Although a large number of small- and medium-sized firms had been privatized through a system of direct sales by auction, the privatization for large enterprises had barely progressed. Besides large-scale privatization, profound structural adjustments still need to be implemented, fiscal discipline should continue, and legislation on the free-market institutional framework has to progress.

REGIONAL COOPERATION

European integration went along three paths for CECs: association with the EC; cooperation with EFTA; and the creation of a central European free-trade area, called CEFTA. The overriding priority for all four CECs is to achieve full membership in the European Community as soon as possible. However, all CECs recognized that regional cooperation is quite complementary and may act as a catalyst. The experience of southern Europe (with Iberian cooperation), as well as the prospects of northern Europe (with EFTA cooperation) soon joining the EC, are sending a clear message: regional integration not only promotes political stability and economic growth, but can also help with integration into the EC.

Closer ties between the CECs and the EC were formalized on 16 December 1991, when the Association Agreements (also known as Europe Agreements) between the three CECs and the EC were signed in Brussels. Some of the EC's national parliaments haven't approved these agreements yet, but interim agreements went into effect in March 1992. These agreements provide for ongoing political dialogue through the Association Councils, and aim at implementing a free-trade area (except for agriculture) within ten years in two stages: within the first five years, most of the EC trade barriers will be removed; and in the following five years, the CECs will provide full access for EC products to their markets.

The EC's protectionism, however, has impeded progress on implementation. In 1991, France blocked a proposal to allow Hungary to export an extra 550 tons of beef to the EC. In December 1992, still with a 30% tariff on east European steel, the EC imposed anti-dumping duties on certain east European steel products and asked for a voluntary export restraint. Further conflicts seem to arise in trade relations regarding sensitive products (food, clothing, textiles, steel), which account for nearly 40% of CECs exports.

Declarations of goodwill are nevertheless continuing. The EC announced a special conference in April 1993 with representatives of all four CECs to discuss how to strengthen economic and political ties. Moreover, a recent EC executive commission report argued that the EC should open up their markets to the central European countries' food, steel and textile sectors and also accept them as formal applicants for membership.

Baldwin (1992) argued that CECs should now opt for membership in EFTA as a first step toward full EC membership. The CECs already maintain close trading relationships with EFTA countries, although a web of bilateral free-trade agreements does not provide a real institutional framework. EFTA membership should not be seen as a replacement for EC membership, but rather as a proven stepping stone.

The four countries initiated regional cooperation in central Europe with the Visegrad Treaty of February 1991. This regional trading zone, called the Visegrad Quadrangle, was further developed as the central European Free Trade Area (CEFTA) in the Cracow Treaty of December 1992. CEFTA, Europe's third trading bloc with 64 million consumers, came into effect in March 1993. The free-trade zone of the four CECs is expected to reverse the trend of declining trade among its members which has persisted after the collapse of the CMEA. Also, it may improve CECs' joint bargaining position in talks on full membership with the EC. This agreement seems especially important for Slovakia, which feared being left out of the European family. Under this pact, tariffs on goods traded among the four members will be reduced to the levels applied to EC goods. Intra-regional tariffs will be reduced in stages and should be eliminated entirely by 2001. The pact will likely reduce government revenues and it will force further restructuring of industries and services within the CEFTA countries.

Trade Structure

Macroeconomic Indicators for Central Europe

Table 8.1 shows some basic economic figures for the three CECs. The population of the CECs taken together is 64 million, about one fifth of the EC(12) population. However, some problems arise in the measurement of some of these indicators, especially regarding the measurement of GNP in CECs. First, only recently have these countries changed their measurement of national income from Net Material

Table 8.1
Economic Indicators of Central European Countries

	CS	HU	PL	CEC(3)	Portugal	EC(12)
Population (millions)	15.6	10.6	38.1	64.3	9.8	333.1
Area (1000 km^2)	128	93	313	534	92	2,233
GNP per capita (US$,WB)	3,400	2,600	1,900	2,380	3,800	14,000
GNP per capita (US$,PPP)	7,880	6,110	4,570	5,627	7,604	14,441
Agriculture/GDP (%)	8	12	14	12	9	8
GDP growth (%)						
1990	−1.1	−3.3	−11.6	−7.7	+4.0	+2.8
1991	−16.0	−10.0	−9.0	−10.9	+2.0	+1.3
1992	−7.5	−6.0	−0.0	−2.8	+1.7	+2.2
Unemployment (%)	10.4	13.5	13.5	12.5	4.2	9.1
Inflation (%)	12	25	45	27	10.5	4.5 (4)
Long-term Interest Rates (%)	18	28	48	31	17.1	10.4 (10)
Budget Deficit/GDP (%)	3	7	7	6	4.6	4.3 (3)
Total Debt/GDP (%)	30	80	40	50	70	60 (60)

Notes: WB = World Bank GDP measure; PPP = purchasing power parity GDP measure; CS = Czechoslovakia; HU = Hungary; PL = Poland; CEC(3) = CS, HU & PL; in the EC(12) column, parentheses denote Maastricht targets. Last available data, in general for the end of 1992. Unemployment in the Czech republic was 2.5%, and in Slovakia 10.4%.
Sources: World Bank 1992; IMF 1992b; CEPR 1992 for PPP data ; EFTA 1992 for World Bank data.

Product (NMP)[7] into Gross National Product (GNP). Second, international comparisons of income levels require the conversion into a common numeraire currency, usually US dollars. The main problem is to find an appropriate exchange rate, and official exchange rates usually do not serve the purpose well, especially in centrally-planned economies and in systems with multiple exchange rates. Market exchange rates are widely used, but, in order to account for shares in real output and not just in price levels, purchasing power parities should be used. Measurement problems also arise: black markets have rapidly grown and up to 20% of GDP in CECs is produced outside the official system. Accounting standards have also changed, and trade data reveal large discrepancies.

Table 8.1 includes two measures of GNP per capita. First, CEPR (1992)

[7] NMP is based on a simplified perception of value and productivity, excluding most of the output of services. NMP is also net of depreciations. The conversion from NMP into GNP is not straightforward and experience has shown that differences can be as large as 10% to 50%.

data based on exchange-rate conversions following the World Bank methodology, showing an average GNP per capita of US$2,380 for CECs, which would put them in the ranks of upper middle-income developing countries such as Brazil or Mexico. Second, EFTA (1992) data based on PPP conversions following the Summers-Heston (1988) methodology, showing an average GNP per capita for CECs of US$5,627 , which would put them in the ranks of poor industrialized countries such as Greece or Portugal. Irrespective of these methods, the ranking of CECs is clear: Poland's economy is about double the size than Hungary's, and the latter is about equal in size to Czechoslovakia's, where the Czech and Slovak shares are approximately in the ratio 3:1. In terms of GNP per capita, Czechoslovakia's income is about 30% larger than Hungary's and about 70% larger than Poland's. Czechoslovakia's GNP per capita is about equal to Portugal's, which is still only 56% of the EC(12) average based on PPP parities. The table illustrates that all CECs went through a deep recession between 1990 and 1992, with real GDP declining cumulatively between 20% and 25%, industrial production declining cumulatively between 32% and 40%, inflation sitting around 30%, and unemployment rising to 13%. Compared with Portugal, all CECs have substantial problems to meet EC(12) convergence criteria for inflation, interest rates, and budget deficits.

Reorientation of Trade Towards The West

The example of Czechoslovakia gives a striking illustration of the radical changes in trade structures in central and eastern Europe. In the 1920s, the country grew at an annual rate of 10%, and by the end of the 1930s, Czechoslovakia was the fourth largest industrial nation in Europe and a major exporter of manufactured products. After the socialist take-over in 1948, trade relations with the West were dramatically reduced, and the strategy of industrialization became one of self-sufficiency and an emphasis on heavy industry. By the 1960s, the total trade of the CMEA bloc with the West accounted for barely 3% of world trade—less than the individual trade of the USSR in the inter-war period. Trade liberalization hence suggests far-reaching consequences both for intra-European trade, and also for the global trading pattern. After the revolutions of 1989, all CECs have rapidly integrated into the world economy. Their economies have opened up dramatically, trade with the West has doubled, but trade with the East has rapidly collapsed. Since the beginning of 1990, exports of CECs to the former CMEA bloc declined in dollar values by 80%–90%.

As shown in Table 8.2, CECs are relatively open economies, but especially Poland is still much more closed than Portugal (openness ratio of 21% versus 37%). By the end of 1991, the trade regimes of CECs were similar to western structures: trade became demonopolized, private activity in the export sector expanded rapidly, licensing and quotas were largely abolished, and tariffs and the exchange rate became the main instruments of trade policy. The boom in trade with the West and the collapse of trade with the East suggests that a considerable reorientation of CECs' trade patterns has taken place. Trade within CECs declined to an average of only 6% of total trade, the share of trade with the former Soviet Union declined by seven percentage points to less than 20%, while trade with the EC increased on average by 17 points, today accounting for nearly half of all CEC trade. The volumes and orientation of CEC trade in 1991 are presented in Figure 8.1.

Key developments in the trade structure of CECs continued in 1992: first, the collapse of the CMEA continued to dramatically switch regional trade away from the former Soviet Union towards the West. Second, regional intra-CEC trade continued to decline, falling to historically low levels. Third, trade with the EC expanded on a large scale: the tightest integration developed with Germany, which captured 20% of total CEC trade; Italy and Austria also aggressively expanded trade relations with CECs (a total of 11%), while other G7-countries lagged behind.

The importance of these developments in CEC trade structures has been tremendous: Rodrik (1992b) disaggregated the Soviet trade shock into three components: a conventional terms-of-trade shock, a shock from the removal of implicit import subsidies, and a shock from the loss of Soviet markets. The combination of these three effects, based on conservative assumptions, amounted to a huge loss of income in CECs, about US$2.2 billion in Poland (3.5% of GDP), US$2.0 billion in Hungary (7.8% of GDP), and US$3.4 billion in Czechoslovakia (7.5% of GDP). Taking the multiplier effects into account, such a trade shock could have caused about one third of the total output decline in CECs.

The Soviet trade shock was partially offset by the good EC-export performance, which has been much better than most analysts had predicted given problems of product quality and rigidities in production. Three explanations are usually given. First, upgraded products have been reoriented from the East to the West; statistics indicate that the quality of the products produced for the Soviet market was highly inferior to the quality of exports bound for the EC. Second, domestic recession and reduced home demand pushed exports up, an argument

Table 8.2
Trade Reorientation of Central European Countries

	CS	HU	PL	CEC(3)	Portugal
Openness Ratio = 0.5(Exp+Imp)/GDP (%)					
1980	34	40	29	33	34
1990	36	30	21	27	37
Change in Trade Volume, 1991 vs. 1990 (%)					
Exports	−6	+10	+8	+5	−1
Imports	−25	+31	+63	+33	+3
Change in Trade Share, 1991 vs. 1989 (%)					
with CEC(3)	−4	−3	−3	−3	+0.1
with FSU	−6	−6	−8	−7	−0.4
with EC(12)	+11	+14	+21	+17	+4.1

Notes: CS = Czechoslovakia; HU = Hungary; PL = Poland; CEC(3) = CS, HU & PL; FSU = former Soviet Union.
Sources: IMF 1992a; EFTA 1992 for GDP data.

supported by Rodrik's (1992b) study. Third, large devaluations and market reforms in CECs made exports competitive. Therefore, it seems that a combination of all three arguments is most plausible. Moreover, the trade policy measures in the 1992 Association Agreements also had a significant impact on trade with the EC.

The substantial change in the destination of exports from CECs implied just as substantial changes in product composition and quality. Hungary may be taken as an example, where exports have been rapidly redirected from eastern to western markets. In 1990, significant increases in all major categories of Hungarian exports to western markets were realized, including machinery, transport equipment and capital goods, which were traditionally directed to CMEA markets. Two reasons can be identified to explain the Hungarian flexibility in redirecting exports from east to west: first, a significant product differentiation and penetration of western markets; and, second, significant improvements in the quality of Hungarian exports.

Traditionally, Hungary had exported different commodities to eastern and western markets: a much larger share of finished products was exported to the East (machinery and equipment accounted for more than half of Hungarian exports to the East) and semi-finished products were mainly exported to the West (including industrial consumer goods, ores minerals and metals, chemicals, food products). A more detailed study, however, shows a substantial degree of product and market diversification. As argued by Maresse (1989), exports in machinery and equipment

Figure 8.1
Trade Volume and Orientation of Eastern European Countries

(a) Czechoslovakia, 1991 Trade (US$)

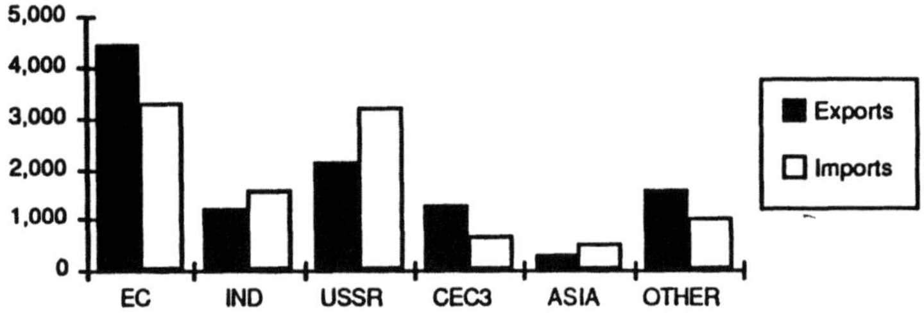

(b) Hungary, 1991 Trade (US$)

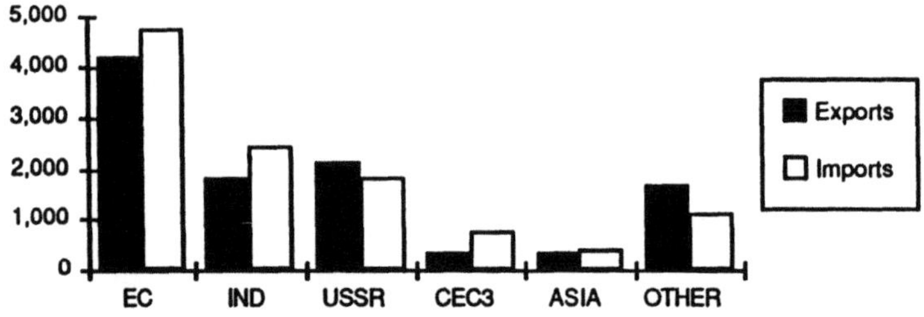

(c) Poland, 1991 Trade (US$)

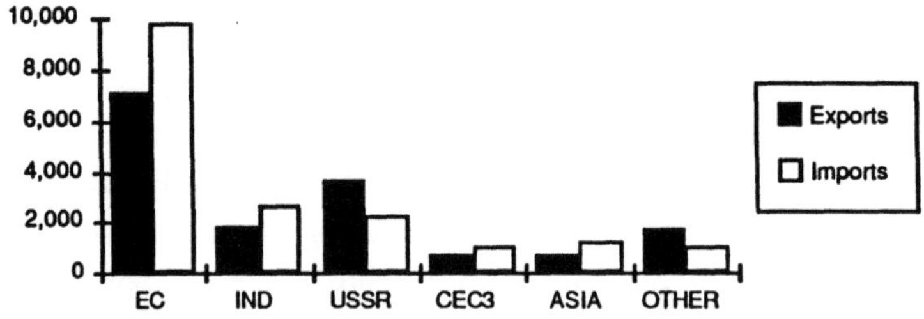

Source: IMF 1992a.
Notes: EC = European Community; IND = other industrial countries; USSR = former Soviet Union; CEC3 = Visegrad Countries; ASIA = Asia without Japan; OTHER = other countries.

to the West increased significantly, showing the production of high-quality goods and the knowledge of western markets and marketing practices.[8]

There is no conclusive evidence whether CEC trade has become primarily labor- or capital-intensive, and whether it is rather inter- or intra-industry trade. It seems that there continues to exist a large share of exports from the CECs to the EC in natural-resource intensive commodities and in labor-intensive commodities, which is mainly inter-industry trade. On the other hand, a substantial portion of CEC exports have become intra-industry trade, especially concentrated in commodities that are intensive in capital and human capital. Bigues and Ilzkovitz (1992) estimated the share of intra-industry trade at 50% for Hungary, 46% for Czechoslovakia, and 42% for Poland, the latter being roughly the same level as in Portugal.

The volume of trade with the EC has more than doubled since 1989, while CMEA markets widely collapsed. The structure of CEC trade has become more intra-industry oriented, with increasing shares for human capital intensive products. In 1993, the level of intra-industry trade of CECs is similar to Portugal's. For the future structure of CEC trade, a southern European path of labor-intensive inter-industry trade, as well as a northern European path of capital-intensive intra-industry trade both seem a distinct possibility.

TRADE POTENTIAL OF CENTRAL EUROPE

Given the importance of trade for the economic development of CECs, it seems a challenging question to ask how much trade with which partners would develop once CECs have fully transformed to market economies. The importance of this question is only matched by its difficulty. It is very difficult to predict the impact of such drastic regime changes as they occur now in CECs, and even in market economies it is very hard to predict future patterns of trade. Initial assumptions are in general of foremost importance. In the literature, four approaches have been suggested to study the trade potential of central Europe. First, we can look at historical trends prior to the socialist experiment. Second, we can build a trade model based on data for current resource endowments, assuming that the trade

---

[8] Maresse (1989) also studied the improvements in the quality of Hungarian exports more in detail, dividing goods in four categories of "hardness." Three main results can be seen: First, the overall composition of exports has shifted towards much higher quality products, nearly all of which are exported to western markets. Second, the destination of lower quality products has shifted even more extremely to eastern markets. Third, exports of middle quality products to western markets have increased, revealing quality upgrades of these previously inferior products.

potential in the near future reflects countries' different endowments of factors of production, in accordance with the theory of comparative advantage. Third, we can choose an incremental approach, studying the misallocation of today's resources and inferring the future efficient allocation of these resources. Finally, we can draw some lessons from today's West European trade patterns, assuming that CECs will develop similar structures.

Looking at the historical background of CECs, we can recognize that the trade structures prior to autarky widely reflected patterns of Heckscher-Ohlin comparative advantage. Looking at Russia, exports of agricultural products and raw materials clearly reflected her relative abundance of natural resources. Russia was a major supplier of agricultural products to the West. Russian and American grain were competing in the European market prior to World War One. Russian oil fields in Baku were the most productive in the world, their oil production was more than half of the world oil production.[9] Looking at CECs, Czechoslovakia played an especially important role as exporter of manufactured products prior to World War Two, reflecting an export-led industrialization with relatively low wages and a corresponding relative abundance of skilled labor.

Collins and Rodrik (1991) have used the historical approach to predict future trade patterns of CECs. They used a procedure to estimate how large CECs aggregate trade flows would be if they had western structures, and then they updated the 1928 trade matrices of CECs to determine predicted bilateral trade flows. Figure 8.2 illustrates their results compared with actual trade data of CECs. However, this approach has not been tested on any other countries or any other time periods.

The second approach of modelling trade is based on current resource endowments. However, there is a major problem with data collection and comparison: CECs have maintained high investment in their autarchic structures, but the stock of capital does not embody best-practice technology and is of very little value today. Hence it is nearly impossible to assess the current capital base of central Europe. Looking at other factors of comparative advantage, three observations can be made. First, large parts of central and eastern Europe continue to reveal abundant natural resources with huge areas of agricultural land, energy reserves, and natural resource deposits. Second, some countries, especially CECs, continue to have a relative abundance of labor, suggesting a comparative advantage

[9] Quoted in CEPR 1990.

Figure 8.2
Trade Potential and Orientation of Eastern European Countries

(a) CEC3 Exports: Actual and Potential (US$)

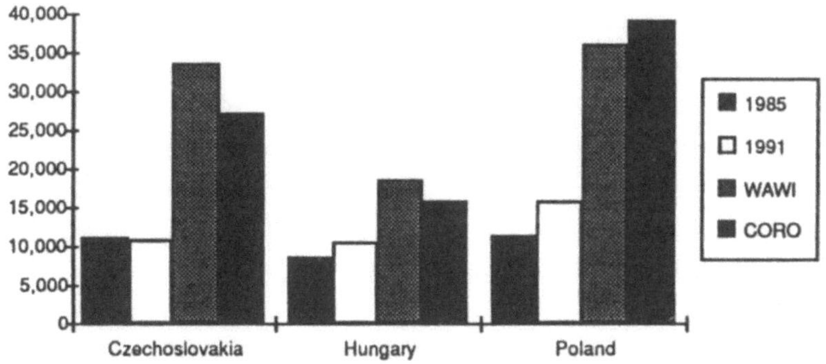

(b) CEC3 Exports: By Destination (US$)

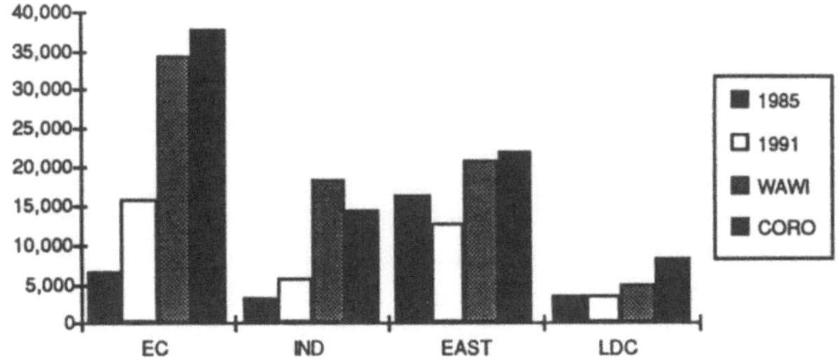

Sources: IMF 1992a; Wang and Winters 1991; Collins and Rodrik 1991.
Notes: 1985 = DOT data in current terms. 1991 = DOT data in current terms. WAWI = estimates of export potential accoring to Wang and Winters 1991; in upper graph revised data, in lower graph original data. CORO = estimates of export potential according to Collins and Rodrik 1991. EC = European Community; EAST = all Central and Eastern European countries; IND = other industrial countries; LDC = developing countries.

in labor-intensive industries. Third, the labor force is highly skilled in some CECs, and international comparisons put them in the range of middle-income newly industrialized countries, suggesting that some comparative advantage in CECs could develop in high-tech industries, rather than in skill-intensive production.

Wang and Winters (1991) as well as Hamilton and Winters (1992) used this approach of comparative advantage, and used the countries' GNP, population, and relative geographic position as proxies to estimate current resource endowments. They utilized the so-called gravity model which does an excellent job in explaining the world's actual bilateral trade flows, but lacks a sophisticated theoretical underpinning. Using data for 76 countries, these two studies predicted CECs bilateral trade patterns after they become fully integrated into the world economy. Figure 8.2 illustrates their results and shows very similar predicted trade patterns compared with the study by Collins and Rodrik.

Figure 8.2 indicates that on average the CECs exports are expected to triple after they fully integrated in the world economy, with the largest relative increase expected for Czechoslovakia. The share of trade with the EC is likely to exceed 50% of CECs exports, and the share of exports to eastern markets is expected to remain at about 25%. That would imply that the level of 1991 exports of the four CECs into the EC would at least double, bringing them in the range US$35 billion (or 2.4% of total EC imports) maybe by the year 2000. These results suggest that rather than accounting for a mere 7% of world merchandise trade, eastern Europe and the former Soviet Union would, even at their current levels of income, have accounted for 18%. Moreover, when incomes in central Europe increase, every 1% of GNP growth should boost imports by 1% and exports by 1.2% (*Oxford Analytica,* 20 March 1992).

However, both the first and the second approach have not yet been fully elaborated. The outcomes are very sensitive to the values of current GNP and all use PPP-converted GNP estimates. Moreover, as indicated in the third and fourth approach, some misallocations in the production of CECs may persist, not all of their trade can be explained by history and comparative advantage, and most importantly, trade policy was left out. In reality, the EC has severely restricted imports of sensitive products (food, clothing, textiles, iron and steel) from CECs and is expected to raise major problems regarding agricultural imports. Therefore, the large potential increase in CEC trade with the EC may take longer to materialize, whereas the depressed trade within CEFTA and with the FSU states may expand sooner than expected.

The third and fourth approaches may give some additional insights which would modify our previous results. First, many resources in CECs were misallocated, especially through the emphasis on heavy industry, so that future trade in these areas may be overstated, unless some comparative advantage remained "by accident." Second, productivity in agriculture was severely depressed, suggesting a very large potential for future improvements. Third, the domestic capital stock in heavy industry is of little value and a large share of domestic savings is likely to be absorbed in investments in infrastructure, suggesting that capital needs may be much higher than expected. Fourth, with an even longer time horizon, more trade is expected to become intra-industry trade, as observed in the evolution of the EC's Common Market. The above models (based on Heckscher-Ohlin structures) are most useful with a medium-term perspective, and their projections are realistic for a time period when the CECs have transformed to market economies but have not yet fully integrated into the EC's Common Market.

Industrial Structure

Competitiveness of Central European industries

As in the southern European and east Asian transitions, trade policy and industrial policy have been closely interrelated: domestic restructuring and industrial policy are one side of the coin, and on the other side we have external stabilization and trade policy. CECs have already been operating a de facto industrial policy, to the extent that they often refuse to allow market forces to close down loss-making state-owned enterprises.

According to our previous results, the long-neglected service sector should revive and expand in CECs, and employment in agriculture should continue to decline. Regarding the industrial sector, substantial structural adjustment is necessary and painful decisions on the closure of some inviable enterprises must be made in order to adapt the structure of production to new domestic and world market conditions. How should industrial policy in CECs be shaped and which criteria should form the basis for firm closures?

After four decades of state planning, any new industrial policy smacks of past intervention. Still, all market economies have developed some kind of industrial policy, to a smaller extent in the United States and to a larger extent in Japan. Eventually, the decision to close certain firms and to keep others operating has to be based on certain criteria, which themselves form the basis of industrial policy. Most economists suggest that CECs should choose an industrial policy which actively promotes the restructuring process and which is based on each country's comparative advantage.[10] Where "strategic" sectors have been identified, industrial policy may become even more sophisticated, and it maybe useful to draw some lessons from the Japanese (MITI) experience.

In practice, any improved industrial policy has to be implemented at the level of individual firms, since key decisions on closure, reorganization, new investment and privatization are taken at this level. Any restructuring induces social costs and unemployment usually increases during restructuring periods. Besides high transitional costs, restructuring is expected to produce substantial net benefits in the medium and longer term. Therefore, some kind of assessment of competitiveness at the branch and individual firm levels must be made. Hughes and Hare (1992) developed a methodology to assess the competitiveness of branches in the industrial sector and argued that this methodology must be based on world prices, since domestic prices are still highly distorted by taxes and subsidies and are poorly correlated to world prices. Some caution must be used in interpreting the results from these studies, since radical changes are ongoing and the Hughes-Hare database is from 1989, the starting point of the restructuring process. Data are disaggregated by three-level ISIC code, giving detailed information on competitiveness at the branch level, although individual firms may show different results. Especially in sectors with both private and state-owned firms, the overall coefficient of competitiveness is highly misleading, since some restructured or private firms may be competitive in a widely uncompetitive sector. In choosing world market prices as a basis, it is hard to adjust these prices for quality differences. However, comparing these data across the three CECs, some ranking can be done and the overall picture becomes clearer.

Table 8.3 shows the value-added of industrial sectors for the three CECs, based on world prices and net of labor costs. This share is available to cover capital costs, which are very difficult to estimate. A negative value indicates that on average, firms in the sector are making losses (net of subsidies and other distortions) and need to get the cost of intermediate inputs well below the gross value of their output in order to become profitable. This can be done in two ways: either the quality of production at existing cost levels is substantially improved

[10] This argument is especially promoted by Hughes and Hare 1992. See also Hughes and Hare 1991; Estrin et al. 1992; and Misala 1992.

Table 8.3
Competitiveness of Central European Industries

ISIC code	Sector	Value-added at world prices less labor costs (% of world price) Czechoslovakia	Hungary	Poland
301	Meat, fish and dairy products	−40.5	−15.4	−13.7
302	Fruit and vegetable products	−37.9	−23.6	−56.4
304	Cereal products	−19.5	+7.8	+29.4
314	Tobacco products	−36.8	+2.7	+6.1
323	Leather products	−23.0	+20.1	−4.2
324	Footwear	+15.5	+20.6	−16.6
331	Wood products	+12.4	+21.4	−5.5
356	Plastic products	+27.5	+10.9	−3.8
361	Pottery and chinaware	+26.3	−1.8	−2.9
362	Glass and glassware	+21.2	+12.8	−12.1
363	Cement	−0.0	+22.0	−24.1
371	Ferrous metallurgy	+19.0	−20.2	−0.5
382	Machinery	+22.9	+14.2	+0.5
385	Instruments	+14.0	+22.0	+11.8
	All industries	+9.2	+4.3	−3.9

Sources: Hughes and Hare 1991, 102.

(improved technology), or the cost of intermediate inputs per unit of output is significantly reduced, maintaining the existing quality level of output (reorganization and labor shedding). The sectors with negative value added at world prices are a far more significant fraction of total output than had been anticipated (for instance by McKinnon 1991). Again, data in Table 8.3 refer to pre-1989 conditions and may change significantly once the ongoing restructuring is incorporated. Moreover, unit labor costs have also changed: they declined by 10% in Czechoslovakia and increased by 20% in both Hungary and Poland during 1989–91 (Estrin et al. 1992).

Still, the data show some interesting results. On average for the entire industrial sector, value added at world prices less labor costs (in percent of world prices) was negative in Poland (−3.9%), slightly positive in Hungary (+4.3%) and positive in Czechoslovakia (+9.2%). Czechoslovakia shows a generally strong performance in engineering and heavy industry, and has an especially weak performance in the food-processing sector. Hungary has very few sectors with negative value added, and stands out in light industry (especially clothing and leather products), building materials and precision engineering. Poland's performance seems the weakest overall: only some sectors of food processing show positive value added, and some relative advantage is revealed in textiles and wooden furniture. Another very interesting result is the low correlation between the sectors of comparative advantage in these three countries. Rank correlations are generally below 0.3, suggesting that an industrial policy based on comparative advantage and closure of the least profitable firms in all CECs would create few conflicts between these countries. On the other hand, the apparent complementarity between the "optimal" production profiles of the three countries implies that there would be substantial benefits for the region from mechanisms to foster intra-regional trade (Brabant 1991; Rosati 1992).

Three points stand out. First, CECs should develop a comprehensive industrial policy which is consistent with the region's trade policy, actively promotes the restructuring process, and based on a well-founded analysis of long-term competitiveness. Second, some specific sectors with comparative advantage exist in each of the CECs. Third, substantial benefits could be derived for the CECs by expanding intra-regional trade in an environment of complementary industrial policies.

Sectoral Impacts of the Association Agreements

So far, the comparative advantage of CECs has been studied only in a regional context, but it should also be evaluated in comparison to western European benchmarks. Several suggestions on the appropriate methodology have been made. The calculation of Revealed Comparative Advantage (RCA) indices seems a promising approach (Balassa 1991; Tovias 1991). It is based on the assumption, that trade between CECs and the EC is done on a convertible currency basis and is relatively free of distortions. By construction, any RCA index smaller than one indicates that there is no comparative advantage for that good. However, the RCA index has neither cardinal nor ordinal properties, hence no conclusion on the extent of comparative advantage is possible. On a very aggregated scale, the countries of central and eastern Europe prior to 1989 only revealed comparative advantage in natural-resource intensive goods. The Asian newly industrialized economies (Hong Kong, Malaysia, Singapore, South Korea, Taiwan) shifted their comparative advantage away from natural-resource intensive goods into the sector of labor-intensive goods during the 1980s. The EC and other industrialized countries have shown comparative advantage in technology-intensive goods and in capital-intensive goods.[11]

Tovias (1991) took a more microscopic approach, comparing Hungary's RCA indices with those of eastern Germany, Portugal, and Spain, using export data disaggregated at the four-level SITC level. He concluded that Hungary has lost its comparative advantage in many sectors, for instance in some agricultural products, cattle, wood charcoal and brooms, but it appears that Hungary has retained revealed comparative advantage in some textile and clothing products.[12] Spain and Portugal have been competing with Hungary in key areas of exports, and Tovias compared their respective RCA indices for the years 1986–87. The main overlap with Spain exists in many agricultural products, such as meats, fruits and juices, vegetables and wine, but also in some manufactured products, such as wood products, footwear, iron and steel, and furniture. Regarding Portugal's RCAs, the overlap includes no agricultural products. Instead, Hungarian and Portuguese RCAs overlap in other sensitive areas, such as various textile, clothing, and footwear items. These overlaps obviously carry enormous importance in the decision process within the EC to approve the full membership request of the CECs.

The unification of Germany and integration of former East Germany into the EC has also major implications for Hungary, which will create new trade barriers between these two countries and much stiffer competition for Hungarian exports to the EC market. Comparing the respective RCA indices, little overlap appeared in agricultural products. However, Hungarian and East German exports revealed strong overlap of RCAs in footwear, minerals, iron and steel, machinery, furniture, travel goods, and clothing.[13]

---

[11] See Misala 1992 for a more detailed study of worldwide RCA indices.

[12] However, the assumption of undistorted trade may not hold, since EC non-tariff barriers imposed on Hungary's agricultural products, the main export sector, have significantly increased after the southern enlargement of the EC in 1986. On the other hand, southern European countries received large transfers from the EC for reforms in their agricultural sectors. Spanish and Portuguese manufactured exports were given duty-free access to EC and EFTA in July 1989.

[13] Tovias (1992) also studied the effects of eventual integration into the EC. Only considering changes in trade policy and access to the EC market, Tovias estimated that Hungary's membership in the EC would expand its exports to the EC by at least 48%, with the following sectors being the main beneficiaries: meat, iron and steel, fruit and vegetables, textiles, and clothing. This calculation

On the other hand, integration with the EC does not bring only benefits. Competition will be much more severe, imports are expected to rise rapidly and factors will become more mobile. Using the framework of Porter (1990), Czinkota (1991) evaluated the total impact on CECs and concluded that government-imposed entry barriers are expected to decrease, while natural barriers to entry (due to increased competition) are expected to increase. Evaluating the "national comparative advantage," CECs main strengths are human resources and skilled labor, whereas major liabilities are infrastructure, domestic demand conditions, industrial structures, and management skills.

Regional Integration in Central Europe: CEFTA

After decades of continuing progress in multilateral trade negotiations, regionalism is again viewed as a solution to major international economic problems. In theory, regionalism is only a second-best solution to multilateral integration, but political reasons often block the first-best choice and leave regionalism as the best available alternative. This is also the case for central Europe: integration into the EC is at least one decade away, so that in the meantime it seems most profitable to integrate as a region of CECs, which could accelerate the process of integration into the EC, as observed in the case of EFTA countries. From an economic perspective, integration is a process and a means by which a group of countries strive to increase its level of welfare by promoting the division of labor and the free movement of factors within the integrated area, and by restricting these movements to outside countries. Different stages of integration are free trade areas, customs unions, common markets, and economic unions. The main economic argument for regional integration is that the additional trade created exceeds the old trade diverted. However, besides this static concept, significant dynamic gains from integration can arise, due to economies of scale, faster growth and new market structures.

Recently, Guzek et al. (1992) have studied the potential effects of a regional bloc in central Europe, specifically a free-trade area comprising Czechoslovakia, Hungary and Poland. This free trade area was established with the Cracow Treaty in December 1992 and came into effect in March 1993. Unfortunately, Guzek et al. limit their study to conventional static concepts and hence ignore potential

---

does not include any structural funds or other EC transfers, which may be substantial. The next best alternative, according to Tovias, would be membership in EFTA, which would still have 60% of the trade effects attributed to EC membership.

dynamic effects. As a result, the estimated benefits of regional integration are rather small, less than one percent of GDP in the CECs. However, their study gives valuable insights into the effects on different sectors and the political economy of integration. Using input-output tables and trade statistics of 1990, the authors concluded that the reduction of regional trade barriers may lead to a 30% increase in the volume of trade. Focusing especially on Poland, the sectoral implications would be substantial declines in prices, which would reduce the profitability of the involved industries. The most affected sectors would be transport, wood and paper products, engineering and electronic products, light industry, synthetic fibers, and mineral products.

Under CEFTA, competition would be increased and rapid restructuring would be required, otherwise the expected increase in trade would not materialize. Benefits may become much larger once the analysis is built on a dynamic model and when the free-trade area is expanded to a customs areas or even a common market. CEFTA could be beneficial overall, but it would also involve costs in reduced fiscal revenues and substantial adjustment costs in certain industries.

Factor Mobility

The integration of central Europe into the world economy not only implies radical changes in their trade and industrial structures, it also enables a certain mobility of factors. Within the Common Market, the objective was to ensure full mobility of all factors (labor, capital, goods and services) by January 1993. For CECs, this mobility is much more restricted, but we have observed massive migration to the West, especially from East to West Germany. Capital has flowed only slowly into CECs, one of the major bottlenecks for central European transformations. Politically, the argument is forcefully made that people can stay if capital moves in. Three main hypotheses have been established. First, the transfer of capital can prevent the migration of labor. Second, free trade can reduce pressure for migration of labor and can provide additional capital. Third, it is in the interests of both the EC and the CECs to promote both the transfer of capital to central and eastern Europe and the growth of free trade in order to achieve political stability and to prepare for economic integration into the EC.

LABOR MOBILITY

During the period 1986–88, western Europe was the destination for about 400,000 immigrants each year, or 0.12% of the entire population. However, during

1989–1990, nearly 400,000 immigrants came just to Germany, which equals 0.75% of the West German population.[14] The main attractions are the large wage differentials. Today, workers could increase their salary more than ten times by migrating from the CECs to Germany, provided they could find jobs. The natural barriers to migration are still high: a different language, different culture, and uncertain prospects of finding a job. Still, compared to migrations in other areas of the world, the incentives are relatively high to migrate from the CECs to the EC, given cultural similarities, social security networks in the EC, and the relatively high skills of people in CECs.

Economic implications are different for the sending country and for the receiving country. The sending country, here the CEC, experiences reduced unemployment in the short term, but qualified workers or entrepreneurs are lost for the future, and the infrastructure continues to be depleted. Human capital is given up for short-term improvement. The receiving country, here the EC, experiences social costs and adjustment costs in the short term, such as problems in construction of housing and higher spending for social services, but gains a dynamic advantage in the long term with the increased human capital. Short-term adjustment problems are incurred for improved prospects of future growth.

This analysis has only outlined economic motives, but it seems that political instability, as currently experienced in the former state of Yugoslavia, is by far the largest incentive to migrate. Press reports in 1990 indicated that millions of Russians were sitting on their suitcases ready to migrate west in the case of political turmoil. Therefore political stability may be the single most important factor for avoiding large-scale migration from eastern to western Europe.

Capital Mobility

As outlined above, substantial transfers of capital to central Europe are essential to support the transformation process, build up the capital stock and the quality of infrastructure, create new potential for growth and avoid massive migration of people to the West. In the first three years of the transformation, 1989–92, capital transfers have been much lower than expected, mainly due to low efficiency of

[14] Exactly 397,000 *aussiedler* and 75,000 asylum seekers entered Germany during 1990. Compared with the huge flood of immigration to the USA at the turn of the century these are comparable ranges. However, the USA then provided a country full of labor opportunities, whereas Germany today is struggling with a recession and 8% unemployment. According to Siebert 1991, immigration to the United States was 0.53% of population per year during 1891–1900 and 1.04% of population per year during 1901–1910.

disbursement and limited capacities of absorption, but the significant inflow of foreign direct investment has been encouraging.

It is very hard to estimate how much capital CECs would need to catch up with the West, and it is not even clear how to estimate their current capital stock. CEPR (1990) assumed an annual growth rate of 7% for CECs, and, based on several assumptions of capital intensity, the authors estimated yearly net capital inflows necessary to support that growth at between US$103 billion and US$226 billion per year. Collins and Rodrik (1991) presented more substantive research to illuminate the expected capital and investment flows associated with the integration of the CECs into the world economy. They considered a yearly inflow of capital into all eastern European countries of US$55 billion as realistic, but estimated an inflow of US$344 billion as desirable to enable a fast growth track of 7% per annum. In 1990, the German Finance Ministry expected transfers to eastern Germany in 1992 to be DM28 billion or 13% of the region's GDP—now it has been revealed that the actual transfers in 1992 just to cover subsidies exceeded DM100 billion or 40% of the region's GDP, or about 4% of total German GDP. An IMF report estimated necessary investment in eastern Germany at DM100–130 billion per year until 2000, in order to achieve 80% of West German productivity levels (Lipschitz and McDonald 1990; *Oxford Analytica,* 1 September 1992).

Siebert (1991) took another approach based on historical analogies: He calculated that the Marshall aid of US$12.4 billion in 1948–51 to the sixteen western European countries accounted for approximately 2% of the recipient countries' GNP. Based on official GNPs for CECs, the equivalent amount of transfers to CECs today would be US$3 billion per year; but based on an average of 1% of donor countries' GNP, the equivalent could be as high as US$143 billion per year.

These back-of-the-envelope calculations are neither very consistent nor realistic. After the Paris summit in 1989 and until the end of 1991, a total of US$33.8 billion has been verbally committed to the four CECs by more than thirty countries and international organizations (including US$10.4 billion from the IMF and the World Bank, and US$10.6 billion from EC countries), but only a small fraction of this amount has actually been disbursed. In 1990, only an average of 13% of the committed funds was spent, ranging from 27% in Poland, 16% in Hungary, to only 4% in the former Czechoslovakia. Multilateral funds had the highest disbursements, but bilateral funds have shown large variations, ranging from 60% of UK aid (especially from the UK-Know-How-Fund) to only 6% of US aid (data for 1990).[15]

More important than the volume of capital flowing into central Europe is its efficiency. Flows of foreign direct investment have been encouraging, often bringing along new technology and western management know-how. Technical assistance programs have shown a wide variation of efficiency. Multilateral aid has often lacked comprehensive coordination, and could not always be absorbed in CECs. Therefore it seems more promising to focus on the efficient use of foreign assistance than on its volume. Moreover, any aid is likely to be temporary, and the growth of the private sector and the inflow of foreign direct investment should be longer-term objectives. This requires a focus on structural and institutional reforms, and a very efficient use of available financial resources.

Prospects for the Eastern Enlargement

Finally, it is time to evaluate the prospects of the four central European economies for achieving full membership in the European Community. These four CECs aspire to start accession negotiations in 1996 and to become full members of the EC by the year 2000, but no timetable for membership has yet been provided. The demands of CECs are becoming more forceful, claiming that they fulfil the basic criteria for entry—stable democracies and growing market economies. Still, the EC government put forward five arguments for keeping the CECs waiting.

First, membership is a question of financial means. Budget transfers from the EC's regional fund (accounting for 25% of the EC budget) plus expenditures

---

[15] The nature of this assistance was diverse. Grants amounted on average to a mere 14% of the total, another 15% went to Polish debt relief, and the rest was less favorable assistance with at least a 25% share of non-returnable funds. The bulk of trade credits and enterprise loans made on a commercial basis are therefore not included in this category of assistance. Foreign direct investment is another category, totaling about US$3 billion in 1991 and US$4.5 billion in 1992 for the CECs, accounting for up to 6% of GNP per year in the case of Hungary. Especially limited by the lack of financial institutions, CECs have shown a limited absorption capacity for foreign capital. The coordination of these multiple governmental and non-governmental aid programs has been virtually non-existent. Although the EC created the so-called G24 Coordination Unit, its impact was negligible. The most significant single item in G24 aid was the writing off of US$17 billion of Polish debt in April 1991. Further multilateral aid during 1990–91 included US$10.4 billion from IMF and World Bank programs, US$1.3 billion from the EC's technical assistance program PHARE, and just US$0.3 billion form the European Bank for Reconstruction and Development (EBRD). Bilateral lending accounted for 60% of assistance to Poland, 50% for Hungary, and just 20% for Czechoslovakia, with by far the largest share being provided by Germany (*Oxford Analytica,* 13 July 1992). Regarding the level of aid flowing to central Europe, US$34 billion in two years is a considerable amount. However, compared to transfers of the EC in structural funds (US$14 billion per year) and agricultural support (US$31 billion per year), this aid seems rather modest, especially given the fact that a large portion of this assistance was not even spent.

for supporting farmers under the Common Agricultural Policy (accounting for 50% of the EC budget), would amount to additional annual funding between ECU 7.8 billion (CEPR 1992) and ECU 18.4 billion (Baldwin 1992), out of a total Community budget of ECU 41 billion. These numbers amount to political dynamite: rich countries strictly refuse to carry the extra burden and poor countries strongly resist sharing their benefits with even poorer CECs. On the other hand, this represents only one side of the coin. Substantial benefits may develop when the CECs are integrated into the EC, in particular through increased exports of the EC to CECs' markets and through improved growth potential. Moreover, the costs of the alternative of closing the door may far outweigh the costs of opening the door. Once political stability in CECs is quantified as an asset for the EC, the alternative cost in case of political turmoil in eastern Europe becomes an important part of the calculation.

Second, membership is a question of domestic politics as well. Large exports in sensitive products into the EC may hurt the German steelmaker, the French farmer, and the Portuguese textile worker—and this perceived threat shapes domestic politics. Trade in these products has already been severely restricted in the Association Agreements, and long transitional periods will be required in the case of membership. However, that threat may be overstated: on average only 6% of EC imports are coming from CECs, and only up to 10% in some sensitive products. Much of CECs' export growth is actually coming from new private companies, often concentrating on high-technology goods. Intra-industry trade also creates less friction than inter-industry trade, especially if it is conducted within multinational companies. Still, the threat is taken for real, and the painful adjustments after the southern European integration are remembered.

Third, as a more long-term concern, the EC allows free movement of people within its borders. Membership of the CECs may increase incentives for their workers to migrate in a westward direction to highly paid jobs. This argument is unlikely to hold since membership treaties usually impose transitional restrictions on migration and since workers in CECs may prefer to stay in a prosperous and growing environment at home, rather than face the risk of unemployment abroad.

Fourth, early membership in the EC may hurt CECs, since they may need longer transitional periods to transform their economies than widely expected. southern European countries took up to three decades for liberalization, and the scope of the necessary transformation may be larger in central Europe. Entire sectors may be crushed by import competition if they do not establish a competitive position before EC integration. Moreover, macroeconomic stabilization has been one key factor in southern European integration, with Greece still facing high costs of large trade deficits and macroeconomic imbalances. The high inflation and large budget deficits in some CECs should be reduced before an application for membership is submitted. Judging from the four basic Maastricht criteria, the Czech Republic would meet all but the inflation target, but Poland and Hungary would only meet one of four targets as of 1992.

Last but not least, the institutional structure would need substantial reform once new members are admitted to the EC. Designed originally for six members, key institutions are already facing problems and institutional reforms have always created conflict within the EC. The debate about horizontal versus vertical integration has already started. On the other hand, the widening of EC membership would fundamentally change the character of the EC: it would become a truly European family of nations, and not only a club of advanced western European states. That was Monnet's and Schumann's original idea, and their vision should guide the decision for future membership.

References

Balassa, B. 1986. The Determinants of Intra-industry Specialization in United States trade. *Oxford Economic Papers* 38: 220–233.

Balassa, B. 1991. Economic Integration in Eastern Europe. The World Bank. PRE Working Paper, no. 636.

Baldwin, R. 1989. The Growth Effects of 1992. *Economic Policy* 11: 247–281.

Baldwin, R. 1992. An Eastern Enlargement of Efta: Why the East Europeans Should Join and the Eftans Should Want Them. CEPR Occasional Paper, no.10.

Bigues, P., and F. Ilzkovity. 1992. Central and Eastern European Countries: Basic Facts and Main Issues: Trade. *Commission of the EC.* DG-II. I/125/92-EN.

Brabant, J. M. van. 1991. Renewing Economic Cooperation in Eastern Europe and Foreign Assistance. *Economic Systems* 15: 243–264.

Cecchini, P. 1988. *The European Challenge, 1992: The Benefits of a Single Market.* Aldershot: Brookfield.

CEPR (Centre for Economic Policy Research). 1990. *Monitoring European Integration: The Impact of Eastern Europe.* London: CEPR.

CEPR. 1992. *Is Bigger Better? The Economics of EC Enlargement*. London: CEPR.

Collins, S. M., and D. Rodrik. 1991. *Eastern Europe and the Soviet Union in the World Economy*. Washington, D.C.: Institute for International Economics.

Czinkota, M. 1991. The EC 92 and Eastern Europe: Effects of Integration vs. Disintegration. *Columbia Journal of World Business* 26: 20–27.

Montesquieu. C.I. de. 1748. *Complete Works*. Dublin.

Diamandouros, P. N. 1986. The Southern European NICs. In E. Comisso. *Power, Purpose, and Collective Choice: Economic Strategy in Socialist States*. Ithaca, N.Y.: Cornell University Press.

Estrin, S., et al. 1992. Enterprise Adjustment in Transition Economics: Czechoslovakia, Hungary, and Poland. IMF Conference Paper (June).

EBRD (European Bank for Reconstruction and Development). 1992. *Quarterly Economic Review* (June).

EFTA (European Free Trade Association). 1992. Economic and Monetary Union (EMU): A Survey of the EMU and Empirical Evidence on Convergence for the EC and the EFTA Countries. EFTA Occasional Paper, no. 36.

Fratzscher, O. 1993. European Integration: Experience of the South and Prospects for the East. Harvard University. Photocopy.

Guzek, M., et al. 1992. Creation of a Free Trade Area Czechoslovakia-Hungary-Poland: Consequences for the Polish Economy. CEPR Discussion Paper, no. 659.

Hamilton, C. B., and L. A. Winters. 1992. Trade with Eastern Europe. *Economic Policy* 12: 77–116.

Hine, R. C. 1989. Customs Union Enlargement and Adjustment: Spain's Accession to the European Community. *Journal of Common Market Studies* 28: 1–27.

Hirschman. A. O. 1945. *National Power and the Structure of Foreign Trade*. Berkeley: University of California Press.

Hughes, G., and P. Hare. 1991. Competitiveness and industrial restructuring in Czechoslovakia. Hungary and Poland. *European Economy*. Special Edition, no. 2.

Hughes. G., and P. Hare. 1992. Industrial Policy and Restructuring in Eastern Europe. *Oxford Review of Economic Policy* 8: 82–104.

IMF (International Monetary Fund). 1992a. *Direction of Trade Statistics*. Washington, D.C.

IMF. 1992b. *Economic Survey*. Washington, D.C.: IMF.

Krugman, P. M. 1987. Economic Integration in Europe: Some Conceptual Issues. In T. Padoa-Schioppa. *Efficiency, Stability and Equity*. New York: Oxford University Press.

Lipschitz, L., and D. McDonald. 1990. German Unification: Economic Issues. International Monetary Fund. Occasional Paper, no. 75.

Marrese, M. 1989. The Separability of Hungarian Foreign Trade with Respect to the Soviet Union, the Rest of the CMEA, and the West. *Comparative Economic Studies* 23.

McKinnon, R. I. 1991. *The Order of Economic Liberalization*. Baltimore: Johns Hopkins University Press.

Misala, J. 1992. Openness and Competitiveness of Economies of the East European Countries and the Former Soviet Union. Universität Kiel. Institut für Weltwirtschaft. Working Paper, no. 501.

Oxford Analytica. 1992. Various issues.

Palankai, T. 1991. The European Community and Central European Integration: the Hungarian Case. Institute for East-West Security Studies. Occasional Paper, no. 21.

Porter, M. 1990. *The Competitive Advantage of Nations*. New York: The Free Press .

Rodrik, D. 1992. Foreign Trade in Eastern Europe's Transition: Early Results. CEPR Discussion Paper, no. 676.

Rosati, D. K. 1992. Problems of Post-CMEA Trade and Payments. CEPR Discussion Paper, no. 650.

Siebert, H. 1991. Die Integration Osteuropas in die Weltwirtschaft. Universität Kiel. Institut für Weltwirtschaft. Working Paper, no. 491.

Summers, R., and A. Heston. 1988. What Have We Learned from International Comparisons: 1987. *American Economic Review. Papers and Proceesings* 78: 467–78.

Tovias, A. 1991. EC-Eastern Europe: A Case Study of Hungary. *Journal of Common Market Studies* 29: 291–315.

Tovias, A. 1992. Hungary's Export Prospects in the EC Market. *Open Economies Review* 3: 181–202.

Wang, Z. K., and L. A. Winters. 1991. Eastern Europe's Trading Potential. CEPR Discussion Paper, no. 610.

Winters, L. A. and A. Venables. 1991. *European integration: trade and industry*. New York: Cambridge University Press.

World Bank. 1992. *World Development Report*. New York: Oxford University Press.

9 Reforming the Financial System

Timothy D. Lane

9.1 Introduction

Reform of the financial system is at the heart of the transformation of formerly centrally-planned economies into market economies. In a market economy the financial system plays a coordinating role that is a necessary complement to the decentralization of economic decisions. In centrally-planned economies resources are allocated through a combination of fiat and bargaining, and enterprises' access to resources does not depend on their solvency. State enterprises face "soft budget constraints" and can continue to operate regardless of continuing losses, as their operations continue to be financed through easy credit and subsidies (Kornai 1980). If the centralized allocation of resources is eliminated, but enterprises' solvency constraints are not enforced, the result is a "no-man's land" in which firms' demand for credit is unlimited at any interest rate—because they never anticipate having to service their debts—and only quantitative credit controls can restrain their borrowing (Beksiak 1989; Dooley and Isard 1991). Unless these credit controls are so detailed as to be tantamount to central planning, they will result in an arbitrary allocation of resources across different activities which is antithetical to a transformation to a market economy. The transition to a market economy thus depends on establishing financial discipline by building a sound financial system.[1]

Financial discipline is important in a functioning market economy, but it is particularly important during the transition. This is because much of the state sector needs to wither away. In many cases, state enterprises are too large, inefficiently organized, or engaged in activities that are not their comparative advantage at world

---

Views expressed are those of the author, and do not represent the official position of the IMF. The author is solely responsible for any errors.

[1] Some general issues related to market-based financial discipline are discussed in Lane 1993.

market prices. Many of the inefficiencies in allocation were not apparent before the reform process began: many firms with low or even negative value added were ostensibly profitable, due to distorted input and output prices (Hughes and Hare 1991); shortages also created spillovers of demand which led inferior products to be purchased; and demand for some goods (notably armaments) was boosted by large state purchases.

As prices were freed and trade barriers lowered many of these inefficiencies were exposed, but the existing financial institutions then continued to issue credit to enable the existing state enterprises to stay in operation. In addition to this reliance on credit from the banking system, there was an explosion of inter-enterprise arrears as many enterprises simply failed to pay for their inputs. This depended on the passivity of the creditor enterprises, many of which would ship goods without requiring evidence of the purchaser's ability to pay—anticipating that they would be bailed out by the authorities sooner or later (Mitchell 1993). The use of credit, both from the banking system and from other enterprises, to capitalize interest on outstanding loans and bail out unprofitable enterprises pre-empted credit that could have been used more productively by other, more efficient enterprises, and especially by the private sector; this was particularly a problem since in many of these countries, notably Poland and the former Soviet Union (FSU), inflation was associated with a sharp decrease in the total real quantity of credit in the economy (Calvo and Coricelli 1992). In many cases, inflation was a tax on households and the private sector, and a subsidy for those state enterprises that continued to have access to credit at negative real interest rates. The transition of the economy thus requires that the financial system stop perpetuating the old economic structure, and that credit be allocated away from many old loss-making state enterprises and toward more efficient firms.

There are also other respects in which financial sector reform is crucial to the transition. Savings have to be mobilized to finance the investment required for economic restructuring, and an efficient financial system is needed to allocate these savings among competing uses. The financial sector may also be important in transferring ownership from the state to the private sector, as well as enabling private owners to transfer their ownership claims. A sound banking system is also needed in order to prevent the systemic disruptions associated with bank collapses, or the fiscal consequences of repeated bailouts to prevent such collapses, which reforming socialist economies can ill afford. In addition, the financial system is needed as the basis for creation of a sound means of payment in the economy, which is essential to the exchange of goods, services, and financial assets.[2]

In this paper, the objectives of and constraints on financial reform will be discussed. First, the legacy of the old regime will be characterized, including the monobank system, passive finance, and bad debt. The next section discusses solutions to the bad debt problem, pointing out that some overhang of old debt may play a salutary role during the transition. Then the implications for the sequencing of reform are drawn out and the appropriate role of the banking system and of non-bank finance are discussed. It is argued that while banks are necessarily central to the financial system in economies in transition, the soundness of the system depends on placing some limitations on banks' activities. The last section draws some general conclusions.

9.2 The Legacy

In considering the financial reforms that are needed in formerly centrally-planned economies, it is important to characterize the legacy of the old regime. The financial sectors of these economies were underdeveloped partly because finance was not given a high priority, as it was regarded as an unproductive activity. The Marxian analysis according to which the interest rate is related to the rate of exploitation rather than to the time value of money was also inimical to the establishment of efficient mechanisms for the pricing and allocation of credit. This failure to accord a time value to money also inhibited the development of the short-run aspects of the banking system: no great effort was made to develop payments systems to expedite clearing and settlement of transactions, nor to establish money markets that could channel available funds to their most urgent uses in the short run (Folkerts-Landau, Garber, and Lane 1993).

Another important aspect of the legacy is the shortage economy. Many goods, services, and inputs were in short supply, and enterprises' output was typically constrained by their inputs rather than by considerations of profitability. Similarly, at least in principle, households' purchases were constrained by the availability of consumer goods, rather than by their budgets. In effect, shortages meant that money was not fungible among alternative uses. The system was characterized as having two separate monetary circuits: household and enterprise—roughly corresponding to cash and credit circuits. Money passed

---

[2] This includes the creation of facilities for clearing and settling payments associated with international trade and investment, key to the country's integration into the world economy.

between the two circuits through the payment of wages in cash, and back again through households' purchase of consumer goods and their deposits in state savings banks. Cash and credit were not freely convertible one to another. Consumer credit was rare, as was payment-by-check by households. In many cases households were required to accumulate savings in special bank deposits to purchase scarce goods, such as automobiles; these deposits were essentially partial pre-payment for the goods rather than generalized purchasing power.

In practice both firms and households often hoarded inputs and consumer goods, which thus partly supplanted money as a store of value. Uncertainty about the availability of goods, however, also meant that money might be held for precautionary purposes, in case desired goods turned up in the official shops. As a result, even though in most cases there was probably not a "liquidity overhang" in the sense of money being held involuntarily for lack of anything to spend it on—there were usually some goods available, and money could be exchanged for goods or foreign exchange in the black market—the demand for money was probably different in a shortage economy than in a market economy (Lane 1992b). All the above implies that price liberalization is expected to lead to a change in the structure of money and credit in the economy.

The issuance of credit by the banking system had nothing to do with credit-worthiness, and did not constrain enterprises' ability to purchase inputs; purchases were constrained only by whether or not they were provided for in the plan. Inputs were allocated centrally, and the credit issued to finance their purchase was created passively, as a record-keeping device. This meant that evaluating credit-worthiness was not part of the banks' terms of reference. It also meant that the accumulation of debts was largely arbitrary—since they were a by-product of the allocation of inputs according to the plan, and these inputs were evaluated at prices that were also somewhat arbitrary. The enterprise sector as a whole typically earned profits (in an accounting sense), which was the most important base for taxation. At the beginning of these countries' reform programs, these debts were in some cases largely wiped out in real terms through inflation (notably in Poland and the FSU); in others (notably East Germany) they made many of the enterprises, and hence banks, insolvent.

Another important feature of the old system was the *monobank*, meaning that a single bank combined the functions of central banking and commercial banking. Most transfers of funds were among different branches of the monobank and, needless to say, there was no competition. Alongside the monobank, there were usually several specialized banks, including a state savings-bank, a foreign-exchange bank, and some other sectoral banks (foreign trade, agricultural, investment, and the like). At the outset of the reform programs the monobanks were broken up and their commercial banking functions devolved onto newly-formed commercial banks—usually erstwhile branch offices of the monobanks. This process created problems for the emerging system as the new banks were not internally integrated, and payments systems and interbank markets for transferring funds among them were non-existent or ill-developed. There was often little real competition since the newly-formed banks had local monopolies, and since the payments system was so inefficient that it could take weeks for a disgruntled customer to take his business elsewhere. However, in some countries (notably Poland and Russia) new banks were also allowed to establish, often with fairly weak requirements with regard to capitalization, links with major debtors, and prudential standards: for example, in Russia, groups of enterprises could set up "association banks," which would channel central-bank credit to those enterprises. In such cases, the system changed from a completely centralized one to a weakly-regulated one with easy entry—but where banks often still had access to central bank credit, as well as an implicit commitment by the government to bail them out in case of failure.

9.3 Bad Debts

The overhang of bad debts, including both bank loans and inter-enterprise claims, may be a particularly burdensome part of the socialist legacy. Although in some cases, these historic debts have been largely eradicated by inflation, they have generally accumulated substantially after the fall of Communism, as these economies have begun their liberalization and reform programs. Price and trade liberalization have exposed the fact that many enterprises are not viable at world prices (Hughes and Hare 1991); the breakdown of trading arrangements within the Council for Mutual Economic Assistance (CMEA) has also led to the contraction of enterprises in sectors that specialized in selling in the sheltered CMEA market (Rodrick 1992). In several countries the state enterprises have been labor-dominated and have chosen to protect workers from the risk of unemployment, maintaining their employment despite a sharp contraction in the demand for their output (Lane 1991). In most countries the monetary authorities also attempted to establish positive real interest rates, and in the absence of financial discipline this has led credit to burgeon through interest capitalization. All these developments increased the demand for credit, and in the absence of financial discipline, this demand has largely been satisfied—if not through the banking system then through the accumulation of inter-enterprise arrears (Clifton and Khan 1992). The result has been an overhang of bad debt that in many countries has been so large that banks' solvency has been in doubt; in some cases the tangle of inter-enterprise claims has made it difficult to assess any enterprises' credit-worthiness, and impeded the legitimate use of trade credit.[3]

The magnitude of the bad debt problem is impossible to assess accurately in the absence of financial discipline when the payment or non-payment of loans conveys limited information about creditworthiness: an insolvent borrower can continue to service debt by borrowing, while a solvent one can run up arrears with impunity, using this as a means of financing other activities. Notwithstanding, estimates of bad debt have been relatively high—in many cases estimated at between a third and two-thirds of total bank debt.[4]

The solvency of banks and other institutions is essential to their efficient operation due to a moral-hazard problem. An insolvent institution has the incentive to take excessive risks: if a risky venture is successful, the bank may be able to regain solvency and keep a portion of any gains, while if the venture fails it is only its creditors who lose. This moral hazard problem applies not only to banks—whose opportunity to participate in risky ventures is almost unlimited—but also to any other firm whose liability is limited. This problem makes it imperative that most banks and enterprises either be brought to solvency somehow, be shut down, or be controlled very directly and strictly in all their activities; the third alternative is obviously incompatible with transition to a market economy.

One solution would be for the authorities simply to enforce debt contracts and use the bankruptcy process used to deal with insolvent debtors. An exception might be made in the case of banks, whose central role in the payments system, together with the obvious political difficulty of wiping out a sizeable fraction of bank deposits, may warrant some measures to recapitalize them rather than shutting many of them down. This response would be designed to send a clear and credible signal that debt contracts will henceforth be enforced, immediately imposing

[3] The seriousness of the problem of inter-enterprise arrears has varied across countries: in Hungary at end-1991 gross arrears were relatively modest (6 percent of GDP), larger in Czechoslovakia, Poland, and Yugoslavia (from 17 to 22 percent of GDP), and enormous in Romania (53 percent of GDP). In Russia, arrears reached 3.5 trillion rubles by mid-1992. It is possible that some of these arrears may be voluntary, as the classification of arrears—usually as trade credits that remain unpaid after a specified period of time—is arbitrary.

[4] Estimates of the magnitude of bad debts are discussed in Calvo and Kumar 1993.

discipline on borrowers.

An alternative approach is to wipe the slate clean, either by erasing all outstanding debts or by socializing them—that is, taking them on as a liability of the government (Begg and Portes 1992; Levine and Scott 1992). Bankruptcy is a costly mechanism, which should only be used to the extent that it is an efficient means of weeding out inviable enterprises, as well as to the extent that the *prospect* of bankruptcy disciplines borrowers and lenders. To the extent that old debts are an artifact of the old regime—including the highly distorted prices that determined enterprises' profitability in the past—they do not convey much information about the borrowers' current viability.

There is also another consideration: enterprises that are actually insolvent—whether because of the non-viability of their economic activities or because of a crippling debt burden—have no incentive to maximize profits, and unless they are shut down immediately, will constitute a further drain on the economy. If it is not known which enterprises are fundamentally inviable, universal debt cancellation or debt socialization could, simply by increasing the proportion of enterprises that are solvent, increase the fraction of economic activity that is guided by the profit motive, and thus bring about some increase in economic efficiency.

Moreover, there is a general rule about bailouts: if there must be a bailout, there should be only one, and it should be now. Clearly, market discipline would be impaired much less by implementing a general bailout immediately—while creating the conditions for avoiding any future bailouts—than by attempting to maintain an unsustainable situation in which there is a transparent need for a bailout in the future. One qualification to this argument is that avoiding future bailouts, and making this determination clear to borrowers, is easier said than done—particularly after the authorities have already carried out one large bailout.

One possible counter-argument to debt cancellation is that debt may itself serve as a disciplining device, in an environment in which the managers' interests may not coincide with those of the firm's ultimate owners. Such a divergence of interests is an example of the agency problem, whose solution requires setting appropriate incentives for the agent (the manager) to serve the interests of the principal (the owner). This problem occurs even within private companies, whose managers may seek their own rewards or aggrandizement at their shareholders' expense; in well-functioning market economies a complex set of incentive mechanisms limits—but can never completely eliminate—this divergence of interests. It is usually even more of a problem in state enterprises in reforming socialist economies, where managers are often beholden to workers and may seek to raise wages and engage in "featherbedding" with respect to employment, at the expense of the enterprise's titular owner, the state.

In this context, debt may play a particularly important role in disciplining managers and constraining them to behave in a way that is more in line with the objectives of the enterprise's owners. Once hard budget constraints have been established, debt requires that periodic interest payments be made to creditors and that further borrowing must be agreed to specifically. An important function of debt is therefore to impound a firm's free cash flow, which management might otherwise try to appropriate or to channel into projects or acquisitions whose return is low but which increase the resources under the management's control. This function of debt has been identified in market economies (Jensen 1986). It appears to be particularly important in sectors of the economy that may be generating high revenues but in which investment should be shrinking.[5] The state sectors of reforming socialist economies surely have these characteristics: many state enterprises enjoy market power, are potentially quite profitable, and may have substantial assets, including physical and specific human capital; however, the long-run inefficiency of state ownership, and the obsolete capital with which many of these enterprises are equipped, suggests that they should shrink over time—particularly as the reforms progress, bringing wage levels up toward levels in developed Western countries, and thus making these enterprises' wasteful techniques increasingly unsuitable. The ability of management, workers, and other insiders to appropriate the company's assets is also scarcely checked, given the weak supervision of these enterprises. Under these circumstances, an overhang of debt may serve a valuable function: to force the enterprises to pay out some of their revenues, rather than allowing them to use these revenues to maintain a larger-than-efficient scale, or allowing various insiders to appropriate them.

The potential disciplinary role of debt may be the basis for a case against writing off all enterprise debts or shifting them onto the state budget. The benefits of such a debt write-off may be reaped immediately by workers and managers

---

[5] Jensen (1986) identified the U.S. oil and tobacco industries as sectors with these characteristics. He cited the (largely unsuccessful) diversification of large firms in these sectors away from their primary areas of activity as illustrating the dangers of free cash flow, and the subsequent debt-creating buyouts of some of these firms as an example of the creation of debt to discipline management.

through higher wages, salaries, and other benefits. In the case of unprofitable firms which have accumulated debts to finance their losses, a debt write-off might enable them to accumulate new debts in order to postpone painful restructuring and in some cases to delay their inevitable demise. This appears, for example, to have been the consequence of the real debt write-off—the sharp reduction in the real value of outstanding debt—that was associated with the initial price jump at the start of the 1990 reform program in Poland, and to a lesser extent in other countries. The resulting "paper profits" appear to have enabled many enterprises to pay wages in excess of the legal norm, to postpone needed adjustments and, in most cases, to avoid shutdown (Lane 1992a).

How will the situation differ after privatization? It is often implicitly assumed that, as the enterprises are privatized, they will immediately begin to behave as profit-maximizing entities.[6] However, it is only realistic to recognize that any of the proposed schemes for mass privatization will give rise to rather weak control of management by shareholders—either because shareholding is widely dispersed across individuals; because it is channelled though mutual funds and other institutions whose incentives to monitor management are less strong than those of private owners; or because the government (or governmental institutions such as pension funds) retains a large interest in the ostensibly-privatized companies. There is evidence that widely-held private companies are less able to solve the agency problem than are more narrowly-held ones; Demsetz and Lehn (1985) found a highly-concentrated ownership structure to be particularly conducive to efficiency in industries that are subject to a high degree of uncertainty—which surely typifies industries in formerly centrally-planned economies. Freeing the newly-privatized enterprises of their old debt, while it sounds like a laudable objective, has the drawback of removing the management's need to pay out some of its returns to debt-holders—and increases the danger that the management can turn most of these enterprises' assets to their own rather than their shareholders' benefit.

This argument suggests that bad debt impairs financial discipline, but good debt may strengthen it. This makes the bad debt problem much more difficult to solve, since it implies that one must be judicious in determining what fraction of

---

[6] Some proposals for privatization are discussed; for example, see by Borensztein and Kumar 1990; Lipton and Sachs 1990; Blanchard and Layard 1990; and Frydman and Rapaczynski 1990. While all these authors discuss the incentive problems—which provide the rationale for complex privatization schemes rather than a simple uniform distribution of shares to the whole population—they cannot claim to solve them.

enterprise debt to write off. This means that enterprises should not be left with such a large debt burden that most of them will be unlikely to be able to service it; but it also means that they should be held responsible for as much of their debt as they are likely, ultimately, to be able to service.

The other main reason for being judicious in any debt cancellation is the fiscal burden. Any write-off or socialization of enterprise debts—unless it is combined with a corresponding write-off of deposits or other liabilities—entails an increase in the debt that must be serviced by the state budget. If enterprises (including banks) were to be privatized by selling shares in a large and efficient equity market, any debt write-off would, of course, be fully offset by an increase in privatization proceeds; but if equity markets are not efficient, and especially if privatization takes place largely through giveaways, debt cancellation or socialization inevitably increase the fiscal burden. This is of concern in any country, but especially so in a reforming socialist economy, whose tax base is narrow, its tax administration cumbersome, and its access to either domestic or foreign capital markets for financing limited.[7] A large, unnecessary socialization of debt would therefore mean an increase in distortionary taxation, probably including increased resort to the inflation tax.[8]

The conclusion of this discussion is that there is no good alternative to undertaking a speedy but careful assessment of the magnitude of the bad debt problem in each country. Such an assessment should then be used as the basis for an immediate reduction of enterprise debts outstanding as of a particular cut-off date—a reduction which should be partial, but should be judged sufficient to remove the need for any further general bailout. After this has been done, attempts should be made to enforce credit contracts, and to make it clear that they will be enforced.

Debt can only work as a disciplining device if creditors insist that debts be serviced, and grant new credit only to credit-worthy borrowers. Under current conditions in Central and Eastern Europe what is noteworthy about creditors, including both banks and other enterprises, is their *passivity*—their unwillingness to press their debtors for payment (Mitchell 1993). The argument that debt should play a positive role in pressing state enterprises to restructure themselves depends on giving creditors the right incentives to collect on existing debts and to extend new credit judiciously. In this regard, restructuring the banks is of vital importance.

---

[7] This is illustrated, for example, by the piecemeal approach that the U.S. authorities have recently been taking to failures of banks and Savings and Loan Associations.

[8] The weaknesses of the tax structure of formerly planned economies is reviewed by Tanzi 1991.

This means taking uncollectable debts off the banks' books at an early stage and injecting funds as necessary in order to restore banks' capital to safe levels—in effect, *decoupling* the banks' bad asset problem from the enterprises' bad debt problem (Blommestein 1992). Another priority is privatization, which is widely viewed as an essential step in increasing banks' efficiency: private owners would care about banks' profitability and could exert pressure for market-oriented lending decisions (Thorne 1991). Other reforms may also be needed to establish an efficient banking structure. This approach implies a sequence of reforms: restructure the banks *first* and then use the banks as an engine for restructuring the rest of the economy.

9.4 Banking Reform

Banking reform begins with the rather haphazard two-tier banking system that resulted from the devolution, during the period 1987–90, of central banks' commercial banking activities onto newly established institutions. In some countries, new banks, either private or state-owned, domestic or foreign, have also entered. Bank restructuring has received a good deal of attention in Central and Eastern Europe including technical and other assistance from international financial institutions.

A fundamental issue of bank restructuring is whether viable banking firms can be created out of what are in many cases the district operations of the former monobank. The problems are not just how to cope with bad loans and recapitalize the banks, as discussed in the previous section. Some action may also be needed to rectify the portfolio imbalances that have arisen because the existing banks have been made to specialize in a particular class of borrowers or lenders, and often to specialize in either borrowing or lending but not both. This has resulted in poor diversification, both geographically and across sectors, as well as in many cases heavy dependence on the central bank for funds. In some cases, these imbalances should be allowed to work themselves out through ongoing lending and, where possible, through inter-bank transactions; in others, they may necessitate some kind of general portfolio restructuring.

While these imbalances have not yet been addressed, a great deal of energy has been put into the improving the existing banking systems. To start with, there has been attention to making these banks' operations more efficient: by training their management and staff, improving their computing facilities, introducing "twinning" arrangements to facilitate technology transfer, and so forth.

Another priority is prudential supervision, such as introducing standardized accounting systems to provide reliable data to be used by regulators, as well as establishing the relevant legal and administrative structures. Prudential regulation focuses on the establishment and enforcement of capital-adequacy standards, as well as banks' diversification (including their exposure to large loan risks), their liquidity, and the adequacy of their provisions for loan losses.

Competition is another concern. In most of the reforming socialist economies there are few banks of any substantial size and competition among these banks has been limited by their geographical and functional specialization, as well as by entrenched customer relationships with state enterprises.[9] The enormous interest-rate spreads in many countries—with borrowing rates at some banks far in excess of lending rates at others—attest to a segmentation of the markets which limits competition. Increasing competition may entail breaking up regional banking monopolies. The entry of new banks must also play an important role, although an appropriate balance must be sought: if entry is made too easy, the soundness of the new banks may be dubious.

Although these measures to improve the banking system are all useful, and many necessary to develop a sound and efficient system, they will come to nothing unless the bad asset problem is resolved.[10] A well-diversified portfolio is of little use to an insolvent bank. Technical improvements will be accepted only grudgingly by a bank that expects that either it or its losses will be liquidated, while competition is also a dull spur for such a bank. Likewise, prudential regulation of banks with negative capital has little meaning; for such banks, much more pervasive controls are needed to prevent imprudent behavior. Privatization also generally requires that banks be recapitalized first: there are precedents in other countries for the sale of insolvent banks, at negative prices, but that would require that there be enough other solvent institutions to be the purchasers—otherwise, the outcome would be larger, less competitive, but still perhaps insolvent institutions.[11]

9.5 Banks, Securities Markets, and Corporate Control

The evident difficulty of creating sound and efficient banks out of the existing

---

[9] An extreme example is the "pocket banks" owned and controlled by particular enterprises, that are numerous in Russia and elsewhere.

[10] Or unless it is discovered that this problem is not fatal; that is, that most banks are still solvent.

[11] There are examples of this procedure in the resolution of failed banks and Savings and Loan Associations in the U.S. Some approaches to dealing with problem banks are discussed in Fries 1990.

banking system make it tempting to look elsewhere for the key to financial sector reform. What about securities markets?

Some progress has been made in establishing securities markets in reforming socialist countries. Central banks in some countries have begun to establish money markets, issuing Treasury Bills and central-bank paper and entering into repurchase agreements for bills of exchange and other short-term instruments, all of which can play a role in the provision of liquidity to banks and provide instruments that may later be used for market-based implementation of monetary policy.

In several reforming socialist countries, stock exchanges have also been established, trading initially in shares of privatized or mixed-ownership companies. To some extent, the latter development reflects the power of a stock exchange as a symbol of the rebirth of capitalism.[12] Can a stock exchange in a reforming socialist country be more than a symbol, and play a significant role in the allocation of savings in the economy?

To address this question, it is important to consider how a stockmarket, despite a widely-diffused structure of ownership, creates incentives for the efficient allocation of resources in a market economy. Shareholders can influence management through their possibility of "exit" through the sale of their shares, a basic link that allows the stock market to act as a market for corporate control.[13] Dissatisfied shareholders sell their shares, driving the price down and making it advantageous for an outside group to buy up the shares and take over the management (Manne 1965). Several conditions are required for this to work. One is that relevant information be available to shareholders. This means both that the information must be made public—that is, that accounts providing relevant data on the firms' performance be published—and that the shareholders must have an incentive to monitor the firm's performance. If ownership is widely diffused—as is likely in reforming socialist economies, due to the relatively egalitarian distribution of wealth—any one shareholder's incentive to engage in such monitoring is relatively weak.[14] In developed market economies institutions such as market-information services have emerged to reduce individual investors' cost of obtaining information, and institutional investors such as mutual funds play a role

---

[12] This is illustrated by the fact that the Warsaw stock exchange is located in the former Communist Party Headquarters building.

[13] "Exit" in the sense used by Hirschman 1970.

[14] Demsetz (1986) discusses the importance of concentrated ownership holdings in providing incentives for shareholders to monitor management performance.

in concentrating interest in obtaining such information. All these arrangements, however, take time to emerge.

For securities markets to become a market for corporate control it is also necessary that they be liquid, so that shares can be sold at short notice at the prevailing market price. Without this condition—which securities markets in economies in transition do not seem likely to be able to satisfy soon—the shareholder's right of exit is hardly meaningful. Liquidity is also essential in encouraging investors to hold equities to begin with; if shares cannot be readily bought and sold at the prevailing price, they will be unattractive as a store of value, and this will make it difficult for firms to raise funds by issuing equity. Liquidity feeds on itself: if a market is deeper, assets traded there become more attractive, bringing more prospective buyers and sellers into the market, and further deepening the market. Markets typically must be in existence for some time before this synergy begins to work.

Moreover, the liquidity of stock markets generally depends on the financing available to specialist traders or dealers who make markets in equities and other securities—which typically depends, in turn, on the liquidity of money markets, and on banks' flexibility in supplying funds at short notice to these traders. Therefore, the development of securities markets cannot be viewed as an alternative to the development of an efficient banking sector; rather, the latter is a prerequisite for the former to go very far.

Some observers have suggested that, because of the limitations of securities markets, banks must play the dominant role in corporate control as well as in providing financing to enterprises. They have urged that formerly centrally-planned economies adopt an "insider" model of corporate finance—something like the German model of universal banking, or the Japanese main-bank system—in which banks have an intimate relationship with the firms to which they lend, having extensive shareholdings and placing their representatives on companies' governing boards (Corbett and Mayer 1991; Hoshi, Kashyap, and Loveman 1992), and where there are extensive cross-shareholdings among different companies. Such systems are alleged to have several virtues: they avoid the "free rider" problem in monitoring enterprise performance, since the banks' stake as major creditors and in some cases as shareholders is sufficiently large to give them the incentive to monitor; they give banks a longer-term perspective by locking them into loan contracts, rather than shares that they can sell tomorrow; they avoid the waste of resources in launching and fighting hostile takeovers; they create a greater incentive to restructure troubled enterprises, rather than simply letting them fail; and they circumvent the problem of asset valuation, which may be thorny because of the uncertainties associated with economic transition and the novelty of equity markets.

Clearly, banks play an important controlling role in all modern capitalist financial systems—in the "Anglo-Saxon" systems as well as in the "Teutonic" and Japanese ones. The role they play has been characterized as *delegated monitoring* which is particularly important in an environment with asymmetrical information, where firms' managers know more about their own operations than outsiders do (Diamond 1984). Banks watch their borrowers closely, which enables them to enter into more efficient risk-sharing arrangements without being cheated. Because banks are able to diversify the risks associated with their borrowers' activities they can issue fixed-interest claims which they will satisfy on pain of cumbersome and costly bankruptcy proceedings. Banks' specialization in monitoring is related to the fact that they typically issue short-term "inside" debt. In this context, inside debt means that the bank has access to information about the firm that is not publicly available (including the behavior of the firm's deposit accounts). It has been argued that it is important that this debt be short-term so that the borrower's ability to pay must be re-evaluated frequently (Fama 1985).

Given the uncertainties of transition and the time it takes to develop other non-bank financial institutions and markets, bank lending will perforce be particularly important in reforming socialist economies. However, there are some dangers in introducing a full-fledged insider system of the German or Japanese variety in the context of Central and Eastern Europe. For one thing, banks there typically do not even have the internal organizational efficiency and expertise needed to function effectively as outside lending institutions, let alone the extensive managerial and financial skills needed to participate directly in enterprise management in the capacity of universal banks. Moreover, to the extent that an insider system would expose banks to more of the risks associated with the state enterprises they would have to be adequately capitalized to bear this risk; this might be difficult to ensure, given the bad asset problem and the budgetary constraints that already make it difficult adequately to recapitalize the banks.

Another potential drawback of the insider system, even if it is combined with privatization and competition, is the threat to the soundness of the banking system that may result from extensive shareholdings by banks and from inside dealings. This was illustrated by the 1970s bank reforms in Chile, which liberalized its banking sector according to the universal-banking model while maintaining government guarantees on deposits. Industrial firms were allowed to own banks, and banks were allowed to lend to their parent firms, allowing enormous scope for self-dealing and for imprudent behavior at public expense.[15] Much of this behavior was uncovered in the financial collapse that occurred with the onset of the debt crisis in 1982 (Velasco 1988). There is no reason to doubt that entrepreneurs in Central and Eastern Europe would be equally adept at exploiting the opportunities associated with unrestricted cross-ownership of shares, particularly given that the regulatory and supervisory structures are in their infancy.

Another danger is that bank ownership and control of companies and cross-shareholdings might be viewed as an easier substitute for privatization—amounting to a more relabelling of the *status quo*. This phenomenon has been discussed by Kornai, who calls it "pseudo-reform." He characterizes such arrangements—including enterprise cross-ownership, ownership by state-owned banks, and "institutional ownership" by state pension funds, insurance companies or city councils—as "hand[ing] over the ownership rights held by this state organization to another state organization, which in turn continues to spend the money of the state irresponsibly" (Kornai 1990, 71). Thus, although an insider system might have certain benefits once private property, competition, and bank supervision have been firmly established, there is the danger that it would sidetrack the reforms on the way to a market economy.[16] This is a particularly salient issue given the fact that most of these countries had insider systems under socialism as well. Breaking the control of the old insider networks (the former *nomenklatura*) may be important to the reform process, to the extent that these networks represent a large relationship-specific investment for their participants, which may make them hostile to changes in economic structure that would reduce the value of their investment. Breaking down the old networks is also regarded as an important political goal in many reforming socialist countries.

In conclusion, it would be unrealistic to base all hopes for financial development on securities markets. Securities markets themselves depend on the existence of an efficient banking system to permit them to become liquid enough to play an important role in financing and in enterprise control. Moreover, banks' function of delegated monitoring is important in all advanced market economies.

---

[15] One example was an arrangement called the "bicycle," whereby a firm would use a bank loan to buy a controlling interest in the same bank.

[16] Competition in banking and in product markets is a precondition for an insider system to work, according to Corbett and Mayer 1991.

This suggests that scarce resources should be devoted to developing the banking system first, and only later to the development of equity and other securities markets. However, it seems risky to promote an insider model of enterprise control in an environment in which banks are weakly capitalized, privatization has not yet taken place, competition in banking and product markets has not yet been established, adequate regulatory safeguards against self-dealing have not yet been introduced, and the existing insider networks involving state banks and state enterprises have not yet been broken.

9.6 Conclusion

The financial system is not just another inefficient state-owned sector in need of restructuring, although that is part of the problem. It is a sector that was particularly neglected under central planning, since there it played mainly an inconspicuous, passive role. It is a key sector in a market economy, however: without a functioning financial system, there can be no financial discipline; and without financial discipline, an economy based on decentralized decision-making cannot function.

By beginning to exert pressure on the state enterprises to service their debts, and by basing future lending decisions on credit-worthiness criteria, financial intermediaries could help reallocate resources from inefficient state enterprises that need to shrink to other firms that need credit to expand their productive activities. Through this reallocation, they could play a vital role in the transition process.

Thus, reforms are needed to create sound and efficient banks. This suggests that, where possible, banks should be privatized. It also requires addressing the banks' bad asset problem at an early stage, decoupling it from the vast problem of enterprise restructuring which will necessarily take longer to address. The development of prudential supervision and regulation is also essential to maintain banks' soundness; while in many cases it would be desirable to promote greater competition as a spur to heightened efficiency.

Only once sound banks have been established can they begin to act as an engine for economic transition—but until the banks begin to work efficiently, it will be difficult for other financial intermediaries and securities markets to play a meaningful role in resource allocation and corporate control. In undertaking these reforms, however, a degree of realism is required. In particular, given that banks are poorly capitalized and the structures for regulating and supervising them inadequate, it would be risky to saddle them to early with a prominent role in controlling enterprise management—as implied, for example, by models of universal banking or by the use of debt-equity swaps to shift the state enterprises' debt problems onto the banks. The banks must first be reformed before they can be considered equal to this role. Reforming the financial system, starting with banks, should therefore be given a high priority in formulating economic policy in a nascent market economy.

References

Begg, D., and R. Portes. 1992. Enterprise Debt and Economic Transformation: Financial Restructuring in Central and Eastern Europe. CEPR Discussion Paper.

Beksiak, J. 1989. Role and Functioning of the Enterprise in Poland. *United Nations Economic Commission for Europe: Economic Studies* 1.

Blanchard, O., and R. Layard. 1990. Economic Change in Poland. In Centre for Research into Communist Economies. *The Polish Transformation: Programme and Progress*. London: Centre for Research into Communist Economies.

Blommestein, H. 1992. Financial Sector Reform and Monetary Management in Central and Eastern Europe. Paper presented at colloquium, Société Universitaire Européenne de Recherches Financières (SUERF), Berlin.

Borensztein, E., and M. S. Kumar. 1990. Proposals for Privatization in Eastern Europe. *IMF Staff Papers* 38: 300–26.

Calvo, G. A., and F. Coricelli. 1992. Stagflationary Effects of Stabilization Programs in Reforming Socialist Economies: Enterprise-Side versus Household-Side Effects. *World Bank Economic Review* 6: 71–90.

Calvo, G. A., F. Coricelli, and M. S. Kumar. 1993. Financial Markets and Intermediation. In IMF. Financial Sector Reforms and Exchange Arrangements in Eastern Europe. IMF Occasional Paper, no. 102.

Clifton, E., and M. S. Khan. 1992. Inter-Enterprise Arrears in Transforming Economies: The Case of Romania. IMF. Photocopy.

Corbett, J., and C. P. Mayer. 1991. Financial Reform in Eastern Europe: Progress with the Wrong Model. CEPR Discussion Paper, no. 603.

Demsetz, H. 1986. Corporate Control, Insider Trading, and Rates of Return. *American Economic Review—Papers and Proceedings* 76: 313–16.

Demsetz, H., and K. Lehn. 1985. The Structure of Corporate Ownership: Causes and Consequences. *Journal of Political Economy* 93: 1155–77.

Diamond, D. W. 1984. Financial Intermediation and Delegated Monitoring. *Review of Economic Studies* 51: 393–414.

Dooley, M., and P. Isard. 1991. Establishing Incentive Structures and Planning Agencies that Support Market-Oriented Transformations. IMF Working Paper, no. WP/91/113.

Fama, E. F. 1985. What's Special About Banks? *Journal of Monetary Economics* 15: 29–39.

Folkerts-Landau, D., P. Garber, and T. Lane. 1993. Payment System Reform in Formerly Centrally-Planned Economies. *Journal of Banking and Finance*. Forthcoming.

Fries, S. M. 1990. Issues in the Reform of Deposit Insurance and Regulation of Depository Institutions. IMF Working Paper, no. WP/90/74.

Frydman, R., and A. Rapaczynski. 1990. Markets and Institutions in Large-Scale Privatizations: An Approach to Economic Transformations in Eastern Europe. New York University. Photocopy.

Hirschman, A. O. 1970. *Exit, Voice, and Loyalty: Responses to Decline in Firms, Organizations, and States*. Cambridge: Harvard University Press.

Hoshi, T., A. Kashyap, and G. Loveman. 1992. Lessons from the Japanese Main Bank System for Financial System Reform in Poland. Paper presented at conference, Bank Structure and Competition. Federal Reserve Bank of Chicago.

Hughes, G., and P. Hare. 1991. The International Competitiveness of Industries in Bulgaria, Czechoslovakia, Hungary and Poland. CEPR Discussion Paper.

Jensen, M. C. 1986. Agency Costs of Free Cash Flow, Corporate Finance, and Takeovers. *American Economic Review—Papers and Proceedings* 76: 323–29.

Kornai, J. 1980. *Economics of Shortage*. Amsterdam: North-Holland.

Kornai, J. 1990. *The Road to a Free Economy. Shifting from a Socialist System: The Case of Hungary*. New York: W. W. Norton & Co.

Lane, T. D. 1991. Wage Controls and Employment in a Reforming Socialist Economy. IMF Working Paper, no. WP/91/111.

Lane, T. D. 1992a. Inflation Stabilization and Economic Transformation in Poland: The First Year. *Carnegie-Rochester Conference Series on Public Policy* 36: 105–56.

Lane, T. D. 1992b. Household Demand for Money in Poland: Theory and Evidence, *IMF Staff Papers* 39: 825–54.

Lane, T. D. 1993. Market Discipline, *IMF Staff Papers* 40.

Levine, R., and D. Scott. 1992. Old Debts and New Beginnings: A Policy Choice in Transitional Socialist Economies. World Bank, Financial Policy and Systems Policy Research Working Paper, no. WPS 876.

Lipton, D. and J. Sachs. 1990. Privatization in Eastern Europe: The Case of Poland. *Brookings Papers on Economic Activity* 2: 293–341.

Manne, H. G. 1965. Mergers and the Market for Corporate Control. *Journal of Political Economy* 73: 110–20.

Mitchell, J. 1993. Creditor Passivity and Bankruptcy: Implications for Economic Reform. In C. P. Mayer and X. Vives, eds. *Financial Intermediation in the Construction of Europe*. Cambridge: Cambridge University Press.

Rodrik, D. 1992. Making Sense of the Soviet Trade Shock in Eastern Europe: A Framework and Some Estimates. Harvard University. Photocopy.

Tanzi, V. 1991. Tax Reform in Economies in Transition: A Brief Introduction to the Main Issues. IMF Working Paper, no. WP/91/23.

Thorne, A. 1991. Issues in Reforming Financial Systems in Eastern Europe: The Case of Bulgaria. World Bank. Photocopy.

Velasco, A. 1988. Liberalisation, Crisis, Intervention: the Chilean Financial System 1975–85. IMF Working Paper, no. WP/88/66.

10 Human Development and Women's Lives in a Restructured Eastern Bloc: Lessons from the Developing World

Stephan Klasen

10.1 Introduction

Most of the economic literature on restructuring eastern Europe and the former Soviet Union has centered on macroeconomic adjustments, privatization and price liberalization (for example, Kornai 1992a; Sachs 1992; Fisher and Frenkel 1992). The importance of those policy discussions is obvious enough. What appears at times to be lost in these discussions, however, is that the ultimate goal of economic transformation is improving the quality of life for the people of the former Soviet bloc and not merely the introduction of a functioning market economy.

If a swift transition to a free market and resumed economic growth were synonymous with rising quality of life, then the exclusive emphasis on the technicalities of transformation would be fully justified; but experiences of economic transformation in other parts of the world—most notably China and other parts of Asia—as well as the impressive achievements of a number of very poor developing countries in terms of what Amartya Sen refers to as "basic functionings" teach a different lesson: namely that high levels of basic functionings such as longevity, education, adequate nutrition and low infant mortality can be achieved at very low levels of income per capita, and that some successful market economies do very poorly in terms of human development indicators (Streeten 1981; Drèze and Sen 1989; UNDP 1992).

In fact, the former Soviet-bloc countries themselves had, at one stage, quite an impressive track-record in terms of a number of these human development indicators in spite of their mediocre economic performance. The current transition to a market reform with the attendant emphasis on structural adjustment,

I would like to thank Amartya Sen and Jeffrey Williamson for helpful comments on earlier versions of this chapter.

retrenchment of the state, and reduced budgets for social programs might seriously jeopardize these achievements and lead to a deterioration in crucial education, health, nutrition and mortality indicators (UNICEF 1992; Sen 1991).[1]

This is also true for the economic and social position of women in eastern Europe and the former Soviet Union. While the reality of economic and social achievements for women under the communist regimes certainly fell short of the official rhetoric (Tatur 1979; Butenschön 1977b; Blau and Ferber 1986; Wolf 1985), first indications from eastern Europe and the Commonwealth of Independent States (CIS) show that women's position in the labor market is deteriorating rapidly (Gora 1991; Paukert 1991; DIW 1991; Bren 1992; Brown 1992). Household-bargaining models, as well as a wealth of studies from developing and developed countries, suggest that high female unemployment rates and falling labor-force participation spells smaller shares of household resources with potentially harmful effects for women's health and nutrition as well as their economic and social position (Banister 1992; Sen 1990b; Blau and Ferber 1986).

Presently, I will try to spell out the potential adverse effects of current transformation efforts on human development and women's lives. In contrast to many other studies, this paper will not only highlight the social consequences of the transformation process itself, but also discuss the potential long-term effects on human development of the new economic and social structures that are replacing the socialist systems in the former communist bloc. Section 10.2 discusses the concept and measurement of human development. Section 10.3 reviews the most important policy-lessons regarding the enhancement of the quality of life from the experience of pre-and post-transition China (as well as other developing countries) and highlights the opportunities and potential pitfalls awaiting eastern Europe. Section 10.4 discusses the level of human development in pre-transformation eastern Europe and the Soviet Union and outlines current trends.

Subsequently, I turn to the economic and social position of women. Section 10.5 discusses the theoretical and empirical literature linking the labor market position of women to the intrahousehold distribution of resources among males and females. Section 10.6 reviews the pre-transformation situation of women in eastern

---

[1] This is not to say that the fall of the regimes in eastern Europe has not been desirable. In particular, there is little doubt that the *political* changes in eastern Europe were beneficial and have a direct positive impact on the quality of life of the people in these countries. In fact, some have argued that the most important failings of the eastern European systems were political rather than economic (Sen 1991).

Europe and, based on the theoretical insights and current developments in the region, spells out potentially adverse effects of the current reform process. The final section summarizes the argument and discusses policy options.

10.2 Human Development: Concept and Measurement Issues

The concept of human development, as introduced by the United Nations Development Program (UNDP), and the idea of basic functionings as discussed by Sen (1985, 1988, 1991) are two related ways of conceptualizing actual human achievements in a country. They stand in contrast to the traditional focus on output expansion as the overriding goal of development policy. Sen (1988) states that income is not intrinsically valuable but rather a means to achieve desirable ends. Thus it might be much more useful to focus on expanding achievements rather than trying to focus on the expansion of income as one of several means to that end.

To Sen, the desirable ends are "functionings" which he defines as "an achievement of a person: what he or she manages to do or to be" (Sen 1985, 10). While many of these functionings are very valuable, there are undoubtedly some functionings that should be considered more "basic" than others. Lists of these basic functionings typically include longevity, adequate nourishment, good health and basic education (Drèze and Sen 1989; Sen 1988). In fact, Sen goes one step further and argues that the truly desirable state-of-affairs in a country is to give all people the capability to choose from many combinations of functionings and a variety of methods of achieving these functionings.[2]

The UNDP defines human development in very similar terms stressing that "the real objective of development is to increase people's development choices" including health, education, a good physical environment, freedom, as well as expanding incomes (UNDP 1991, 13). The plurality of these desirable development outcomes immediately raises the question of valuation and ranking of the various goals (Sen 1988). In contrast to the income measures where the market, for better or worse, decides on the weights attached to each good, it is not immediately clear how much an increase in average life-expectancy is worth in terms of, say, income or educational improvements. Some attempts have been made to create composite indices incorporating health, education, income and freedom indices to arrive at an

---

[2] For an in-depth discussion of these concepts see Sen 1985, 1988; and Drèze and Sen 1989. Clearly, the socialist system did better in terms of functionings than capabilities. Although most basic functionings were provided, the population had exceedingly small liberties in choosing between bundles of functionings and ways to achieve them (Kornai 1992b).

aggregate measure of human development.[3] One may easily dispute the valuations implicit in these aggregate indices and one can think of a number of equally plausible valuations. But, clearly, each of these goals (whether aggregated or not) deserves attention when planning and measuring progress in the development process.

This is not to say that income expansion cannot lead to improvements in these other development goals. There is a positive correlation between per-capita income and achievements in human development such as longevity, education and political and social liberties (Dasgupta and Weale 1992; Stewart 1985; Streeten 1981). But the relation is far from perfect and much can be learned from the outliers. Table 10.1 presents data on life expectancy, infant mortality, overall and female adult literacy in a selected number of countries. The countries are listed in ascending order of income per capita as reported by the World Bank.[4] The table shows that some extremely poor developing countries do very well in terms of life expectancy, infant mortality and adult literacy. In fact, some low-income countries such as Sri Lanka and the Indian State of Kerala do better in all non-GNP indicators than all nations in the upper-middle-income category, some of which command an income per person more than ten times greater.

Similarly, the relationship between the *growth* of per-capita income and the expansion of health-related indicators is far from perfect. Dasgupta and Weale correlate data from over 50 developing nations for 1970 and 1980 and find only a moderate correlation between income growth and improvements in life expectancy and that there is no perceptible link between income growth and expansion of adult literacy at all (Dasgupta and Weale 1992). In fact, at times, the link between income growth and expansion of life expectancy can be apparently paradoxical. Table 10.2 reports data on decadal expansion of life expectancy in England and Wales and growth of per-capita income in the United Kingdom between 1901 and 1960. The largest expansions in life expectancy occurred during periods of slow or even negative income growth, while during high income-growth decades life

---

[3] For examples, see Morris 1979; UNDP 1992; and Dasgupta and Weale 1992.

[4] The data are transferred into US-Dollars using official exchange rates which often give a distorted picture of purchasing power of people in many poor countries (Perkins 1992a; Balassa 1974). Using purchasing power parity estimates, China's GDP per capita allegedly stands at $2,656 and India's at $910 in 1990 (UNDP 1992). Perkins considers this estimate for China too high and puts the PPP-level of GDP per capita at $1,020 in 1990 (Perkins 1992a).

Table 10.1
GNP and Human Development, 1990

	GNP per capita (US$)	Life expectancy (Years)	Infant mortality (per 1000)	Adult literacy (%)	Female literacy (%)	Fertility (children per woman)
Low income						
Kerala	272	70	42	91	87	2.3
India	350	59	94	48	34	4.2
China	370	70	30	73	62	2.4
Sri Lanka	470	71	26	88	83	2.6
Mauritania	500	47	122	34	21	6.5
Indonesia	570	62	71	77	68	3.3
Lower mid-income						
Congo	1010	53	69	57	44	6.3
Cuba	1170	75	14	94	93	1.9
Jamaica	1500	73	16	>95	>95	2.5
Costa Rica	1900	75	18	93	93	3.1
Chile	1940	72	20	93	93	2.7
Botswana	2040	67	63	74	65	6.7
Algeria	2060	65	68	57	45	5.1
Iran	2490	63	46	54	43	5.0
Upper mid-income						
South Africa	2530	62	67	70	n.a.	4.3
Brazil	2680	66	60	81	80	3.3
Gabon	3330	53	99	61	48	5.2
South Korea	5400	71	30	>95	>95	1.7
Saudi Arabia	7050	64	65	62	48	7.1

Notes: Income and life-expectancy data for Kerala are for 1989; literacy data for 1991; fertility data for 1986–88; infant mortality data for 1981.
Sources: World Bank 1992; UNICEF 1992; Registrar General 1991; UNDP 1992; Sen 1993; Bhat and Rajan 1990.

expectancy hardly improved at all.[5]

These surprising results are not simply statistical anomalies that confound an otherwise clear trend. In fact, there are a number of economic reasons why the correlation between income and human-development achievements is far from perfect. First, the translation of income into desirable functionings or human-

[5] Similarly, improvements in income in the antebellum United States did nothing to improve life expectancy, which fell between 1820 and 1860 (Pope 1991; Williamson 1990).

Table 10.2
Income Growth and Life Expectancy in Britain, 1901–60

	Increase in life expectancy	Growth of per-capita real income (%)
1901–11	4.0	5.9
1911–21	6.5	–12.0
1921–31	2.4	15.8
1931–40	1.4	33.4
1940–51	6.8	7.9
1951–60	2.8	22.2

Note: Growth figures refer to United Kingdom, while life expectancy data are from England and Wales. England and Wales made up more than 75% of UK population throughout the century.
Sources: Drèze and Sen 1989; Maddison 1982.

development achievements depends on a variety of factors such as the distribution of income between households, within households, and the ability of individuals to translate income into functionings (Sen 1988, 1990a; Stewart 1985). Second, a great number of desirable functionings such as health, education, and a clean environment have aspects of public goods and tend to be underprovided by the private sector. Thus high incomes may not translate into high achievement in health, education, and environmental clean-up unless these goods are provided collectively, typically by the state (Sen 1988, 1991; Caldwell 1986). Conversely, very poor countries can achieve very high levels of basic functionings if they are made a priority of state intervention, a topic to which I shall return to later (UNDP 1991; Sen 1991; Caldwell 1986).[6] Third, important human-development goals such as political and civil liberties might bear little relation to national income or growth of income per capita while they most certainly influence the quality of life in a given country (Dasgupta and Weale 1992).

The key lessons to emerge from this discussion are that many human-development achievements do not automatically follow from rising opulence; nor

[6] These two reasons incidentally account for the apparently inverse relation between life expectancy and growth in Britain. The improvements are largest during the decades that encompass the two world wars since war-time rationing during both wars sharply reduced inequality in access to food and other basic commodities. In addition, the introduction of the National Health Service in the aftermath of World War Two provided free, quality health-care regardless of the individual's ability to pay and contributed to the large improvements in life expectancy in the 1940s. Public action was considerably more successful than rapid income growth in delivering human development improvements (Drèze and Sen 1989).

are low incomes an insurmountable obstacle to high levels of human development; instead, it is crucial to analyze the various strategies countries have chosen to achieve high levels of human development.

10.3 Human-Development Strategies: Lessons from the Developing World

Drèze and Sen (1989) distinguish between two successful strategies to achieve high levels of human development. The first they call "growth-mediated" security. Successful examples include Singapore, Hong Kong, Kuwait, the United Arab Emirates (UAE) and South Korea. While the experiences of Kuwait and UAE are not easily emulated—since the basis of their growth and prosperity was rapidly rising oil revenues—the examples from three of the East Asian tigers, and South Korea in particular, prove instructive.

South Korea's real income per capita grew at 7.1% per year between 1965 and 1990, which, according to the World Development Report, is the fastest rate of any country in this time period (World Bank 1992). At the same time, life expectancy at birth expanded by 16 years between 1960 and 1990, reaching 70 years in 1990. The adult literacy rate expanded to 96%, a rate comparable to advanced industrialized countries.

In light of these improvements, one should not, however, be led into thinking that rapid growth *alone* achieved these impressive results in terms of human development. Table 10.3 compares growth performance with an index of improvements in life expectancy for a number of developing countries.[7] It shows that some fast-growers, such as Brazil and Iraq, were unable to translate growth into large improvements in the index of life expectancy.

The difference between South Korea, Brazil, and Iraq is that in South Korea government intervention was aimed at spreading the benefits of growth as widely as possible. Government policies fostered universal education, with an emphasis on labor-intensive growth and low unemployment (Drèze and Sen 1989; Mason et al. 1989).[8] In contrast, Brazil started off with high inequality and maintained it

---

[7] The improvement index is taken from Dasgupta and Weale (1992) and is predicated on the fact that improvements in life expectancy are less costly and easier to achieve when life expectancy is very low. The index of improvements in life expectancy (*LE*) captures this and is defined as follows:

$$\frac{(LE_{1980} - LE_{1960}) * 100}{80 - LE_{1960}}$$

[8] In addition, South Korea embarked on its rapid growth-path with relatively low inequality (Mason et al. 1985; Drèze and Sen 1989).

Table 10.3
Growth and Human Development in the Developing World

	Annual growth of GDP per capita, 1960–80 (%)	Life expectancy, 1980	Change in life expectancy, 1960–80	Improvement index, 1960–80
Singapore	7.5	72	8	50.0
South Korea	7.0	65	11	42.3
Iraq	5.3	56	10	29.4
Brazil	5.1	63	8	32.0
Costa Rica	3.2	70	8	44.4
Mexico	2.6	65	7	31.8
South Africa	2.3	61	8	29.6
Chile	1.6	67	10	43.5

Note: Improvement Index is defined in footnote 7.
Sources: World Bank 1982, 1983.

throughout. While, in South Korea, the bottom 40% of households command about 15.4% of total income, the corresponding share in Brazil was 8.1% in 1988 (UNDP 1991; World Bank 1992). Thus growth, without an emphasis on spreading its benefits as widely as possible, may yield only limited progress in furthering human development.

The second strategy Drèze and Sen discuss is called *support-led security*. Successful examples include Sri Lanka, Chile, Cuba, Jamaica, Costa Rica, China and the Indian state of Kerala. This strategy is predicated on the notion that the fastest way to ensure progress in human development in poor countries is to provide the most important basic functionings through state intervention. All these countries have made the provision of cheap or free health-care, universal education, public health, and, in some cases, the provision of subsidized or free nutrition to vulnerable groups a state priority, and committed state resources to these ends.[9] Table 10.1 demonstrates the success of these policies in spite of low and moderate per-capita incomes in these countries.

There are three particularly promising aspects that recommend such a strategy to poor countries. First, the public health and education sectors, both labor-intensive activities, are part of the non-traded sector of the economy. Since wages in the non-traded sector tend to orient themselves to wages and productivity in the

[9] For details, see Caldwell 1986; Streeten 1981; UNDP 1991; Stewart 1985; and Drèze and Sen 1989, 1990.

traded sector, efforts to improve health and education of the population can be achieved at relatively low cost (Caldwell 1986; Sen 1991). Table 10.4 shows that Costa Rica, Sri Lanka, Chile and Botswana were able to achieve impressive improvements in health and education with only modest government outlays.[10] Second, investments in health and education might improve the growth performance of a country. Both can be seen as investments in human capital that might pay off in terms of improved productivity and faster income growth (Becker 1975; Easterlin 1981; Streeten 1981; Mason et al. 1989). Third, investments in basic needs are mutually reinforcing and further a number of other desirable development goals. In particular, research has shown that improved education for women pays off in terms of lower infant and child mortality as well as reduced fertility (Streeten 1981; Stewart 1985; Caldwell 1981; Preston and Haines 1991). All countries in Table 10.1 that exhibit high female literacy (with the exception of Botswana) have undergone a sharp reduction in fertility rates in the past decades. Similarly, the state of Kerala has achieved a much lower birth rate than the Indian national average (Bhat and Rajan 1990). Reduced fertility diminishes dependency burdens and facilitates improved investments in health, education, and employment, thereby creating a mutually reinforcing cycle of increasing human development.

The experience of China is particularly instructive for policy-makers in eastern Europe and the CIS since it also has a legacy of decades of communist rule and recently experienced a radical transformation of its economy towards markets. There is little doubt that the economic record of China's post-1979 transformation is enviable. In contrast to eastern Europe and the CIS, China was able to transform its economy without any appreciable contraction in economic activity. Instead, it was immediately able to embark on a path of extremely rapid growth of upwards of 8% per year (Perkins 1992b). Agricultural production nearly doubled, exports tripled, rural and urban incomes rose dramatically, and the availability of food and consumer goods in both urban and rural areas improved tremendously. Table 10.5 summarizes a few of China's major economic achievements in the past decade. The question then arises whether this resounding economic success translated into equally impressive human development improvements. Before answering this question, it may be useful to briefly review China's pre-transition record of human

[10] Conversely, highest spending does not necessarily buy lowest mortality. The United States spends, even as a percentage of GDP, more than any other country on health care (13% of GDP in 1991) and has only the 9th highest life expectancy (only one year higher than Costa Rica's) and trails 21 other nations in infant mortality (UNDP 1991; UNICEF 1992).

Table 10.4
Government Expenditure on Health and Education (% of GNP)

	Health		Education	
	1972	1990	1972	1990
Costa Rica	0.8	7.1	5.4	5.0
Sri Lanka	1.6	1.5	3.3	2.8
South Korea	0.2	0.3	2.8	2.9
Chile	4.3	1.9	6.3	3.3
Botswana	2.0	2.0	3.4	8.5
Brazil	1.9	2.6	2.4	1.9
India	0.2	0.3	0.2	0.5

Source: World Bank 1992.

development. When the Communists took control in 1949, life expectancy at birth barely reached 40 years, infant mortality stood at 175 per 1000 live births, and the average number of children per women was 6. By 1979, the year when the transition to a more market-oriented economy began, life expectancy at birth had reached between 65 and 70 (depending on the estimate chosen), infant mortality had dropped to 40 per 1000, and the fertility rate stood at 2.7 children per women (Banister 1987; World Bank 1982). These improvements came in spite of the fact that agricultural production per capita had not risen since the 1950s and had actually fallen for some key food crops (Smil 1986; Banister 1987, 1992).

The key to these impressive human development achievements seems to have been an effective land reform; sanitation and epidemic control measures; immunization campaigns; the build-up of a rural public health system consisting of 775,000 trained midwifes and 1.6 million so-called "barefoot doctors"; disaster relief and government distribution of grain to deficit areas; a cooperative health insurance system covering 90% of the rural production brigades; and heavy emphasis on the promotion of education (Banister 1987, 1992). Thus China under the pre-1979 economic and social regime is another classic case of support-led security.

Post-transition China presents a polar opposite case to the developments pre-1979. While the economy boomed, human development stagnated. Table 10.6 shows the contrasts in achievements between the pre- and post-transition phase. Life expectancy at birth has virtually stagnated since 1979. In fact, it fell in the first few years of reform, apparently due to a steep rise in childhood infectious diseases,

Table 10.5
Economic and Consumption Indicators in China

Economic data	1978	1983	1988	1990	Growth (%)
Real GNP (b. renminbi)	655	938	1592	1738	165
Agriculture (index)	252	341	434	476	89
Exports (index)	182.2	398.2	735.6	n.a.	304
Consumption/Cap. rural	100.0	148.5	215.2	212.7	113
Consumption/Cap. urban	100.0	122.3	177.4	179.3	79
Food and consumer goods	1980	1985	1990		
Meat (kg/cap) rural	2.48	7.74	11.34		
Eggs (#/cap) rural	1.2	2.05	2.41		
Color TV urban	0.59	17.21	59.04		
Color TV rural	n.a.	n.a.	4.72		
Bicyles urban	135.9	152.27	188.59		
Bicycles rural	36.87	80.64	118.33		

Note: Data on color TVs and bicycles are per 100 households.
Sources: Perkins 1992a; State Statistical Bureau 1991.

which resulted in higher infant and early-childhood mortality (Davis 1990). Life expectancy has since turned up again, although infant mortality, particularly for females, continued to rise (see Section 10.5).

What prompted this poor health-performance in spite of otherwise impressive growth? Three factors appear to be particularly important. First, although economic liberalization is certain to have reduced income inequality *between* rural and urban areas, it appears to have contributed to an increase in inequality *within* rural and *within* urban areas (Ling 1991; Perkins 1992b; China Yearbook 1991). Second, and probably more important, there has been a breakdown of the rural health delivery-system and an increasingly unequal distribution of health resources. The number of doctors, midwives, and other rural medical workers fell by more than 50% (Henderson 1990; Davis 1990). Between 1979 and 1981 alone, half a million "barefoot doctors" are reported to have discontinued practice (New 1986).[11] Third, the rural health insurance system collapsed, covering only about 9% of rural residents in 1987 (Davis 1990). This came at the same time as charges for medical care doubled due to higher wages for medical staff, the introduction of expensive

[11] The two most prominent reasons for the decline were tougher training requirements for rural medical workers and economic incentives to move to urban areas where salaries for medical professionals were rising quickly (New 1986; Henderson 1990).

Table 10.6
China's Pre-and Post-Transition Achievements

Economic indicators	1953–76	1977–84	1978–90
Annual growth in NMP per capita (%)	2.1	7.1	7.0
Annual improvements in life expectancy	1.0	0.0	0.1
Annual reduction in infant mortality rate	5.6	−0.7	−1.8
Education indicators	1957–79	1979–87	
Annual increase in promotion rate (%) from primary to middle school	1.8	−1.8	
Education indicators	Promotion rate, primary to lower middle school (%)	Promotion rate, lower middle to upper middle school (%)	Promotion rate, upper middle school to university (%)
1957	44	40	6
1970	71	39	4
1979	83	38	25
1984	66	38	25
1987	69	36	—
Health indicators	Life expectancy	Infant mortality	Fertility rate
1953	40.3	174.6	6.01
1970	61.4	70.4	5.82
1979	65.0	39.4	2.75
1981	64.8	43.7	2.69
1984	64.6	50.1	2.16
1990	66.7	60.8	2.4

Note: The 1978–1990 income growth figure refers to real GNP per capita.
Sources: Perkins 1986, 1992a; Banister 1987, 1992; UNDP 1991; Davis 1990.

technologies, as well as reduced state subsidies (Henderson 1990). The combined effect of three factors has been to increase inequality in the delivery of health care. For those who did not benefit as much in the growth boom, health care became increasingly unaffordable and unavailable.[12]

[12] Paradoxically, the government's retrenchment in the promotion of rural public health came at a time of rising government spending on health care. According to the Ministry of Health, spending for health care between 1978 and 1984 rose at twice the rate of overall government spending. Most of this increase went into capital-construction expenditures and higher wages for medical professional

Similar to the worsening health situation, Table 10.6 shows that the promotion of education has stalled. The percentage of primary-school graduates going to lower middle-school fell by 8 percentage points between 1979 and 1983 with most of the decline concentrated in rural areas. This is partly due to increasing inequality in access to education. Government funding for primary and secondary school was increasingly shifted to the local level making the availability of education dependent on the prosperity of the locality. In addition, the economic reforms have led to a surge in the demand for child-labor which led to a drop in the completion rates (Davis 1990). The decline in the educational opportunities for rural children might block future improvements in health or further declines in fertility.[13]

A key lesson to emerge from the Chinese experience is that even a very successful economic transformation can lead to little or no improvements in human-development indicators. Rapidly rising incomes in China have apparently not counterbalanced increasing inequality in the availability of health care and education. Given that the governments in eastern Europe and the CIS are very unlikely to match China's growth performance in the near future (Perkins 1992b), transformation might lead to even more drastic declines in human development due to a combination of shrinking incomes and a break-down of the social security and health-care system. Only through continued government involvement in the delivery of basic functionings can the high level of human development be maintained in the face of a rapid transformation to a market economy.

10.4 Human Development in Eastern Europe and the CIS: Historical Trends and Current Developments

Human development, as defined by the United Nations Development Program, has been high in all eastern European countries and the Soviet Union. In terms of the Human Development Index, all countries of the region, with the exception of Albania, are in the category "high human development" (UNDP 1992). Table 10.7 summarizes the main achievements. Given the relatively modest levels of per-capita incomes, the high levels of life expectancy, literacy, and the low infant mortality

---

staff to modernize health delivery in urban areas (Henderson 1990). Thus higher spending did little to improve the health performance of the population.

[13] As can be seen from Table 10.6, fertility began to decline rapidly in the 1970s, prior to the enunciation of the one-child policy. The aggressive one-child family campaign has led to further declines in fertility, albeit at a considerable human cost (see Section 10.5).

are impressive. They are only slightly worse than the levels of human development in the much wealthier industrialized countries of western Europe.

The data from the former Soviet Union deserve closer scrutiny. First, it has to be noted that the data in Table 10.7 mask some very crucial regional differences. Infant mortality rates for 1987, for example, vary from a low of 11.3 per 1000 in Latvia to a high of 56.4 per 1000 in Turkmenia. There is a corresponding spread in the life expectancy at birth in 1985–86 ranging from 64.8 in Turkmenia to 73.3 in Armenia.[14] Similarly, the fertility rate in 1986–87 varies from a low of 2.1 in Belarus to a high of 5.8 in Tadzhikistan (Anderson and Silver 1989b; Jones and Grupp 1987).

The literacy rate is also likely to be an overestimate given that more than 23% of adult men and 29% of adult women in 1989 had less-than-incomplete secondary education.[15] But, quite clearly, big strides have been made to increase literacy and lengthen schooling in the former Soviet Union. While in 1970 only about 65% of all employed men and women had some secondary education, that rate had climbed to over 90% in 1989 (Ryan 1992).

While the reality of human development achievements in the Soviet Union might have been considerably more modest, particularly in the Southern tier of the Soviet Union, even there impressive gains had been made in cutting mortality rates, improving education and reducing fertility (World Bank 1993). However, while improvements in mortality continued in the high mortality regions, there were no further reductions in overall mortality in the rest of the Soviet Union since the early 1970s and male mortality rose between 1971 and 1980. Deteriorating environmental conditions, worsening health habits (smoking, alcoholism), and a stagnating health care system might have contributed to the slow-down or reversal of progress in Soviet vital statistics (Anderson and Silver 1986a, 1986b, 1989a; Jones and Grupp

[14] Life expectancy data from the former Soviet Union, particularly in the Southern tier, might be biased upward due to incomplete death registration and a different way of distinguishing between stillbirths and infant mortality. Thus average life-expectancy in the Soviet Union might be lower and the spread in life expectancy considerably larger (Anderson and Silver 1986; Jones and Grupp 1983).

[15] Moreover, the fact that absolutely no data was published on the number of people without any or only incomplete primary education leads one to believe that number is substantial (Pockney 1991).

Table 10.7
Human Development in Eastern Europe and the former USSR

	GDP per capita, 1990 ($)	Life expectancy, 1990 (years)	Infant mortality, 1990 (‰)	Adult literacy, 1990 (%)	Fertility rate, 1990
Romania	1,640	70	27	96	2.1
Poland	1,690	71	16	98	2.2
Bulgaria	2,250	73	14	93	1.9
Hungary	2,780	71	15	99	1.8
Yugoslavia	3,060	72	20	93	1.9
Czechoslovakia	3,140	72	11	99	2.0
USSR	4,550	71	23	99	2.3
	GDP per capita, 1991 ($)	**Life expectancy, 1985–86 (years)**	**Infant mortality, 1987 (‰)**	**Fertility rate, 1986–87**	
Estonia	3,830	70.4	16.1	2.2	
Latvia	3,410	70.2	11.3	2.2	
Russia	3,220	69.3	19.4	2.2	
Belarus	3,110	71.4	13.4	2.1	
Lithuania	2,710	71.5	12.3	2.2	
Kazakhstan	2,470	68.9	29.4	3.1	
Ukraine	2,340	70.5	14.5	2.1	
Moldavia	2,170	71.6	24.3	2.3	
Armenia	2,150	73.3	22.6	2.6	
Turkmenistan	1,700	64.8	56.4	4.8	
Azerbaydzhan	1,670	69.9	28.6	3.0	
Georgia	1,640	71.6	24.3	2.3	
Kirghizia	1,550	67.9	37.8	4.2	
Uzbekistan	1,350	68.2	45.9	4.7	
Tadzikistan	1,050	69.7	48.9	5.8	
For comparison	**GDP per capita, 1990 ($)**	**Life expectancy, 1990 (years)**	**Infant mortality, 1990 (‰)**	**Adult literacy, 1990 (%)**	**Fertility rate, 1990**
Iran	2,490	63	46	54	5.0
Iraq	2,340	63	63	60	6.2
Turkey	1,630	67	69	81	3.5
Pakistan	796	56	104	35	6.2
India	350	59	94	48	4.2
Afghanistan	280	42	167	29	6.8

Notes: Income data for USSR is estimated GNP per capita in 1980. Income data for Iraq and Afghanistan are for 1987.
Sources: World Bank 1992, 1993; UNICEF 1992; UNDP 1992; Pockney 1991; Anderson and Silver 1989.

1983).[16]

Nevertheless, the level of human development achieved in all countries of the former Communist bloc is larger than that of many countries of comparable prosperity. The main ingredients of this relative success are quite clear. The socialist system guaranteed employment and, therefore, a minimum level of income to all able-bodied citizens, and provided state-administered pensions to the old and disabled. At the same time, necessities including food and housing were heavily subsidized and available at very low cost. Inflation was suppressed. Education was mandatory and free. And, last but not least, health care was free, and the governments invested heavily in public health, sanitation, and insured that immunizations reached the levels prevalent in western Europe (Kornai 1992a; UNICEF 1992; Gaudier 1991).[17] Similar to the record of many developing countries, free health-care was achieved at a remarkably low cost to the state. Public expenditure on health care as a percentage of GDP in 1987 ranged from a low 1.9% in Romania to a high 4.2% in Czechoslovakia (UNDP 1992; Helmstadter 1992; Kornai 1992a).[18]

In the current process of transition, many of the elements of this security system will necessarily fall by the wayside. They will include an end to guaranteed employment, liberalization of most prices (including some or all basic necessities), and potentially an end to free health care for all. The question then becomes whether and how alternative institutional arrangements will fill the void left by the inevitable dismantling of the old security system.

The need to establish an alternative safety net-arrangement has been clearly

---

[16] Average life expectancy for the entire Soviet Union reportedly remained at 73 years for females between 1960 and 1986; it is reported to have fallen for males from 65 in 1968 to 62 in 1978, after which it went back up to 65 (Anderson and Silver 1989a). A factor in this was that infant mortality reportedly increased from 22.9 per 1000 in 1971 to 30.8 per 1000 in 1975 (Jones and Grupp 1983) and only dropped down to the former level again in 1990 (UNICEF 1992). Moreover, adult mortality, particularly for males, was on the rise in the 1970s, particularly in the Russian Republic (Anderson and Silver 1986a, 1989a). While a large portion of these apparent deteriorations are artifacts of improved vital registration systems in the higher mortality regions of the Southern tier, it is clear that there were little or no improvements in mortality rates in large parts of the Soviet Union in the 1970s and only modest improvements in the second half of the 1980s (Jones and Grupp 1983; Anderson and Silver 1986b).

[17] While nominally, every citizen was entitled to the same quality care, there were substantial inequalities in the health-care delivery system (Helmstadter 1992; Kornai 1992b).

[18] Since prices in the entire economy in the eastern bloc did not reflect relative scarcities in the economy, these numbers may not be entirely comparable with western figures. Also, the numbers do not include tips and bribes to doctors which were commonly used in a number of countries to secure higher quality care (Pataki 1992; Kornai 1992b).

recognized and some attempts have been made to implement a new social security system (Fisher and Frenkel 1992; Kornai 1992a). For example, unemployment insurance is now established in all eastern European countries including all republics of the former Soviet Union (Slay 1992a; Gaudier 1992). In order to soften the blow of price liberalization, prices for some basic commodities continue to be subsidized in many countries.

Nevertheless, there are signs that some of the developments that led to stagnating and deteriorating levels of human development in China are also occurring in the eastern bloc. There are a number of reports of rapidly rising inequality and increasing poverty in many parts of eastern Europe (Ferge 1991; Gaudier 1991; Kornai 1992a). Price liberalization, inflation and rapidly-falling incomes have eroded the purchasing power of many groups of the population —particularly the elderly, the disabled and children—in many countries of eastern Europe including Czechoslovakia, Hungary, Poland and Russia (Engelbrekt 1992; Gaudier 1991), trends likely to lead to deteriorating health and nutrition among those sectors of the population. In the country hit worst by the transformation, Albania, infant mortality has already doubled in the past two years (UNICEF 1992).

Maybe the most important changes concern the health-care systems of the former eastern bloc. There is considerable pressure to terminate or drastically reduce the socialized health-care sector (Helmstadter 1992; Kornai 1992a; Pataki 1992). While most eastern European countries appear to favor a system of universal health-insurance similar to the one existing in Germany, that appears not to be the case in the republics of the former Soviet Union. There, price liberalization in Russia dramatically increased costs for medical supplies which has led to subsequent cutbacks in services by hospitals and doctors. In addition, the government was only able to fund 60% of the health care budget for 1992. Early reports indicate that, due to a rapid erosion of the state-run health care system, 35% of the Russian population and 65% of the population in Moscow is already paying the full costs of medical services out of their own pockets. This *de facto* privatization of health care and the retrenchment of the state has been blamed for the rise in the mortality rate in Russia by about 5% in 1991, with further increases feared for 1992 (Helmstadter 1992). Moreover, reductions in state-run immunization programs are linked to the first large-scale diphtheria epidemic in Russia and the Ukraine since the 1960s. The epidemic has already struck 4,000 by the end of 1992 and public health officials fear that it will continue to spread rapidly (Bohlen 1993).

The dismantling of the state-run health-care system could, if continued, have devastating effects on mortality and life expectancy in the former Soviet Union. In contrast to China, where the termination of the collective health-care system was countered by rapidly rising rural incomes, the destruction of Soviet health-care comes at a time when the economy contracted by 17% in 1991 and is likely to have suffered a similar contraction in 1992 (Slay 1992b).

The worst problems are likely to appear in the Southern tier of the former Soviet Union. They already had the lowest life expectancy, highest infant mortality, highest fertility, and lowest income per capita of all the Soviet Republics (Shokhin 1991; see also Table 10.7). A dismantling of the state-run health-care system, which was largely responsible for the improvements in human development, might push down the human-development performance of the new countries to levels closer to those of their immediate neighbors (see Table 10.7). The human cost of such a deterioration would be considerable.

It is too early to tell what the impact of the current transition will be on human development in eastern Europe and the CIS. Early reports point to a deteriorating situation in many parts of the former Communist bloc, particularly in the CIS, which mirror similar experiences in China. Unless drastic steps are taken to ensure the continued support for health care and income maintenance, much of the human-development gains achieved over the past few decades may be lost.

10.5 Women's Economic and Human Development

The earlier sections have stressed the importance of inequality in the distribution of crucial welfare-related resources as one of the important obstacles to high levels of human development. While the discussion so far usually referred to *inter*-household inequality, I will now turn to another important factor influencing human development: *intra*-household inequalities with particular emphasis on the distribution of household resources between the sexes.

This particular aspect of distributional concerns critically influences human development in several ways. First, given that women make up between 45% and 55% of every population, female deprivation is a significant societal problem. Second, success in achieving many other desirable functionings such as low infant mortality, reduced fertility, and improved educational opportunities for children depend critically on the intra-household distribution of resources.[19]

Demographic data from developing countries indicate that the intra-household distribution of basic functionings is, and has been, highly unequal in many countries. Table 10.8 shows that many regions of the developing world—particularly North Africa, and West, South, and East Asia—have fewer females than males, although biomedical evidence and data from sub-Saharan Africa, Latin America and Southeast Asia suggest that women have, in the absence of discrimination, a considerable survival advantage vis-a-vis men. Careful research has shown that such differences in sex ratio are indeed a result of excess female mortality, particularly—but not exclusively—among children. A comparison between the actual sex ratio and the one that should prevail in the absence of gender discrimination shows that more than 90 million additional women should be alive today in the countries that exhibit excess female mortality. The problem of "missing women" is worst in Bangladesh, Pakistan, India and China (D'Souza and Chen 1980; Chen et al. 1981; Coale 1991; Sen 1990b, Sen 1993; Klasen 1992).[20]

In order to understand which economic forces lead to such inequalities, it is important to conceptualize intra-household distribution. One way to model unequal distribution of resources between the sexes among children has been to pose a joint family utility function where children are treated as investment goods. Consequently, calculations by parents may lead them to neglect girls in favor of boys in places where boys have higher expected earnings as child laborers and/or as adults (Rosenzweig and Schultz 1982). Clearly this kind of thinking is likely to influence parental allocation rules among their children, particularly in regions where they rely heavily on their children for old-age insurance.[21] But this model is inadequate, in and of itself, for a number of reasons. First, it ignores the

---

[19] I have already commented on the influence of female literacy on infant mortality and fertility. Moreover, there is a clear correlation between the level of female education and their children's education (Streeten 1981; Stewart 1985; Drèze and Sen 1989; Easterlin 1981).

[20] Apart from such drastic cases of discrimination in survival chances, there are less-glaring inequalities that reduce women's human development. They include such diverse issues as unequal distribution of work burden within the household; lower earnings for the same work; unequal political representation and power; inequalities in education; and other remaining social and legal barriers. For data on these issues and further discussion, see United Nations 1991; UNDP 1992; Blau and Ferber 1986; and Tinker 1990.

[21] Additional socio-economic and cultural factors (which, in themselves, might have an economic foundation: see Boserup 1970) may reinforce these calculations. If, for example, a dowry needs to be paid for the woman, and she will leave and settle with her husband's family (patrilocal marriage), parents have higher costs and few expected returns from investment in girls and depend even more on the well-being of their sons (Dyson and Moore 1983).

Table 10.8
Female-Male Ratios and Women's Labor Force Participation, 1990

	Female-male ratios	Female share of labor force (%)	Women's labor-force participation rate (%)
South Asia	0.935	20	22
West Asia	0.941	19	21
East Asia	0.947	40	59
North Africa	0.986	16	17
Latin America and Caribbean	1.004	39	32
South-East Asia	1.005	34	48
Sub-Saharan Africa	1.020	37	47
North America	1.044	41	50
Europe, Japan, Australia and New Zealand	1.045	38	43
USSR	1.109	48	60

Note: Women's labor force participation refers to the percentage of women above age 15 who are considered economically active.
Sources: United Nations 1991; United Nations Population Division 1992.

question of unequal distribution of resources among parents. Moreover, the assumption of a joint family utility function blurs the crucial problem of conflicting interests and implicitly assumes that girls have consented to the discrimination against them (Hartmann and Folbre 1991).

Another way to conceptualize intra-household distribution is Sen's (1990b) model of cooperative conflict. This game-theoretic formulation of household relations also argues for the existence of gains from marriage. At the same time, it states that there is an inherent conflict over the distribution of these gains between the members of the family. The resolution of these conflicts will depend on three factors. First, the so-called *breakdown position,* which refers to the notion that the distributional share a person receives within marriage depends on what that person's resources would be outside of marriage. For example, a woman will get a better distributional deal within marriage the greater her potential access to resources should she decide (and be able) to get divorced (Nash 1950; Sen 1990b). Second, the higher the *perceived contributions* of a person to joint household-production the better their share in the distributional bargain, on account of the greater perceived legitimacy of their claim to their share of the resources.[22] Third, intra-household resource allocation will be affected by *perceived interests*: if a wife puts the family's well-being ahead of her own, while her husband only values his individual well-being, she may be willing to settle for fewer resources so long as the welfare of the family is maximized. Such notions of women's sacrifice for the good of the family might lead to a reduced allocation of resources to women (Sen 1990b).

If such considerations are important in the distributional struggle between husband and wife, they may translate into unequal allocation among children via similar mechanisms. If the mother believes she needs and deserves a smaller share than her male counterpart, it is not hard to imagine that she would assume the same for her female daughter. However, while this model seems to capture distributional issues between parents quite well, it is not entirely satisfactory in its explanation of female disadvantage among children. In particular, it fails to explain that female disadvantage among children is not uniform, but depends importantly on family composition and birth order (Das Gupta 1987; Muhuri and Preston 1991).

In the following, I wish to combine the insights from these two theories to better understand distributional issues within the household. As far as distribution between the parents is concerned, I propose to apply the cooperative-conflict model which, in my view, best captures the congruent and divergent interests of husbands and wives in their struggle over intra-household distribution. But one of the areas of congruence is that both have an interest in maximizing the benefits and minimizing the costs of their children, particularly in places where they depend on their children for old-age insurance. Consequently, the notion of a joint utility-function for the parents when considering their allocation rules vis-à-vis their children might adequately capture this aspect of distribution.[23]

A number of important implications can be derived from this formulation of the model which are apparently borne out by empirical evidence. The first is that any improvement in the outside earnings of women, as a result of higher female

---

[22] Note that the actual contributions might be less important than the perceptions thereof. For example, women's housework may be a very productive, valuable, and time-consuming activity but not recognized as such by neither men nor women. That way it may be explicable that in spite of many surveys showing that women actually work harder and longer in market and home combined than men do, they expect and receive less remuneration for it in terms of household resources (Sen 1990b; United Nations 1991; Tinker 1990; Waring 1988).

[23] Note, however, that in contrast to Schultz and Rosenzweig, the joint utility function of the parents is not a family utility function. Thus while it may be optimal for the parents to allocate more resources to boys and fewer to girls (particularly high birth-order girls), in no sense does this imply that it is optimal for everyone concerned and the female children might have consented to it.

labor-force participation or higher female-male earnings ratios, will improve the situation of women and girls in the family through a number of important mechanisms. It will likely improve the situation of a woman since it improves her breakdown position. It is likely to improve her own and her husband's perception of her contribution.[24] It might also change her perceived interests as outside work is likely to raise her independence. At the same time, increases in the outside earnings of women raises the potential value of female children and might therefore lead to a reduction in discrimination against them.[25]

Table 10.8 supports the impression that, with the exception of China, the higher the labor-force participation of women the higher the female-male ratio of the population. Table 10.9 presents the same kind of data for the 17 largest states and territories in India in 1981. An OLS regression linking female labor-force participation and the (migration-adjusted) female-male ratio shows that women's labor-force participation significantly influences the female-male ratio in the expected direction and accounts for 40% of the (very large) variation in female-male ratios.[26]

In addition, a wealth of studies from developed countries have shown that increased female labor-force participation coincided with a number of important advances for women such as rising female-male earnings ratios; declining occupational and pay discrimination; higher rates of female political participation; and some redistribution of domestic work burdens (Blau and Ferber 1986; Becker 1981; Goldin 1991; United Nations 1991; Davis 1984).

While raising the outside-earnings potential of women might be a particularly promising strategy for furthering women's human development, it is by no means the only one. The model also predicts that institutional, legal and cultural changes might help women and girls considerably. For example, the legalization of divorce and the institution of an effective alimony and child-support structure would, once again, improve the breakdown position of women. Rising divorce rates in western countries and sharply reduced fertility are further indications of increased independence for women which have translated into reduced inequality in the intra-household distribution of benefits and burdens (McCrate 1987; Becker

[24] Work outside the home is typically valued much more than housework and the contribution to the household made by outside work is much easier to quantify (Waring 1988; Drèze and Sen 1989).

[25] In addition, improved economic "value" of girls may reduce or even eliminate female-specific costs such as dowries which should, once again, raise their survival chances (Boserup 1970; Dyson and Moore 1984).

[26] See also Bardhan 1987 for a similar calculation using data from Indian states.

1981).

Similarly, enabling women to better control their fertility via easy access to birth control and abortions, as well as facilitating child-rearing by instituting parental leave with job guarantee and child care, are other steps to improve their economic and social position. These measures enable them to enter, remain or return to the workforce and pursue careers similar to men's in much greater numbers (Goldin 1991; Blau and Ferber 1991; Davis 1984). Sweden has been particularly generous in implementing these policies and has achieved the highest female labor-force participation-rate as well as the highest female-male earnings ratio in the western world (Blau and Ferber 1986; UNDP 1992).

Moreover, the introduction of old-age insurance might drastically reduce the incentive to favor boys and thereby reduce discrimination against girls by giving parents alternative investment calculations. Cultural and institutional changes such as moving from patrilocal to matrilocal marriages would raise the value of a girl as a potential provider in old age, as would the ability of women to inherit property (Dyson and Moore 1984). Changing perceptions on the value of child-rearing and housework could also go a long way to improve the position of women in the household by raising their perceived contributions (even if their actual contributions remained the same) and, possibly, changing their perceived interests (Sen 1990b; Waring 1988).

Finally, state intervention might partially make up for discrimination against girls and women. Access to free health-care and free nutrition for those in need might eliminate the most egregious forms of inequities in the distribution of health care and nutrition. The example of the Indian state of Kerala might be instructive here. Although women have a relatively low labor-force participation-rate, access to public health-care and public distribution of food might be at the heart of Kerala's success in providing more equitable survival chances than any other state in India (Table 10.9).[27] The same holds for Sri Lanka where public provisioning of health and subsidized food have contributed to turning a male advantage in life expectancy in the early 1950s to a female advantage by the early 1970s (Nadarajah 1983; Caldwell 1986).

The development of discrimination in China provides another illustration of

---

[27] The exceptionally high level of female education might also have contributed to an improved position of women in Kerala (Drèze and Sen 1989; Caldwell 1986). In general, however, the link between literacy and discrimination against females is unclear and heavily debated in the literature (Rosenzweig and Schultz 1982; Muhuri and Preston 1991).

Table 10.9
Female-Male Ratios and Female Labor-Force Participation in India, 1981

Indian states	Female labor-force participation rate, 1981 (%)	Migration-adjusted female-male ratio, 1981
Andhra Pradesh	27.87	0.975
Maharashtra	24.63	0.959
Madhya Pradesh	22.63	0.945
Tamil Nadu	22.57	0.973
Karnataka	19.23	0.966
Himachal Pradesh	18.80	1.002
Kerala	12.79	1.019
Gujarat	11.85	0.942
Orissa	10.88	0.977
Rajasthan	9.44	0.911
Bihar	9.16	0.930
Tripura	9.08	0.954
Dehli	6.39	0.893
Uttar Pradesh	6.02	0.870
West Bengal	5.97	0.933
Haryana	4.82	0.909
Punjab	3.09	0.887

Note: The reported female-male ratios were adjusted for net migration (from birthplace) within India. Regressing migration-adjusted female-male ratio (FMR) on female labor-force participation rate (FLFP) yields the following results (standard error in parenthesis):

$$\underset{}{FMR = 0.900 + \underset{(0.00104)}{0.00334}\ FLFP} \qquad R^2=0.406$$

Sources: Registrar General 1981, 1988.

the role the state may play in enhancing or reducing women's and girls' human development. Women in pre-revolutionary China suffered from various types of discrimination ranging from no access to property or education, arranged marriages, complete legal subordination to their fathers and husbands, to footbinding and considerably higher mortality rates. Once the Communists took over, they vowed, among other things, to ensure equal rights for women. In the Marriage Law Campaign of 1950 they gave equal rights to men and women, allowed divorce, forbade arranged marriages, legalized the remarriage of widows, allowed women to own property and made them beneficiaries of the 1949 land reform (Johnson

1983; Wolf 1985; Banister 1987).

While many of these reform were never implemented in many parts of rural China due to the heavy resistance of the male population, they were reasonably successful in reducing women's discrimination in the areas where they were instituted (Johnson 1983). In addition, repeated campaigns to mobilize women for the workforce led to rapidly rising female labor-force participation rates.

Apart from these legal and economic campaigns, the creation of free medical care and public health facilities in all of China, combined with the income and food security provided by the communes and backed by the central government, ensured that girls and women had improved access to medical care and food. Table 10.10 shows that these policies were quite successful, not only in raising overall life expectancy, but also in enhancing women's health. While in 1953, women outlived men by just 1 year, the gap in life expectancy rose to 3.2 in 1964.[28]

Table 10.10 also shows that, in this aspect, women have benefitted relatively little from the economic transformations that began in 1978. Life expectancy rose by only one year between 1978 and 1990, and female infant-mortality more than doubled in the same period.[29] Once again, it is government policy that is largely responsible for this deterioration. In particular, the dismantling of the collective health-care system has apparently led to heightened discrimination in the access to medical care. This is consistent with the analysis of the model described above. If you turn an essentially free good into a scarce good in a society that continues to have a high son-preference, females are likely to suffer (Banister 1987; Davis 1990). Moreover, the implementation of the one-child policy combined with severe financial penalties for having more children has led to increasing discrimination against girls who are now considered even more undesirable than previously.[30]

The preceding discussion shows that women's roles in the labor market, as well as a number of government policies legislating family, fertility, health and welfare, can have considerable influence on the economic and human development of women.

---

[28] To be sure, this relatively small gap in life expectancy is an indication of continued discrimination against women. In countries with little or no discrimination, the gap in life expectancies usually ranges from 5 to 8 years (United Nations Population Division 1992)

[29] Mortality rates have fallen in other age brackets (Banister 1992).

[30] There is some debate as to whether these girls are born and then simply have higher mortality rates and thus disappear or whether they are hidden, illegally adopted, or otherwise kept out of sight of government officials. Most likely, a combination of both is at work (Johansson and Nygren 1991; Banister 1992).

Table 10.10
Gender-Specific Vital Statistics in China

	Infant mortality (per 1000)		Life expectancy (years)		Female-male ratio
	Male	Female	Male	Female	
1953	179.3	169.5	39.8	40.8	0.930
1964	89.4	81.7	55.5	58.7	0.944
1970	70.3	70.4	60.2	62.5	0.944
1978	36.8	37.7	64.1	66.0	0.943
1982	34.9	57.5	64.7	64.7	0.942
1984	33.9	67.2	64.9	64.1	0.940
1990	39.7	83.1	66.4	67.0	0.938

Sources: Banister 1987, 1992; Coale 1991.

10.6 Women's Economic and Social Position in Eastern Europe and the CIS

As in China, the regimes in eastern Europe and the Soviet Union also guaranteed legal and economic equality to women and were, at least verbally, committed to achieving equality between the sexes (Jancar 1976). Marriage contracts were egalitarian, birth control and abortion were legalized and made available, child care and family leave was instituted, educational opportunities were equalized, women were allowed and encouraged to join the political system, and women were enlisted in the workforce in increasing numbers (Lapidus 1978; Blau and Ferber 1986; Kornai 1992b). Table 10.11 demonstrates that some of these policies were quite successful, particularly in education: women had achieved equality or even surpassed men at all levels, including university studies. Female enrollment in higher education surpassed male enrollment earlier and to a larger degree than anywhere in the western world (Tatur 1979; Butenschön 1977a).[31]

In addition, Table 10.11 shows that women's labor force participation rates were very high, higher than in all European countries with the exception of Sweden (ILO 1992; Kornai 1992b). One factor that aided the high labor force participation of women was that child care was more readily available than in western European countries encompassing between 30% of all children in Bulgaria up to 60% in Hungary. Moreover, paid family-leave and sick-leave policies were generous and allowed reentry into the labor force at any time (Jancar 1976; Butenschön 1977b;

[31] In the Soviet Union, there was considerable regional variation in the educational attainments of women with the Southern tier lagging behind the rest (Ryan 1992).

Table 10.11
Economic and Demographic Indicators for Eastern European Women

	Labor-force participation rate			Tertiary-education enrollment ratio
	Women (%)	Men (%)	Ratio (W/M)	
Czechoslovakia	45.6	54.3	0.840	0.84
Poland	43.2	54.5	0.793	1.12
Romania	42.6	51.0	0.835	n.a.
Hungary	39.5	51.1	0.773	1.06
East Germany	49.3	60.0	0.822	n.a.
USSR	45.8	55.0	0.833	1.06
For comparison				
USA	44.3	56.8	0.778	1.06
West Germany	36.6	60.7	0.603	0.86
Sweden	49.7	55.0	0.904	1.06

	Crude birth rate (per 1000)	Abortion-birth ratio	Contraceptive prevalence (%)	Divorce rate (per 1000 population over 25)
Czechoslovakia	13.3	0.77	95	4.1
Poland	14.9	0.18	75	2.2
Hungary	11.7	0.73	73	4.3
East Germany	12.0	0.37	n.a.	5.0
Bulgaria	12.5	1.18	76	2.2
USSR	17.7	1.30	n.a.	5.8
For comparison				
USA	15.7	0.36	68	8.0
West Germany	11.0	0.11	n.a.	3.5
Sweden	13.6	0.34	78	3.2

Note: Tertiary education enrollment-ratio is female over male and refers to 1988–89. Labor force participation data refer to number of people in labor force divided by all people. They are from 1991 (Czechoslovakia, USA); 1990 (Hungary, Romania, Sweden); 1989 (USSR); 1988 (Poland); 1987 (West Germany); 1981 (East Germany). Crude birth rate data is for 1990. Abortion-birth ratios only refer to legally induced abortions and are from 1988 (East Germany, Poland); 1987 (USA); and 1989 (all others). Contraceptive prevalence is for 1976 (Bulgaria), 1977 (Czechoslovakia, Poland), 1990 (all others). Divorce rates are for 1985-87.
Sources: ILO 1989–90, 1992; UNDP 1992; UN Population Division 1992; UNICEF 1992.

Lapidus 1978; Kornai 1992b).

This is not to suggest that women had actually achieved equality vis-à-vis men in eastern Europe and the Soviet Union. In fact, they were struggling with much the same issues that concern women in the West. While labor-force participation was high, there was considerable occupational segregation between men and women. Women dominated the health and education profession while they were underrepresented in industry (Lapidus 1978; Tatur 1979; Dunn 1978). Similarly, within occupations, women were concentrated in the lower rungs of the hierarchies while they were heavily underrepresented in leading positions (Jancar 1976; Butenschön 1977a; Dunn 1978). Consequently, there were considerable pay differentials between men and women. Estimates of the ratio of women's to men's earnings range from about 70% to 75%, which is in the range of pay inequality in western countries (Tatur 1979; UNDP 1992; Bren 1992; Paukert 1991; Blau and Ferber 1986).

Moreover, women were still largely responsible for bringing up the family and, therefore, essentially carried a double burden. Butenschön (1977b) presents survey results showing that women had to perform up to six hours or more of housework a day apart from their full-time jobs. Waiting in line (due to persistent shortages), the low level of technology in the household, and the refusal of most men to help in the home made the life of a working woman particularly difficult. Thus it is no surprise that some women had an ambivalent attitude towards their labor-force participation. Surveys done in the 1970s showed that about 25% of women would rather have worked part-time or not at all if they could have afforded to (Jancar 1976; Butenschön 1977a). Nevertheless, women's high labor-force participation-rates contributed considerably to their economic and social independence. In fact, the policies to enlist as many women as possible in the labor force, although mainly initiated to satisfy rapidly rising labor demand as a result of "forced growth," were explicitly seen and presented as attempts to ensure economic and social equality between the sexes (Kornai 1992b; Jancar 1976). As I have argued in the last section, there is considerable merit to that view. In fact, demographic data from the former Soviet Union indicate that female labor-force participation had a direct impact on the relative health and mortality of women. Similar to the situation in the Indian states, there is a close link between female labor-force participation-rates and the sex ratio and the ratio of life expectancies in the Soviet Republics. Table 10.12 presents data for 1985 and shows that the regressions between labor-force participation, sex ratio, and life expectancy ratio

Table 10.12
Work, Life Expectancy and Survival in the Former Soviet Republics

	Female-male ratio, 1985	Female labor-force participation rate, 1985 (%)	Female-male life-expectancy ratio, 1985–86	
Ukraine	1.172	39.3	1.131	
Latvia	1.157	48.3	1.137	
Russia	1.154	45.8	1.160	
Estonia	1.146	48.4	1.144	
Belarus	1.140	42.8	1.132	
Lithuania	1.121	43.2	1.136	
Georgia	1.118	36.5	1.114	
Moldavia	1.109	38.2	1.101	
Kazakhstan	1.067	38.7	1.145	
Azerbaydzhan	1.048	26.3	1.117	
Kirghizia	1.047	29.5	1.109	
Armenia	1.045	37.9	1.074	
Uzbekistan	1.030	22.8	1.091	
Turkmenistan	1.029	20.5	1.104	
Tadzhikistan	1.029	18.4	1.068	
For comparison				"Missing women" (millions)
Turkey, 1991	0.974	23.4	1.055	0.55
Iran, 1986	0.956	5.5	1.013	0.99
Afghanistan, 1979	0.944	4.9	1.024	0.58
India, 1981	0.934	14.4	1.006	26.05
Pakistan, 1990	0.905	8.2	1.000	4.13

Note: Due to heavy male war-losses during World War Two, the female-male ratios are higher than expected in the former Soviet Republics. Given equal treatment, women are expected to outlive men. Female labor-force participation rate refers to number of women working divided by total number of women. "Missing Women" are calculated by comparing non-discriminatory expected sex ratios with actual sex ratios (see Coale 1991; Klasen 1992). Life-expectancy ratios for non-Soviet countries are for 1990, female-male ratio and "missing women" for Turkey are for 1986. Regressing the female-male ratio (FMR) of the former Soviet Republics on female labor-force participation rates (FLFP) yields the following results (standard error in parenthesis):

$$FMR = 0.925 + \underset{(0.0754)}{0.4704}\ FLFP \qquad R^2 = 0.749$$

Using FLFP to predict the female-male life-expectancy ratio (FMLE) yields:

$$FMLE = 1.048 + \underset{(0.051)}{0.194}\ FLFP \qquad R^2 = 0.527$$

Sources: Pockney 1991; UNDP 1991, 1992; UNICEF 1992; Klasen 1992; UN Population Division 1992; ILO 1992.

have an extremely good fit with women's labor-force participation being a highly significant predictor of the sex ratio or the ratio of life expectancies. The table also shows considerable regional variation in the female-male and the life-expectancy ratio. Women in the central Asian republics, who had by far the lowest labor-force participation, also had the lowest female-male ratio and female-male life-expectancy ratio.

Another sign of economic and social independence was that divorce rates in eastern Europe and the Soviet Union were comparable to western levels and that women had high control over their fertility as shown by the birth rate data, the rate of contraception use, and the ratio of abortions to live births.[32] In fact, the high divorce, low fertility, and high abortion rates can be seen as attempts by women to limit or reject the double burden they were expected to carry (Jancar 1976).[33]

All in all, it appears that women had achieved a considerable amount of economic and social autonomy in eastern Europe and the USSR. The question then becomes how the transformation to a market economy might influence this. First impressions from eastern Europe suggest that the current transition is hurting women in a variety of ways. The first and foremost problem is in the labor market where women are being pushed out of the labor force in increasing numbers. The most reliable data come from the former German Democratic Republic, now part of unified Germany. Table 10.13 traces the development of unemployment from 1990 to the end of 1992. In December 1990, unemployment for women stood at 8.2% in contrast to 6.4% for men; by June 1992 it had risen to 20.1% for women and has ever since been about double the rate for men.

Initial reports from other countries point to similar developments. In Poland, the ratio of vacancies to job seekers among women turned from more than 10 to 1 in 1989 to 1 to 40 in 1992. The ratio of vacant jobs available for men to the number of applicants was "only" 1 to 14 in 1992 (Kornai 1992b, 215; Brown 1992, 54; Gora 1991). 60% of Poland's unemployed are women and most of the available

[32] Since liberal divorce and abortion legislation depressed birth rates, it ran counter to attempts to increase labor-force growth. For that reason, Rumania outlawed abortion and divorce in 1967 (Jancar 1976; Kornai 1992b).

[33] To be sure, there is nothing to be celebrated about high divorce rates. But the fact that the majority of divorces were demanded by women (Butenschön 1977a) indicates that women were able to secure an independent economic existence for themselves which is likely to have improved their bargaining position within marriage. Similarly, the exceptionally high rates of abortions in eastern Europe and the Soviet Union is to a large extent a sad commentary on the availability and quality of birth control and male attitudes towards using it. Nevertheless it indicates a high degree of women's control over their fertility.

jobs are reserved for men (*Economist,* 1992). In Czechoslovakia, female and male unemployment rates diverged in 1991 with women making up 60% of the unemployed (Paukert 1991; Bern 1992). These figures might represent an underestimate. An ILO survey done in 1991 found that about half of the women who have become unemployed are so discouraged about job prospects that they have dropped out of the labor force altogether (Paukert 1991). Moreover the female-male earnings ratio is reported to have dropped by 7 percentage points to less than 0.7 in the past year (Bren 1992). Only 29% of all jobs advertised in Slovakia in early 1991 were open to female applicants (Bren 1992, 59).[34]

There is little reliable data on the republics of the former Soviet Union. Also, much of the labor-shedding that accompanies the transformation has not yet taken place so that in Russia, for example, the overall official unemployment rate was below 1% by the end of 1992 (Weir 1993). The little data there is, however, points to the same problems for women in the labor market as everywhere else in eastern Europe. Between 1989 and 1990, the labor force participation rate of women in Estonia declined from 51.3% of all women to 47.5% (ILO 1992, 39–40). In addition, women made up about 75% of the unemployed in 1991 (ILO 1992, 630). Similarly, more than 70% of the registered jobless in Russia in late 1992 were women (Weir 1993).

A combination of factors appears to have contributed to this rapid absolute and relative deterioration of women's labor-market situation. One is that many of the services (and protective legislation) that enabled high women's labor-force participation have been discontinued. Due to fiscal pressures in former East Germany and Czechoslovakia, many state-run child-care facilities have been closed or the prices for the services rendered have been drastically increased (DIW 1991; Bren 1992; Pearson 1991). Similarly, many company-run child-care facilities, accounting for about 80% of all day-care places in Russia, are closed or in the process of privatization or liquidation (Weir 1993). As child care becomes increasingly unavailable or unaffordable, many women with small children are forced out of the labor market. Available female labor-force participation data show that the largest declines are among women of child-bearing years (ILO 1992).

---

[34] These figures should be treated with some caution. The official unemployment rate is partially a function of the generosity of the unemployment benefit system. Also, people working in the informal sector, many of which may be women, are often counted as unemployed (Brown 1992). In Hungary, the problem appears to be less pronounced with women making up only 40% of the unemployed. At the time of writing this article, there was no reliable data from Rumania, Bulgaria, and Albania.

Table 10.13
Unemployment Rates in Eastern Germany

		Male (%)	Female (%)
December	1990	6.4	8.2
March	1991	8.0	10.0
June	1991	8.0	11.2
September	1991	9.1	14.3
December	1991	8.9	14.7
March	1992	11.2	20.1
June	1992	10.0	18.9
September	1992	9.6	19.0
November	1992	9.4	18.5

Source: Bundesanstalt für Arbeit 1992.

Second, the largest number of new jobs is created in small companies that are either unwilling to grant child care, maternity leave and other benefits to women or, in places where they are required to do so, they simply refuse to hire women (Bren 1992).

Third, the concentration of women in lower rungs of the hierarchies in state-run enterprises makes them considerably more vulnerable to the mass lay-offs that have accompanied privatization efforts. Their virtual absence in the corporate hierarchies has also prevented them from influencing decision-making in employment policies.

Fourth, open and hidden discrimination have led to increased lay-offs among women. Since men were naturally assumed to be the main bread-winner in any family, concern for the social costs of lay-offs leads many employers to fire women first and try to retain men as long as possible. Some have even argued that pushing women instead of men out of the workforce is a hopeful strategy to soften the blow of transformation (DIW 1991; Weir 1993).[35]

Fifth, there has been virtually no political organizing and action on the part of women's groups to defend their labor market position. In fact, the political muscle of women is exceedingly small given that their representation in the political system has declined sharply since transformation (Bren 1992; Adamik 1991; UNDP

[35] This is in spite of the fact that, prior to the transition, women had nearly the same labor-force participation-rate as men, and only wage and occupational discrimination had prevented them from earning more than their husbands.

Table 10.14
Percentage of Women in Parliament

	1988	1990
Czechoslovakia	42	10
Poland	25	16
Hungary	52	4
Bulgaria	27	9
Romania	26	8
USSR	53	17
For comparison		
USA	6	7
West Germany	24	26
Sweden	45	62

Note: 1990 data are for unified Germany.
Source: UNDP 1991, 1992.

1992; Weir 1993). Table 10.14 shows the changes in women's representation in parliament between 1988 and 1990.

Finally, some countries have begun to restrict the availability of abortions, thereby sharply reducing women's control over their fertility. Most notably, Poland has banned abortions under all circumstances, and Hungary is considering similar legislation (Newman 1991).[36]

Taken together, these factors have made it much harder for women to carry the double-burden of home and work.[37] Given that unemployment has not peaked in many parts of eastern Europe, much more retrenchment for women's labor-market position is in store unless specific policies are designed to shield them from discriminatory employment policies (Adamik 1991; Pearson 1991).

It is difficult to assess precisely what the consequences of these developments will be for the intra-household distribution of benefits and burdens. Following from the earlier discussion in Section 10.5, it is quite clear that they could worsen women's bargaining positions within the household considerably: both their breakdown position, as well as their perceived contributions are likely to drop,

[36] On the other hand, Rumania has now legalized abortions for all women in the first trimester. Also, it is hoped that the availability of reliable birth control is going to increase in the process of transformation to a market economy (Newman 1991).
[37] One countervailing tendency might be that the availability of part-time labor, which was virtually unavailable under socialist rule, will increase as the economic transformation continues (DIW 1991).

leading to a redistribution disfavoring women in the family. This is not to say that I expect women's mortality to go up in eastern Germany, Hungary, or Poland. There the problems might manifest themselves in terms of reduced economic and social independence, less ability to leave an undesirable marriage-situation, and less access to consumption goods.

In the central Asian and Transcaucasian parts of former Soviet Union, however, the effects might be much more dramatic. In particular, a combination of a sharp reduction in women's labor-force participation and a reduction or termination of the state-run pension system may lead to a situation similar to those prevalent in neighboring India, Pakistan, Afghanistan, and Turkey, where parents have a considerable economic incentive to favor boys over girls in the allocation of food and medical care. Consequently, women and girls may suffer from the kinds of discrimination that cause millions of "missing women" in South and West Asia (Table 10.12).

10.7 Policies to Preserve Human Development in Eastern Europe and the CIS

I have outlined potential dangers for human development in eastern Europe and the CIS. The current transformation process can lead to severe reductions in the relatively impressive human-development achievements of eastern European countries. In particular, rising inequality and reduced access to health care and education may lead to increases in mortality, illiteracy, and fertility. While these concerns may apply all over eastern Europe, they are likely to be most pressing in the Southern tier of the former Soviet Union.

Women may be the biggest losers of the monumental economic changes taking place in the former communist bloc. In particular, they may lose much of the economic and social independence they achieved as a result of their high involvement in the labor market. Again, the problems might be most severe in the central Asian republics, where increasing female-male mortality rates and heightened discrimination against women and girls might be on the horizon.

The theoretical arguments and the empirical evidence suggest that the state can play a very important role in forestalling these adverse developments. Policies that aim at reducing inequality, as well as strategies to make basic functionings as widely available as possible, could do much to preserve and enhance human development. The evidence from poor developing countries shows that these policies can be successfully implemented at a modest cost to society. Moreover, continued support for women's involvement in the workplace, such as investment in child care and maternity leave, anti-discrimination policies, and access to fertility control, can do much to preserve and enhance women's economic and social roles. In addition, equitable access to health, education, and other basic functionings can do much to protect women's entitlements and prevent some of the adverse effects brought about by their worsening labor-market position.

It would be foolish to suggest, however, that these successful policies can be easily implemented in eastern Europe and the CIS. In particular, three problems present themselves that make the situation in parts of the former eastern bloc considerably more difficult. One is that the demographic situation in eastern Europe and in the European republics of the former Soviet Union makes any policy to protect and enhance entitlements considerably more costly than in developing countries. Due to decades of low birth rates and low retirement ages (ranging from 52 for women in Bulgaria to at most 60 anywhere else in eastern Europe), the ratio of non-productive old people to the working population is very high. Consequently, any policy to enhance human development must be financed by a rather small pool of working people and be distributed among a large group of non-working old people who, in addition, have higher medical and social needs (Engelbrekt 1992; United Nations Population Division 1992).

Second, a crucial precondition for enacting such policies is the achievement and maintenance of internal peace and security. If civil wars and internal strife continue as they do now in many parts of eastern Europe and the CIS, there is little hope that effective programs to enhance basic functionings can be implemented in these war-torn regions.

Finally, it is important to recognize that the success of policies to enhance human development depends on the existence of a well-functioning state willing and able to put these policies effectively into practice. In the context of eastern Europe, this is far from guaranteed. Janos Kornai puts it thus:

> We are dealing neither with the philosopher-statesmen of Plato, who rise above all selfish criteria, nor with the expert, law-abiding, punctilious bureaucracy of Max Weber. Nor are we dealing with the political decision-makers described in studies of welfare economics, who exclusively serve the public interest. Therefore, any economist arguing that market forces should be curtailed must soberly consider that *this* is the kind of state to which he now wishes to assign a function, and this is the kind of state it will remain for some time to come. (Kornai 1992a, 3–4)

Thus recognizing the need for policies to preserve and enhance human development in eastern Europe is only a first step towards reaching the goal.

Creating institutions that are willing and capable of implementing these policies effectively is an equally important task.

References

Adamik, M. 1991. Hungary: A Loss of Rights? *Feminist Review* 39: 166–170.

Anderson, B. A., A. J. Coale, and E. Härm. 1979. *Human Fertility in Russia Since the Nineteenth Century*. Princeton, N.J.: Princeton University Press.

Anderson, B. A., and B. D. Silver. 1986a. Infant Mortality in the Soviet Union. *Population and Development Review* 12: 705–738.

Anderson, B. A., and B. D. Silver. 1986b. Sex Differentials in Mortality in the Soviet Union. *Population Studies* 40: 191–214.

Anderson, B. A., and B. D. Silver. 1989a. Patterns of Cohort Mortality in the Soviet Union. *Population and Development Review* 15: 471–501.

Anderson, B. A., and B. D. Silver. 1989b. Demographic Sources of the Changing Ethnic Composition of the Soviet Union. *Population and Development Review* 15: 609–656.

Balassa, B. A. 1973. Just How Misleading are Official Exchange Rate Conversions? A Comment. *Economic Journal* 83: 332.

Banister, J. 1987. *China's Changing Population*. Stanford, Calif.: Stanford University Press.

Banister, J. 1992. China: Recent Mortality Levels and Trends. Photocopy.

Bardhan, P. K. 1987. On the Economic Geography of Sex Disparity in Child Survival in India: A Note. Paper presented at BAMANEH/SSRC Workshop, Differential Female Mortality and Health Care in South Asia, Dhaka.

Becker, G. S. 1975. *Human Capital*. New York: NBER.

Bhat, M., and I. Rajan. 1990. Demographic Transition in Kerala Revisited. *Economic and Political Weekly* (1–8 September).

Blau, F. D., and M. A. Ferber. 1986. *The Economics of Women, Men, and Work*. Englewood Cliffs, N.J.: Prentice-Hall.

Bohlen, C. 1993. Diphtheria Epidemic Sweeps Russia. *New York Times* (29 January).

Boserup, E. 1970. *Women's Role in Economic Development*. London: Allen and Unwin.

Bren, P. 1992. The Status of Women in Post-1989 Czechoslovakia. *RFE/RL Research*

Report (16 October).

Brown, B. 1992. Transforming Postcommunist Labor Markets: The Polish Case. *RFE/RL Research Report* (14 August).

Bundesanstalt für Arbeit. 1993. Eckwerte des Arbeitsmarktes im Bundesgebiet Ost. *Mitteilungen*. Nürnberg.

Butenschön, M. 1977a. Frauenemanzipation in der UdSSR: Anspruch und Wirklichkeit (I). *Osteuropa* 27: 91–104.

Butenschön, M. 1977b. Frauenemanzipation in der UdSSR: Anspruch und Wirklichkeit (I). *Osteuropa* 27: 192–209.

Caldwell, J. C. 1981. *The Theory of Fertility Decline*. London: Academic Press.

Caldwell, J. C. 1986. Routes to Low Mortality in Poor Countries. *Population and Development Review* 12: 171–220.

Chen, L. C., E. Huq, and A. D'Souza. 1981. Sex Bias in the Allocation of Food and Health Care in Rural Bangladesh. *Population and Development Review* 7: 55–70

Coale, A. J. 1991. Excess Female Mortality and the Balance of the Sexes in the Population: An Estimate of the Number of Missing Females. *Population and Development Review* 17: 517–523.

Das Gupta, M. 1987. Selective Discrimination against Female Children in Rural Punjab, India. *Population and Development Review* 13: 77–100.

Dasgupta, P., and M. Weale. 1992. On Measuring the Quality of Life. *World Development* 20: 119–131.

Davis, D. 1990. Chinese Social Welfare: Policies and Outcomes. *China Quarterly* 119: 577–598.

Davis, K. 1984. Wives and Work: The Sex Revolution and its Consequences *Population and Development Review* 10: 397–417.

Deutsches Institut für Wirtschaftsforschung (DIW). 1991. Frauenpolitische Aspekte der Arbeitsmarktentwicklung in Ost- und Westdeutschland. *DIW Wochenbericht* 30/91.

Drèze, J., and A. K. Sen. 1989. *Hunger and Public Action*. Oxford: Clarendon Press.

Drèze, J., and A. K. Sen, eds. 1990. *The Political Economy of Hunger*. Oxford: Clarendon Press.

D'Souza, S., and L. C. Chen. 1980. Sex Differential in Mortality in Rural Bangladesh. *Population and Development Review* 6: 257–270.

Dunn, E. 1978. Die Stellung der Frau in ländlichen Gebieten der Sowjetunion. *Osteuropa* 28: 997–1013.

Dyson, T., and M. Moore. 1983. On Kinship Structure, Female Autonomy, and Demographic Behavior in India. *Population and Development Review* 9: 35–57.

Easterlin, R. A. 1981. Why Isn't the Whole World Developed? *Journal of Economic History* 41: 1–20.

Economist, 1992. (12 December).

Engelbrekt, K. 1992. Growing Poverty among Bulgaria's Pensioners. *RFE/RL Research Report* (28 February 28).

Fisher, S., and J. A. Frenkel. 1992. Macroeconomic Issues of Soviet Reform. *American Economic Review* 82: 37–42.

Folbre, N., and H. I. Hartmann. 1988. The Rhetoric of Self-Interest: Ideology and Gender in Economic Theory. In A. Klamer, D. McCloskey, and R. Solow, eds. *The Consequences of Economic Rhethoric*. Cambridge: Cambridge University Press.

Gaudier, M. 1991. Economic Reform, Social Change and Institutional Perspectives in Central and Eastern Europe. *Labour and Society* 16: 439–467.

Goldin, C. D. 1991. *Understanding the Gender Gap*. Cambridge: Harvard University Press.

Gora, M. 1991. Shock Therapy for the Polish Labour Market. *International Labour Review* 130: 145–163.

Helmstadter, S. 1992. Medical Insurance in Russia. *RFE/RL Research Report* (31 July).

Henderson, G. 1990. Increased Inequality in Health Care. In D. Davis and E. Vogel, eds. *Chinese Society on the Eve of Tiananmen*. Cambridge: Harvard University Press.

ILO (International Labour Organization). 1989–90, 1991, 1992. *Yearbook of Labour Statistics*. Geneva: ILO.

Jancar, B. 1976. Zur Rolle der Frau in der kommunistischen Gesellschaft. *Osteuropa* 26: 528–548.

Johansson, S., and S. Nygren. 1991. The Missing Girls of China. *Population and Development Review* 17.

Johnson, K. A. 1983. *Women, the Family and Peasant Revolution in China*. Chicago: University of Chicago Press.

Jones, E., and F. W. Grupp. 1983. Infant Mortality Trends in the Soviet Union.

Population and Development Review 9: 213–246.

Jones, E., and F. W. Grupp. 1987. *Modernization, Value Change and Fertility in the Soviet Union*. Cambridge: Cambridge University Press.

Klasen, S. 1992. Missing Women: When, Where, and How Many? Harvard University. Photocopy.

Kornai, J. 1992a. The Postsocialist Transition and the State: Reflections in the Light of Hungarian Fiscal Problems. *American Economic Review* 82: 1–21.

Kornai, J. 1992b. *The Socialist System*. Princeton, N.J.: Princeton University Press.

Lapidus, G. W. 1978. *Women in Soviet Society*. Berkeley: University of California Press.

Ling, Z. 1991. *Rural Reform and Peasant Income in China*. London: Macmillan.

Maddison, A. 1982. *Phases of Capitalist Development*. Oxford: Oxford University Press.

Mason, E. S., M. J. Kim, D. H. Perkins, K. J. Kim, and D. C. Cole. 1989. *The Economic and Social Modernization of the Republic of Korea*. Cambridge: Harvard University Press.

McCrate, E. 1987. Trade, Merger and Employment: Economic Theory on Marriage *Review of Radical Political Economics* 19: 73–89.

Morris, M. D. 1979. *Measuring the Condition of the World's Poor: The Physical Quality of Life Index*. London: Pergamon.

Muhuri, P., and S. H. Preston. 1991. Effects of Family Composition by Sex Among Children in Matlab, Bangladesh. *Population and Development Review* 17: 415–434.

Nadarajah, T. 1983. The Transition from Higher Female to Higher Male Mortality in Sri Lanka. *Population and Development Review* 9: 317–325.

Nash, J. F. 1950. The Bargaining Problem. *Econometrica* 18.

New, P. 1986. Primary Health Care in the People's Republic of China: A March Backward? *Human Organization* 45: 147–153.

Newman, K. 1991. Eastern Europe: Update on Reproductive Rights. *Ms*. (July/August).

Pataki, J. 1992. Reform of the Hungarian Health-Care System. *RFE/RL Research Report* (7 February).

Paukert, L. The Economic Status of Women in the Transition to a Market System. *International Labour Review* 130: 613–633.

Pearson, R. 1991. Questioning Perestroika: A Socialist-Feminist Interrogation. *Feminist*

Review 39: 91–96.

Perkins, D. H. 1986. *China: Asia's Next Economic Giant?* Seattle: University of Washington Press.

Perkins, D. H. 1992a. China's Economic Boom and the Integration of the Economies in East Asia. Harvard University. Photocopy.

Perkins, D. H. 1992b. China's Gradual Approach to Market Reforms. Harvard University. Photocopy.

Pockney, B. P. 1991. *Soviet Statistics since 1950.* New York: St. Martin's Press.

Pope, C. L. 1992. Adult Mortality in America before 1900. In C. Goldin and H. Rockoff, eds. *Strategic Factors in 19th Century American Economic History*. Chicago: University of Chicago Press.

Preston, S. H., and M. R. Haines. 1991. *Fatal Years*. Princeton, N.J.: Princeton University Press.

Registrar General. 1981. *Census of India 1981: Provisional Population Totals*. New Delhi: Ministry of Home Affairs.

Registrar General. 1988. *Census of India 1981: Internal Migration in India 1961–81*. New Delhi: Ministry of Home Affairs.

Registrar General. 1991. *Census of India 1991: Provisional Population Totals*. New Delhi: Ministry of Home Affairs.

Rosenzweig, M. R., and T. P. Schultz. 1982. Market Opportunities, Genetic Endowments, and Intrafamily Resource Distribution: Child Survival in Rural India. *American Economic Review* 72: 803–815.

Ryan, M. 1991. *Contemporary Soviet Statistics*. London: Edward Elgar.

Sachs, J. D. 1992. Privatization in Russia. *American Economic Review* 82: 43–48.

Sen, A. K. 1985. *Commodities and Capabilities*. Amsterdam: North-Holland.

Sen, A. K. 1988. The Concept of Development. In H. Chenery and T. Srinivasan, eds. *Handbook of Development Economics*. Amsterdam: North-Holland.

Sen, A. K. 1990a. Justice: Means Versus Freedoms. *Philosophy and Public Affairs*, Spring 1990.

Sen, A. K. 1990b. Gender and Cooperative Conflicts. In I. Tinker, ed. *Persistent Inequalities*. New York: Oxford University Press.

Sen, A. K. 1991. What Did You Learn in the World Today? *American Behavioral Scientist* 34: 530–548.

Sen, A. K. 1993. The Economics of Life and Death. *Scientific American*. 268: 40–47.

Shokhin, A. 1991. The Social Aspects of Economic Reform in the USSR. *Labour and Society* 16: 359–380.

Slay, B. 1992a. International: Unemployment Provision in the Former Communist Countries. *RFE/RL Research Report* (10 January).

Slay, B. 1992b. The Polish Economy: Between Recession and Recovery. *RFE/RL Research Report* (11 September).

Smil, V. 1986. Food Production and Quality of Diet in China. *Population and Development Review* 12: 25–45.

State Statistical Bureau. 1991. *China Statistical Abstract 1991*. Beijing: State Statistical Bureau.

Stewart, F. 1985. *Planning to Meet Basic Needs*. London: Macmillan.

Streeten, P. 1981. *First Things First*. New York: Oxford University Press.

Tatur, M. 1979. Merkmale der Erwerbstätigkeit der Frauen in Polen. *Osteuropa* 29: 220–237.

Tinker, I., ed. 1990. *Persistent Inequalities*. New York: Oxford University Press.

UNICEF. 1992. *The State of the World's Children 1992*. New York: Oxford University Press.

United Nations. 1991. *The World's Women 1970–1990*. New York: United Nations.

UNDP (United Nations Development Program) 1991, 1992. *Human Development Report*. New York: Oxford University Press.

United Nations Population Division. 1992. *Demographic Yearbook*. New York: United Nations.

Waring, M. 1988. *If Women Counted*. New York: Harper and Row.

Weir, F. 1993. The Kitchen Counterrevolution. *In These Times* (22 March).

Whitlock, E. 1992. Midyear Update on Russian Economic Indicators. *RFE/RL Research Report* (28 August).

Williamson, J. G. 1990. *Inequality, Poverty, and History*. New York: Oxford University Press.

Wolf, M. 1985. *Revolution Postponed*. Stanford, Calif.: Stanford University Press.

World Bank. 1982, 1992, 1993. *World Development Report*. New York: Oxford University Press.

11

Foreign Direct Investment in Eastern Europe: The Case of Telecommunication

Sophia Eltrop

11.1 Introduction

Joseph Stalin once vetoed a plan to extend Russia's telephone network, saying he could "think of no better instrument of counter-revolution" (*Economist*, 8 February 1992). In centrally-organized economies like those of eastern Europe communication between private people was not encouraged. Telephones were considered a luxury and modern telecommunication techniques were unknown.[1] The only communication links that were promoted were those in offices and factories between superiors and subordinates.[2] Superiors gave orders to their immediate subordinates, who performed their tasks as they were told and reported back only to their superiors. Although such vertical links were important, no further horizontal communication was encouraged. On the contrary, information was often kept a secret within each office and the secrecy was mostly welcome as a means to avoid criticism. Naturally, in such a communication structure few phones were needed.

Following the revolutionary developments since 1989 the situation has turned around completely. All of a sudden "communication" and "information" have become keywords for the transformation of former communist countries into democracies and market economies. This follows immediately from the new and different requirements of a market economy. When people are no longer told what

---

My thanks to Graham Allison for encouraging me to write this paper, to Gary Müller for valuable help and discussions and to David Allen for support in finding interview partners.

[1] Current telephone penetration levels in central and eastern European countries range between 9 and 22 direct exchange lines (DEL) per 100 inhabitants, well short of the OECD average of 40 per cent DEL density (EBRD 1991, 50).

[2] In the GDR, the Ministry of Energy and its subordinate plants had a whole telephone system of their own to ensure that communication in this crucial sector was free of friction.

to do, but are expected to make their own individual plans and decisions, they need access to information regarding their choices and cannot tolerate limitations to their private and professional contacts. A newcomer in a business needs to find and reach his suppliers as quickly and easily as his clients need to be able to reach him. Otherwise he cannot establish a market for his goods. Moreover, telephones are only one basic element in the set of all possible communication links that allow markets to develop. The communication structure in a country has also important social and political implications. A modern telecommunication system is a prerequisite for a functional and more decentralized government system. For the formation of a civic society telephones are equally important. Tolerance can only be learned through frequent conversation, and pluralism will only be appreciated by people who have access to information about others. Telephone, perhaps Cable Television, and even communications by satellite will be crucial in forming an environment of openness and in providing a wide variety of information opportunities.

A modern telecommunication structure will be crucial for a successful reorganization of former communist societies and centrally-planned economies. But not only western observers of eastern Europe understand this; leaders of the countries of eastern Europe and the Former Soviet Union (FSU) themselves seem dedicated to put the improvement of telecommunication before most other needs. Of the 388 million ecus ($545 million) that the European Bank for Reconstruction and Development (EBRD) committed to eastern Europe last year, about 70 percent (268 million ecus) went into telecommunication projects (*Economist*, 8 February 1992). Telecommunication ministers are eager to get the latest technologies, and because eastern European telecommunication companies have neither the technology nor the know-how for modern telecommunication, they are forming joint ventures with western companies in practically all areas of telecommunication. Many small improvements have already been made.[3]

Some new services have been introduced by international telecommunication companies without the need for money from governments or development banks. With the permission of each respective country, international companies have

---

[3] New switches which replace hand switching or very primitive switching methods have been installed to increase the capacity of telephone systems significantly. Modern digital telecommunication networks have been started and will later enable users to employ the whole range of new computer technologies through their telephone connections. Long-distance links are being built right now which will increase the capacity for international calls.

installed mobile telephone networks for cities like Moscow, Budapest or Gdansk. They have also put up satellite stations, significantly relieving congestion in local and international calls.[4] In those cities most foreign business-people would not have come if there had not been a cellular network with international connections through satellites.

The telecommunication industry all over the world seems enthusiastic about investment in eastern Europe.[5] Many managers in the business expect remarkable growth in the economic activities of those countries and a subsequently large market for telecommunication.[6] Nevertheless, telecommunication companies are not dependent on eastern Europe in order to expand and find new markets. The efforts of former eastern-bloc countries to construct a communication infrastructure comes at a time when western countries have also started to rebuild and improve their telecommunication systems. To attract and sustain foreign investment in telecommunication will require constant efforts from governments in eastern Europe; after all, because of the many uncertainties, foreign direct investment in many other sectors has hitherto failed to appear.

This work presents an effort to explain some of the surprising developments in telecommunication in eastern Europe. There is one obvious reason for optimism among international companies. Telephones have been shown to be a necessity rather than a luxury good everywhere in the world.[7] Poor people spend a relatively larger part of their income on telephone calls than do the rich. Therefore, in the long run, the telecommunication business is always profitable. In the short run, profits are rather easily predictable, even in regions of poverty and in times of

---

[4] In 1991, a contract to install a cellular mobile communications network for the whole area of Poland for up to 100,000 lines was awarded to a consortium bringing together Ameritech from the US and France Telecom (*Financial Times*, 7 October 1991). US West set up systems in Hungary, Czechoslovakia, St. Petersburg and Moscow (US West, News Releases). Nokia, a Finnish firm, also installed a mobile network in Moscow, but offered its service only to foreign businessmen and diplomats (*Economist*, 8 February 1992, 74). In the three Baltic states, a cellular telephone system is built by Televerket (Sweden), and Telekom Finland. Swedish Telecom recently began work on a cellular telecommunications system linking European countries with Latvia, Lithuania and Estonia. NEC Earth stations were even set up in remote places like Vladivostok, Tashkent and Azerbaijan (*Nikkei Weekly*, week ending 1 February 1992).

[5] Companies involved in such deals include Britain's Cable and Wireless; AT&T; U.S.West; NEC and international consortia such as one Danish group comprising GN Great Nordic, Telecom Denmark and NKT.

[6] For example the president of PTT Telecom which is now involved in the Ukraine, Ben Verwaayen (*Public Network for the European Telecommunication Management* 2 (February 1992): 10).

[7] This information is from an interview with Frank Oltscher, Generaldirektion, Deutsche Bundespost Telecom.

economic recession. Many western companies involved in eastern European countries seem to trust in that evidence and aim to win the race for the best projects in eastern Europe and the FSU.

Yet this answer alone is not sufficient to explain the speedy developments. The question arises, are there further lessons that can be learned from telecommunication and applied to other areas of infrastructure? Is it for example the lack of regulation, the freedom that international telecommunication companies enjoy in those first days of new market economies that attract foreign investment in this area?

Section 11.2 deals with factors that attract foreign investment and examines different ways to finance projects. In order to find out how government regulation, or lack thereof, influences investment decisions, different projects are categorized according to their profitability for international companies.

Some of those findings will lead to the question whether present regulation is optimal in the sense of general welfare. In Section 11.3 some of the developments will be closely examined to assess their actual benefit. There is a bias towards projects that have a short pay-off period. I ask: Could the fact that international companies are concentrating on services with inelastic demand lead to an unbalanced combination of services?[8] Can the lack of competition within services lead to undesirable long-term results?[9]

Some telecommunication projects will have to be financed by governments or by loans to governments from institutions such as The World Bank and the EBRD; but in the long run these projects will have to be paid for by the public. Hence governments should take their need for capital into account during project appraisal. Section 11.4 deals with governments' needs to raise capital and the role that direct foreign investment can play in this process. How can taxes and other fees be levied on the telecommunication sector without deterring investment? Since international companies are so eager to invest, one can assume that their expected rent is high; European countries' have an urgent need for capital, in particular for the part of telephone service that international companies find less popular. Are

[8] In Budapest, for example, the cellular mobile telephone network has successfully become a substitute for the regular network and is being used by all international business people. Not only international businessmen, but most Hungarian businesses have a cellular mobile telephone, because the regular network is so poor. Private people, though, can hardly afford one of the mobile phones and are therefore completely excluded from enjoying the new network externalities.

[9] Poland provides a good example of how investments of international companies could be channeled into other more desirable areas by bringing in competition.

there measures that would divert some of the international companies' rent to governments? Are there other means to effect an improved capital allocation?

In view of both the possible need to channel investment into certain areas and the possible opportunity to raise revenue from international companies, conclusions will be drawn about how certain projects should be regulated. Section 11.5 summarizes the main findings.

11.2 Methods of Financing

The Agents in the Telecommunication Market

Since telecommunication has natural-monopoly properties and large network externalities, it is subject to regulation by the state and, in some aspects, by supranational agencies. Thus, when looking at how telecommunication projects are financed, we have to distinguish between several players.

The government usually enters in two functions: firstly as regulator of the whole industry; and secondly as a supplier of services. In many eastern and western countries telecommunication used to be connected to the postal service under the supervision of a Ministry of Posts and Telecommunications. Now, domestic telecommunication services have been mostly split off from the postal service and new domestic telecommunication companies have been founded.[10] Telecommunication companies are still government agencies, but plans for privatizing them abound.[11]

A second group of players consists of private companies that enter the market as suppliers of specific services. Most of the companies we will focus on are from the west. Eastern companies with their backward technology have very little to contribute unless they switch to new technologies, which happens mostly in cooperation with western companies.

Western firms are involved in joint ventures for specific projects (*Financial*

---

[10] In Poland, for example, a law was passed in 1991 that split the state-owned Polish Post Telegraph and Telephone Company (PPTT) into two units. The newly-formed Telekomunikacja Polska SA will provide the telecommunication services (*Financial Times*, 7 October 1991).

[11] The World Bank is preparing a study on this issue for the main eastern European countries whose Post and Telecommunication ministries they are consulting. In Poland, the new telecommunications law explicitly gives private operators the right to provide domestic services that were formerly in public hands (*Financial Times*, 7 October 1991). Only international phone links are to remain under direct state control.

Times, 23 March 1992[12]) or have acquired licenses for operating parts of the infrastructure independently. One example of a case where private companies have taken over the operation of a whole new service is cellular mobile telephone. No eastern companies were able to provide such a service. Nevertheless, mobile telephone was a very attractive service for eastern European economies. Accordingly, governments let western firms set up these services completely on their own, with little regulation and the assurance that no other companies would be let in (*Economist,* 8 February 1992, 74).[13]

Hard Currency from Traffic Fees

Improvement of the switching system is one of the primary capital-needs facing domestic telecommunication companies. Many new switching systems have already been installed since 1991. These switches were supplied by international companies and had to be paid for in hard currency.[14] It is rather easy for eastern European companies to pay for switches that connect international calls, since they generate plenty of profit. Switches that improve connections from eastern Europe to the West increase telephone traffic and thus pump in hard currency from the western telephone partner.

Eastern European telecommunication companies get their share of the telephone revenue in hard currency through bilateral arrangements between the respective national telecommunication companies. The western client pays his phone bill by sending a check to his national phone company. But this company is obligated to compensate the eastern telecom company for participating in establishing the connection. So, even if the telephone call did not originate from its area, the eastern company gets revenue for letting the call come in. This

[12] The article is about telecommunication projects and is titled: Joint Ventures Abound in Former Communist Bloc.

[13] US West won an exclusive right to modernize the St. Petersburg telephone system. In an interview US West stated that this right concerned mobile telephones only.

[14] Switches for international calls have been provided for Warsaw by AT&T. Siemens of Germany is to provide a new international exchange for Katowice; Poznan will be served by a new exchange from Alcatel CIT (*Financial Times,* 7 October 1991). According to an agreement between US West International Holdings, Inc., and the Soviet Union Ministry of Post and Telecommunications (MPT) US West will invest about $18 million in the financing and operational support of three new international-gateway telephone switching-systems in the Soviet Union over two years. Installation of the switches was expected to begin 1991 with completion estimated by late 1992 (US West, News Release, 16 July 1991). US West International and the Kaunas Enterprise of the Lithuanian PTT Communications Ministry (KPTT) formed a joint venture to install and operate the first international telecommunications gateway in Lithuania (US West, News Release, 11 October 1991).

arrangement works in both directions; but statistics show that traffic between a developed and an underdeveloped country originates mostly from the developed country.[15] Thus, simply by operating their part of the connection, eastern European phone companies gain a share of the hard currency revenue in the rich country. Thus, the arrangement clearly works to the advantage of the poorer country.

Aside from new switches, additional long-distance connections are needed to increase the capacity for long-distance calls. In the area of the former Soviet Union the need is acute. Because of the central nature of the former regime, all international calls were fed through Moscow, regardless of the distance.[16] Thus, congestion in Moscow was, and still is, inevitable.

Building new long-distance cables is a necessary, but an expensive and slow process. To a limited degree satellite connections can substitute for long-distance cables. Satellite connections have the huge advantage of needing little prior investment to be set up. All that is needed is a satellite station in the country and permission to use certain frequencies. Thus, satellite connections can be established very quickly.

Armenia was one of the first former-Soviet republics to receive a modern satellite connection. It was established through Intelsat and can eventually be upgraded to carry 500 direct connections. Investment amounted to $1.7 million. The project is financed by AT&T, but has been supported greatly by Armenians living in the United States (*Frankfurter Allgemeine,* 9 December 1991). Here was an investment by a major international telecommunication-company that involved little actual risk. With so many Armenians living in the United States and willing to spend their hard currency on telephone calls to relatives in Armenia, an eventual profit for this project is secure. This also illuminates how crucial demand from hard currency countries can be. The investment would have been less likely to materialize, if only Armenians from Armenia had backed it.[17]

In the long run, the FSU and eastern Europe will need more international connections than can be efficiently provided for by satellite connections. Increasingly many new telecommunication technologies require capacities that can

---

[15] Interview with Frank Oltscher, Generaldirektion, Deutsche Telecom.

[16] Currently, there is only one international gateway location using analog switches to serve the entire Soviet Union (US West, News Release, 16 July 1991).

[17] More satellite connections have been established by now in Uzbekistan, Tashkent, Vladivostok and Azerbaijan, but they were financed in a slightly different manner (see later).

only be provided by modern cables. Unfortunately, some of the cables in use in eastern Europe were laid even before World War Two and need to be replaced completely. Eventually, profit from building new long-distance cables is relatively secure. But in the case of fiber-optic cables, for example, the pay-off period is rather long, and the investment bears a high risk for international companies.

Nevertheless, all countries aspire to have fiber-optic cables. Together with state-owned Telecom Denmark, GN Great Nordic has signed a contract to lay the first fiber-optic cable system between the Soviet Union and western Europe.[18] The whole investment is expected to be paid for by traffic fees (*Financial Times*, 9 June 1991). According to one source (*Economist*, 8 February 1992, 74), the investment needed for this project amounted to £44 million, but probably this is only a fragment. Another source claims it is a $500 million project (*Business Week*, 25 June 1990).[19] Before any of these sums are paid off from traffic fees, the whole cable must be laid and connected to the general network, and it will take several years before any cash flow comes out of the project. This explains why most international companies are reluctant to start with such an ambitious project. The more investment is needed before actual operation can generate cash flow, the less appealing the project.

Capital in Return for Shares in Companies

There are many projects in telecommunication that have a long-delayed pay-off period. Some require very high initial investment but little maintenance (long-distance fiber-optic cables); others need time for enough subscribers to participate to make them profitable (ISDN). To get international companies interested in such projects, additional incentives are needed besides the promise to pay as soon as cash flow comes in.

Some international companies have used this situation successfully to become more than mere suppliers of equipment. Due to the urgent need for foreign capital and technology transfer, international companies were allowed to become shareholders in national and local telecommunication companies; that is, they are actually becoming owners of large shares of other countries' key infrastructure

[18] Apparently no actual construction for this fiber-optic cable has been started. According to Business Week, U.S.West is co-leader of the consortium (*Business Week*, 25 June 1990, 104). But in an interview, US West indicated that they had given the lead of the first part to a Scandinavian company and to their knowledge no actual construction had started.

[19] Note that the estimated market value of existing or approved foreign operations is based on cash-flow projections.

networks. This is a vast step forward relative to former state-controlled telecommunication and a great opportunity for national telecommunication companies to enter markets in other countries. For decades even western European countries have sheltered their telecommunication infrastructure in national monopolies. These monopolies are dissolving only slowly. By contrast, in eastern Europe foreign companies are now welcome to enter the market in key positions.

In mid-January, American Telephone & Telegraph (AT & T) announced that, in exchange for providing Ukraine with some $58 million worth of telephone exchanges, it is taking a 39% stake in the country's national telephone operator. PTT Telecom, the Dutch carrier, will take another 10%. American influence on telecommunication standards in Ukraine will grow in the future. And the deal has another advantage for AT&T and PTT Telecom: instead of waiting for traffic fees to pay for their investment, they have immediate access to cash flow from already-established operations. The same incentive is used for attracting investment on local levels. Last year Britain's Cable and Wireless agreed to build a £200 million ($356 million) digital telecommunications network in the Polish port of Gdansk, in exchange for a license to operate a telephone system for 25 years (*Economist,* 8 February 1992, 74).

The most dramatic example of foreign involvement in setting up infrastructure in eastern Europe is the case of cellular mobile telephone. This technology, which can at the same time be a substitute and an extension for basic telephones, was not formerly available in former eastern Europe, but has now proved indispensable. In addition, it generates profit surprisingly quickly. Despite secure profit prospects, there is no eastern European phone company involved in setting up this modern technology. Instead, western companies are already turning profit from it. US West has been most aggressive in seeking cellular contracts in eastern Europe (*Warren Publishing,* 22 January 1991). They have established cellular radio networks in several eastern European countries and in Russia.[20] In

[20] US West is a partner in cellular licenses in Hungary, Czechoslovakia, St. Petersburg and Moscow (*New York Times,* 7 October 1991). In Hungary, US West built a nationwide cellular network in partnership with the Hungarian Telecommunications Company (*Economist,* 8 February 1992, 74). WesTel, the joint venture that developed and manages the system, was initially offering service to 3,000 Budapest customers and added capacity for another 3,000 by February 1991. Plans also called for expansion to Miskoloz and the main corridor highway between Budapest and Vienna by the end of 1993. (US West, News Release, 15 October 1990). Together with Bell Atlantic, US West also took a stake in a new Czech mobile network, predicted to cost $80 million over the first five years (*Economist,* 8 February 1992, 74). The first call was placed on September 12, 1991 in Prague. Earlier, the same day, service was inaugurated in Bratislava and Brno (US West, News Release, 12

an interview, a representative from US West explained that their investment in Hungary actually paid off after only one year; from then on, the cash flow from operation was used to upgrade capacities. In Moscow, they expected to turn a profit in two years. Their clients are not only international businesspersons. In Hungary, cellular telephone is used as a substitute for the dilapidated regular network and Hungarian businesspersons—not foreigners—form the majority of users. Economic development in Russia is going much slower and international businesspersons—not Russians—form the majority of clients in Moscow. On the other hand, cellular phones in Moscow are actually used for their mobile functions. The system has not substituted for the normal telephone network as completely as in Hungary.

Clients for mobile telephone have to pay their bills in hard currency. St. Petersburg's cellular system, a joint venture between US West International Holdings and several local Russian companies called Delta Telecom, will charge $195 a month for access to the cellular network.[21] There are also plans to offer this service against national currencies. Delta expects to introduce a ruble pricing plan in the near future (US West, News Release, 9 September 1991). Cellular telephone was introduced in Moscow a few months later and under similar conditions.[22] Likewise, new telephones in holiday resorts in Moscow and Bulgaria are only available for hard currency; GPT is erecting the telephone boxes and customers operate them using dollar-bought telephone cards.[23]

Searching for National Hard Currency Reserves

Natural resources form an important source of hard currency in former communist countries. There are few cases, though, where natural resources have been bartered for equipment or technology transfer. Western companies from the United States

September 1991).

[21] This includes 210 minutes of calling, detail billing, call waiting, call forwarding and three-way calling. After the 210 minutes of calling have been used, each additional minute will cost $0.65. Delta Telecom will lease the cellular phone-sets for prices ranging from $50 to $75 per month depending on the model. There is a one-time connection fee of $995.

[22] The first commercial cellular telephone service in Moscow began a limited trial on Dec. 16, 1991. It is operated by Cellular Communications (MCC). The service initially was limited to 100 customers, but was expanded in early 1992, and will have an ultimate capacity of 60,000 customers within five years. Monthly service will cost $50 and each minute of usage will be billed at 60 cents. Long-distance charges are in addition to the monthly and usage fees. Cellular phone-sets can be either leased or purchased. Purchase prices range from $1,000 to $1,300. Also, there will be a one-time connection fee of $995, which will be waived during the trial period (US West, News Release, 16 December 1991).

[23] GPT is 40% owned by Siemens and 69% by Britain's GEC.

and Europe are generally not interested in barter trades.[24] Nevertheless, some businesses contemplate breaking this habit. Randal Tobial from AT&T is one of those who have thought about swapping telephone exchanges for Russian oil, timber or for maintenance work on their company's cable-laying ships (*Economist*, 8 February 1992).

Japanese corporations have a very different approach in their effort to enter the eastern European telecommunication market. They only deliver equipment if immediate payment is guaranteed and none of them have made any effort to acquire shares of corporations. Japanese decision makers are keenly aware of the financial risk involved in unstable soft-currency countries. They try to act as a subcontractor to one of their well-established trading firms which can negotiate credit arrangements with governments or international institutions.[25] Thus, the Japanese undertook projects in eastern Europe or the FSU (whether telecommunications projects or otherwise) in exchange for hard currency. Only occasionally did they deliver on a barter basis; in those cases, compensation was accepted in the form of lumber, petroleum, coal, and other minerals.

If hard currency is not immediately available, Japanese companies look for it. Big Japanese trading companies are involved in searching for hard currency. When successful they employ subcontractors to deliver equipment.[26] The satellite system in Tashkent, Uzbekistan was purchased by the republic's export-import organization and was paid for by the hard currency that a Japanese trading company had located.[27]

Help from Development Banks

For some parts of the telecommunication infrastructure neither traffic fees in hard currencies, nor the opportunity to gain shares in companies, nor barter opportunities can attract foreign direct investment. National telephone networks are the most neglected, including cables and switches. Even though there are newspaper reports about projects to renovate local telephone networks, most of them actually deal with

---

[24] From an interview with NEC.
[25] From an interview with NEC.
[26] In 1991, KDD (Kokusai Denship Denwa Co.) struck the accord with Uzbekistan to form a telecommunications link between Japan and the republic via the Intelsat satellite by 1992. NEC delivered the Earth stations to the republic's capital, Tashkent, in March 1992. The link was the second direct international line between an industrial democracy and a republic other than Russia (*Nikkei Weekly*, week ending 1 February 1992).
[27] From an interview with NEC.

cellular telephones and not any regular telephone network.[28] The task of renovating local and domestic networks is left to domestic telephone companies. Obviously, these domestic companies are dependent on financial help from the international community.[29] In Poland, Mr. Jerzy Slezak, the communications minister, is looking for credit to pay $120 million for seven transit switches for Warsaw to be supplied by Alcatel Sesa of Spain. To finance the switches is clearly more difficult than in the case of international switches since they cannot be expected to raise revenue in hard currency. The Ministry of Communication of Poland would also like to see some 10 million new telephone lines installed by the end of the century at an estimated cost of up to $15 billion. As of October 1991, the ministry had been able to raise only $600 million from western governments and commercial sources, including the World Bank and the EBRD (*Financial Times,* 7 October 1991). The largest portion of the required capital is still missing.

Because formal ties between international companies and national posts and telecommunications ministries matter, political support from outside the country is as crucial for successful projects as good management in the ministries. As a reflection of the United States' and Germany's very positive stance in offering economic assistance to eastern Europe and the FSU, American and European vendors were much more aggressive in pursuing business opportunities in difficult markets than their Japanese counterparts. Very often projects seemed to capitalize directly on diplomatic or political ties.[30] But supporting governments and international companies have to be able to clearly identify with whom they should communicate. In the beginning they only had to deal with Post and Telecommunication ministries or public entities which had financial capabilities. Now, at the beginning of the disintegration and privatization of public entities, authorities or initiatives have been shifted down to state, municipal, and private levels, and it has become difficult to identify the proper negotiation partner.[31] Therefore, efforts to locate hard currency and complete contracts succeed on a first-

---

[28] From an interview with US West. The project in St. Petersburg is based on cellular telephone.

[29] In Poland, in early 1991, The World Bank approved a $120 million loan to finance a national digital network which would overlay the present system. This is being co-financed by the EBRD with a $90 million loan to provide phones for 70,000 businesses and improve services for 900,000 private subscribers (*Financial Times,* 7 October 1991).

[30] From an interview with NEC.

[31] For example, in April 1991, Bell Atlantic said it had won an exclusive franchise to modernize St. Petersburg's telephones. The existing local-telephone-operator had already granted US West permission to launch a mobile service. In the ensuing muddle, US West emerged as the contract winner (Economist, Feb. 8, 1992: 74).

come-first-serve basis.[32] The result is an unbalanced, piecemeal investment-and-development strategy.

11.3 Structural Aspects of Foreign Direct Investment in Telecommunication

Network Externalities

The shortcomings inherent in the present pick-and-choose scheme of investment opportunities should now be more apparent. Firstly, because of the perceived political instability in eastern Europe and especially in the FSU, international business concentrates on satisfying inelastic demand first and prefers projects with a short pay-off period to long-term projects with high initial investment.[33] This means, for example, that the telecommunication needs of large businesses or foreign companies with an ability to pay in hard currency are satisfied before any other. Secondly, wherever hard currency is available, international companies are present to make a fast deal. This uses up hard currency for projects that could perhaps be financed otherwise.[34] Thirdly, over time network externalities can lead to strategic pricing by service providers. Private providers could increasingly engage in rent-seeking activities. This is particularly true as long as there is no competing service.

Instead, a welfare-optimal development of telecommunication infrastructure would focus on taking advantage of network externalities by providing access to the network from all sides. 'Network externalities' describes the social benefits from an increased number of subscribers. Additional subscribers not only reduce the average cost per subscriber, they also expand the circle of people who can be reached and thus increase the economic value of the whole communication network. Thus, network externalities are similar to dynamic economies of scale. In telecommunication they cannot be measured easily. They contain all the consequences of increased business activities that would not have taken place without the telephone. At the present low stage of development in eastern Europe network externalities are still immense. Every new subscriber adds significantly to the range of participating people.

Network externalities are a special concern for the small and medium-sized

[32] From an interview with NEC.

[33] This is frequently mentioned by business leaders such as for example David de Pury, Chairman of BBC Brown Boveri (April 8th, 1993).

[34] From an interview with NEC. A Japanese trading company found out where hard currency is available, then another Japanese company come in as subcontractor and supplied a equipment against immediate payment.

enterprises who are just starting and need to make themselves known. Providing telephone lines to the general public in eastern Europe would support small and medium-sized enterprises, because their clients tend to be individuals. In Budapest, where a cellular mobile-telephone network is already operating successfully as a substitute for the regular network, there are still twice as many requests for regular telephones as can be satisfied daily. Satisfying this demand faster could probably lead to a substantial increase in business activities.

However, concentrating efforts on cellular mobile telephone (which does not need physical telephone lines and is consequently cheaper to set up) has drawbacks. Firstly, because the most urgent demand for telephones is satisfied through this system there is less pressure to improve the regular network. Consequently, small businesses and individuals who cannot afford the expensive mobile telephone cannot contribute to further network externalities: they are left out. Secondly, frequencies are scarce, so mobile telephone will eventually suffer from congestion or stay expensive. Since all operators of cellular mobile telephone in eastern Europe have exclusive licenses they are likely to act like monopolists and keep prices high, keeping this telephone network exclusive. Therefore, special emphasis must be put on laying new cables and providing new lines.

Individuals can still place calls to businesses over public phones. Therefore, more access to private phones at home does not rank high in the list of priorities for business; besides, the costs of installing new lines are high. $1,599 was the estimated average cost of one new private access to the telephone network in eastern Europe (*Financial Times,* 23 March 1992). This amount is so high because the telephone systems in eastern Europe were installed in the last century and need complete replacement. Of course, the cost per access varies widely depending on the circumstances.[35] The estimated cost for Poland's plan to have some ten million new lines installed by the end of the century amounts to $15 billion (*Financial Times,* 7 October 1991). Most individuals are not willing to pay the high price that would be charged for getting phones into their homes faster. Their price elasticity for demand is higher than that of business. Without outside support for private phone use access to private telephones for the general population is far from sight (*Financial Times,* 23 March 1992).[36]

---

[35] Poland and Romania are piloting the use of radio to connect homes to local exchanges (*Economist,* 8 February 1992, 18). If successful, this could make individual phone access substantially cheaper.
[36] One example of help is that provided by international organizations, such as the World Bank-EBRD loan to finance a national digital network in Poland which would overlay the present system.

Furthermore, eastern Europe is still far from getting one of the most promising new technologies in long-distance telecommunication: fiber-optic cables. Because of their high capacities, they are the base for extending modern digital-telecommunication techniques all over eastern European countries. There are actually some talks about running another fiber-optic line from Germany to Warsaw and then on to Moscow (*Warren Publishing Communications Daily*, 22 January 1991). US West is supposed to be co-leader of the consortium to build a $500 million fiber-optic cable through the Soviet Union (*Business Week,* 25 June 1990, 104), but there has been no actual construction yet on the part of US West. The Danes have taken the leadership in the first section, but it has not started yet either. Together with state-owned Telecom Denmark, GN Great Nordic had signed a contract to lay (parts of) the first fiber-optic cable system between the former Soviet Union and the rest of the world.[37]

Monopolistic Trends

The problem of monopolistic trends in telecommunication in eastern Europe has not yet been sufficiently addressed by governments.[38] There is a dangerous tendency in the pattern of contracts with international companies. Foreign companies either overhaul the existing state monopoly or build new monopolies in areas untouched by the state company, such as cellular mobile telephone. Eventually, this trend could block the road to fully competitive markets in the future.

State monopolies in telecommunication formally guaranteed that a network could be financed through cross subsidization. By letting international telecommunication companies offer services, countries of eastern Europe have abandoned that old principle. The driving force behind this was the perception that only many private companies together could perform the huge task of developing telecommunication in eastern Europe fast enough. But private companies do not have an incentive to cross subsidize among themselves in order to establish structures similar to a state monopoly: they only try to maximize their own profit. Thus, giving them a dominant market position can easily lead to monopolistic prices and quantities.

Western Europe is just now engaging in a big effort to abolish such monopolistic structures, since they are hindering fast innovation. It would be unwise

---

[37] The investment of about £44 million was supposed to be paid for by traffic fees (*Financial Times,* 9 June, 1991).

[38] The following analysis draws on *Economist* (8 February 1992: 18).

for eastern Europe not to follow that same pattern as fast as possible, considering that they aim at the same level of technological sophistication as the west. Nevertheless, nowhere have newcomers been invited to set up competing fixed-wire networks. The only arrangement which is close to competing networks can be found in Moscow. Sovintel, a joint venture between GTE and Sovam, both from the United States, is putting in a competing network alongside the existing public network. It is a fixed overlay network, separate from the country's public network, but it is designed for Moscow's international business community (*Financial Times,* 23 March 1992). If some of the former CMEA-countries are too small to allow efficient competition of several providers of competing services, the problem might be solved by neighboring countries offering joint licenses to providers; this would also help to establish common standards in the region, but it requires that governments be willing to accept regional co-operation.

The lack of competition is especially severe in the mobile phone service. France Telecom and Ameritech, one of America's seven big regional operators, have won the right to sell mobile-telephone services throughout Poland. This right, awarded in 1991 is exclusive (*Economist,* 8 February 1992). There is no good reason why the right should not have been shared by at least two competitors, but it cannot now be taken away from them without breaking contracts.

This leads to another important issue, the duration of a license. Without long-term contracts such mistakes could be corrected in a short time; but long-term commitments fix the competitive structure of the market for a long time. Two examples illustrate this: the joint venture to operate the first international telecommunication gateway in Lithuania has been granted an exclusive 15-year license to provide international PSTN access in Lithuania, only excepting existing links (US West, News Release, 11 October 1991); Britain's Cable and Wireless agreed to build a £200 million ($356 million) digital telecommunications network in Gdansk in exchange for a license to operate a telephone system for 25 years (*Economist,* 8 February 1992, 74). In many other countries such structures are just now being dissolved. Competition is being introduced and soon consumers will profit from decreasing prices due to the increased competitive pressure. If eastern Europe is to follow the western example, time limits on monopolistic rights should be considered for all areas of telecommunication. Allowing a five-year moratorium on competition for example, would give universal-service providers an incentive to phase out cross-subsidies (*Economist,* 8 February 1992, 18) and at the same time give every potential entrant a clearly-established planning horizon. Since certain investment projects have only a long-term prospect of being profitable, some compromises about the lifetime of licenses might be advisable in order to keep foreign direct investment attractive. Advantages from immediate competition have to be weighed against the need to attract investors, but a period of twenty five years for the right to operate a cellular mobile radio is clearly too long. Such a project can turn a profit after only a couple of years; therefore, companies would be willing to bid for shorter licenses. Long-lasting, exclusive rights for the operation of mobile radio, as they presently exists in some areas, do not serve a social purpose.

In addition to all this, political considerations have to be considered closely. Investment decisions in eastern Europe are so sensitive to political change that long-term perspectives of twenty years or more are not feasible. International companies must take, for example, the possibility of repatriation into account when they engage in eastern Europe. Political coups could complicate foreign involvement before eastern Europe sees a well-developed telecommunication infrastructure and companies have educated their own technicians and managers to operate it. Poland is anticipating complications from repatriation: thus, the share of any foreign capital in telecommunication companies must not exceed 49 percent. Ukraine has limited foreign participation in the joint venture with AT&T and PTT Telecom to a minority stake. The country's State Committee of Communications will own 51% of the venture (*Public Network for European Telecommunications Management* 2 (February 1992)). All this will keep international companies from committing themselves for more than ten years. Giving them licenses for more than ten years is an unnecessary one-sided commitment by eastern Europe.

Standards

To a large degree, international telecommunication companies consider investment in eastern Europe as a means to get into the west European market.[39] Projects such as delivering switching systems are not necessarily expected to pay off by themselves, but only once they provide the wanted market access into the west European market.

Whoever can cover a large area with equipment of a certain kind can get a considerable advantage over other companies. Operators have an interest in sticking

[39] Richard Callahan, executive vice-president of US West, stated that "Eastern Europe is our way of getting into Western Europe, and there is a lot of money in both places" (*New York Times*, 7 October 1991).

to certain equipment suppliers once they chose them. Because each kind of switching equipment needs its own group of expert technicians and its own replacement equipment, operators usually stick to one supplier. This does not hinder free flow between systems. Different equipment in different countries are compatible at rather low cost, but every company that can cover a major area with its own type of equipment has an advantage due to economies of scale. Thus, eastern Europe's choice of switching equipment has consequences for western Europe.

There is a race going on among international telecommunication companies to set standards. Ericsson of Sweden, for example, tried to enter the switching-equipment market in Poland. It looked as if Ericsson would be shut out when Poland refused to accept its AXE 10 switching equipment. However, fierce lobbying by the Swedes caused the ministry to change its decision. Meanwhile another joint venture to produce equipment is being considered for the Telecom Telfa plant in Bydgoszcz (*Financial Times,* 7 October 1991, 24).

Because of their long-term consequences, decisions about the predominant equipment standard are crucial. Eastern European countries might get a good bargain with their present choices, but might regret them as soon as the service turns out to be unsatisfactory. Lobbying efforts from countries that want to support their own industry should therefore be checked carefully. The shifting of authorities will complicate the picture in eastern Europe. For example, Poland is one of the first countries to privatize whole local networks (*Financial Times,* 7 October 1991). In the future, many decisions will be made at the local level and coordinating them will be even more difficult.

11.4 Sources for Government Revenue

Despite some promising developments, the preceding analysis makes clear that governments will have to find some way to take care of those parts of the infrastructure that are presently neglected by international investors. This will require capital. In western Europe, the existence of state monopolies in telecommunication allowed a universal service financed by cross subsidization between profitable and non-profitable parts of the network to develop. In eastern Europe, the emergence of miscellaneous private engagements in telecommunication requires a different approach.

Governments could finance neglected parts of the network with further help from the EBRD and the World Bank, but the presence of so many international telecommunication companies in their countries leads one to question if those international companies could generate some of that capital. Since there are so many factors that make eastern Europe attractive for international companies, revenue could be extracted from them without stopping their engagement in these countries. It is very important, though, to find those kinds of fees that do not stop investment and do not lead to distortions in the market.

A decision would have to be made between imposing one-time fees or regular user-fees; another choice could be seen between selling existing monopolies or selling restricted licenses. Regular fees promise more revenue in the long run but might increase telephone prices more significantly or reduce incentives to invest. Privatizing state companies is often like selling monopoly rights, whereas licenses can be handled flexibly and given to more than one company.

Poland provides a good example of making profit from selling licenses. Poland asked bidders for its nationwide mobile license to make cash "donations" towards the cost of updating its wire-based network, a direct competitor. The winner was also required to reimburse the government for the cost of administering the auction. In June 1991, France Telecom and Chicago-based Ameritech, one of America's seven big regional operators, announced they had jointly won the Polish license for an undisclosed sum. Rumors put the size of their "donations" at $80 million (*Economist,* 8 February 1992).

This way of raising fees provides a good example of how money can be raised with as little distortion as possible. The companies that had to pay these fees afterwards had to consider them sunk costs. Thus they will not influence further pricing. In addition to this advantage of bidding, the competition between several bidders led to a price higher than could have been achieved in negotiations with only one candidate. Many other licenses might be worth considering for such a process. Fifteen year-long rights to operate telephone systems could be worth more than expected: this can only be determined in an auction.[40]

Since cellular mobile telephone has been such a success in eastern European

---

[40] See also US West, News Release, 11 October 1991. US West International and the Kaunas Enterprise of the Lithuanian PTT Communications Ministry (KPTT) formed a joint venture to install and operate the first international telecommunications-gateway in Lithuania. The joint venture has been granted an exclusive fifteen-year license to provide international PSTN access in Lithuania, excepting existing links.

countries, it also should be considered a strong candidate for auctions.[41] It requires the use of frequencies. Right now frequencies might seem ample. In the former communist regimes the military was the predominant user of frequencies and it can be assumed that a lot of these frequencies are available right now. In the long run, frequencies will become as rare as they are already in the western world, where the auctioning of frequencies has been seriously considered for quite a while.[42] Licenses could also be re-auctioned after a certain period, perhaps shorter than the time periods seen in western Europe.[43] Cellular mobile telephone is also a good example which illustrates the choice between selling monopolies whole, or selling restricted licenses that allow competition, perhaps at a later date. In any case investment will not be deterred: an auction will always find a price that is acceptable for its bidders.

The right to sell mobile-telephone service throughout Poland awarded to France Telecom and Ameritech in 1991 was exclusive. Poland was able raise a sum of about $80 million from this auction. Only knowing that they would have a secure monopoly for several years to come, could France Telecom and Ameritech afford to bid so high. But even if Poland had wanted to raise a large sum of money quickly, it could have held auctions for non-exclusive licenses; that might have only reduced the immediate price of licenses for such areas where competition will be added in the near future. In the long run, the country will benefit from competition much more than from an initially high auction revenue (*Economist,* 8 February 1992, 18).

11.5 Summary

As we have seen, part of the amazing development in the telecommunication sector in eastern Europe and the FSU comes from recognizing telecommunication as an indispensable necessity for the development of private business. No matter how

---

[41] From an interview with US West. The cellular mobile telephone-network investment of US West, set up in Hungary, has come to a break-even point after only one year. Subsequently cash flow was used to enlarge the network.

[42] CSP International: Deregulation of the spectrum in the UK, study commissioned by the Department of Trade and Industry, London, 1987.

[43] As far as I could find out, licenses have been given for periods as long as 15 to 25 years. In the USA, the life of the usage rights is separated from the term of the licenses for radio communication services. For certain services, a new round of negotiations for the frequencies is held roughly every five years. Permission to operate these services extends, by contrast, to some 20 years, so as to ensure the necessary planning security (The Federal Minister of Posts and Telecommunications, 1991).

desperately hard currency is needed for other areas, it will always be spent on telecommunication. Most leaders in eastern Europe understand this and act accordingly.

Equally important is the fact that telecommunication generates hard currency and can therefore attract foreign investors. For example, switching systems: the governments in eastern Europe gave first priority to new switching systems. Most of them were easy to finance, because switches that improve and increase international telephone traffic generate income from abroad. According to standard international arrangements, substantial parts of the money from the bills of western telephone customers go to the eastern company that participates in establishing the connection. International companies also provided switches in return for receiving shares in eastern European domestic telephone companies. The same dealing applied to equipment and technical help for the renovation of old telephone networks. By being actual owners of eastern European telephone operators, international companies received immediate revenue from their engagement.

In some places, cellular mobile-telephone networks, set up by foreign companies which charge fees in hard currency, have replaced regular telephone networks. Mobile phone networks are quickly installed, in high demand by business people and already very profitable. For some time their success might distract from the regular telephone, but the improvement of regular telephone networks remains indispensable. There are clear disadvantages to mobile phones. Capacities are limited and prices are so high that only few can afford them. In a similar way, satellite connections can replace long-distance cables to some extent. They are also relatively cheap to set up and have been installed in many countries and former republics.

In contrast to the above systems, some parts of the overall telecommunication network have been neglected. The installation of fiber-optic cables is expensive and therefore has not yet passed the stage of pure planning, and the renovation of local wire-based telephone systems is least popular among international investors, because it requires high initial investment. Governments have to take over the responsibility of channeling money into the problematic areas of telecommunications infrastructure in order to ensure balanced development of the communication system and the exploitation of network externalities. Without deterring foreign investment, a lot of capital could be raised by governments through international auctions of licenses (such as the profitable cellular mobile telephone licenses). The lifetime of licenses should be as short as possible in order to facilitate a restructuring of the market later on. In cases where foreign direct investment can only be attracted through long-term licenses, these licenses should be linked to a clear plan stipulating when more competition will be admitted to the market. License auctions will not deter foreign investors, because bidding prices always reflect willingness to pay. Licenses for monopolies will generate high immediate returns. Nevertheless, if necessary to promote fast innovation, licenses should be split up among several competitors.

Because of high network externalities in the telecommunication market, over time there is a high probability of strategic pricing by service providers. Private providers could increasingly invest in rent-seeking activities. There is no incentive for them to cross-subsidize into other areas—as there would be for state providers. Since state provision is no longer a feasible option, competing provision of services is critical for the development of a competitive telecommunication network.

Despite widespread activity in telecommunication in eastern Europe and the FSU, a continuation of this example of east-west cooperation is constantly jeopardized by political instabilities. Therefore, political support by the international community for these countries' efforts to modernize will prove crucial for future success.

References

European Bank for Reconstruction and Development (EBRD). 1992. *Annual Report*. London: Royal Institute of International Affairs.

The Federal Minister of Posts and Telecommunications. 1991. *Frequency Regulation in the Federal Republic of Germany*. Report by the Committee of Experts on Basic Frequency Regulation Matters in Civil Telecommunications. Bonn: The Federal Minister of Posts and Telecommunications.

De Pury, D. 1993. *The Importance of Saving the World Trading System*. Speech delivered at Harvard University, Kennedy School of Government, Institute of Politics, 8 April.

12 The Breakdown of the Soviet Oil Empire and its International Ramifications

Eugene M. Khartukov and
Dmitry A. Surovtsev

12.1 Introduction

By the time of the failed August 1991 coup in Moscow, the ailing national oil industry had just passed the peak of its inter-republican integrity: at the threshold of the 1990s the fifteen republics of the fabulous "unbreakable union" achieved the highest degree of their oil interdependence with an obvious reliance upon Russia's oil supplies. In 1990, in particular, the Russian Federation accounted for 90 percent of Soviet production of crude oil and gas condensate, 65 percent of the country's refined products output, and 95 percent of its foreign trade in liquid fuels. Furthermore, Russia occupied a unique position in that it was the only Soviet republic with a surplus of both crude and products, supplying excess oil to all the Soviet "have nots" (Figure 12.1). The second largest oil producer, Kazakhstan, responsible for a much smaller share of national oil production (4 percent), had to import Siberian crudes to feed two of its three refineries and could not fully satisfy its own products needs. Meanwhile, the other four oil-processing republics (Belarus, Azerbaijan, Lithuania, and Turkmenia), which hosted about 16 percent of the country's refinery runs and enjoyed product surpluses, had to rely on Russian feedstock supplies. At the same time, other Soviet republics, including the traditional oil-producing and refining states of Ukraine, Uzbekistan and Georgia, were heavily (if not exclusively) dependent on deliveries of both crude and product surpluses from Russia. As for 1991, disaggregated data on crude oil balances of the republics in the former Soviet Union (FSU) show a substantial divergence in the degree of self-sufficiency in crude, which ranged from around 150 percent for Russia and Kazakhstan to some 70 percent for Azerbaijan and Turkmenistan, to less

The authors are grateful to Fereidun Fesharaki and David Fridley for their invaluable comments and assistance in preparing a draft of this paper.

Figure 12.1
Oil Self-Sufficiency of Former Soviet Republics, 1990 (○) and 1991 (●)

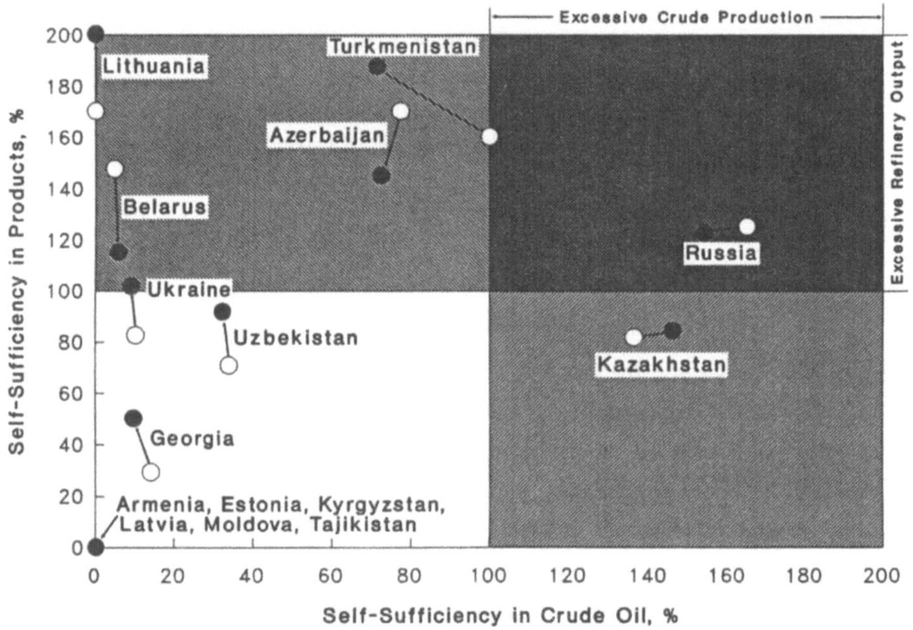

than 33 percent for Uzbekistan, to between 5 and 10 percent for Belarus, Ukraine, and Georgia, and to zero in case of Lithuania and those ex-Soviet republics which have no refinery capacity (Table 12.1).

In turn, due to an even more uneven distribution of the FSU refining industry, republic-by-republic self-sufficiency in oil products differed to an even greater extent. In 1991 six of the former Soviet republics (Russia, Ukraine, Belarus, Azerbaijan, Lithuania, and Turkmenistan) were self-reliant in products, with self-sufficiency ratios varying from 1.0 to 2.0. At the same time the other oil-processing republics (Uzbekistan, Kazakhstan, and Georgia) could only partly cover their own needs for liquid fuels, while the remaining six (including two Baltic states) were completely dependent on refined products imported from the nearest republics with product surpluses and, first of all, from Russia, which remained the largest exporter of liquid fuels both inside and outside of the Soviet Union (Table 12.2).

Nevertheless, despite mismanagement of the huge national oil complex and

Table 12.1
Crude Oil Balances of the Former Soviet Republics, 1991

Republic	Gross output (mmbd)[1]	Refinery capacity (mmbd)	Refinery thruput (mmbd)	Capacity utiliza-tion (%)	Net outflow (mmbd)	Total inland demand (mmbd)[2]	Self-suffici-ency (%)[3]
Russia	9.26	6.44	5.75	89.3	3.26	6.00	154.0
Kazakhstan	0.54	0.39	0.38	95.5	0.17	0.37	146.0
Azerbaijan	0.23	0.40	0.33	81.7	−0.09	0.32	72.2
Turkmenia	0.11	0.24	0.15	62.5	−0.04	0.15	71.1
Ukraine	0.10	1.25	1.20	96.0	−1.01	1.11	8.9
Uzbekistan	0.05	0.17	0.17	94.0	−0.10	0.15	32.5
Belarus	0.04	0.83	0.79	94.0	−0.68	0.72	5.9
Georgia	0.00	0.10	0.04	40.4	−0.03	0.04	9.6
Kyrgyzstan	0.00	—	—	n.a.	0.00	0.00	n.a.
Tajikistan	0.00	—	—	n.a.	0.00	0.00	n.a.
Lithuania	—	0.27	0.24	89.5	−0.22	0.22	0.0
Others[4]	—	—	—	n.a.	—	—	n.a.
Totals	10.37	10.10	9.08	89.8	1.22	9.15	113.5

[1] Including field losses and condensate. [2] Including own and direct use, losses and stock changes. [3] As applied to Total Inland Demand. [4] Latvia, Estonia, Armenia, and Moldova.
Note: Totals may not add up due to independent rounding.

dwindling supplies of Russian (mainly West Siberian) crudes, before the country began to break apart and, especially, until the August coup, the integrated oil industry of the Soviet Union remained fairly coordinated and functioned relatively smoothly. Surprising as it might seem (in view of the absence of market mechanisms), virtually all available (that is, produced and unlost) oil was promptly and properly transported, processed and distributed to numerous (and quite complacent) consumers in all fifteen republics. The underlying reason for this remarkable harmony was rooted in the tight and strict centralized control of the industry, which saw the first "cracks of democratization" only at the beginning of the 1990s. Furthermore, the developed infrastructure of technologically interdependent oil fields, pipelines, refineries and distribution bases spread throughout the country would never have let the nationwide oil complex fall apart on the day after the declaration of the republics' independence. That is why, even after the official funeral of the USSR in December 1991 the anachronisms of central command-management of the industry and its trans-border technological integration still kept

Table 12.2
Oil Product Balances of the Former Soviet Republics, 1991

Republic	Gross output (mmbd)[1]	Net outflow (mmbd)	Total inland demand (mmbd)[2]	Self-sufficiency (%)
Russia	5.67	1.06	4.61	123.0
Ukraine	1.19	0.01	1.18	101.0
Belarus	0.78	0.10	0.68	115.0
Kazakhstan	0.37	−0.07	0.44	84.0
Azerbaijan	0.32	0.10	0.22	145.5
Lithuania	0.24	0.12	0.12	200.0
Uzbekistan	0.16	−0.02	0.18	91.5
Turkmenistan	0.15	0.07	0.08	188.0
Georgia	0.04	−0.05	0.09	50.0
Latvia	0.00	−0.11	0.11	0.00
Moldova	0.00	−0.11	0.11	0.00
Armenia	0.00	−0.09	0.09	0.00
Kyrgyzstan	0.00	−0.05	0.05	0.00
Tajikistan	0.00	−0.05	0.05	0.00
Estonia[3]	0.00	−0.05	0.05	0.00
Totals	8.93	0.86	8.07	110.7

[1] Including refinery fuel (but excluding refinery losses). [2] Including refinery fuel, storage and distribution losses, chemical feedstock, and stock changes. [3] Without account of domestically produced oil shale products.
Note: Totals may not add up due to independent rounding.

the FSU oil complex from complete balkanization—even though they could not prevent the more frequent oil supply disruptions and widening imbalances in republican (and regional) oil supply and demand.

The spreading shortages of liquid fuels, which have hit virtually all regions of the FSU (particularly the republics with permanent product deficits), were actually caused by the rapid breakdown of centrally-controlled distribution of basic goods which was not yet replaced by emerging market links between producers and consumers. By the end of 1991, when the central management crisis was exacerbated by the dissolution of the USSR, the former nationwide distribution system was finally dismantled into fifteen disabled fragments, while the newly-established direct, producer-consumer links experienced additional centrifugal pressures from the republics' oil nationalism.

By mid-November the Russian government, preoccupied with its own

Table 12.3
Authorized 1992 Exports of Russian Crude Oil to Other Ex-Soviet Republics[1]

Importing Republic	Exporting Region					
	W. Siberia	Volga-Urals	N. Caucasus	Kaliningrad	Others[2]	*Totals*
Ukraine	168	63	3	11	58	302
Belarus	262	28	—	—	—	290
Kazakhstan	191	—	—	—	—	191
Lithuania	56	—	—	—	—	56
Uzbekistan	42	—	—	—	—	42
Turkmenia	27	—	—	—	—	27
Azerbaijan	25	—	—	—	—	25
Georgia	11	—	—	—	—	11
Totals	781	91	3	11	58	944

[1] Units are kbd. In accordance with export quotas defined on 23 January 1992. [2] Swap deliveries from Kazakhstan (in exchange for West Siberian crude supplied to eastern and southern Kazakhstan). Note: Totals may not add up due to independent rounding.

economic problems and seeking to prevent any re-export of Russian oil in the form of petroleum products produced by other ex-Soviet republics (especially by Ukraine, Belarus, or Lithuania), temporarily banned the "inside" export of Russian liquid fuels and introduced a strict export quota-and-license system which applied as well to all the "brother" republics of the FSU. By the end of January 1992, when the ban was finally lifted, the disappointed FSU republics, now treated as foreign states, discovered that Russian oil export quotas for 1992 left them on a starvation diet. The authorized supplies of Russian crude oil were curtailed by more than half compared to the levels of at least 2 mmbd in the preceding years (Table 12.3).[1] As a result, in the event of excess requirements, the reduced deliveries of Russian crude had to be augmented by hard-currency or barter-based imports from other oil-exporting countries.

12.2 International Ramifications

Although the oil shortages which occurred in some of the former Soviet republics

[1] Actual deliveries of Russian crude to other oil-processing republics of the FSU went down from 2,374 kbd in 1991 to 1,505 kbd in 1992, of which Ukraine received 668 kbd; Belarus, 339 kbd; Kazakhstan, 227 kbd; Uzbekistan, 82 kbd; Lithuania, 80 kbd; Turkmenistan, 19 kbd; Azerbaijan, 17 kbd; and Georgia, 13 kbd. As for "inside" exports of Russian oil products, in 1992 their deliveries to other FSU republics decreased by 30 percent (to about 390 kbd).

during 1991 and the first half of 1992 appeared as if they had been purposely created by the Russian leadership with the object of political blackmail, it would be unreasonable to assume that unavoidable political conflicts between the newly-declared sovereign states result in inevitable oil supply disruptions. First, such a potential consequence of the Soviet Union's fragmentation will be counteracted by the market-induced integration of the economically interdependent states, which is developing virtually in reverse proportion to the rapid breakup of the Soviet Empire. Second, at least until the start of the next millennium, the integrity of the FSU oil market will be supported by the existing infrastructure, which ties the national oil industries into a single technological complex. And, finally, the official fragmentation of the USSR oil industry will be dampened by the dominant position of Russian oil on the present and, most likely, future petroleum market of the FSU (see below).

In this light the rumors of possible oil export disruptions which could be caused by political clashes between Russia and the other oil-transporting republics (notably, Ukraine and the Baltic states) seem greatly exaggerated. As soon as their sovereign claims are formally satisfied and the issue of political independence is *de jure* settled, none of the neighbor states will be interested any longer in blocking or hindering the movement of Russian oil through their own territories. This is partly due to their heavy dependence on these vital supplies (Figure 12.2) and partly to much desired transit payments. This does not ensure, however, completely smooth, conflict-free development of new inter-republican relations that are sure to be complicated by inevitable economic frictions and possible trade wars.

What can really affect the world oil market is the rapid decentralization of the Soviet oil trade, which used to be virtually monopolized by the all-Union foreign-trade agency *Soyuznefteexport* (SNE).[2] Since 1990 this traditional oil-trade monopoly has been actively undermined by a growing number of independent sales handled by other trading companies (both national and partly foreign-owned) or directly by FSU oil producers and, especially, by quite aggressive and independent-minded national refineries. Thus, in 1990 some 10 percent of all exported Soviet oil (more than 320 kbd) actually bypassed SNE, which was not involved in these "democratic" deals even as a broker or a commission agent. Every fourth barrel of these decentralized deliveries (including 14 kbd of crude and 66 kbd of products) was counter-traded in barter deals with their estimated shadow

[2] In 1992 SNE was renamed *Nafta Moskva*.

Figure 12.2
Dependence on Russian Crude Oil, 1991–92:
Share of Russian Crude Oil in Total Refinery Thruput

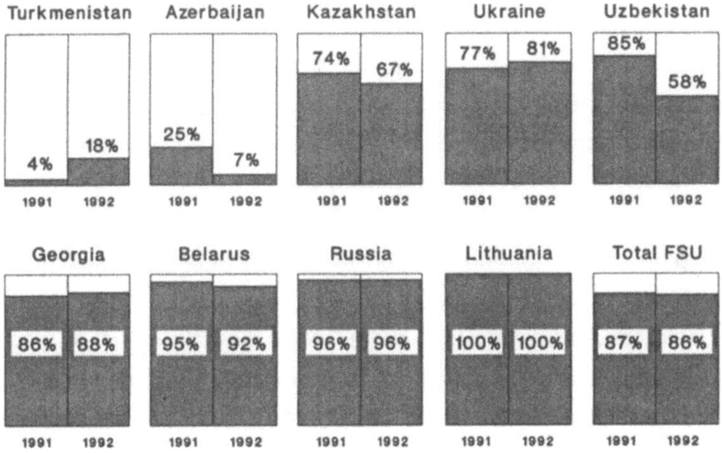

prices being, on the average, four times lower than the corresponding world-market prices. In 1991 the share of decentralized oil exports amounted to 20 percent of the country's oil trade (about 420 kbd out of a total 2.08 mmbd), and the share of non-centrally controlled supplies of refined products exceeded 40 percent of the country's product exports (370 kbd out of 880 kbd).[3]

Further decentralization, which may result from the direct marketing of the ever-growing decontrolled oil streams, is likely to bring forth many new currency-starved national exporters which, unless bound by sensible government regulations or production-sharing agreements with their foreign partners, may add substantially to international market competition, further undercut unstable world oil prices and trigger another damaging price war. In this context, the possibility arises that the governments of the oil-producing republics, which are sure to be involved in related international agreements and cooperative schemes, might resist an unrestrained

[3] According to preliminary data, in 1992 export sales of "freely-traded" Russian crude accounted for more than 38 percent of all Russian exports of crude oil (508 kbd out of 1,320 kbd) while decentralized deliveries of oil products provided about 44 percent of Russia's product exports (235 kbd out of 540 kbd).

liberalization of oil trade both on the Commonwealth and republican levels.[4]

The growing government concern about the negative consequences of national oil-industry decentralization has led to the establishment of a new monopolistic structure which was called upon to replace the disappearing USSR Ministry of Oil and Gas Industries. In October 1991 the Russian government approved an earlier "democratic" decision "to form on a voluntary basis" the Russian State Oil and Gas Corporation. This state-run entity united all the operational and research amalgamations (associations) producing crude oil, oil-wells and offshore gas establishments, as well as oil-transporting and petroleum-manufacturing equipment on all Russian territory. Dubbed *Rosneftegaz*, the newly born corporation was empowered with almost unlimited authority and the unprecedented privilege of controlling "state-ordered" production, distributing allocated export quotas and advising the Russian administration on the domestic pricing of oil and gas. In December 1991 the monopolistic position of *Rosneftegaz* was safeguarded and reinforced by a decree from Gaidar which actually banned any further decentralization of the national energy sector and stipulated that all its (recently "destated" or partly privatized) enterprises should be reconverted into wholly state-owned holding companies. In the same vein, in June 1992 the Russian government undertook another tightening of control by depriving oil producers of their independent legal status and by appointing a new, hard-line Vice Premier to take charge of the energy complex.

The recent appointment of former Soviet Gas Industry Minister Viktor Chernomyrdin to govern anarchic oil producers signified a definite shift to more centralized and consequently stricter management of the ailing industry, which may hence be given more generous financial support but less freedom to dispose of its own products (especially, on international markets). At the same time the inauguration of a strong-handed ruler, who can hide neither his negative attitude to any form of "destructive liberalization" nor his rather xenophobic feelings towards "unnecessary" foreign companies, will hardly accelerate the ongoing corporatization and envisaged partial privatization of the industry and will likely close some doors

[4] In December 1992 Russia and Kazakhstan began active consultations on the creation of their bilateral "mini-OPEC" (open, however, for any other FSU members). In January 1993 Ukraine set afloat an idea of an oil refiners' union (with Russian, Belarusian and Kazakh enterprises invited to participate). At the beginning of February 1993, a tentative plan to form a Kazakh-Azeri oil cartel was made public. And, finally, in March 1993, the Intergovernmental Oil and Gas Council of the former Soviet Republics was established for mutual assistance in developing their hydrocarbons industry.

once opened to foreign investors (Khartukov and Fesharaki 1992).

The breakup of the USSR forever shelved long-awaited Soviet petroleum legislation and redirected efforts of FSU law-makers towards drafting and discussing republican bills. Though this multinational law-making process has just started and no special petroleum-related laws have been adopted yet in any of the former Soviet Republics, foreign oil companies interested in doing business in the FSU may soon find themselves dealing with several national legislatures.[5] However, due to common mental horizons and a lack of national legal traditions, general rules and regulations which could be imposed by related republican laws will most likely differ little. Nevertheless, specific terms and conditions for petroleum-related activities and fiscal regimes for foreign investors are sure to vary substantially by republic and will certainly reflect varying national interests in achieving a higher level of self-sufficiency in oil.

12.3 Market Reforms and the World Oil Market

The most decisive factor adding so much uncertainty to the already complicated prospects for FSU oil exports is that now, under the growing pressure of market reforms, the export equation (that is, indigenous supplies, domestic requirements and the export policy itself) is no longer determined solely by fairly predictable physical constraints and/or by somewhat understandable (though less predictable) political pretensions of the command administration. Rather, it is influenced to an ever greater extent by emerging economic and social forces conducted by Adam Smith's "invisible hand." In other words, foreseeable oil developments in the FSU (including their impact on world oil markets) will greatly depend on the pace, speed and depth of the country's marketization.

The dramatic political, economic and social events that occurred in the FSU after the August 1991 coup have proved our earlier choice of the "slow marketization" and "economic shock" scenarios to be the most useful models of medium-term development of the FSU economy and its petroleum sector (Khartukov and Fesharaki 1991; Khartukov and Surovtsev 1992). Furthermore, the preceding two-year period of radical political and market reforms made it possible

[5] In addition to the national laws on foreign investments that were recently enacted in many of the FSU republics, at the end of March 1992 the Russian president signed the Law on Mineral Resources which codified general rules for the use of the nation's mineral wealth and is to be supplemented eventually by more specific petroleum (oil and gas) legislation. Two months later, on 30 May 1992, Russia's action was repeated by the Supreme Council (parliament) of Kazakhstan which adopted the republic's Code on Mineral Resources and Processing of Mineral Raw Materials.

to refine our 1991 forecast by taking into account their actual implementation. Since the ex-Soviet oil industry (and FSU economy as a whole) is now definitely vacillating between the "economic shock" and "slow marketization" paths, it would be appropriate to concentrate on these most probable scenarios, which are presented in their updated form in Table 12.4.

The "slow marketization" scenario assumes gradual increases of domestic fuel prices in line with estimated marginal (replacement) costs, the introduction of external convertibility of the rouble by 1995 and its full convertibility by 2000, and a quite limited involvement of Western oil companies until the probable end of their present "wait-and-see" attitude by the mid-1990s. Under these economic conditions, by 1995 ex-Soviet oil production will decline to 7.7 mmbd and then, by the end of the century, will get back to the level of 8.4 mmbd; in turn, domestic oil consumption, after falling to 6.7 mmbd in 1993, will experience modest growth up to less than 8 mmbd; and the national exportable surplus will recover from its low-point of zero in 1995 to some 0.6 mmbd by the year 2000.

The "economic shock" (or accelerated marketization) scenario differs from the above case in that the mentioned market reforms are forcibly and aggressively introduced into the ailing economy which becomes subject to economic "shock therapy." In this scenario, by the end of the century indigenous oil production, after falling to its low of 7.8 mmbd in 1994, will exceed 10 mmbd; domestic consumption, depressed by both economic slowdown and inflated energy prices, will nose-dive in the mid-1990s to less than 6 mmbd before recovering to some 7.5 mmbd by the year 2000; and net oil exports, relied upon to patch widening economic holes, will peak at almost 3.5 mmbd in the late 1990s.

As for the international ramifications of the possible changes in the FSU oil trade associated with a more or less rapid marketization, it would be safe to presume that the world petroleum market will neither remain untouched by, nor indifferent to, the market reforms in the once-largest oil-producing country. Moreover, as we have shown elsewhere (Khartukov and Surovtsev 1991a; 1992), the impact of the incremental supplies (or withdrawals) of ex-Soviet oil brought about by the implemented reforms can easily outweigh the influence of another, medium-size crisis in the Middle East and could be fairly comparable with the corresponding effect of conceivable differences in OECD economic growth rates. According to computer simulations of the world oil market with GAPMER's forecasting system, in the late 1990s estimated differences in the world oil price, caused by more or less rapid FSU marketization, could amount to $8 per barrel (in

Table 12.4
Scenarios for FSU Oil Balance, 1992-2000

	Slow Marketization			Economic Shock		
Year	Supply	Demand	Net Exports	Supply	Demand	Net Exports
1992	9.1	7.0	2.1	9.1	7.0	2.1
1993	8.3	6.7	1.6	8.2	6.3	2.0
1994	8.0	7.3	0.7	7.8	6.0	1.8
1995	7.7	7.7	0.0	8.1	5.8	2.3
1996	7.9	7.6	0.3	8.5	5.9	2.6
1997	8.1	7.7	0.4	9.2	6.4	2.8
1998	8.1	7.8	0.3	10.3	6.9	3.4
1999	8.3	7.9	0.4	10.6	7.2	3.4
2000	8.4	7.8	0.6	10.6	7.5	3.1

Notes: Supply is gross indigenous production, including condensate. Demand is total inland demand, including own and direct use, losses and changes in stocks of crude and products. 1992 is preliminary and estimated data. Totals may not add due to independent rounding. Units are mmbd.

real, constant 1992 dollars).[6] As can be seen in Figure 12.3 and Appendix Tables 12.A and 12.B, the "slow marketization" scenario lifts the (real) world oil price up to the $33/b level. In its turn, the "economic shock" scenario points to a weaker market, with its (real) prices hardly exceeding the $25/b level by the end of the century.

The fragmentation of the USSR necessitates disaggregation of the above-mentioned scenarios with due account of supply-demand balances in each of the now independent states. A republic-by-republic section of our outlook is presented in Table 12.5, which clearly reflects both the growing striving for greater self-sufficiency in oil and the physical restraints to achieving this desired goal. Thus, by the end of this century, almost all the FSU "have nots" can marginally improve their present oil position either through developing their modest petroleum resources or by curtailing wasteful consumption of oil products. At the same time, due to probable substantial increases in indigenous crude production, Uzbekistan may join the "club" of net exporters, while Azerbaijan and Kazakhstan could expand their export potentials. Russia is likely to remain the FSU's largest oil-exporting state, with one-third to one-half of its oil output still available for export.

[6] For description of the medium-term World Oil Market Model, developed by the World Energy Analysis and Forecasting Group (GAPMER), see Khartukov and Surovtsev 1991b.

Table 12.5
Projected Oil Balances of the Former Soviet Republics, 1995 and 2000

	1995 (mmbd)			2000 (mmbd)		
Republic	Supply	Demand	Net Exports	Supply	Demand	Net Exports
Russia	6.3–6.7	3.8–4.6	1.7–2.9	6.7–8.0	4.3–4.6	2.1–3.7
Kazakhstan	0.7	0.4	0.3	0.8–1.0	0.4–0.6	0.3–0.5
Azerbaijan	0.3	0.2	0.1	0.4–0.5	0.2–0.3	0.1–0.3
Turkmenistan	0.1	0.1	0	0.1	0.1	0
Ukraine	0.1	0.7–0.8	−(0.6–0.7)	0.1–0.2	0.7–1.0	−(0.5–0.9)
Uzbekistan	0.1	0.2	−0.1	0.2–0.3	0.2	0–0.1
Belarus	0	0.3–0.4	−(0.3–0.4)	0.1	0.3–0.4	−(0.2–0.3)
Georgia	0	0.1	−0.1	0	0.1	−0.1
Kyrgyzstan	0	0–0.1	−0.1–0	0	0.1	−0.1
Tajikistan	0	0–0.1	−0.1–0	0	0.1	−0.1
Lithuania	0	0.1	−0.1	0	0.1	−0.1
Latvia	—	0.1	−0.1	—	0.1	−0.1
Moldova	—	0.1	−0.1	0	0.1	−0.1
Armenia	—	0.1	−0.1	0	0.1	−0.1
Estonia[1]	—	0.1	−0.1	—	0.1	−0.1

[1] Excluding negligible production and consumption of oil shale products.

12.4 Conclusion

Gorbachev's *perestroika* unintentionally—and unexpectedly—has led to the political disintegration of the Soviet Union and, almost immediately, to the breakup of its formerly "one and indivisible" oil industry. However, while current geopolitics continue to tear the FSU to sovereign pieces, economic integration begins to reassemble the politically fragmented region, which may eventually find itself glued together again by emerging market forces. Thus, in the short term, the FSU oil industry will suffer from inevitable imbalances, regional oil shortages and gluts spreading toward neighboring international markets. In the medium term, however, the desired smooth interaction of the independent national oil industries will become possible on the basis of civilized trade and business grounds. Simultaneously and in the longer term, the cooperating parts of the former Soviet oil empire and, above all, its frontier regions (including those of Russia itself—the Russian Far East, for example) will become more self-reliant or infrastructurally independent and will speed up their natural growth and integration into the neighboring petroleum markets of Europe, the Near and Middle East, Central Asia and the Far East.

Figure 12.3
Price of Arab Light Under Various FSU Reform Scenarios, 1992 $/b

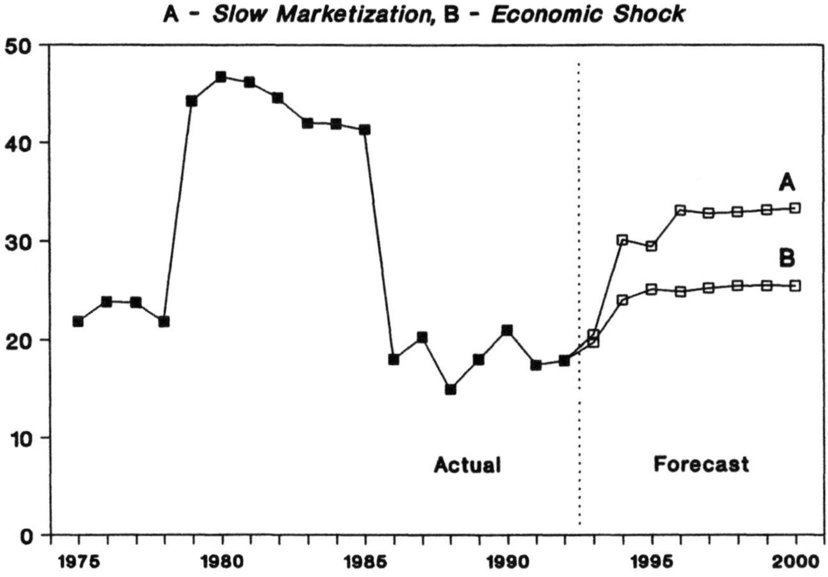

Appendix Table 12.A
World Oil Market Outlook, 1992–2000: Economic Shock Case

	1992[1]	1993	1994	1995	1996	1997	1998	1999	2000
Free World oil consumption[2]	54.5	55.7	57.2	56.0	56.4	56.2	56.7	57.8	59.6
Non-OPEC oil production	27.0	27.3	27.3	27.0	27.0	27.0	27.1	27.2	27.3
CPE Net oil exports	1.1	0.9	0.2	0.4	0.4	0.4	0.7	0.4	−0.1
including FSU net oil exports	*2.1*	*2.0*	*1.8*	*2.3*	*2.6*	*2.8*	*3.4*	*3.4*	*3.1*
OPEC NGL production	2.2	2.2	2.3	2.5	2.6	2.7	2.8	2.9	3.0
Call on OPEC crude[3,4]	24.2	25.3	27.4	26.1	26.4	26.1	26.1	27.2	29.3
Free World stock change	0.2	−0.5	0.8	0.6	0.3	0.2	0.2	0.3	0.4
OPEC crude production[3,5]	24.4	24.8	28.2	26.7	26.7	26.3	26.3	27.5	29.7
available capacity[6]	*25.5*	*28.0*	*29.2*	*29.6*	*30.1*	*30.9*	*31.4*	*31.8*	*32.0*
minimum requirements	*17.0*	*16.3*	*16.8*	*16.7*	*18.2*	*19.0*	*19.5*	*20.0*	*20.5*
Market price of Arab Light (constant 1992 $/b)[7]	17.9	19.7	24.0	25.1	24.9	25.2	25.5	25.5	25.4
Major assumptions									
OECD GDP real growth rate (%)[8]	1.5	2.0	2.6	1.8	2.8	1.9	2.9	3.7	4.7
Middle East political instability (1988 = 100)	92	100	100	100	100	100	100	100	100

[1] Actual. [2] Excluding refinery gains. [3] Including Ecuador. [4] Including required stock changes. [5] Beginning from 1993, assumed to balance global supply and demand. [6] Average. [7] Fob Ras Tanura. [8] Assumed and subsequently adjusted for oil price changes.

Note: Units are mmbd except as indicated. Totals may not add due to independent rounding. CPE = Former Centrally Planned Economies (including East Germany). Free World refers to non-CPE countries.

Appendix Table 12.B
World Oil Market Outlook, 1992–2000: Slow Marketization Case

	1992[1]	1993	1994	1995	1996	1997	1998	1999	2000
Free World oil consumption[2]	54.5	55.6	56.4	54.1	53.6	52.7	52.4	52.7	53.7
Non-OPEC oil production	27.0	27.2	27.2	26.9	26.9	27.0	27.3	27.6	27.9
CPE Net oil exports	1.1	0.4	−0.9	−1.9	−1.9	−2.0	−2.4	−2.6	−2.6
including FSU net oil exports	*2.1*	*1.6*	*0.7*	*0.0*	*0.3*	*0.4*	*0.3*	*0.4*	*0.6*
OPEC NGL production	2.2	2.2	2.3	2.5	2.6	2.7	2.8	2.9	3.0
Call on OPEC crude[3, 4]	24.2	25.7	27.8	26.7	26.0	25.0	24.7	24.8	25.4
Free World stock change	0.2	−0.9	1.2	0.6	0.4	0.0	0.0	0.1	0.2
OPEC crude production[3, 5]	24.4	24.8	29.0	27.3	26.4	25.0	24.7	24.9	25.6
available capacity[6]	*25.5*	*28.0*	*29.0*	*28.8*	*29.5*	*30.4*	*31.0*	*31.1*	*31.0*
minimum requirements	*17.0*	*16.0*	*15.8*	*16.2*	*17.7*	*19.4*	*19.8*	*20.0*	*20.1*
Market price of Arab Light (constant 1992 $/b)[7]	17.9	20.5	30.2	39.5	33.1	32.3	32.4	32.7	32.8
Major assumptions									
OECD GDP real growth rate (%)[8]	1.5	2.0	2.5	1.7	2.7	1.6	2.6	3.7	4.7
Middle East political instability (1988 = 100)	92	100	100	100	100	100	100	100	100

[1] Actual. [2] Excluding refinery gains. [3] Including Ecuador. [4] Including required stock changes. [5] Beginning from 1993, assumed to balance global supply and demand. [6] Average. [7] Fob Ras Tanura. [8] Assumed and subsequently adjusted for oil price changes.
Note: Units are mmbd except as indicated. Totals may not add due to independent rounding. CPE = Former Centrally Planned Economies (including East Germany). Free World refers to non-CPE countries.

References

Khartukov, E., and Fesharaki, F. 1991. Soviet Oil Industry: Update and Outlook to 2000. *EWC Petroleum Advisory* 73.

Khartukov, E., and Fesharaki, F. 1992. The Control of Russian Oil: Changing Management Patterns. *EWC Energy Advisory* 102.

Khartukov, E., and Surovtsev, D. 1991a. World Oil Market Post-Gulf War: A View from Moscow. *Energy Policy* 19: 610–14.

Khartukov, E., and Surovtsev, D. 1991b. World Oil Prices—Scenario Outlook to 2000. In *International Energy Market Modelling*. Proceedings of the 32nd International Conference of the Applied Econometrics Association, Montpellier, 23–25 October.

Khartukov, E., and Surovtsev, D. 1992. Ex-Soviet Oil on the Global Market: Beware of the Dog. *OPEC Bulletin* 23 (6): 13–24.

MIX
Papier aus verantwortungsvollen Quellen
Paper from responsible sources
FSC® C105338

If you have any concerns about our products,
you can contact us on
ProductSafety@springernature.com

In case Publisher is established outside the EU,
the EU authorized representative is:
Springer Nature Customer Service Center GmbH
Europaplatz 3, 69115 Heidelberg, Germany

Printed by Libri Plureos GmbH
in Hamburg, Germany